The American Revolution, 1763–1783

The American Revolution, 1763–1783

A Bicentennial Collection

Edited by

RICHARD B. MORRIS

University of South Carolina Press
Columbia, South Carolina

Contents

Introduction

THE TASK of encompassing within a single volume the essential documentation of an occurrence so comprehensive and complex as the American Revolution imposes singular restraints upon the editor. As a movement of decolonization the American Revolution began considerably before 1776, while as a transforming social event it has not yet run its course. Its military phase may have been initiated at Lexington; but before the war was over, it had been waged on four continents and on most of the seven seas, while its diplomacy had involved all the great powers of that day.

Before winnowing the chaff from the wheat, one must sift an enormous body of contemporary records, state papers, legislative journals, newspaper accounts, personal diaries, orderly books, and letters, all of which cast light on the multifaceted War of Independence. The winnowing involves some hard decisions, such as where to begin, where to end, and what to omit. One might heed John Adams' retrospective comment that the Revolution was "in the minds of the people, and this was effected, from 1760 to 1775, in the course of fifteen years before a drop of blood was drawn at Lexington." Contrariwise, one might accept Benjamin Rush's distinction in 1787 between "the late American War" and the "American Revolution." "The American War is over," he declared, "but this is far from being the case with the American Revolution. On the contrary but the first act of the great drama is closed."

Were one to accept Adams' interpretation, one would document merely the preliminaries and leave out the events leading to the winning of independence. Benjamin Rush's interpretation would require a full documentation of the struggle for equality from the beginnings down to our own day. Neither course would be sensible or satisfactory. Prudence and balance have dictated the setting of the chronological limits for this book. It opens with the pre-Revolutionary tensions which marked the closing years of the French and Indian War, and continues through the definitive treaty of peace of September 3, 1783; a few selections from a later date give a retrospective view.

The book is focused on facets and issues of the Revolutionary Era that still have a compelling relevance to our own time: the issues that impelled the colonists to secede from the Empire, the rise of antimonarchical and republican sentiment, the growth of revolutionary organizations, and the restraints imposed upon social violence by the Revolutionary elite which directed, from beginning to end, the first successful movement of decolonization in modern times. Consideration is given as well to the ideological principles that spurred the colonists toward revolution and that inspired their notions of constitutionalism, prompted them to seek limitations on governmental authority, and cautioned them to be doubly sure that civil liberties be explicitly safeguarded. Lastly, documentation illuminates, or at least suggests, the egalitarian, social, and cultural transformation that the American Revolution triggered.

In order adequately to cover the War for Independence—its political and constitutional aspects as well as its economic and social ramifications—one must, for reasons of space, curtail the perhaps more familiar account of military and naval events. Thus, while this collection treats the major battles, it cannot provide a blow-by-blow account of military and naval events. The scope of the war on land and sea deserves the kind of full-dress treatment that this editor (in collaboration with Henry Steele Commager) has sought to provide in The Spirit of Seventy-Six.[1] Similarly, the negotiations by the United States to secure financial assistance and military supplies, along with recognition as an independent nation, and the operations of the peacemakers of all the various belligerents and the self-appointed mediators from the neutral powers, involved extraordinary documentation, the kind and variety that this editor drew upon in writing The Peacemakers: The Great Powers and American Independence.[2] All that we have room for here are the treaty of alliance with France, an account of the British peace mission of 1778, the definitive treaty of 1783, and the

1. One-volume edition, Harper & Row, New York, 1967.
2. Harper & Row, New York, 1965.

defense of the respective roles pursued in accomplishing the last-named by two of the chief protagonists in the drama of the peace-making.

Today historians are generally agreed that the friction between colonists and mother country climaxed by Lexington and Concord began at least fifteen years before the first military clashes of the Revolution and can be clearly traced to the closing years of the French and Indian War. They are also agreed that a broad background of events between 1660 and 1763 must be kept in perspective if one is to understand the depth of the colonists' determination to maintain that wide area of autonomy that they had carved out for themselves. During that earlier period the royal governors had declined in authority while the colonial legislatures were becoming virtually omnipotent; American shipping interests had become accustomed to a venal and inefficient customs service which made evasion of the revenue laws, notably of the Molasses Act of 1733, a normal and accepted practice. On more than one occasion in this earlier period had the issue been raised of how much power inhered in the separate colonies. In the 1720's and 1730's political leaders like Justice David Lloyd of Pennsylvania and John Randolph of Virginia had spoken up on behalf of the legislative supremacy of the colonial representative assemblies; and in 1750 the Reverend Jonathan Mayhew pushed orthodox Whiggism to the edge of subversion when he argued that oppressive government might be dissolved when a sovereign exceeded constitutional limitations.

The challenge to accepted imperial relationships began almost imperceptibly. Indeed, one could argue that a new conception of the British Empire was initiated at Whitehall rather than in America. In August 1753, Charles Townshend, as a junior minister, drafted instructions for Sir Danvers Osborn, the Governor of New York, which aimed at checking the virtually uncontrolled power over the public purse which had been seized by that province's Assembly. The instructions directed the Assembly to make permanent provision for the salaries of royal officials and for the security of the province and any foreseeable changes. The money was to be applied by warrants from the governor on advice of the Council, while the Assembly would be merely permitted "from time to time to view and examine" accounts. Had Townshend's instructions been carried out, the royal executive would have been rendered financially independent of the colonial Assembly, and the issues of Parliamentary taxation which marked the next decade would never have arisen in the particular manner they did.

The Seven Years' War, which broke out first in the Ohio country as an encounter of settlers with the French and the Indians, demonstrated to imperial administrators the need to tighten the reins on the colonies. The British government, properly horrified at the extensive trade that the colonists carried on with the enemy during the conflict, determined to keep trade within legitimate bounds and to stamp out smuggling. By the latter part of the last intercolonial war, advocates of a tougher policy toward the colonies were at the helm of the Privy Council and the Board of Trade. This change was reflected in revised instructions to royal governors and in the disallowance of colonial laws. It is not by chance, then, that three issues which provoked great irritation in the colonies were very much alive prior to the enactment of the Grenville revenue program. These were the issuance of general search warrants, the disallowance by the King in council of the Virginia Two-Penny Act, and the drafting and transmission of instructions for the future appointment of judges at the pleasure of the Crown.

The war put heavy burdens upon the budget makers, and at its end England was left with a huge debt. Even had the British statesmen seriously considered raising the taxes of Englishmen, they would have been quickly disillusioned by the people themselves, who complained that they were already overtaxed. Perhaps shortsightedly but quite understandably, the statesmen turned to the colonies to pay their share of the cost of maintaining the military establishment required in America to patrol the huge territories wrested from France by the Treaty of Paris.

The issues between colonies and mother country were quickly joined and, from debates on specific taxes or administrative measures, were transmuted into arguments on the nature of the British Constitution and on the rights of Englishmen. Granted that the colonists generally opposed taxation for revenue purposes rather than as a weapon of trade regulation, and did so from the beginning of the controversy, and that the distinction between internal and external taxes was really spurious, one would still find it difficult to defend the contention, which has been repeatedly advanced recently, that the colonists adopted a consistent constitutional line. Originally the American Whigs recognized Parliament's right to regulate trade and to legislate for the colonies. As John Dickinson argued the case in 1767, Parliament could under the Constitution levy taxes for purposes of regulation only. By 1774, American Whigs had moved leftward and had denied any legislative authority of Parliament over them; by July 1776 they formally abrogated the authority of the King over his subjects in America. Few, if any, of the colonists had reached such extreme positions as early as the Stamp Act controversy. Few, if any, had contemplated secession at the start. One might regard the Anglo-American controversy as concerned from its inception with defining the limits of government and the relationship of colonies to metropolis; and these concerns were paramount in drafting both the state constitutions, beginning in 1776, and the Articles of Confederation.

The American cause was imbued with a strong moral overtone. The Patriots convinced themselves that they were engaged in a righteous struggle to uphold the British Constitution and the time-honored rights of Englishmen against arbitrary and capricious acts of a government ruled by corrupt, dissolute men who did not, and could not, represent them and, to compound the evil, were engaged in a conspiracy to subvert their liberties. The Loyalists or Tories, as the supporters of the Crown were called by their enemies, cherished the equally strong conviction that the American Whigs had hatched a conspiracy to overthrow the British Constitution and secede from the empire.

Whether one puts down the final breach to burgeoning cultural separatism, as did David Ramsay and other first-generation historians of the Revolution, or to mismanagement rather than evil intent, as do the more recent crop of historians of the "imperial school," or, more dubiously, to the exploitation of the colonials through the operation of the British mercantilist system, there is no gainsaying the fact that the American Revolution was, first of all, a political and constitutional struggle over sovereignty, a battle where who was right was more important than whose pocketbook was being pinched. But the Revolution transcended a struggle for political independence. It was the first major anticolonial war of modern times, and thus heralded not only the Revolutionary Age but also the gradual dissolution of the great world empires.

Retrospectively, the effort to achieve republican and egalitarian institutions—an effort that was central to the developing revolutionary movement—overshadows the issues of home rule and who should rule at home. No one would at this date deny the intensity of sectional, economic, and even class conflicts in the Revolutionary Era. The existence of such conflicts serves to refute some recent historians who have depicted American society as a seamless web of consensus. The issues of frontier security against Indians, tenant exploitation by big landowners, oppressive and arbitrary government in the interests of the seaboard, and law and order on the Southern frontier are set forth in this volume in a series of accounts documenting the complaints of the Paxton Boys, the New York Levellers, and the diverse Regulator movements that emerged on the North and South Carolina frontiers. The fact that there was a fear of leveling influences and of mob rule—a fear shared by property-conscious Whigs as well as by Tories—is amply supported by the evidence in this collection. The war on the home front to maintain the wage-price line and to curb war profiteers expressed the conviction of the less affluent, as well as of dedicated patriots like Washington, that patriotism should come before profits.

Finally, the divisions on the home front were brought into focus by the struggle to achieve more democracy, for legislative supremacy, and for limitations on the power of government. On some of these issues a Patriot such as John Adams might well differ with another Patriot like Thomas Paine. How to reconcile these differences and achieve a republican society along egalitarian lines was a preoccupation of a number of statesmen. Thus, while Theophilus Parsons, the reputed author of the *Essex Result* (1778), might, on the one hand, deplore the intensity of class divisions and the prospect of parties along special interest lines; on the other, he did not lose sight of basic goals and reminded his readers that, while they were contending for freedom, they should see to it, "Let us all be equally free. It is possible, and it is just." Indeed, the outlook of Americans generally—regardless of specific instances of friction between some landlords and some tenants, some creditors and some debtors, some easterners and some frontiersmen—was shaped by a conviction that permanent class groupings or status had no place in America. This did not mean that when the Founding Fathers talked about equality, they advocated social leveling. Quite the contrary. One and all affirmed the superior position that men of virtue and talents should hold in the state. The aim of a political society, Parsons contended, was not to secure equality of property but to maintain equality of rights.

In one way or another reformers of the Revolutionary Era devoted considerable attention to the ownership of property and sought to bring about its redistribution. While great landlords could be found on both the Patriot and the Tory sides of the Revolutionary controversy, the Patriots soon recognized the dangers of an emerging land monopoly. Admittedly the immediate purpose in confiscating the immense Tory estates was fiscal relief for the hard-pressed new Revolutionary states rather than the creation of a nation of small freeholders. While in some cases, notably in urban areas, Loyalists' properties passed into the hands of the affluent who could part with cash, in many areas of the country, and certainly on estates where the legislatures had established the principle of tenant pre-emption, there was a good deal of redistribution of property and many more landholders were created by the confiscation program than had existed before it was initiated. In addition, the opening up of the Crown lands of the West, obtained by the Patriots at the peacemaking in Paris, provided an unrivaled opportunity to create a society of relatively small freeholders. To prevent land jobbers and monopolizers from completely taking over, statesmen like Thomas Jefferson sought legislation curbing ownership of unappropriated lands. The great issue of the land jobber versus the individual settler was not settled in the Revolutionary Age, but the broad land policy of the emerging United States was to tip the scales in favor of the freeholder and against the speculative land company.

The enactment of Jefferson's proposals to end primogeniture and entailed estates crowned the efforts of the Virginia law reformer to supplant "an aristocracy of wealth" by an "aristocracy of virtue and talent." All the other states quickly emulated Virginia. There are those who question the effectiveness of Jefferson's blows against land monopoly, and who point to the fact that most Southern planters had, even before Jefferson's program, made ample provision in their wills for the younger children in their families. They also cite a number of legal devices, already in widespread use, for breaking entails. However, other legal instruments to perpetuate future interests in land were used by the larger landowners, particularly in New York. Not only was Jefferson concerned that, in a debtor society like Virginia, property owners needed to be free to liquidate all kinds of property to keep solvent, but he regarded primogeniture and entailments as poor examples for the egalitarian society that he envisioned for America.

We are accustomed to associating recent revolutions, whether the Bolshevik Revolution of 1917 or the Cuban Revolution of 1959, with violent social upheaval. In contrast, the American Revolution, with its sober and affluent leadership and its emphasis on legitimacy and moderation, seemingly accomplished its social transformation in a less explosive, if at least as durable, a fashion. To men who were forced to emigrate and whose property was seized, the social revolution seemed violent enough, to be sure. Loyalist émigrés, like Van Schaack, Jonathan Boucher, and Thomas Hutchinson, whose views of the conflict are recorded herein, numbered, according to some estimates, as many as one hundred thousand; and perhaps an equal number of black people joined the exodus. As one perceptive scholar of revolutions has pointed out, the percentage of displaced persons was far higher in the American than in the French Revolution.

The American Revolution was characterized by a remarkable transformation of white society while it failed to confront honestly the issue of black inequality. The wealthy South Carolinian Henry Laurens, an ex-slave trader himself and later president of the Continental Congress, declared, in a letter quoted herein, that the principles enunciated by the Declaration of Independence must have relevance to the Negro as well as to the white man. Others not only put such sentiments down on paper but took measures to implement their views. Jefferson tried unsuccessfully to write into the 1776 Virginia Constitution a provision that "no person hereafter coming into the state would be held in slavery." In his draft of the Declaration he included the slave trade as one of the evils ascribed to George III, but his fellow delegates had the reference stricken out. Even before the great Declaration the North took steps to end slavery, a process which the war accelerated; while the close of the war saw a burgeoning of manumission societies in the North as well as widespread manumission of slaves by planters in some of the southern states.

The harsh fact is that the Patriot side claimed most of the big slaveowners of the South, who were intensely provoked by Lord Dunmore's Proclamation offering freedom to indentured servants and slaves enlisting in the Royalist cause. Such offers indeed proved irresistible to some slaves who saw no other way of bettering their lot, although they were eventually disillusioned. Others enlisted in the Patriot army, some as front-line soldiers, some in labor battalions. To men with strong antislavery convictions, statesmen like

John Jay, the failure of the American Revolution to end slavery and discrimination against the Negro made the Declaration of Independence a continuing commitment. By failing to deal with black inequality in the Revolution and by evading the issue during the Federal Convention, the Founding Fathers postponed to some remote time the implementation of the principles and promises embodied in the Declaration of Independence. The long history of the antislavery and civil rights movements in the United States provides continuous and abundant proof that men of conscience in America considered equality for the Negro to be the great unfulfilled commitment of the American Revolution.

The American Revolution, 1763–1783

I

Early Tensions

Tensions between the colonies and the mother country antedate the inauguration of a new imperial program in 1763. In 1761, James Otis, Jr., unsuccessfully opposed the issuance by the Massachusetts courts of writs of assistance, or general search warrants. However, no account of Otis's inflammatory speech attacking the constitutionality of the writs was published until 1773. The writs were issued in Massachusetts and were explicitly authorized in the Townshend Acts passed in 1767. Thereafter their issuance was successfully contested in most of the colonies. They were specifically condemned by the Virginia Bill of Rights of 1776, and the Fourth Amendment to the Constitution makes general search warrants illegal. Otis here in fact struck the first blow in America for what has recently been called the right of privacy.

The issue of constitutional limits was also raised at this time by Patrick Henry of Virginia. As counsel for the defendant in the Parson's cause, described below in a letter from the Reverend James Maury to the Reverend John Camm, Henry attacked the legality of the English Privy Council's disallowance in 1759 of a Virginia statute, the Two-Penny Act, which had commuted the pay of Anglican ministers into currency at a rate of twopence per pound of tobacco, when, owing to the failure of the tobacco crop, the market price was much higher. The jury ignored the ruling of the bench that the act was "no law," and returned a mere nominal verdict for the plaintiff minister of one penny—in effect a victory for the colony.

Still another controversial issue involved the tenure of judges. When disputes arose in New York and New Jersey regarding judicial appointments, the governors in the royal colonies were instructed not to appoint judges during good behavior but only at the King's pleasure. The attempt on the part of the Crown to secure greater control over the judges of the colonial higher courts must be listed as a serious grievance of the American colonists, and the Declaration of Independence denounced the King for naming judges dependent upon his will for their tenure and salaries.

1. The Writs of Assistance: Speech of James Otis Against the Writs of Assistance February 24, 1761

1. THIS WRIT IS against the fundamental principles of law. The privilege of the House. A man who is quiet, is as secure in his house, as a prince in his castle—notwithstanding all his debts and civil processes of any kind. But—

For flagrant crimes and in cases of great public necessity, the privilege may be infringed on. For felonies an officer may break upon process and oath, that is, by a special warrant to search such a house, sworn to be suspected, and good grounds of suspicion appearing.

Make oath *coram* Lord Treasurer, or Exchequer in England, or a magistrate here, and get a special warrant for the public good, to infringe the privilege of house.

General warrant to search for felonies. Hawkins, Pleas of the Crown. Every petty officer, from the highest to the lowest; and if some of them are common, others are uncommon.

Government justices used to issue such perpetual edicts. With what particular reference? But one precedent, and that in the reign of Charles II., when star chamber powers and all powers but lawful and useful powers, were pushed to extremity.

The authority of this modern practice of the Court of Exchequer. It has an Imprimatur. But what may not have? It may be owing to some ignorant Clerk of the Exchequer. But all precedents, and this among the rest, are under the control of the principles of law. Lord Talbot. Better to observe the known principles of law than any one precedent, though in the House of Lords.

As to Acts of Parliament. An act against the Constitution is void; an act against natural equity is void; and if an act of Parliament should be made, in the very words of this petition it would be void. The executive Courts must pass such acts into disuse.

SOURCE: C. F. Adams, ed., *The Works of John Adams* (10 vols., Boston, 1850–1856), II, 521 *et seq.*

8 Rep. 118 from Viner. Reason of the common law to control an act of Parliament. Iron manufacture. Noble Lord's proposal, that we should send our horses to England to be shod. If an officer will justify under a writ, he must return it. 12 Mod. 396, perpetual writ. Statute Charles II. We have all as good right to inform as customhouse officers, and every man may have a general irreturnable commission to break houses.

By 12 of Charles, on oath before Lord Treasurer, Barons of Exchequer, or Chief Magistrate, to break, with an officer. 14 C. to issue a warrant requiring sheriffs, &c. to assist the officers to search for goods not entered or prohibited. 7 & 8. W. & M. gives officers in plantations same powers with officers in England.

Continuance of writs and processes proves no more, nor so much, as I grant a special writ of assistance on special oath for special purpose.

Pew indorsed warrant to Ware. Justice Walley searched House. Province Law. p. 114.

Bill in chancery. This Court confined their chancery power to revenue, &c.

2. In the first place, may it please your Honors, I will admit that writs of one kind may be legal; that is, special writs, directed to special officers, and to search certain houses, &c. specially set forth in the writ, may be granted by the Court of Exchequer at home, upon oath made before the Lord Treasurer by the person who asks it, that he suspects such goods to be concealed in those very places he desires to search. The act of 14 Charles II, which Mr. Gridley mentions, proves this. And in this light the writ appears like a warrant from a Justice of the Peace to search for stolen goods. Your Honors will find in the old books concerning the office of a Justice of the Peace, precedents of general warrants to search suspected houses. But in more modern books you will find only special warrants to search such and such houses specially named, in which the complainant has before sworn that he suspects his goods are concealed; and you will find it adjudged that special warrants only are legal. In the same manner I rely on it, that the writ prayed for in this petition, being general, is illegal. It is a power, that places the liberty of every man in the hands of every petty officer. I say I admit that special writs of assistance, to search special places, may be granted to certain persons on oath; but I deny that the writ now prayed for can be granted, for I beg leave to make some observa-

tions on the writ itself, before I proceed to other acts of Parliament. In the first place, the writ is universal, being directed "to all and singular Justices, Sheriffs, Constables, and other officers and subjects"; so, that, in short, it is directed to every subject in the King's dominions. Every one with this writ may be a tyrant; if this commission be legal, a tyrant in a legal manner also may control, imprison, or murder any one within the realm. In the next place, it is perpetual; there is no return. A man is accountable to no person for his doings. Every man may reign secure in his petty tyranny, and spread terror and desolation around him. In the third place, a person with this writ, in the daytime, may enter all houses, shops, &c. at will, and command all to assist him. Fourthly, by this writ not only deputies &c. but even their menial servants, are allowed to lord it over us. Now one of the most essential branches of English liberty is the freedom of one's house. A man's house is his castle; and whilst he is quiet, he is as well guarded as a prince in his castle. This writ, if it should be declared legal, would totally annihilate this privilege. Custom-house officers may enter our houses, when they please; we are commanded to permit their entry. Their menial servants may enter, may break locks, bars, and every thing in their way; and whether they break through malice or revenge, no man, no court, can inquire. Bare suspicion without oath is sufficient. This wanton exercise of his power is not a chimerical suggestion of a heated brain. I will mention some facts. Mr. Pew had one of these writs, and when Mr. Ware succeeded him, he endorsed this writ over to Mr. Ware; so that these writs are negotiable from one officer to another; and so your Honors have no opportunity of judging the persons to whom this vast power is delegated. Another instance is this: Mr. Justice Walley had called this same Mr. Ware before him, by a constable, to answer for a breach of Sabbath-day acts, or that of profane swearing. As soon as he had finished, Mr. Ware asked him if he had done. He replied, Yes. Well then, said Mr. Ware, I will show you a little of my power. I command you to permit me to search your house for uncustomed goods. And went on to search his house from the garret to the cellar; and then served the constable in the same manner. But to show another absurdity in this writ; if it should be established, I insist upon it, every person by the 14 Charles II. has this power as well as custom-house officers. The words are, "It shall be lawful for any person or persons authorized," &c. What a scene does this open! Every man, prompted by revenge, ill humor, or wantonness, to inspect the inside of his neighbor's house, may get a writ of assistance. Others will ask it from self-defence; one arbitrary exertion will provoke another, until society be involved in tumult and in blood.

Again, these writs are not returned. Writs in their nature are temporary things. When the purposes for which they are issued are answered, they exist no more; but these live forever; no one can be called to account. Thus reason and the constitution are both against this writ. Let us see what authority there is for it. Not more than one instance can be found of it in all our law-books; and that was in the zenith of arbitrary power, namely, in the reign of Charles II, when star-chamber powers were pushed to extremity by some ignorant clerk of the exchequer. But had this writ been in any book whatever, it would have been illegal. All precedents are under the control of the principles of law. Lord Talbot says it is better to observe these than any precedents, though in the House of Lords, the last resort of the subject. No Acts of Parliament can establish such a writ; though it should be made in the very words of the petition, it would be void. An act against the constitution is void. (vid. Viner.) But these prove no more than what I before observed, that special writs may be granted *on oath and probable suspicion*. The act of 7 & 8 William III. that the officers of the plantation shall have the same powers, &c., is confined to this sense; that an officer should show probable ground; should take his oath of it; should do this before a magistrate; and that such magistrate, if he thinks proper, should issue a special warrant to a constable to search the places. That of 6 Anne can prove no more.

2. The Case of the Parson's Cause:
The Reverend James Maury to the Reverend John Camm
December 12, 1763

DEAR SIR:—

Now that I am somewhat at leisure, than when I wrote to you by Major *Winston*, from *Hanover*, some few days ago, I have sat down to give you the best account I can of the most material

SOURCE: J. P. Kennedy, ed., *Journals of the House of Burgesses of Virginia, 1761–1765* (Richmond, 1907), pp. li–liii.

passages in the trial of my cause against the Collectors in that Court, both to satisfy your own curiosity, and to enable the lawyer, by whom it is to be managed in the General Court, to form some judgment of its merits. I believe, sir, you were advised from Nov'r Court, that the Bench had adjudged the twopenny act to be no law; and that, at the next, a jury, on a writ of inquiry, were to examine whether the Plaintiff had sustained any damages, and what. Accordingly, at *December* Court, a select jury was ordered to be summoned; but, how far they who gave the order, wished or intended it to be regarded, you may judge from the sequel. The Sheriff went into a public room, full of gentlemen, and told his errand. One excused himself (*Peter Robinson of King William*) as having already given his opinion in a similar case. On this, as a person then present told me, he immediately left the room, without summoning any one person there. He afterwards met another gentleman (*Richard Sq. Taylor*) on the green, and, on his saying he was not fit to serve, being a churchwarden, he took upon himself to excuse him, too, and, as far as I can learn, made no further attempts to summon gentlemen. These, You'll say, were but feeble endeavors to comply with the directions of the Court in that particular. Hence, he went among the vulgar herd. After he had selected and set down upon his list about eight or ten of these, I met him with it in his hand, and on looking over it, observed to him that they were not such jurors as the Court had directed him to get, being people of whom I had never heard before, except one, whom, I told him, he knew to be a party in the cause, as one of the Collector's Securities, and, therefore, not fit for a juror on that occasion. Yet this man's name was not erased. He was even called in Court, and, had he not excused himself, would probably have been admitted. For, I cannot recollect, that the Court expressed either surprise or dislike that a more proper jury had not been summoned. Nay, though I objected against them, yet, as *Patrick Henry* (one of the Defendant's lawyers) insisted they were honest men, and, therefore, unexceptionable, they were immediately called to the book and sworn. Three of them, as I was afterwards told, nay, some said four, were Dissenters of that denomination called *New Lights*, which the Sheriff, as they were all his acquaintance, must have known. Messrs. *Gift* and *McDowall*, the two most considerable purchasers in that county, were now called in to prove the price of tobacco, and sworn. The testimony of the former imported, that, during the months of May and June, 1759, tobacco had currently sold at 50s. per hundred, and that himself, at or about the latter end of the last of those months, had sold some hundreds of hhds. at that price, and, amongst the rest, one hundred to be delivered in the month of August, which, however, were not delivered till September. That of the latter only proved, "That 50s. was the current price to tobacco that season." This was the sum of the evidence for the Plaintiff. Against him, was produced a receipt to the Collector, to the best of my remembrance in these words: "Received of Thomas Johnson, Jun'r, at this and some former payments, £144, current money, by James Maury." After the lawyers on both sides had displayed the force and weight of the evidence, pro and con to their Honors, the jurors, and one of those who appeared for the Defendants had observed to them that they must find, (or if they must find, I am not sure which, but think the former) for the Plaintiff, but need not find more than one farthing; they went out, and, according to instruction (though whether according to evidence or not, I leave you to judge), in less than five minutes brought in a verdict for the Plaintiff, one penny damages. Mr. Lyons urged, as the verdict was contrary to evidence, the jury ought to be sent out again. But no notice was taken of it, and the verdict admitted without hesitation by the Bench. He then moved to have the evidence of Messrs. Gift and McDowell recorded, with as little effect. His next motion, which was for a new trial shared the same fate. He then moved it might be admitted to record, "that he had made a motion for a new trial, because he considered the verdict contrary to evidence, and that the motion had been rejected;" which, after much altercation, was agreed to. He lastly moved for an appeal, which, too, was granted. This, sir, as well as I can remember, is a just and impartial narrative of the most material occurrences in the trial of that cause. One occurrence more, tho' not essential to the cause, I can't help mentioning, as a striking instance of the loyalty, impartiality and attachment of the Bench to the Church of England in particular, and to religion at large. Mr. Henry, mentioned above (who had been called in by the Defendants, as we suspected, to do what I some time ago told you of), after Mr. Lyons had opened the cause, rose and harangued the jury for near an hour. This harangue turned upon points as much out of his own depths, and that of the jury, as they were foreign from the purpose; which it would be impertinent to mention here.

However, after he had discussed those points, he labored to prove "that the act of 1758 had every characteristic of a good law; that it was a law of general utility, and could not, consistently with what he called the original compact between King and people, stipulating protection on the one hand and obedience on the other be annulled." Hence, he inferred, "that a King, by disallowing Acts of this salutary nature, from being the father of his people, degenerated into a Tyrant and forfeits all right to his subjects' obedience." He further urged, "that the only use of an Established Church and Clergy in society, is to enforce obedience to civil sanctions, and that the observance of those which are called duties of imperfect obligation; that, when a Clergy ceases to answer these ends, the community have no further need of their ministry, and may justly strip them of their appointments; that the Clergy of *Virginia*, in this particular instance of their refusing to acquiesce in the law in question, had been so far from answering, that they had most notoriously counteracted, those great ends of their institution; that, therefore, instead of useful members of the state, they ought to be considered as enemies of the community; and that, in the case now before them, Mr. *Maury*, instead of countenance, and protection and damages, very justly deserved to be punished with signal severity." And then he perorates to the following purpose, "that excepting they (the jury) were disposed to rivet the chains of bondage on their own necks, he hoped they would not let slip the opportunity which now offered, of making such an example of him as might, hereafter, be a warning to himself and his brethren, not to have the temerity, for the future, to dispute the validity of such laws, authenticated by the only authority, which, in his conception, could give force to laws for the government of this Colony, the authority of a legal representative of a Council, and of a kind and benevolent and patriot Governor." You'll observe I do not pretend to remember his words, but take this to have been the sum and substance of this of his labored oration. When he came to that part of it where he undertook to assert, "that a King, by annulling or disallowing acts of so salutary a nature, from being the Father of his people degenerated into a Tyrant, and forfeits all right to his subjects' obedience," the more sober part of the audience were struck with horror. Mr. *Lyons* called out aloud, and with an honest warmth, to the Bench, "That the gentleman had spoken treason," and expressed his astonishment "that their worship could hear it without emotion, or any mark of dissatisfaction." At the same instant, too, amongst some gentlemen in the crowd behind me, was a confused murmur of Treason, Treason! Yet Mr. *Henry* went on in the same treasonable and licentious strain, without interruption from the Bench, nay, even without receiving the least exterior notice of their disapprobation. One of the jury, too, was so highly pleased with these doctrines, that, as I was afterwards told, he every now and then gave the traitorous declaimer a nod of approbation. After the Court was adjourned, he apologised to me for what he had said, alleging that his sole view in engaging in the cause, and in saying what he had, was to render himself popular. You see, then, it is so clear a point in this person's opinion, that the ready road to popularity here, is, to trample under foot the interests of religion, the rights of the church, and the prerogative of the crown. If this be not pleading for the "assumption of a power to bind the King's hands," if it be asserting "such supremacy in provincial Legislatures" as is inconsistent with the dignity of the Church of *England*, and manifestly tends to draw the people of these plantations from their allegiance to the King, tell me, my dear sir, what is so, if you can. Mr. *Cootes*, merchant on *James* River, after Court said "he would have given a considerable sum out of his own pocket, rather than his friend *Patrick* should have been guilty of a crime, but little, if any thing inferior to that which brought *Simon* Lord *Lovett* to the block;" and justly observed that he exceeded the most seditious and inflammatory harangues of the Tribunes of old Rome.

3. Tenure of Judges: Circular Letter of Instructions to the Royal Governors December 17, 1761

Judges' Commissions During Pleasure Only

Whereas laws have been lately passed or attempted to be passed in several of our colonies in America enacting that the judges of the several courts of judicature or other chief officers of justice in the said colonies shall hold their offices during good behavior, and

SOURCE: L. W. Labaree, ed., *Royal Instructions to British Colonial Governors, 1670–1776* (2 vols., New York, 1935), I, 367–368.

whereas the governors or other chief officers of several of our said colonies have granted commissions to the judges or other chief officers of justice by which they have been empowered to hold their said offices during good behavior contrary to the express directions of the instructions given to the said governors or other chief officers by us or by our royal predecessors; and whereas it does not appear to us that in the present situation and circumstances of our said colonies it would be either for the interest and advantage of the said colonies or of this our kingdom of Great Britain that the judges or other chief officers of justice should hold their offices during good behavior; it is therefore our express will and pleasure that you do not upon any pretense whatever, upon pain of being removed from your government, give your assent to any act by which the tenure of the commissions to be granted to the chief judges or other justices of the several courts of judicature shall be regulated or ascertained in any manner whatsoever. And you are to take particular care in all commissions to be by you granted to the said chief judges or other justices of the courts of judicature that the said commissions are granted during pleasure only, agreeable to what has been the ancient practice and usage in our said colonies and plantations.

II

The Role of the West

The transappalachian West played a significant role in the events leading up to the Revolution. One of the major objectives of the new British tax program after 1763 was to defray the cost of British troops stationed in the West. When, at the end of the Seven Years' War, Parliament debated the peace treaty, William Petty, the Earl of Shelburne, pointed out the advantages of retaining Canada instead of a French sugar island. The decision to incorporate Canada into the Empire marked a decisive turning point in British imperial policy.

The French and Indian War had exposed the insecurity of the frontiers against Indian raids, and the Indians did not readily accept British overlordship. Between the spring and the late fall of 1763, Western posts were overrun in an Indian uprising under the leadership of the Ottowa chief Pontiac. The task of maintaining peace on the frontier and protecting the Indians against land frauds and uncontrolled encroachments by white settlers now commanded much of the time of British officials. The plan attributed to Henry Ellis, former Governor of Georgia, became the basis for the Proclamation of 1763, which established the Appalachians as a temporary boundary line between the colonies and lands reserved to the Indians and created three new provinces: Quebec, East Florida, and West Florida. As a result of treaties negotiated in 1768, lands west of the Appalachian area were purchased from the Indians. Virginia had a large stake in the area, as did Philadelphia merchants who secured huge land grants north of the Ohio to compensate for losses allegedly suffered at the hands of the Indians. In February 1774 the North Ministry restricted land grants within the colonies, and the Quebec Act passed the same year extended Canada's boundaries to the Ohio River, an area where a number of colonies had claims.

4. Canada vs. Guadalupe: Lord Shelburne's Draft of a Speech in the House of Lords in Support of the Preliminary Articles of Peace December 9, 1762

HERETOFORE THE Province of a Statesman was more easy and much less complicated, than It is at this present Period of the State of Europe. The Internal of Antient States was generally extremely simple, and the Relation they stood in to each other obvious to every observer. Of late years the Art of Government is become extreamly complex and difficult. The Interests of Commerce and the easy intercourse which it has introduced has linked all Europe into an Indissoluble System; all the Parts are become relative, and a sort of Ballance has been necessarily introduced between the Various States of this extensive Union. Any particular Nation therefore must no longer think of measuring its Strength singly with that of another, but must look forward through the whole extent of that Chain of Interest which combines the whole and which by degrees must draw every State into the Contention.

Heretofore, the Extension of Limits was the Single Point aimed at. But now the Possession of Territory is but a secondary Point, and is considered as more or less valuable, as It is subservient to the Interest of Commerce, which is now the great object of ambition.

There are Truths with regard to commerce however, which may be depended on, and which may serve as a measure to Judge our Interests. Such as: That the Strength of every nation depends upon the number of Industrious people. That These will increase in proportion to the means of Subsistance and to the demand. That the Products of Land and Tobacco, Corn, and Manufactures, will be in proportion to the people producing, and will be exchanged to procure the Bullion and Products of other Countrys. That the Number of Ships and Sailors will be in proportion to the Exports and Imports. That of all sorts of Wealth Bullion is the most

SOURCE: Lansdowne Papers, Vol. 165, William L. Clements Library, University of Michigan.

convenient, and essential to a Nation in debt. An Able and an Honest Minister will therefore be chiefly attentive to the Attainment of these two great Points, which in general are perfectly coincident.

We have gained over the French and Spaniards this War many Advantages. It is natural to wish for Peace, that we may reap the Fruits of Victory, and recruit the exhausted Nation with Men and Money. Common Sense therefore dictates to us that We must restore some of our conquests. No Nation will make Peace but to obtain some lost Good or to avoid some apprehended Evil. Neither France nor Spain could well apprehend more Evil, than they had already sustained. They could not fear for Paris or Madrid. They therefore could have no Inducement positive or negative to permit us to enjoy our conquests in Peace. Such a Peace would do them no good. It would be the Worst of Evils; and without a Peace we should be at last the Victors of ourselves, and should exhaust our Strength without an Enemy. Something therefore must have been restored, and something so considerable too, as to make Peace desirable to our Enemies. Without this We must have waged Eternal War.

Some Advantages We had a right to retain. The question therefore will be, whether We have been so Judicious as to retain such Things as will best serve to Increase our Wealth, the number of our People, and consequently our Future power. Whether we could have obtained further Advantages is but matter of Guess and Speculation, is an Affair of the Cabinet, can never make a Subject of Party Debate. In the mean time We are Sure by making Peace at this Period, we save Millions of money and Thousands of men; we reap a part, and rescue it from a Caprice of Fortune.

Commerce is circuitous in a course. The advantages or disadvantages of every Conquest must be considered with respect to Gr. Br. as direct and collateral.

The Security of the British Colonies in N. America was the first cause of the War and has been wisely attended to in the Negotiations for Peace. The total Extirpation of the French from Canada, and of the Spaniards from Florida, gives Gr. Br. the universal empire of that extended Coast, makes the Inhabitants easy in their possessions, opens a new Field of Commerce, with many Indian Nations, which have hitherto been Enemies to the repose of British Subjects and prevented the extension of our Settlements, furnishes great additional resources for the Increase of our Naval Power, and is of Millions more consequence than all our other conquests, as it ensures to G. Br. the pleasing hopes of a Solid and lasting Peace.

To prove the above Assertion It is proper to observe, that the exports to N. America for some years past has been ¼ of the British Trade; the annual exports from London only having exceeded 2,000,000 Sterling, and the exports from Bristol, Liverpool, Glasgow, and other out Ports, cannot be so little as 500,000, whereas the Whole Exports from G. B. are computed at 10 Million.

The N. Americans send us in return chiefly Rice Tobacco Corn and Fish, the greatest part whereof is exported to Foreign Markets. Naval Stores Indigo Iron and Furs which may be deemed Materials for Manufactures and therefore bring returns from Foreigners equal to their Value.

Ships and Lumber without which our West Indian Islands cannot subsist, and Flax seed for the Supply of the Linnen Manufacture in G. B. and Ireland, which is of immense consequence. Wherefore It appears that the Value of our exports to N. America as far as they consist of our Manufactures which are the greater part is a clear profit to the Nation, and in its present State may be fairly said to Yield full half the National Ballance G. B. gave by Trade, the annual profits of which are thought not to exceed 2 Million.

If It be objected that France may yet disturb the British Colonies by means of the Mississippi, I answer, that the Climate being unwholesome, the Inhabitants are weakly and not likely to increase; they have no resources for ammunition; the Navigation is so hazardous, and the Winds so adverse, that Ships are frequently 6 Weeks beating up from the Bay of Appellachio to the Gulph of Florida. Supplies from France and Spain must be tedious and uncertain, so that no War can be carried on with Vigour from that quarter, against the robust Inhabitants of our Northern Colonies.

By the acquisition of Canada Britain gains the Cloathing of many Indian Nations, besides 70,000 Acadians, which in so cold a Climate must annually consume full 200,000£ value of British Manufacture; the returns for which must be made part in Fish exported to Foreign markets; about 60,000£ value in Furs (which under proper Regulations will give G. B. almost a monopoly of the Fine Stave Trade,) and be the means of bringing a Profit of treble their Value into the Kingdom, Some Oyle, Whalebone, and Iron.

There are some considerable Iron Forges, one of which at St. Maurice near Trois Rivieres has in some years produced 400 Tuns of Bar and Cast Iron, and if proper encouragement is given this Country might be made to supply all the materials imported from the Baltick, for any quantity of Iron is to be found there which being run into Pigs and Bar Iron would be a good Ballast for Kelp and Flax, for the growth of which the Climate is suitable, and these three Articles being paid for in our own Manufactures instead of Money as they are now paid for to Russia and Sweden would be an immense gain of ½ a Million Sterling. Brittain likewise obtains by this Cession the Sole right of Ship building in America, which is of considerable consequence to our Sugar Colonies, as the returns made by America in Shipping keeps down the Freight of Sugar ¼ lower than it otherwise would be in time of Peace, and enables them to supply the Sugar Islands with Lumber, much cheaper than It could be otherwise procured. It is also of great consequence to the Fishery for the Price of Timber and other materials for Ship building are so much advanced, that small Ships will cost 50 pounds Sterling more in Europe than America, which is sufficient of itself to turn the carriage of Fish to all foreign markets into the hands of British Subjects except what the French take for their own consumption.

The Cession of Cape Breton, St. John's and Gaspia Bay, and the rest of the Fisherys in the river St. Lawrence gives G. Britain ¼ of the French Fisheries, finds employment for 100 sail of 150 Tun each and about 4000 Sea Men, which may [be] reckoned worth 250,000£ Sterling per annum.

By the acquisition of Florida G. Britain has obtained the Cloathing and the command of several Indian Nations, who have long been the Terror of the Inhabitants of S. Carolina and Georgia, and a great hindrance to the Settlement of the latter. She has also the command of the Homes and bound Flotillas from Vera Cruz, may easily make descents from thence on the Spanish Islands, and with the addition of that part of Louisiana on the left of the Mississippi, may in time raise a sufficient quantity of Cochineal and Indigo, for the Supply of our Manufactures, for which Britain and Ireland pay annually to France and Spain 500,000£ Sterling. If Sugar Land was wanted any quantity of Sugar Canes might be raised there.

If to all these considerations It is added, that by the Possession of Canada, G. Britain is secure from any future War in N. America, which may be the Saving of Millions of money and Thousands of Lives and that a Sufficient number of Men may be transported from thence to st[arve] the French and Spanish Islands, in case of a New War, It is therefore manifest, that in comparison of N. America, The Keeping the French Islands, and particularly the Islands of Guadualoupe and Grand Terre so much contended for is a trifling object, which would be but of little value to Britain, under the capitulation. The present possessors thereof being all Frenchmen would enrich themselves by the advantage of the British Markets, and afterwards sell their Lands, Negroes, and Utensils for their full value, and return to France, so that in all probability, England would pay France 4 or 5 Millions Sterling for their acquisition, which would make it a dear purchase. Should any one alledge that G. Britain is in Want of Sugar Land, and therefore Guadauloupe should be kept, The answer is obvious. There is more Sugar Land in Tobago, St. Vincent's, and Dominique, than can be cultivated in many centuries, and Jamaica, if cultivated to the heigh, would produce more sugar than all Europe consumes. At present it produces 60,000 Hogsheads though not ¼ of it properly cultivated. There is treble the quantity of Square Miles yet uncultivated in Jamaica more than those Islands contain.

It is moreover worth consideration that the Sugar Trade is more a Trade of necessity than of Profit. The exports from Britain don't exceed 1 Million whereas the Imports of Sugar and Rum must amount to 2 Millions, which is all exhausted among ourselves and therefore yields no material profit. It is usefull to keep to procure so great a Ballance being paid to Foreigners. It is also worthy Notice, that wherever Sugar grows Population decreases, and that our Sugar Colonies weaken and depopulate our Mother Country. Sugar requiring Moist and Heat are the Causes of Putrefaction.

On the contrary the Northern Colonies encrease Population and of course the consumption of our Manufactures, pay us for them by their Trade with Foreigners, and thereby giving employment to Millions of Inhabitants in G. Britain and Ireland, and are of the utmost consequence to the Wealth, safety, and Independance of these Kingdoms and must continue so for Ages to come.

5. Proclamation of 1763: Governor Henry Ellis' Plan
May 5, 1763

*Hints Relative to the Division and Government of the
Conquered and Newly Acquired Countries in America*

The Country call'd Canada is of such vast Extent, that, for the
greater Convenience of governing its Inhabitants there seems to be
a Necessity of dividing it into two Provinces at least, and of establishing in each a distinct Government.

Quebec, of Course, should be the Capital of the Lower province,
comprehending the Isle of Orleans, the Settlements on the South
Eastern Banks of St. Lawrence to a certain Distance, and all the
Territory on the North West Side of that River, lying to the East-
ward of Trois Rivieres.

Montreal might with equal propriety be made the Capital of the
Upper province, which may include not only that Tract of Land
between Lake Champlain and St. Lawrence but likewise all the
Country on the North West Side of that River above Trois
Rivieres.

The Civil Government of these Provinces would be best administered for some time, by a Governor & Council only, who
should be vested with the same legislative Powers as have been
conferred on the General Assemblies in those provinces where the
Royal Government has been settled in it's greatest purity; and
when Circumstances are so much changed as to render it expedient, His Majesty may indulge His new Subjects in that part of the
World with Representatives in General Assembly which would at
once convert what before was a Despotic Government into one of
Liberty.

In regard to the Ecclesiastical Establishment in Canada there
occurs but two Methods of putting that upon any tolerable footing; One is to make no immediate Alteration, but let the regular
Clergy of the several Communities now subsisting there gradually

SOURCE: Colonial Office Papers, British Public Record Office—
photocopy, Library of Congress.

die off, without suffering them to be replaced, and then grant to
such of the Canadians, as may still adhere to Popery, the same
Indulgence as is allowed to His Majesty's Roman Catholick Subjects in Ireland, who by the Capitulation of Limerick were in
similar Circumstances.

The other Method is, to take the Revenue of the regular Clergy
immediately into the Hands of Government, and allow to the
Individuals of which those Communities are composed, Stipends
or Pensions for Life and Permission to exercise their religious
Functions hereafter only as secular Priests—With respect to the
Secular Clergy: They, it is conceived, may, without any great
Inconvenience be permitted to continue on their usual Footing.

As every part of the British Dominions however circumstanced
should be under some Jurisdiction or other, it is proposed, that all
the Southern Coast of Labradore, from the Island of Anticosti to
Hudson's Streights, may be annexed to the Newfoundland Government, and that in order effectually to assert our Right to that
Coast an Establishment may be immediately formed upon it, at
or near the Streights of Belleisle, where there are many commodious Harbours formerly resorted to by the French and Esquimeaux,
for the Purposes of Traffick and Fishing.

It might also be necessary to fix upon some Line for a Western
Boundary to our ancient provinces, beyond which our People
should not at present be permitted to settle, hence as their Numbers increased, they would emigrate to Nova Scotia, or to the
provinces on the Southern Frontier, where they would be usefull to
their Mother Country, instead of planting themselves in the Heart
of America, out of the reach of Government, and where, from the
great Difficulty of procuring European Commodities, they would
be compelled to commence Manufacturs to the infinite prejudice
of Britain.

All the Country to the Westward of this Boundary may be put
under the immediate Protection and Care of the Officers commanding at the distant posts. But as many of the King's Subjects
will necessarily have Occasion to go beyond this Line for Trade and
other purposes, and may have Disputes among themselves, or with
the Indians, it would be proper that the Decision of such Differences, and indeed, that all Matters cognizable by Law should be
reserved to the Civil Power in any of the Neighboring Provinces.

The Island of St. John in the Gulph of St. Lawrence, and Isle Royal, which are so near to Nova Scotia, should be united to it forthwith, and make a part of that Government.

Georgia, which is at present of too narrow Limits ever to become a flourishing Province, should be extended Southward to the River St. Marys, and a Line running Westward from thence to St. Mark's in the Bay of Apelache, would be a proper Boundary on that Side.

All the Peninsula Southward of this Line ought to be comprized in the Province of Florida, and the Country situated between St. Mark's and the River Mississippi, should be formed into another province.

Perhaps the very best Mode of Government for these new provinces, which 'tis likely, will be settled either by foreign Protestants or the King's natural born Subjects who are intitled to British Liberty, would be that of Georgia or Nova Scotia, which has been the latest formed, is the freest from a Republican Mixture, and the most conformable to the British Constitution of any that obtains amongst our Colonies in North America, and might therefore be adopted at once, without any material Alteration.

Granado, the Granadillo's & St. Vincent's may be put under one Government which may be exactly similar to that of the Leeward Islands, unless, on account of the Number of French already settled upon them, it should be thought more adviseable to adopt the Plan proposed for the Government of the Canadian Provinces.

As Tobago is itself a considerable Island entirely unsettled and lying at a Distance from the Others, it may, with propriety either have a particular Government of it's own or continue as it is, united to that of Barbados, with which it's future Inhabitants can have an easy Intercourse, by means of the Trade Winds, a Convenience which they could not have with respect to Granado, were they connected with that Government.

The Island of Dominica so detached from the King's other Possessions in those Parts, and lying in the Center of the French Sugar Islands may be made a separate and perhaps a military Government at least for the present.

The Fort at Senegal which is not of more Importance than that at Gambia, or those on the Gold Coast may, in time of Peace at least, be put under the Direction of the African Committee in the same Manner as the other Forts are in that Quarter, and it would be extremely proper to have a small Establishment immediately at Portlandie, were it only as a Mark of Possession and Right to that part of the Gum Coast, which, otherwise may one Time, be usurped by the French.

6. Land Speculation: George Washington to William Crawford Mount Vernon, September 21, 1767

DEAR SIR:

From a sudden hint of your Brother I wrote to you a few days ago in a hurry, since which having had more time for reflection, I am now set down in order to write more deliberately, and with greater precision, to you on the Subject of my last Letter; desiring that if any thing in this shoud be found contradictory to that Letter you will wholely be governd by what I am now going to add.

I then desird the favour of you (as I understood Rights might now be had for the Lands, which have fallen within the Pensylvania Line) to look me out a Tract of about 1500, 2000, or more Acres somewhere in your Neighbourhood meaning only by this that it may be as continguous to your own Settlemt. as such a body of good Land coud be found and about Jacobs Cabbins or somewhere on those Waters I am told this might be done. It will be easy for you to conceive that Ordinary, or even middling Land would never answer my purpose or expectation so far from Navigation and under such a load of Expence as those Lands are incumbred with; No: A Tract to please me must be rich (of which no Person can be a better judge than yourself) and if possible to be good and level; Coud such a piece of Land as this be found you woud do me a singular favour in falling upon some method to secure it immediately from the attempts of any other as nothing is more certain than that the Lands cannot remain long ungranted when once it is known that Rights are to be had for them. What

SOURCE: J. C. Fitzpatrick, ed., *The Writings of George Washington* (39 vols., Washington, 1931–1944), II, 467–471.

mode of proceeding is necessary in order to accomplish this design
I am utterly at a loss to point out to you but as your own Lands
are under the same Circumstances self Interest will naturally lead
you to an enquiry. I am told the Land, or Surveyors Office is kept
at Carlyle, if so I am of Opinion that Colo. Armstrong (an
Acquaintance of mine) has something to do in the management of
it, and I am perswaded woud readily serve me to him therefore at
all events I will write by the first oppertunity on that Subject that
the way may be prepard for your application if you shoud find it
necessary to make one to him. Whatever trouble or expence you
may be engagd in on my behalf you may depend upon being thank-
fully repaid. It is possible (but I do not know that it really is the
case) that Pensylvania Customs will not admit so large a quantity
of Land as I require, to be entered together if so this may possibly
be evaded by making several Entries to the same amount if the
expence of doing which is not too heavy; but this I only drop as a
hint leaving the whole to your discretion and good management. If
the Land can only be secured from others it is all I want at present,
the Surveying I would choose to postpone, at least till the Spring
when if you can give me any Satisfactory account of this matter
and of what I am next going to propose I expect to pay you a visit
about the last of April.

The other matter, just now hinted at and which I proposed in
my last to join you in attempting to secure some of the most
valuable Lands in the King's part which I think may be accomplished after a while notwithstanding the Proclamation that re-
strains it at present and prohibits the Settling of them at all for I
can never look upon that Proclamation in any other light (but this
I say between ourselves) than as a temporary expedient to quiet
the Minds of the Indians and must fall of course in a few years
especially when those Indians are consenting to our Occupying the
Lands. Any person therefore who neglects the present oppertunity
of hunting out good Lands and in some measure marking and
distinguishing them for their own (in order to keep others from
settling them) will never regain it, if therefore you will be at the
trouble of seeking out the Lands I will take upon me the part of
securing them so soon as there is a possibility of doing it and will
moreover be at all the Cost and charges of Surveying and Patenting
&c. after which you shall have such a reasonable proportion of the
whole as we may fix upon at our first meeting as I shall find it

absolutely necessary and convenient for the better furthering of the design to let some few of my friends be concernd in the Scheme and who must also partake of the advantages.

By this time it may be easy for you to discover, that my Plan is to secure a good deal of Land, You will consequently come in for a very handsome quantity and as you will obtain it without any Costs or expences I am in hopes you will be encouragd to begin the search in time. I woud choose if it were practicable to get pretty large Tracts to gether, and it might be desirable to have them as near your Settlement, or Fort Pitt, as we coud get them good; but not to neglect others at a greater distance if fine and bodies of it lye in a place. It may be a Matter worthy your enquiry to find out how the Maryland back line will run, and what is said about laying of Neale's (I think it is and Companys) Grant. I will enquire particularly concerning the Ohio Companys that one may know what to apprehend from them. For my own part I shoud have no objection to a Grant of Land upon the Ohio a good way below Pittsburg but woud willingly secure some good Tracts nearer hand first.

I woud recommend it to you to keep this whole matter a profound Secret, or trust it only with those in whom you can confide and who can assist you in bringing it to bear by their discoveries of Land and this advice proceeds from several very good Reasons and in the first place because I might be censurd for the opinion I have given in respect to the King's Proclamation and then if the Scheme I am now proposing to you was known it might give the alarm to others and by putting them upon a Plan of the same nature (before we coud lay a proper foundation for success ourselves) set the different Interests a clashing and probably in the end overturn the whole all which may be avoided by a Silent management and the [operation] snugly carried on by you under the pretence of hunting other Game which you may I presume effectually do at the same time you are in pursuit of Land which when fully discovered advise me of it and if there appears but a bear possibility of succeeding any time hence I will have the Lands immediately Surveyed to keep others off and leave the rest to time and my own Assiduity to Accomplish.

If this Letter shoud reach your hands before you set out I shoud be glad to have your thoughts fully expressd on the Plan I have proposd, or soon afterwards as conveniently may be as I am desirous of knowing in time how you approve of the Scheme. I am, &c.

7. The Quebec Act
May 20, 1774

An Act for Making Effectual Provision for the Government of the Province of Quebec, in North America

May it therefore please Your most Excellent Majesty,

That it may be enacted: [Boundaries defined, Boundaries of Proclamation of 1763 extended to include territory west to the Mississippi, north to the frontiers of the Hudson's Bay territory, and the islands in the mouth of the St. Lawrence.]

. . . And whereas the Provisions made by the said Proclamation, in respect to the Civil Government of the said Province of Quebec, and the Powers and Authorities given to the Governor and other Civil Officers of the said Province, by the Grants and Commissions issued in consequence thereof, have been found, upon Experience, to be inapplicable to the State and Circumstances of the said Province, the Inhabitants whereof amounted at the Conquest, to above Sixty five thousand Persons, professing the Religion of the Church of Rome. . . .

It is hereby declared, That His Majesty's Subjects professing the Religion of the Church of Rome, of, and in the said Province of Quebec, may have, hold, and enjoy, the free Exercise of the Religion of the Church of Rome, subject to the King's Supremacy, declared and established by an Act made in the First Year of the Reign of Queen Elizabeth, over all the Dominions and Countries which then did, or thereafter should, belong to the Imperial Crown of this Realm; and that the Clergy of the said Church may hold, receive, and enjoy their accustomed Dues and Rights, with respect to such Persons only as shall profess the said Religion.

Provided nevertheless, That it shall be lawful for His Majesty, His Heirs or Successors, to make such Provisions out of the rest of the said accustomed Dues and Rights, for the Encouragement of the Protestant Religion, and for the Maintenance and Support of a Protestant Clergy within the said Province, as he or they shall, from Time to Time, think necessary or expedient. . . .

SOURCE: D. Pickering, ed., *Statutes at Large, from Magna Charta to . . . Anno 1761–[1806]* (London, 1762–1806), XXX, 549.

And be it further enacted by the Authority aforesaid, That all His Majesty's *Canadian* Subjects within the Province of *Quebec*, the Religious Orders and Communities only excepted, may also hold and enjoy their Property and Possessions, together with all Customs and Usages, relative thereto, and all other their Civil Rights, in as large, ample and beneficial Manner, as if the said Proclamation, Commissions, Ordinances, and other Acts and Instruments, had not been made, and as may consist with their Allegiance to His Majesty, and Subjection to the Crown and Parliament of *Great Britain;* and that in all Matters of Controversy relative to Property and Civil Rights, Resort shall be had to the Laws of *Canada,* as the Rule for the Decision of the same; and all Causes that shall hereafter be instituted in any of the Courts of Justice, to be appointed within and for the said Province by His Majesty, His Heirs and Successors, shall, with respect to such Property and Rights, be determined agreeably to the said Laws and Customs of *Canada,* . . .

And whereas the Certainty and Lenity of the Criminal Law of *England,* and the Benefits and Advantages resulting from the Use of it, have been sensibly felt by the Inhabitants from an Experience of more than Nine Years, during which it has been uniformly administered; be it therefore further enacted by the Authority aforesaid, That the same shall continue to be administered, and shall be observed as Law, in the Province of *Quebec,* as well in the Description and Quality of the Offense, as in the Method of Prosecution and Trial, and the Punishment and Forfeitures thereby inflicted, to the Exclusion of every other Rule of Criminal Law, or Mode of Proceeding thereon, which did or might prevail in the said Province before the Year of our Lord One thousand seven hundred and sixty-four; any Thing in this Act to the Contrary thereof in any Respect notwithstanding; . . .

And whereas it may be necessary to ordain many Regulations, for the future Welfare and good Government of the Province of *Quebec,* the Occasions of which cannot now be foreseen, nor without much Delay and Inconvenience be provided for, without entrusting that Authority for a certain Time, and upon proper Restrictions to Persons resident there:

And whereas it is at present inexpedient to call an Assembly; be it therefore enacted by the Authority aforesaid, That it shall and may be lawful for His Majesty, . . . and with the Advice of the

Privy Council, to constitute and appoint a Council for the Affairs of the Province of *Quebec*, to consist of such Persons resident there, not exceeding Twenty-three, nor less than Seventeen, as His Majesty, . . . shall be pleased to appoint; . . . which Council, so appointed and nominated, or the major Part thereof, shall have Power and Authority to make Ordinances for the Peace, Welfare, and good Government of the said Province with the Consent of His Majesty's Governor, or, in his Absence, of the Lieutenant Governor, or Commander in Chief for the Time being. . . .

III

A Background of Social
and Regional Conflict

Almost simultaneous with the rise of protest against the new tax policies of Great Britain was the upsurge of frontier and agrarian unrest. These movements varied in form and intensity, but all the agitation was directed toward such objectives as more equitable representation of sectional interests, better and cheaper administration of justice, a reduction of taxes or quit rents, and more secure leaseholds or fee simple. In Pennsylvania a frontier band known as the Paxton Boys threatened to march to Philadelphia unless their demands were met. In New York tenant farmers rebelled against the higher rents charged by their landlords. In South Carolina the law-and-order Regulator movement sought to obtain governmental machinery for the back country, while the North Carolina Regulators took up arms against the colonial authorities in an attempt to redress their many grievances.

The frequent suppression by affluent seaboard interests of such insurgency contributed to the ambivalent stand of frontiersmen and tenant farmers toward the movement for independence—a movement that largely stemmed from seaboard grievances.

8. March of the Paxton Boys: Remonstrance of the Distressed and Bleeding Frontier Inhabitants of Pennsylvania February 13, 1764

To the Honourable John Penn, Esquire, Governor of the Province of *Pennsylvania*, & of the Counties of *New Castle*, *Kent*, and *Sussex*, on *Delaware*, and to the Representatives of the Freemen of the said Province, in General Assembly met:

WE Matthew Smith and James Gibson, in behalf of ourselves and His Majesty's faithful and loyal Subjects, the Inhabitants of the Frontier Counties of Lancaster, York, Cumberland, Berks, and Northampton, humbly beg leave to remonstrate and to lay before you the following Grievances, which we submit to your Wisdom for Redress.

First. We apprehend that as Freemen and English Subjects, we have an indisputable Title to the same Privileges & immunities with His Majesty's other Subjects who reside in the interior Counties of Philadelphia, Chester, and Bucks, and therefore ought not to be excluded from an equal share with them in the very important Privilege of Legislation; nevertheless, contrary to the Proprietor's Charter and the acknowledged principles of common Justice & Equity, our five counties are restrained from electing more than ten Representatives, viz: four for Lancaster, two for York, two for Cumberland, one for Berks, and one for Northampton; while the three Counties and City of Philadelphia, Chester, and Bucks, elect Twenty-Six. This we humbly conceive is oppressive, unequal, and unjust, the cause of many of our Grievances, and an infringment of our Natural privileges of Freedom & Equality; wherefore we humbly pray that we may be no longer deprived of an equal number with the three aforesaid Counties to represent us in Assembly.

SOURCE: *Minutes of the Provincial Council of Pennsylvania* (10 vols., Philadelphia, 1852), IX (1762–1771), 138 *et seq.*

Secondly. We understand that a Bill is now before the House of Assembly, wherein it is provided that such Persons as shall be charged with killing any Indians in Lancaster County, shall not be tried in the County where the Fact was committed, but in the Counties of Philadelphia, Chester, or Bucks. This is manifestly to deprive British Subjects of their known Privileges, to cast an eternal Reproach upon whole Counties, as if they were unfit to serve their Country in the quality of Jurymen, and to contradict the well-known Laws of the British Nation in a point whereon Life, Liberty, and security essentially depend, namely, that of being tried by their equals in the neighborhood where their own, their Accusers', and the Witnesses' Character and Credit, with the Circumstances of the Fact, are best known & instead thereof putting their Lives in the hands of Strangers who may as justly be suspected of partiallity to, as the Frontier Counties can be of prejudices against Indians; and this, too, in favour of Indians only against His Majesty's faithful & loyal subjects. . . .

Thirdly. During the late and present Indian War, the Frontiers of this Province have been repeatedly attacked and ravaged by Skulking parties of the Indians, who have with the most Savage Cruelty murdered Men, Women, and Children without distinction, and have reduced near a thousand Families to the most extream distress. It grieves us to the very heart to see such of our Frontier Inhabitants as have escaped Savage Fury with the loss of their parents, their Children, their Wives or Relatives, left destitute by the public, and exposed to the most cruel Poverty and Wretchedness while upwards of an Hundred and twenty of these Savages, who are with great reason suspected of being guilty of these horrid Barbarities under the Mask of Friendship, have procured themselves to be taken under the protection of the Government, with a view to elude the Fury of the brave Relatives of the murdered, and are now maintained at the public Expence. Some of these Indians now in the Barracks of Philadelphia, are confessedly a part of the Wyalusing Indians, which Tribe is now at war with us, and the others are the Moravian Indians, who, living amongst us under the Cloak of Friendship, carried on a Correspondence with our known Enemies on the Great Island. We cannot but observe with sorrow & indignation that some Persons in this Province are at pains to extenuate the barbarous Cruelties practised by these Savages on our murdered Brethren & Relatives, which are shocking to human Nature, and must pierce every Heart but that of the hardened perpetrators or their Abettors; Nor is it less distressing to hear others pleading that although the Wyalusing Tribe is at War with us, yet that part of it which is under the Protection of the Government may be friendly to the English and innocent. In what nation under the Sun was it ever the custom that when a neighboring Nation took up Arms, not an individual should be touched but only the Persons that offered Hostilities? Who ever proclaimed War with a part of a Nation, and not with the Whole? Had these Indians disapproved of the Perfidy of their Tribe, & been willing to cultivate and preserve Friendship with us, why did they not give notice of the War before it happened, as it is known to be the Result of long Deliberations, and a preconcerted Combination amongst them? Why did they not leave their Tribe immediately, and come amongst us before there was Ground to suspect them, or War was actually waged with their Tribe? No they stayed amongst them, were privy to their murders & Ravages, until we had destroyed their Provisions; and when they could no longer subsist at home, they come not as Deserters, but as Friends to be maintained through the Winter, that they may be able to Scalp and butcher us in the Spring.

And as to the Moravian Indians, there are strong Grounds at least to suspect their Friendship, as it is known they carried on a Correspondence with our Enemies on the Great Island. We killed three Indians going from Bethlehem to the Great Island with Blankets, Ammunition, & Provisions, which is an undeniable Proof that the Moravian Indians were in confederacy with our open Enemies; And we cannot but be filled with Indignation to hear that action of ours painted in the most odious and detestable Colours, as if we had inhumanly murdered our Guides who preserved us from perishing in the Woods, when we only killed three of our known Enemies, who attempted to shoot us when we surprized them. And besides all this, we understand that one of these very Indians is proved by the oath of Stinton's Widow, to be the very Person that murdered her Husband. How then comes it to pass that he alone, of all the Moravian Indians, should join with the enemy to murder that family? Or can it be supposed that any Enemy Indians, contrary to their known custom of making War, should penetrate into the Heart of a settled Country to burn, plunder and murder the Inhabitants, and not molest any Houses in their return, or ever be seen or heard of? Or how can we account for it, that no ravages have been committed in Northampton County, since the removal of the Moravian Indians, when the Great Cove has been struck since? These things put it beyond doubt with us that the Indians now at Philadelphia are His Majesty's Perfidious Enemies, & therefore to protect and maintain them at the Public Expence, while our suffering Brethren on the Frontiers are almost destitute of the necessaries of Life and are neglected by the Public, is sufficient to make us mad with rage, and tempt us to do what nothing but the most violent necessity can vindicate. We humbly and earnestly pray, therefore, that those Enemies of His Majesty may be removed as soon as possible out of the Province.

Fourthly. We humbly conceive that it is contrary to the maxims of good Policy, and extremely dangerous to our Frontiers, to suffer any Indians of what tribe soever to live within the Inhabited parts of the Province while we are engaged in an Indian War, as Experience has taught us that they are all perfidious, and their claim to Freedom & Independency, puts it in their power to act as Spies, to entertain & give intelligence to our Enemies, and to furnish them with Provisions and Warlike Stores. To this fatal intercourse between our pretended Friends and open Enemies, we must ascribe the greatest of the Ravages and Murders that have been committed in the course of this and the last Indian War. We therefore pray that this grievance be taken under consideration and remedied.

Fifthly. We cannot help lamenting that no Provision has been hitherto made, that such of our Frontier Inhabitants as have been wounded in defence of the Province, their Lives and Liberties, may be taken care of and cured of their Wounds at the publick Expence. We therefore pray that this Grievance may be redressed.

Sixthly. In the late Indian war this Province, with others of His Majesty's Colonies, gave rewards for Indian Scalps, to encourage the seeking them in their own Country, as the most likely means of destroying or reducing them to reason; but no such Encouragement has been given in this War, which has damped the Spirits of many brave Men who are willing to venture their Lives in parties against the Enemy. We therefore pray that public rewards may be proposed for Indian Scalps, which may be adequate to the Dangers attending Enterprizes of this nature.

Seventhly. We daily lament that numbers of our nearest & dearest relatives are still in Captivity among the Savage Heathen, to be trained up in all their Ignorance & Barbarity, or to be tortured to death with all the contrivances of Indian Cruelty, for attempting to make their escape from Bondage; We see they pay no regard to the many solemn Promises which they have made to restore our Friends who are in Bondage amongst them. We therefore earnestly pray that no trade may hereafter be permitted to be carried on with them, until our Brethren and Relatives are brought home to us.

Eighthly. We complain that a certain Society of People in this Province, in the late Indian War, & at several Treaties held by the King's representatives, openly loaded the Indians with Presents, and that J. P., a leader of the said Society, in Defiance of all Government, not only abetted our Indian Enemies, but kept up a private intelligence with them, and publickly received from them a Belt of Wampum, as if he had been our Governor or authorized by the King to treat with his Enemies. By this means the Indians have been taught to despise us as a weak and disunited people, and from this fatal Source have arose many of our Calamities under which we groan. We humbly pray therefore that this Grievance may be redressed, and that no private subject be hereafter permitted to treat with, or carry on a Correspondence with our Enemies.

Ninthly. We cannot but observe with sorrow that Fort Augusta, which has been very expensive to this Province, has afforded us but little assistance during this or the last War. The men that were stationed at that place neither helped our distressed Inhabitants to save their Crops, nor did they attack our Enemies in their Towns, or patrole on our Frontiers. We humbly request that proper measures may be taken to make that Garrison more serviceable to us in our Distress, if it can be done.

N.B. We are far from intending any Reflection against the Commanding Officer stationed at Augusta, as we presume his Conduct was always directed by those from whom he received his Orders.

SIGNED on Behalf of ourselves, and by appointment of a great number of the Frontier Inhabitants.

MATTHEW SMITH.
JAMES GIBSON.

9. New York Rent Riots: Journal of Captain John Montresor April 29–August 19, 1766

April 29, 1766

The city alarmed from the approach of the Country Levellers called the West Chester men. The militia ordered to hold themselves in readiness. Letters Received from them in town declaring that if Mr. Courtlandt does not give them a grant forever to his Lands, they will march with their Body now collected and pull down his House in Town and also one belonging to Mr. Lambert Moore.

May 1, 1766

Six men (a Committee from West Chester people being 500 men now lying at King's Bridge) came into town to explain matters. . . . The Military applied to on account of the Levellers on which they dispersed. Sons of Liberty great opposers to these Rioters as they are of opinion no one is entitled to Riot but themselves.

May 6, 1766

Proclamation issued 100£ reward for the taking of Pendergrast, Chief of the Country Levellers and 50£ for either Munro and Finch, two officers, "en second."

June 28, 1766

Advices from the Manor of Livingston that the Levellers have rose there to the number of 500 men, 200 of which had marched to murther the Lord of the Manor and level his house, unless he

SOURCE: "Journals of Capt. John Montresor, 1757–1778," New-York Historical Society, *Collections*, XIV, 363–365, 375–377, 381, 384.

would sign leases for 'em agreeable to their form, as theirs were now expired and that they would neither pay Rent, taxes, &c, nor suffer other Tenants. The Levellers met by Mr. Walter Livingston the Son who made a sally with 40 armed men—the 200 having only sticks—obliged them to retire, not without their threatening a more respectable visit on the return of Col. Livingston of the Manor.

June 29, 1766

Seventeen Hundred of the Levellers with firearms are collected at Poughkeepsie. All the jails broke open through all the counties this side of Albany of the East side of the River by people headed by Pendergrast. 8000 cartridges sent up to the 28th Regt. . . .

July 10, 1766

This morning arrived the 28th Regimt with Pendergrast the principal country Rebel ring leader . . .

August 6, 1766

Accounts from the Circuit, Pendergrast is indicated for High Treason . . .

August 19, 1766

Wm Pendergrast, who was tried at Poughkeepsie and found guilty of High Treason and received Sentence of Death, begged leave of the Court to admit him to deliver a few words viz "That if opposition to government was deemed Rebellion, no member of that court were entitled to set upon his Tryal."

10. North Carolina Regulators: Petition of the Inhabitants of Anson County, North Carolina October 9, 1769

MR. SPEAKER AND GENTLEMEN OF THE ASSEMBLY:
The Petition of the Inhabitants of Anson County, being part of the Remonstrance of the Province of North Carolina,
HUMBLY SHEWETH, That the Province in general labour under general grievances, and the Western part thereof under particular ones; which we not only see but very sensibly feel, being crouch'd beneath our sufferings: and, notwithstanding our sacred priviledges, have too long yielded ourselves slaves to remorseless oppression.—Permit us to conceive it to be our inviolable right to make known our grievances, and to petition for redress; as appears in the Bill of Rights pass'd in the reign of King Charles the first, as well as the act of Settlement of the Crown of the Revolution. We therefore beg leave to lay before you a specimen thereof, that your compassionate endeavour may tend to the relief of your injured Constituents, whose distressed condition calls aloud for aid. The alarming cries of the oppressed possibly may reach your Ears; but without your zeal how shall they ascend the throne. How relentless is the breast without sympathy, the heart that cannot bleed on a View of our calamity; to see tenderness removed, cruelty stepping in; and all our liberties and privileges invaded and abridg'd by (as it were) domesticks who are conscious of their guilt and void of remorse. O how daring! how relentless! whilst impending Judgments loudly threaten and gaze upon them, with every emblem of merited destruction.

A few of the many grievances are as follows, viz.,

1. That the poor Inhabitants in general are much oppress'd by reason of disproportionate Taxes, and those of the western Counties in particular; as they are generally in mean circumstances.

SOURCE: W. L. Saunders, ed., *Colonial Records of North Carolina* (10 vols., Raleigh, 1886–1890), VIII, 75–78.

2. That no method is prescribed by Law for the payment of the Taxes of the Western counties in produce (in lieu of a Currency) as is in other Counties within this Province; to the Peoples great oppression.

3. That Lawyers, Clerks, and other pentioners, in place of being obsequious Servants for the Country's use, are become a nuisance, as the business of the people is often transacted without the least degree of fairness, the intention of the law evaded, exorbitant fees extorted, and the sufferers left to mourn under their oppressions.

4. That an Attorney should have it in his power, either for the sake of ease or interest or to gratify their malevolence and spite, to commence suits to what Courts he pleases, however inconvenient it may be to the Defendant: is a very great oppression.

5. That all unlawful fees taken on Indictment, where the Defendant is acquitted by his Country (however customary it may be) is an oppression.

6. That Lawyers, Clerks, and others extorting more fees than is intended by law; is also an oppression.

7. That the violation of the King's Instructions to his delegates, their artfulness in concealing the same from him; and the great Injury the People thereby sustains: is a manifest oppression.

And for remedy whereof, we take the freedom to recommend the following mode of redress, not doubting audience and acceptance; which will not only tend to our relief, but command prayers as a duty from your humble Petitioners.

1. That at all elections each suffrage be given by Ticket & Ballot.

2. That the mode of Taxation be altered, and each person to pay in proportion to the profits arising from his Estate.

3. That no future tax be laid in Money, untill a currency is made.

4. That there may be established a Western as well as a Northern and Southern District, and a Treasurer for the same.

5. That when a currency is made it may be let out by a Loan office on Land security, and not to be call'd in by a Tax.

6. That all debts above 40s. and under £10 be tried and determined without Lawyers, by a jury of six freeholders impanneled by a Justice, and that their verdict be enter'd by the said Justice, and be a final judgment.

7. That the Chief Justice have no perquisites, but a Sallary only.

8. That Clerks be restricted in respect to fees, costs, and other things within the course of their office.

9. That Lawyers be effectually Barr'd from exacting and extorting fees.

10. That all doubts may be removed in respect to the payment of fees and costs on Indictments where the Defendant is not found guilty by the jury, and therefore acquitted.

11. That the Assembly make known by Remonstrance to the King, the conduct of the cruel and oppressive Receiver of the Quit Rents, for omitting the customary easie and effectual method of collecting by distress, and pursuing the expensive mode of commencing suits in the most distant Courts.

12. That the Assembly in like manner make known that the Governor and Council do frequently grant Lands to as many as they think proper without regard to head rights, notwithstanding the contrariety of His Majesties Instructions; by which means immense sums has been collected and numerous Patents granted, for much of the most fertile lands in this Province, that is yet uninhabited and uncultivated, environed by great numbers of poor people who are necessitated to toil in the cultivation of bad Lands whereon they hardly can subsist, who are thereby deprived of His Majesties liberality and Bounty: nor is there the least regard paid to the cultivation clause in said Patent mentioned, as many of the said Council as well as their friends and favorites enjoy large Quantities of Lands under the above-mentioned circumstances.

13. That the Assembly communicates in like manner the Violation of His Majesties Instructions respecting the Land Office by the Governor and Council, and of their own rules, customs and orders; if it be sufficiently proved that after they had granted Warrants for many Tracts of Land, and that the same was in due time survey'd and return'd, and the Patent fees timely paid into the said office; and that if a private Council was called on purpose to avoid spectators, and peremptory orders made that Patents should not be granted; and Warrants by their orders arbitrarily to have issued in the names of other Persons for the same Lands, and if when intreated by a solicitor they refus'd to render so much as a reason for their so doing, or to refund any part of the money by them extorted.

14. That some method may be pointed out that every improve-

ment on Lands in any of the Proprietor's part be proved when begun, by whom, and every sale made, that the eldest may have the preference of at least 300 Acres.

15. That all taxes in the following counties be paid as in other Counties in the Province, (i.e.) in the produce of the Country and that ware Houses be erected as follows, (viz.) in Anson County, at Isom Haley's ferry landing on Pe Dee river; Rowan and Orange, . . . Cumberland . . . Mecklenburg . . . and in Tryon County. . . .

16. That every denomination of People may marry according to their respective Mode, Ceremony, and custom, after due publication or Licence.

17. That Doctr Benjamin Franklin or some other known patriot be appointed Agent, to represent the unhappy state of this Province to His Majesty, and to solicit the several Boards in England.

11. South Carolina Regulators: Remonstrance and Petition of the South Carolina Back Country November 7, 1767

THE REMONSTRANCE and Petition of the Inhabitants of the Upper and Interior Parts of this Province on behalf of themselves, and all other the Settlers of the Back Country,

Humbly Showeth

That for many years past, the back parts of this province hath been infested with an infernal gang of villains, who have committed such horrid depredations on our properties and estates, such insults on the persons of many settlers, and perpetrated such shocking outrages throughout the back settlements, as is past description.

Our large stocks of cattle are either stolen and destroyed, our cow pens are broke up, and all our valuable horses are carried off. Houses have been burned by these rogues, and families stripped and turned naked into the woods. Stores have been broken open and rifled by them (wherefrom several traders are absolutely

SOURCE: Fulham Palace Transcripts, Library of Congress.

ruined). Private houses have been plundered; and the inhabitants wantonly tortured in the Indian manner for to be made confess where they secreted their effects from plunder. Married women have been ravished, virgins deflowered, and other unheard of cruelties committed by these barbarous ruffians, who, by being let loose among us (and connived at) by the acting magistrates, have hereby reduced numbers of individuals to poverty, and for these three years last past have laid (in a manner) this part of the province under contribution.

No trading persons (or others) or with money or goods; no responsible persons and traders dare keep cash or any valuable articles by them. Nor can women stir abroad but with a guard, or in terror. The chastity of many beauteous maidens have been threatened by these rogues. Merchants' stores are obliged for to be kept constantly guarded (which enhances the price of goods). And thus we live not as under a British government (every man sitting in peace and security under his own vine, his own fig tree), but as if [we] were in Hungary or Germany, and in a state of war, continually exposed to the incursions of hussars and pandours; obliged to be constantly on the watch and on our guard against these intruders, and having it not in our power to call what we possess our own, not even for an hour; as being liable daily and hourly to be stripped of our property.

Representations of these grievances and vexations have often been made by us to those in power, but without redress. Our cries must have pierced their ears, though not entered into their hearts. For, instead of public justice being executed on many of these notorious robbers (who have been taken by us at much labour and expense and committed) and on others (who with great difficulty and charge have been arraigned and convicted), we have to lament that such have from time to time been pardoned; and afresh set loose among us to repeat their villainies, and strip us of the few remaining cattle, horses, and moveables, which after their former visits they had left us.

Thus distressed, thus situated and unrelieved by government, many among us have been obliged to punish some of these banditti and their accomplices in a proper manner; necessity (that first principle) compelling them to do what was expected that the executive branch of the legislature would long ago have done.

We are free men, British subjects, not born slaves. We contribute our proportion in all public taxations, and discharge our duty to the public equally with our fellow provincials, yet we do not participate with them in the rights and benefits which they enjoy, though equally entitled to them.

Property is of no value, except it be secure. How ours is secured appears from the forementioned circumstances, and from our now being obliged to defend our families by our own strength, as legal methods are beyond our reach, or not as yet extended to us.

We may be deemed too bold in saying "That the present constitution of this province is very defective, and become a burden, rather than being beneficial to the back inhabitants." For instance: to have but one place of judicature in this large and growing colony, and that seated not central but in a nook by the seaside; the back inhabitants to travel two, three hundred miles to carry down criminals, prosecute offenders, appear as witnesses (though excluded to serve as jurors), attend the courts and suits of law, the governor and Court of Ordinary, all land matters, and on every public occasion, are great grievances and call loudly for redress. For 'tis not only loss of time which the poor settlers sustain therefrom, but the toil of travelling, and heavy expenses therefrom arising. Poor suitors are often driven to great distresses, even to the spending their last shilling, or to sell their only horse, for to defray their travelling and town costs. After which, they are obliged to trudge home on foot, and beg for subsistence by the way. And after being subpoenaed and then attending court as witnesses or as constables, they oft are never called for on trials but are put off to next court, and then the same services must be repeated. These are circumstances experienced by no individuals under British government save those in South Carolina.

It is partly owing to these burdens on our shoulders that the gangs of robbers who infest us have so long reigned without repression: for if a party hath twenty cattle, or the best of his stallions stolen from him, the time and charge consequent on a prosecution of the offenders is equal to, or greater than his loss, as to prosecute would make him doubly a sufferer. And poor persons have not money to answer the cravings of rapacious lawyers. As proceedings at law are now managed, it may cost a private person fifty pounds to bring a villain to justice; and in civil cases the recovery of twenty pounds will frequently be attended with seventy pounds costs, if not treble that sum.

When cattle and horses are stolen and the thief is publicly known (at [sic] they will commit their robberies openly at noonday). Persons who see and know of these evils are backward in making information as they thereby are certain to subject themselves to much trouble and expense, beside the risk they run of being plundered themselves by the rogues in revenge for informing against them. And in consequence of being subpoenaed to attend the courts of Charleston (under great disadvantages), they are often obliged to sell their substance at half value to defray road charges, the public having made no provision on this head. These long journeys are often required too at some critical juncture, very detrimental to the poor planter; who therefrom, will endeavour to avoid appearing against rogues when they are brought to trial. From which circumstances, many rogues have been acquitted at court for want of evidence, the trials of others delayed, the province (as well as individuals) put to grievous expense; and the gangs of robbers (herefrom recruited and spirited) have still reigned without control, ranging and plundering the country with impunity. We can truly say they reign, as by their menaces they intimidate many whom they have injured from laying hold on and bringing of them to justice.

If we are thus insecure, if our lives and properties are thus at stake, if we cannot be protected, if these villains are suffered to range the country uncontrolled and no redress to be obtained for our losses; all of us and our families must quit the province and retire where there are laws, religion and government. For as the laws now stand, it is of no import to bind lawless profligate persons to their good behaviour. Recognizances are laughed at because never put in suit, nor can be but at the private expense of the suffering party. Wherefrom the clergy, magistracy, and all in public authority (who ought to be protected in execution of the laws and honoured in their public stations) are insulted and abused by licentious and insolent persons without redress.

The trial of small and mean causes by a single magistrate (a wise institution in the infancy of the colony) is now become an intolerable grievance, partly through the ignorance of some justices, and the bigotry and partiality of others. Individuals are rather oppressed than relieved by their decisions, for persons are ofttimes saddled with ten or twelve pounds costs on a debt of as many shillings. Through the indolence, connivance, or corruption of several justices, it is owning that the thieves have gained such strength and risen to such a pitch of audacity. They well know that if warrants are issued out against them that they will be slowly pursued, or that they shall have timely notice given them for to avoid the officers. We could enumerate many flagrant instances of this sort, but as every complaint of this nature from the country have hitherto been disregarded, we can only close this article with saying that through the venality of mean persons now in the Commission, contempt instead of respect is thrown on this so honourable and necessary an office.

By poor persons being obliged to travel to Charleston to obtain patents for small tracts of land or to renew their warrants, his Majesty's kindness to his subjects is defeated as it causes land to come as dear, or prove as expensive in running out, as if for to be purchased, the same fees being paid on a grant of ten as on one of ten thousand acres. The like grievance exists in respect to the proving of wills or taking out letters of administration, the fees on which are treble to what is charged at home, even though clogged with stamps. When effects of a deceased party doth not exceed £40 or £50, half this sum must be expended in court fees, no distinction being made, it being alike the same if the effects are fifty or fifty thousand pounds. These are great hardships on the poor, especially as the fees now claimed at the public offices are double to what were formerly demanded, which merits the serious attention of the legislature.

As the laws are now modelled, any malicious, malevolent party, may arrest any stranger, any innocent person, for any sum whatever, without showing cause of action or making oath of his debt or giving security for joining issue, which often prevents persons from getting bail, for though the debt or balance may not be six pence, yet the sum alleged may be six thousand pounds. This intimidates persons from becoming securities and subjects many to wrongful and injurious imprisonment whereby their credit and families are entirely ruined, health impaired, lives sacrificed by lying in a close and stinking gaol; crowded with thieves and vagabonds! No separation, no distinction made of parties, not hardly even of the sexes. Who can boast of British liberty that is not safe one hour from so dreadful an oppression! A stranger, or vagrant in this province, who can pay a lawyer ten pounds, may at his pleasure or for his frolic, send to prison (at 200 miles distance) the best person here among us without his knowing on what account or for what reason, and this in as arbitrary a manner as in France, by a lettre de cachet, or in Spain, by warrant from the Inquisition. Most sore are these evils! Especially too when a poor wretch who has inadvertently broke the peace (for which in Britain he would be ordered a few lashes or a small fine, and be dismissed) must lie five or six months in this loathsome gaol amidst thieves and robbers, in the heat of summer, and then afterwards be discharged by proclamation. Punishments ought to bear some proportion to trespasses. Nor should small and great offences be treated with equal severity. To be confined six months in Charleston gaol at 200 or 300 miles distance from friends or family, and to live in this hot clime on bread and water is a far heavier punishment than for to be in the French King's galleys, or a slave in Barbary. And for persons to lie there session after session for small sums or petty offences, is contrary to all humanity. And more so (as we observed) when persons of every class and each sex are promiscuously confined together in a space where they have not room to lie, and no distinction made between offenders; but thieves and murderers, debtors to the king, offenders in penal laws, vagrants and idle persons are closely huddled in one mixed crowd.

When persons are unwarrantably arrested by vexatious pettifoggers or litigious miscreants (as such will infest every society), and bail is given; in this case, should the plaintiff discontinue and refuse joining issue and drop the suit, we apprehend (from the sufferings of many) that no remedy at present lies for relief of any innocent person who is so treated, consistent with the liberty of the subject. But the defendant must admit to £40 or £50 charge and loss. Or if he sue for damages or costs expended, or for false imprisonment after being ruined and undone, what satisfaction is to be obtained against insolvent prosecutors?

By our birthright as Britons we ought for to be tried by a jury of our peers. This is the glorious liberty of free-born subjects, the darling privilege that distinguishes Britain from all other nations. But we poor distressed settlers enjoy only the shadow, not the substance of this happiness. For can we truly be said to be tried by our peers when few or no persons on this north side of Santee River (containing half the province) are on the jury list? The juries of every court are generally composed of the inhabitants of Charleston or its environs—persons who never perhaps travelled beyond

Charleston Neck; who know not even the geography, much less the persons and concerns of the back country. These determine boundaries of our lands, without a view, and decide on matters of which they [have] no proper conception. We think these proceedings as absurd as if affairs of shipping and trade were to be settled by twelve residents in our woods who never saw a town, the sea, or a ship in their lives.

Herefrom, the lives and properties of us back settlers, may accidentally be affected through the judge or jurors having no personal knowledge of parties who depose in court, or of their quality, estate, or character they bear where they dwell. All persons, without exception, are now admitted to give evidence, according to the mode of their profession, and stand recta in curia. Now, as we are a mixed people, and many concealed papists among us (especially in the disguise of Quakers), and as such are often admitted as witnesses and jurors, a wrong verdict may often pass through this general admission of persons of all countries' complexions and characters being suffered to be on juries, and so give evidence without distinction or restriction.

Nor can we be said to possess our legal rights as free-holders when we are so unequally represented in Assembly. The south side of Santee River, electing 44 members, and the north side, with these upper parts of the province (containing ⅔ of the white inhabitants), returning but six. It is to this great disproportion of representatives on our part that our interests have been so long neglected, and the back country disregarded. But it is the number of free men, not black slaves, that constitute the strength and riches of a state.

The not laying out the back country into parishes is another most sensible grievance. This evil we apprehend to arise from the selfish views of those whose fortune and estates are in or near Charleston, which makes them endeavour that all matters and things shall centre there, however detrimental to the body politic. Hence it arises that Assemblies are kept sitting for six weeks, to oblige us (against inclination) to choose such persons for representatives who live in or contiguous to Charleston, and to render a seat in the Assembly too heavy a burden for any country planter of a small estate for to bear. From this, our non-representation in the House, we conceive it is that sixty thousand pounds public money (of which we must pay the greater part, as being levied on the consumer) hath lately been voted for to build an Exchange for the merchants, and a ball-room for the ladies of Charleston; while near sixty thousand of us back settlers have not a minister or a place of worship to repair to! As if we were not worth even the thought of, or deemed as savages, and not Christians!

To leave our native countries, friends, and relations, the service of God, the enjoyment of our civil and religious rights for to breathe here (as we hoped) a purer air of freedom, and possess the utmost enjoyment of liberty and independency; and instead hereof, to be set adrift in the wild woods among Indians and outcasts; to live in a state of heathenism, without law or government or even the appearance of religion; exposed to the insults of lawless and impudent persons, to the depredations of thieves and robbers, and to be treated by our fellow provincials who hold the reins of things as persons hardly worthy the public attention, not so much as their Negroes. These sufferings have broken the hearts of hundreds of our new settlers, make others quit the province; some return to Europe (and therefrom prevent others coming this way), and deterred numbers of persons of fortune and character (both at home and in America) from taking up of lands here and settling this, our back country, as otherwise they would have done.

But whatever regulations, whatever emoluments are offered for the embellishment or benefit of the metropolis, such are readily admitted while we are considered by its inhabitants (and if they could, they would make us) hewers of wood and drawers of water, for service of the town; who treat us not as brethren of the same kindred, united in the same interests, and subjects of the same prince, but as if we were of a different species from themselves; reproaching us for our ignorance and unpoliteness, while they themselves contribute to it, and would chain us to these oars, as unwillingly that either us or our posterity should emerge from darkness to light, and from the power of Satan unto God. Their very follies and extravagancies would afford us means of knowledge and refinement. What they waste and throw away would lay for us the foundations of good things. The sums trifled away in a play house there would have raised us fifty new churches. And the heavy annual charges which the public is saddled with, attending the conveying of prisoners to town, summoning juries, and other incident expenses, together with Mr. Provost Marshal's and Mr. Attorney General's bills, would, if thrown together for these last seven years, have defrayed the expense of building gaols and court houses in every parish of the province, and all other public edifices. But this is not comparable to the damage done the mother country and the West India trade by the thieves stealing of all our best horses, and then selling of them to Dutch agents, for to be transported to the French islands to work their sugar mills. Add to this the depression of our lands in value, prevention of their sale and culture of any improvements in planting or public works through the insecurity of all property by incursions of the thieves; the bad character which the back settlements hath gained hereby (both in Britain and America); the rise of provisions through loss of our stocks of meat cattle; the length of time and great expense it will cost us to raise again a fine breed of horses; the dread which persons of condition and character entertain even of their persons should they travel among us (which deters them from sending of any slaves for to improve their lands in the back country through fear of their being stolen), prevents their paying us any attention or regard or attempting any new branches of commerce though excited thereto by the Society of Arts at home. In short, the dread impressed on all travellers, and which prevents itinerants from visiting us (and thereby making cash to circulate); the damp put on our spirits through the disregards shown us by the Legislature which has prevented, as beforesaid, many thousands from settling among us and lessening thereby the weight of taxes, and adding to the increase of provisions and commodities for the market; the drawing of merchants and mechanics among us, thereby lowering the present exorbitant prices of goods and labour, and opening new channels of trade; all these, and other striking circumstances, have been little thought of or considered in Charleston, midst scenes of luxury and dissipation. . . .

Through the nonestablishment of public schools, a great multitude of children are now grown up in the greatest ignorance of everything save vice, in which they are adepts. Consequently they lead idle and immoral lives for they having no sort of education, naturally follow hunting, shooting, racing, drinking, gaming, and every species of wickedness. Their lives are only one continual scene of depravity of manners and reproach to the country, being more abandoned to sensuality and more rude in manners than the poor savages around us. They will learn no trade or mechanic arts whereby to obtain an honest livelihood, or practise any means of industry; or if they know, they will not practise them, but range the country with their horse and gun, without home or habitation, all persons, all places, all women being alike to them. These are other deep roots from which the hordes of mulattoes and villains we are pestered with have shot up, whereas, had we churches and ministers, schools and catechists, children would be early taught the principles of religion and goodness, and their heads and hands be employed in exercises of the manual and useful arts; tradesmen would increase; manufacturers be followed up; agriculture be improved; the country wear a new face, and peace and plenty smile around us.

But in our present unsettled situation, when the bands of society and government hang loose and ungirt about us; when no regular police is established but everyone left to do as seemeth him meet, there is not the least encouragement for any individual to be industrious, emulous in well-doing, or enterprising in any attempt that is laudable or public-spirited. Cunning, rapine, fraud, and violence are now the studies and pursuits of the vulgar. If we save a little money for to bring down to town wherewith to purchase slaves, should it be known, our houses are beset and robbers plunder us even of our clothes. If we buy liquor for to retail, or for hospitality, they will break into our dwellings and consume it. If we purchase bedding, linen, or decent furniture, they have early notice, and we are certain for to be stripped of it. Should we raise fat cattle, or prime horses for the market, they are constantly carried off, though well guarded (as a small force is insufficient for their security). Or if we collect gangs of hogs for to kill and to barrel up for sale, or plant orchards or gardens, the rogues, and other idle, worthless, vagrant people with whom we are overrun, are continually destroying of them, and subsisting on the stocks and labours of the industrious planter. If we are in any wise injured in our persons, fame, or fortune, what remedy have we? What redress can be obtained without travelling two hundred miles to Charleston? Where (through the chicanery of lawyers, slowness of law proceeding, and expenses thence arising), we are greater sufferers than before, and only thereby add evil to evil. Nay, we have had, and daily do see those very horses and creatures which have been stolen from us (and for which we have endeavoured to bring villains to justice); we have seen these our creatures sold before our faces for to raise money to fee lawyers to plead against us and to save rogues from the halter. And what defence are the laws (as they are now dispensed) to us against such as are below the law? For in many cases (as in branding and killing of cattle) fines only being imposed and no provision made for the sufferer, should the injurer be a vagrant, or insolvent, incapable of paying the fine, what redress lies in this case? The confining of the transgressor for six months (at the private expense of the sufferer, beside his charges of prosecution) in the common gaol of Charleston, where it is as agreeable to him to live an idle life in as out of it, work being the article he would avoid at any rate, and we have not a bridewell, whipping post, or pair of stocks in the province, and the workhouse of Charleston is only so in name.

As the back country is now daily increasing by imports of people from Ireland and elsewhere (most of whom are very poor), the number of the idle and worthless must also increase if our settlements long remain in their present neglected state. Many of these new settlers greatly repent their coming out here, to languish away life in a country that falls so very short of their expectations; and the sober part of them would more willingly return than remain here. They have indeed land given them, and may with industry, raise a bare subsistence; but they are discouraged from any bold pursuits or exerting their laudable endeavours to make improvements through the uncertainty that attends us all; i.e., whether in the end they may reap the fruits of their labour; for such number of idle and vagrant persons from the northern colonies traverse and infest this province that if a spot of ground be planted (especially with fruit trees for cider, etc.), the proprietor cannot be certain of gathering the produce but may see it carried off before his face without control. So great is the weakness of government in these parts that our magistrates are weary of committing persons to Charleston for petty offences and they have no authority to inflict punishments. It is therefore in vain for us to attempt the laying out of vineyards, sheepwalks, or bleaching grounds, as it would only be working for these indolent, unsettled, roving wretches.

Property being thus insecure, no improvements are attempted, no new plans can take place, nothing out of the common road can be executed, till legislation is extended to us. A damp is now put on all spirited endeavours to make matters run in their proper channel. And (shameful to say), our lands (some of the finest in

America) lie useless and uncleared, being rendered of small value from the many licentious persons intermixed among us whom we cannot drive off without force or violence.

But these our lands would be of infinite value, and in time, the most desirable in the province, were proper regulations to take place, and good manners and order be introduced among us. Our soil is not only fruitful but capable of producing any grain whatever. Our vales and woods are delightful, our hills healthful and pleasant. This single consideration merits the public attention. For, was the country to be once cleared of lawless and idle people (or were they only for to be put under proper restraint), were courts of justice once established, the roads repaired and improved, bridges built in proper places, and travelling rendered safe and commodious, we should no longer be pestered with insolvent and licentious persons from the neighboring governments. Nor would this province be the sink (as now it is) of the refuse of other colonies. Such abandoned wretches would no longer seek shelter or find protection here, nor set bad examples to our rising progeny. We should chase them away as beasts of prey. And was the country once cleared of such vermin, it would induce genteel persons to make the tour of their native country and not embark annually for Rhode Island or New York for the benefit of cool air. They may breathe equal as salubrious on our hills. And the specie which is now carried out of the province by our travelling gentry (never to return!) would circulate among the poor back inhabitants and quickly find its way down to Charleston.

IV

Imperial Policy Innovations
and Colonial Opposition

Prior to the Seven Years' War, opposition in the colonies to British policy had been sporadic and largely isolated in character, save perhaps for the widespread positive response in America to the Revolution of 1688 in England. The English tradition that there were limitations on government, a tradition rooted in common law, in recollections of the Commonwealth period, and of the final overthrow of the Stuarts had never died out, however. Occasions such as the commemoration of the anniversary of Charles I's execution fanned the flames of latent republicanism. On one such anniversary, in January 1750 the Reverend Jonathan Mayhew, the rational, Unitarian-leaning Puritan preacher of the West Church in Boston, defined the grievances upon which civil disobedience could be supported.

Mayhew's remarks have a prophetic ring, but the testing of his preachments were deferred for some fifteen years. The conclusion of the Seven Years' War in 1763 left Great Britain with a staggering war debt and the prospect of continuing budgetary outlays for the defense of the newly enlarged Empire. The vigorous protest against the cider tax in England forced the Grenville Ministry to shift some of the financial burden to the colonies. The first measure enacted by Grenville was the Sugar Act, which called for a tax of threepence per pound of imported sugar and provided for strict enforcement. The strongest opposition to this act came from the New York Assembly, which declared it unconstitutional.

The second step in the Grenville program was the Stamp Act. As reported by Jared Ingersoll, the agent for Connecticut, few in Parliament originally opposed it. However, news of the passage of the Stamp Act touched off a violent reaction in America. The Virginia House of Burgesses led by Patrick Henry adopted a set of resolves condemning the measure, and other legislatures soon followed suit. In some cities, such as Boston, angry mobs damaged the property of stamp distributors and defenders of the act. The letter here of Governor Bernard reports the Boston riot of August 15, 1765, when the mob forced Andrew Oliver to resign as stamp collector. Eleven days later mobs sacked the home and library of Chief Justice Hutchinson and burned the records of the court of vice-admiralty.

In October 1765 representatives from eleven colonies met in New York to deal with the crisis. This Stamp Act Congress displayed a high degree of colonial solidarity, but the resolves that it adopted, though firm, were conciliatory.

12. The Case for Civil Disobedience: Jonathan Mayhew's Sermon, "A Discourse Concerning Unlimited Submission and Non-Resistance to the Higher Powers" 1750

THERE is one very important and interesting point which remains to be inquired into; namely, the extent of that subjection to the higher powers, which is here enjoined as a duty upon all christians. Some have thought it warrantable and glorious, to disobey the civil powers in certain circumstances; and, in cases of very great and general oppression, when humble remonstrances fail of having any effect; and when the publick welfare cannot be otherwise provided for and secured, to rise unanimously even against the sovereign himself, in order to redress their grievances; to vindicate their natural and legal rights: to break the yoke of tyranny, and free themselves and posterity from inglorious servitude and ruin. It is upon this principle that many royal oppressors have been driven from their thrones into banishment; and many slain by the hands of their subjects. It was upon this principle that *Tarquin* was expelled from *Rome*; and *Julius Cesar*, the conqueror of the world, and the tyrant of his country, cut off in the senate house. It was upon this principle, that King *Charles* I, was beheaded before his own banqueting house. It was upon this principle, that King *James* II. was made to fly that country which he aimed at enslaving: And upon this principle was that *revolution* brought about, which has been so fruitful of happy consequences to *Great-Britain*. But, in opposition to this principle, it has often been asserted, that the

SOURCE: Jonathan Mayhew, *A Discourse Concerning Unlimited Submission and Non-Resistance to the Higher Powers* (Boston, 1750), pp. 12–34.

scripture in general (and the passage under consideration in particular) makes all resistance to princes a crime, in any case whatever.—If they turn tyrants, and become the common oppressors of those, whose welfare they ought to regard with paternal affection, we must not pretend to right ourselves, unless it be by prayers and tears and humble intreaties: And if these methods fail of procuring redress, we must not have recourse to any other, but all suffer ourselves to be robbed and butchered at the pleasure of the *Lord's anointed;* lest we should incur the sin of rebellion, and the punishment of damnation. For he has God's authority and commission to bear him out in the worst of crimes, so far that he may not be withstood or controuled. Now whether we are obliged to yield such an absolute submission to our prince; or whether disobedience and resistance may not be justifiable in some cases, notwithstanding any thing in the passage before us, is an inquiry in which we are all concerned; and this is the inquiry which is the main design of the present discourse.

Now there does not seem to be any necessity of supposing, that an absolute, unlimited obedience, whether active or passive, is here injoined, merely for this reason, that the precept is delivered in *absolute terms,* without any *exception* or *limitation* expressly mentioned. We are enjoined, (ver. 1) to be *subject to the higher powers:* and (ver. 5) to be *subject for conscience sake.* And because these expressions are absolute and unlimited, (or, more properly, general) some have inferred, that the subjection required in them, must be absolute and unlimited also; At least so far forth as to make passive obedience and non-resistance, a duty in all cases whatever, if not active obedience likewise. Though, by the way, there is here no distinction made betwixt active and passive obedience; and if either of them be required in an unlimited sense, the other must be required in the same sense also, by virtue of the present argument; because the expressions are equally absolute with respect to both. But that unlimited obedience of any sort, cannot be argued merely from the indefinite expressions in which obedience is enjoined, appears from hence, that expressions of the same nature, frequently occur in scripture, upon which it is confessed on all hands, that no such absolute and unlimited sense ought to be put. For example, *Love not the world; neither the things that are in the world;*[1] *Lay not up for yourselves treasures*

1. 1 John ii. 15.

upon earth;[2] *Take therefore no thought for the morrow;*[3] are precepts expressed in at least equally absolute and unlimited terms: but it is generally allowed that they are to be understood with certain restrictions and limitations; some degree of love to the world, and the things of it, being allowable. . . .

There is, indeed, one passage in the new-testament, where it may seem, at first view, that an unlimited submission to civil rulers, is injoined. *Submit your selves to every ordinance of man for the Lord's sake.*[4] To every *ordinance of man*. However, this expression is no stronger than that before taken notice of, with relation to the duty of wives—*So let the wives be subject to their own husbands—* IN EVERY THING. But the true solution of this difficulty (if it be one) is *this: by every ordinance of man*[5] is not meant every command of the civil magistrate without exception; but *every order of magistrates appointed by man;*—whether superior or inferior: For so the apostle explains himself in the very next words— *Whether it be to the king as supreme, or to governors, as unto them that are sent,* etc. But although the apostle had not subjoined any such explanation, the reason of the thing itself would have obliged us to limit the expression [*every ordinance of man*] to such human ordinances and commands, as are not inconsistent with the ordinances and commands of God, the supreme lawgiver; or with any other higher, and antecedent, obligations.

It is to be observed, in the next place, that as the duty of universal obedience and non-resistance to the *higher powers*, cannot be argued from the absolute unlimited expressions which the apostle here uses, so neither can it be argued from the scope and drift of his reasoning, considered with relation to the persons he was here opposing. As was observed above, there were some professed *christians* in the apostolic age, who disclaimed all magistracy and civil authority in general, *despising government*, and *speaking evil of dignities;* some under a notion that *jews* ought not to be under the jurisdiction of *gentile* rulers; and others, that they were set *free* from the temporal powers, by Christ. Now it is with

2. Matt. vi. 19.
3. Matt. vi. 34.
4. Peter ii. 13.
5. Literally, every human institution, or appointment. By which manner of expression the apostle plainly intimates that rulers derive their authority immediately, not from God, but from men.

persons of this licentious opinion and character, that the apostle is concerned. And all that was directly to his point, was to show, that they were bound to submit to magistracy *in general.* . . .

And if we attend to the nature of the argument with which the apostle here enforces the duty of submission to *the higher powers,* we shall find it to be such an one as concludes not in favor of submission to all who bear the *title* of rulers, in common; but only, to those who *actually* perform the duty of rulers, by exercising a reasonable and just authority, for the good of human society. This is a point which it will be proper to enlarge upon; because the question before us turns very much upon the truth or falshood [*sic*] of this position. It is obvious, then, in general, that the civil rulers whom the apostle here speaks of, and obedience to whom he presses upon christians as a duty, are *good rulers*[6] such as are, in the exercise of their office and power, benefactors to society. Such they are described to be throughout this passage. Thus it is said, that they are not *a terror to good works, but to evil;* that they are *God's ministers for good; revengers to execute wrath upon him that doth evil; and that they attend continually upon this very thing.* St. Peter gives the same account of rulers: *They are for a praise to them that do well, and the punishment of evil doers.* It is manifest that this character and description of rulers, agrees only to such as are rulers in fact, as well as in name: to such as govern well, and act agreeably to their office. And the apostle's argument for submission to rulers, is wholly built and grounded upon a presumption that they do in fact answer this character; and is of no force at all upon supposition to the contrary. If *rulers are a terror to good works, and not to the evil;* if they are not *ministers for good* to society, but for evil and distress, by violence and oppression; if they *execute wrath upon* sober, peaceable persons, who do their duty as members of society; and suffer rich and honourable knaves to escape with impunity; if, instead of *attending continually upon* the good work of advancing the publick welfare, they *attend* only upon the gratification of their own lust and pride and ambition, to the destruction of the public welfare; if this be the case, it is plain that the apostle's argument for submission does not reach them; they are

6. By *good rulers,* are not intended such as are good in a *moral* or *religious,* but only in a *political,* sense; those who perform their duty so far as their office extends; and so far as civil society, as such, is concerned in their actions.

not the same, but different persons from those whom he character-
izes; and who must be obeyed according to his reasoning. . . .

If it be said, that the apostle here uses another argument for
submission to the *higher powers*, besides that which is taken from
the usefulness of their office to civil society, when properly discharged and executed; namely, that their *power is from God; that
they are ordained of God*; and that they *are God's ministers*: And if
it be said, that this argument for submission to them will hold
good, although they do not exercise their power for the benefit, but
for the ruin, and destruction of human society; this objection was
obviated, in part, before. Rulers have no authority from God to do
mischief. They are not *God's ordinance*, or *God's ministers*, in any
other sense than as it is by his permission and providence, that they
are exalted to bear rule; and as magistracy duly exercised, and
authority rightly applied, in the enacting and executing good
laws,—laws attempered and accommodated to the common welfare of the subjects, must be supposed to be agreeable to the will of
the beneficent author and supreme Lord of the universe; whose
kingdom ruleth over all,[7] and whose *tender mercies are over all his
works*.[8] . . .

Thus, upon a careful review of the apostle's reasoning in this
passage, it appears that his arguments to enforce submission, are of
such a nature, as to conclude only in favor of submission *to such
rulers as he himself describes*; i.e., such as rule for the good of
society, which is the only end of their institution. Common
tyrants, and public oppressors, are not intitled to obedience from
their subjects, by virtue of any thing here laid down by the inspired
apostle.

I now add, farther, that the apostle's argument is so far from
proving it to be the duty of people to obey, and submit to, such
rulers as act in contradiction to the public good[9] and so to the
design of their office, that it proves *the direct contrary*. For, please
to observe, that if the end of all civil government, be the good of
society; if this be the thing that is aimed at in constituting civil

7. Psal. ciii. 19.
8. Psal. xclv. 19.
9. This does not intend, their acting so in a *few particular instances*, which
the best of rulers may do through mistake, etc. but their acting so *habitually*;
and in a manner which plainly shows, that they aim at making themselves
great, by the ruin of their subjects.

rulers; and if the motive and argument for submission to government, be taken from the apparent usefulness of civil authority; it follows, that when no such good end can be answered by submission, there remains no argument or motive to enforce it; if instead of this good end's being brought about by submission, a contrary end is brought about, and the ruin and misery of society effected by it, here is a plain and positive reason against submission in all such cases, should they ever happen. And therefore, in such cases, a regard to the public welfare, ought to make us with-hold from our rulers, that obedience and subjection which it would, otherwise, be our duty to render to them. If it be our duty, for example, to obey our king, merely for this reason, that he rules for the public welfare, (which is the only argument the apostle makes use of) it follows, by a parity of reason, that when he turns tyrant, and makes his subjects his prey to devour and to destroy, instead of his charge to defend and cherish, we are bound to throw off our allegiance to him, and to resist; and that according to the tenor of the apostle's argument in this passage. Not to discontinue our allegiance, in this case, would be to join with the sovereign in promoting the slavery and misery of that society, the welfare of which, we ourselves, as well as our soveriegn, are indispensably obliged to secure and promote, as far as in us lies. It is true the apostle puts no case of such a tyrannical prince; but by his grounding his argument for submission wholly upon the good of civil society; it is plain he implicitly authorises, and even requires us to make resistance, whenever this shall be necessary to the public safety and happiness. . . .

All civil rulers, as such, are the ordinance and ministers of God; and they are all, by the nature of their office, and in their respective spheres and stations, bound to consult the public welfare. With the same reason, therefore, that any deny unlimited and passive obedience to be here injoined under a republic or aristocracy, or any other established form of civil government; or to subordinate powers, acting in an illegal and oppressive manner; (with the same reason) others may deny, that such obedience is enjoined to a king or monarch, or any civil power whatever. For the apostle says nothing is peculiar to kings; what he says, extends equally to all other persons whatever, vested with any civil office. They are all, in exactly the same sense, the ordinance of God; and the ministers of God; and obedience is equally injoined to be paid to them all.

For, as the apostle expresses it, *there is* NO POWER *but of God:* And we are required to *render to* ALL *their* DUES, and not MORE than their DUES. And what these *dues* are, and to *whom* they are to be *rendered,* the apostle *sayeth not;* but leaves to the reason and conscience of men to determine.

Thus it appears, that the common argument, grounded upon this passage, in favor of universal, and passive obedience, really overthrows itself, by proving too much, if it proves any thing at all, namely, that no civil officer is, in any case whatever, to be resisted, though acting in express contradiction to the design of his office; which no man, in his senses, ever did, or can assert.

13. Protest Against the Cider Tax in England: Petitions from Southams and Hereford June 6, 1763

Petition from Southams

Sir,

The farmers in this country, dreading the excisemen, have had several meetings, and have come to several resolutions, the purport of which are as follow:

That since it appears by the cyder-act, that *all cyder,* good or bad, strong or weak, is to be charg'd at the pound's mouth with the exorbitant duty of 4s. a hogshead, and that this money must be raised and paid within six weeks after making, without the least drawback or deduction for the great loss and waste in racking from the gross lee, for the shrinking afterwards, or for what may leak out, or turn ropy, casky, &c. the duty *called* 4s. will, in *truth,* amount to 6 or 7s. a hogshead on all the clean cyder which in the spring of the year shall be found fit for sale or use.

That this being, therefore, a burthen intolerable, and a tax impossible to be paid, they resolve, that unless they can have an assurance of being released from it by a repeal of the act in the next

SOURCE: *Gentleman's Magazine,* XXXIII (June 1763), 302, 304.

session, they will rather let the apples rot under the trees, than make any cyder this year; and consequently they will make no entry with the exciseman of their mill houses, as they will not use them themselves, or permit others to use them.

That rather than ride after excisemen, and suffer such spies and informers to come into their houses, they will take their leave of cyder, by drinking out, in their own families, what is at present in their cellars, and as this is chargeable with no duty (unless sold or removed) they will make no entry of the quantity already by them, or which they may lay in their cellars before the 5th of July.

That having thus no business with the excisemen, nor the excisemen with them, they will wait till the parliament meets.—If the cyder act is intended to be repealed, it may be done (they say) time enough to save some of the latter fruit.—If not, that all the orchards shall be demolished in the next winter that can be taken up, and be turned back into pasture, as the duty cannot possibly be paid.

Petition from Hereford

To Sir John Morgan, Bart. and Velters Cornewall, Esq. Knights of the Shire for the County of Hereford

The Gentlemen, Clergy, and Free-holders of the County of Hereford, highly sensible of your diligence and steadiness in your opposition to the late Tax upon Cyder and Perry,[1] return you their warmest thanks. The many inconveniences, and indeed hardships, attending this tax, are so visible to those of his majesty's subjects, who are more particularly affected thereby, that they cannot help looking upon it as the offspring of precipitation, rather than of expedience: Such an extension of the Excise Laws, so alarming to the nation, will greatly disturb the ease and quiet of the people; the disproportion of this tax to the duty upon malt liquor brewed in private houses, affords matter for complaint; the immediate pay-ment of the duty from the mill, must distress many numerous families, which for their subsistence depend upon the profits of small farms; consequently, the landed property will decrease in value, and the weight of the land-tax be more severely felt.

It is humbly hoped, that a proper representation of the whole of

1. Pear cider.

these our grievances, and of the uncertain produce of the tax, will induce the wisdom and moderation of a *British* parliament to raise the supplies necessary for government by some other means, less burthensome to the cyder counties, less irksome to his majesty's faithful subjects.

You, therefore, whose abilities and integrity we have experienced, are, as the representatives of this county, intreated to use every constitutional measure, to obtain a repeal of so much of the late act as lays an additional tax on Cyder and Perry; Thus shall your fellow-countrymen rejoice in peace, as well private as public; thus will they be enabled the more easily to preserve that rule and good order, so beneficial to every nation, so much recommended by that sovereign, whom they honour as a parent, and whose parliament they revere as the guardian of their liberties.

14. Sugar Act: Petition of the New York Assembly October 18, 1764

To the Honourable the Knights, Citizens and Burgesses, Representing the Commons of Great-Britain, in Parliament Assembled

The Representation and Petition of the General-Assembly of the Colony of New-York.

Most humbly Shew,

That from the Year 1683, to this Day, there have been three Legislative Branches in this Colony; consisting of the Governor and Council appointed by the Crown, and the Representatives chosen by the People, who, besides the Power of making Laws for the Colony, have enjoyed the Right of Taxing the Subject for the Support of the Government.

Under this Political Frame, the Colony was settled by Protestant Emigrants from several Parts of Europe, and more especially from Great-Britain and Ireland: And as it was originally modelled with

SOURCE: *Journal of the Votes and Proceedings of the General Assembly of the Colony of New York* (New York, 1764–1766), II, 776–779.

the Intervention of the Crown, and not excepted to by the Realm of *England* before, nor by *Great-Britain*, since the Union, the Planters and Settlers conceived the strongest Hopes, that the Colony had gained a civil Constitution, which, so far at least as the Rights and Privileges of the People were concerned, would remain permanent, and be transmitted to their latest Posterity.

It is therefore with equal Concern and Surprize, that they have received Intimations of certain Designs lately formed, if possible, to induce the Parliament of *Great-Britain*, to impose Taxes upon the Subjects *here*, by Laws to be passed *there*; and as we who have the Honour to represent them, conceive that this Innovation, will greatly affect the Interest of the Crown and the Nation, and reduce the Colony to absolute Ruin; it became our indispensible Duty, to trouble you with a seasonable Representation of the Claim of our Constituents, to an Exemption from the Burthen of all Taxes not granted by themselves, and their Foresight of the tragical Consequences of an Adoption of the contrary Principle, to the Crown, the Mother Country, themselves and their Posterity. . . .

An Exemption from the Burthen of ungranted, involuntary Taxes, must be the grand Principle of every free State.—Without such a Right vested in themselves, exclusive of all others, there can be no Liberty, no Happiness, no Security; it is inseparable from the very Idea of Property, for who can call that his own, which may be taken away at the Pleasure of another? . . . [T]he People of this Colony, inspired by the Genius of their Mother Country, nobly disdain the thought of claiming that Exemption as a *Privilege*.— They found it on a Basis more honourable, solid and stable; they challenge it, and glory in it as their Right. That Right their Ancestors enjoyed in *Great-Britain* and *Ireland*; their Descendants returning to those Kingdoms, enjoy it again: And that it may be exercised by his Majesty's Subjects at Home, and justly denied to those who submitted to Poverty, Barbarian Wars, Loss of Blood, Loss of Money, personal Fatigues, and ten Thousand unutterable Hardships, to enlarge the Trade, Wealth, and Dominion of the Nation; or, to speak with the most unexceptionable Modesty, that when as *Subjects*, all have equal Merit; a Fatal, nay the most odious Discrimination should nevertheless be made between them, no Sophistry can recommend to the Sober, impartial Decision of Common Sense. . . .

No History can furnish an Instance of a Constitution to permit one Part of a Dominion to be taxed by another, and that too in Effect, but by a Branch of that other Part; who in all Bills for public Aids, suffer not the least Alteration.—And if such an absurd and unequal Constitution should be adopted, who, that considers the natural Reluctance of Mankind to burthens, and their Inclination to cast them upon the Shoulders of others, cannot foresee, that while the People on one Side of the *Atlantic*, enjoy an Exemption from the Load, those on the other, must submit to the most unsupportable Oppression and Tyranny.

Against these Evils, the Indulgence of the present Parliament, of which we have had such large Experience, cannot provide, if the grand Right to tax ourselves is invaded. Depressed by the Prospect of an endless Train of the most distressing Mischiefs, naturally attendant upon such an Innovation, his Majesty's *American* Subjects, will think it no inconsiderable Augmentation of their Misery, that the Measure itself implies the most severe and unmerited Censure, and is urged, as far as they are acquainted, by no good Reasons of State.

They are unconscious of any Conduct, that brings the least Imputation upon their Love and Loyalty, and whoever has accused them, has abused both the Colonies and their Mother Country; more faithful Subjects his Majesty has not, in any Part of his Dominions, nor *Britain* more submissive and affectionate Sons.

And if our Contributions to the Support of the Government upon this Continent, or for the Maintenance of an Army, to awe and subdue the Savages should be thought necessary, why shall it be presumed, without a Trial, that we more than others, will refuse to hearken to a just Requisition from the Crown? To Requisitions for Aids salutary to our own Interests? Or why should a more incorrigible and unreasonable Spirit be imputed to us, than to the Parliament of *Ireland*, or any other of his Majesty's Subjects?

Left to the Enjoyment of our antient Rights, the Government will be truly informed when a Tax is necessary, and of the Abilities of the People; and there will be an equitable Partition of the Burthen. And as the publick Charges will necessarily increase with the Increase of the Country, and the Augmentation or Reduction of the Force kept up, be regulated by the Power and Temper of our barbarian Enemy, the Necessity for continuing the present Model must appear to be most strongly inforced.—At the remote Distance of the *British* Commons from the sequestered Shades of the interior Parts of this Desart, false Intelligence of the State of the *Indians* may be given; whereas the Vicinity of the Colonies will enable them, not only, to detect all false Alarms, and check all fraudulent Accounts, but urge them by the never failing Motive of Self-Preservation, to oppose any hostile Attempts upon their Borders.

Nor will the Candour of the Commons of *Great-Britain*, construe our Earnestness to maintain this Plea, to arise from a Desire of Independency upon the supreme Power of the Parliament. Of so extravagant a Disregard to our own Interests we cannot be guilty.— From what other Quarter can we hope for Protection? We reject the Thought with the utmost Abhorrence; and a perfect knowledge of this Country will afford the fullest Proof, that nothing in our Temper can give the least Ground for such a Jealousy.

The peaceable and invariable Submission of the Colonies, for a Century past, forbids the Imputation, or proves it a Calumny.— What can be more apparent, than that the State which exercises a Sovereignty in Commerce, can draw all the Wealth of its Colonies into its own Stock? And has not the whole Trade of *North-America*, that growing Magazine of Wealth, been, from the Beginning, directed, restrained, and prohibited at the sole Pleasure of the Parliament? And whatever some may pretend, his Majesty's American Subjects are far from a Desire to invade the just Rights of *Great-Britain*, in all commercial Regulations. They humbly conceive, that a very manifest Distinction presents itself, which, while it leaves to the Mother Country an incontestible Power, to give Laws for the Advancement of her own Commerce, will, at the same Time, do no Violence to the Rights of the Plantations.

The Authority of the Parliament of *Great-Britain*, to model the Trade of the whole Empire, so as to subserve the Interest of her own, we are ready to recognize in the most extensive and positive Terms. Such a Preference is naturally founded upon her Superiority, and indissolubly connected with the Principle of Self-Preservation.—And therefore, to assign one Instance, instead of many, the Colonies cannot, would not ask for a Licence to import woolen Manufactures from *France*; or to go into the most lucrative Branches of Commerce, in the least Degree incompatible with the Trade and Interest of *Great-Britain*.

But a Freedom to drive all Kinds of Traffick in a Subordination to, and not inconsistent with, the *British* Trade; and an Exemption from all Duties in such a Course of Commerce, is humbly claimed by the Colonies, as the most essential of all the Rights to which they are intitled, as Colonists from, and connected, in the common Bond of Liberty, with the uninslaved Sons of *Great-Britain*.

For, with Submission, since all Impositions, whether they be internal Taxes, or Duties paid, for what we consume, equally diminish the Estates upon which they are charged; what avails it to any People, by which of them they are impoverished? Every Thing will be given up to preserve Life; and though there is a Diversity in the Means, yet, the whole Wealth of a Country may be as effectually drawn off, by the Exaction of Duties, as by any other Tax upon their Estates.

And therefore, the General Assembly of *New-York*, in Fidelity to their Constituents, cannot but express the most earnest Supplication, that the Parliament will charge our Commerce with no other Duties, than a necessary Regard to the particular Trade of *Great-Britain*, evidently demands; but leave it to the legislative Power of the Colony, to impose all other Burthens upon it's own People, which the publick Exigences may require.

Latterly, the Laws of Trade seem to have been framed without an Attention to this fundamental Claim.

Permit us, also, in Defence of our Attachment to the Mother Country, to add, what your Merchants (to whom we boldly make the Appeal) know to be an undoubted Truth; that this Continent contains some of the *most useful* of her Subjects.—Such is the Nature of our Produce, that all we acquire is less than sufficient to purchase what we want of your Manufactures; and, be the Policy of your Commerce what it will, all our Riches must flow into *Great-Britain*.—Immense have been our Contributions to the National Stock.—Our Staple, Industry, Trade and Wealth, all conduce to the particular Advantage of our fellow Subjects there.—The natural State of this Country, necessarily forms the Ballance of Trade in her Favour.—Her growing Opulence must elevate her above all Fear and Jealousy of these Dependences. How much stronger then the Reasons for leaving us free from ungranted Impositions? Whoever will give full Scope to his Meditations on this Topic, will see it the Interest of *Great-Britain*, to adopt the Maxim, that her own Happiness is most intimately connected with the Freedom, Ease and Prosperity of her Colonies: The more extensive our Traffic, the Greater her Gains; we carry all to her Hive, and consume the

Returns; and we are content with any constitutional Regulation that inriches her, though it impoverishes ourselves. . . .

The honourable House will permit us to observe next, that the Act of the last Session of Parliament, inhibiting all Intercourse between the Continent and the foreign Sugar Colonies, will prove equally detrimental to us and *Great-Britain.—That* Trade, gave a value to a vast, but now alas unsaleable Staple, which being there converted into Cash and Merchandize, made necessary Remittances for the *British* Manufactures we consumed: . . . And when we consider the Wisdom of our Ancestors in contriving Trials by Juries, we cannot stifle our Regret, that the Laws of Trade in general, change the Current of Justice from the common Law, and subject Controversies of the utmost Importance to the Decisions of the Vice-Admiralty Courts, who proceed not according the old wholesom Laws of the Land, nor are always filled with Judges of approved Knowledge and Integrity.—To this Objection, the aforementioned Statute will at first View appear to be so evidently open, that we shall content ourselves with barely suggesting, that the amazing Confidence it reposes in the Judges, gives great Grief to his Majesty's *American* Subjects. . . .

The General Assembly of this Colony have no desire to derogate from the Power of the Parliament of *Great-Britain*; but they cannot avoid deprecating the Loss of such Rights as they have hitherto enjoyed, Rights established in the first Dawn of our Constitution, founded upon the most substantial Reasons, confirmed by invariable Usage, conducive to the best Ends; never abused to bad Purposes, and with the Loss of which Liberty, Property, and all the Benefits of Life, tumble into Insecurity and Ruin: Rights, the Deprivation of which, will dispirit the People, abate their Industry, discourage Trade, introduce Discord, Poverty and Slavery; or, by depopulating the Colonies, turn a vast, fertile, prosperous Region, into a dreary Wilderness; impoverish *Great-Britain*, and shake the Power and Independancy of the most opulent and flourishing Empire in the World.

All which your Petitioners (who repose the highest Confidence in your Wisdom and Justice) humbly pray, may be now taken into your seasonable Consideration, and such Measures pursued, as the Event may prove to have been concerted for the Common-Weal, of all the Subjects of *Great-Britain*, both at home and abroad.

15. Stamp Act: Jared Ingersoll's Account of the Debate in the House of Commons in a Letter to Governor Thomas Fitch of Connecticut February 11, 1765

Since my last to you I have been honoured with yours of the 7th of December in which you inform me that the General Assembly have been pleased to desire my assistance while here in any matters that may concern the colony. Be so good, sir, in return as to assure the Assembly that I have not only a due sense of the honour they have done me by placing this confidence in me, but that I have ever since my arrival here, from motives of inclination as well as duty, done everything in my power to promote the colony's interests.

The principal attention has been to the stamp bill that has been preparing to lay before Parliament for taxing America. The point of the authority of Parliament to impose such tax I found on my arrival here was so fully and universally yielded that there was not the least hopes of making any impressions that way. Indeed it has appeared since that the House would not suffer to be brought in, nor would any one member undertake to offer to the House any petition from the colonies that held forth the contrary of that doctrine. I own I advised the agents if possible to get that point canvassed so that the Americans might at least have the satisfaction of having the point decided upon a full debate, but I found it could not be done, and here, before I proceed to acquaint you with the steps that have been taken in this matter, I beg leave to give you a summary of the arguments which are made use of in favour of such authority.

The House of Commons, say they, is a branch of the supreme legislature of the nation, and which in its nature is supposed to

SOURCE: Jared Ingersoll, *Mr. Ingersoll's Letters Relating to the Stamp-Act* (New Haven, 1766).

represent, or rather to stand in the place of the Commons; that is, of the great body of the people who are below the dignity of peers; that this House of Commons consists of a certain number of men chosen by certain people of certain places, which electors, by the way, they insist are not a tenth part of the people, and that the laws, rules, and methods by which their number is ascertained have arose by degrees and from various causes and occasions, and that this House of Commons therefore is now fixed and ascertained and is a part of the supreme unlimited power of the nation, as in every state there must be some unlimited power and authority; and that when it is said they represent the commons of England it cannot mean that they do so because those commons choose them, for in fact by far the greater part do not, but because by their constitution they must themselves be commoners and not peers, and so the equals, or of the same class of subjects, with the commons of the kingdom. They further urge that the only reason why America has not been heretofore taxed in the fullest manner has been merely on account of their infancy and inability; that there have been, however, not wanting instances of the exercise of this power in the various regulations of the American trade, the establishment of the post office, etc., and they deny any distinction between what is called an internal and external tax as to the point of the authority imposing such taxes. And as to the charters in the few provinces where there are any, they say in the first place the king cannot grant any that shall exempt them from the authority of one of the branches of the great body of legislation, and in the second place say the king has not done or attempted to do it. In that of Pennsylvania the authority of Parliament to impose taxes is expressly mentioned and reserved; in ours 'tis said, our powers are generally such as are *according to the course of other corporations in England* (both which instances by way of sample were mentioned and referred to by Mr. Grenville in the House); in short, they say a power to tax is a necessary part of every supreme legislative authority, and that if they have not that power over America, they have none, and then America is at once a kingdom of itself.

On the other hand, those who oppose the bill say it is true the Parliament have a supreme unlimited authority over every part and branch of the king's dominions, and as well over Ireland as any other place, yet we believe a British Parliament will never think it prudent to tax Ireland. 'Tis true they say that the commons of

England and of the British Empire are all represented in and by the House of Commons, but this representation is confessedly on all hands by construction and virtually only as to those who have no hand in choosing the representatives, and that the effects of this implied representation here and in America must be infinitely different in the article of taxation. Here in England the member of Parliament is equally known to the neighbour who elects and to him who does not; the friendships, the connections, the influences are spread through the whole. If by any mistake an Act of Parliament is made that prove injurious and hard, the member of Parliament here sees with his own eyes and is moreover very accessible to the people; not only so, but the taxes are laid equally by one rule and fall as well on the member himself as on the people. But as to America, from the great distance in point of situation, from the almost total unacquaintedness, especially in the more northern colonies, with the members of Parliament, and they with them, or with the particular ability and circumstances, of one another, from the nature of this very tax laid upon others not equally and in common with ourselves, but with express purpose to ease ourselves, we think, say they, that it will be only to lay a foundation of great jealousy and continual uneasiness, and that to no purpose, as we already by the regulations upon their trade draw from the Americans all that they can spare. At least they say this step should not take place until or unless the Americans are allowed to send members to Parliament; for *who of you*, said Col. [Isaac] Barré nobly in his speech in the House upon this occasion; *who of you reasoning upon this subject feels warmly from the heart* (putting his hand to his own breast) *for the Americans as they would for themselves or as you would for the people of your own native country?* And to this point Mr. Jackson produced copies of two Acts of Parliament granting the privilege of having members to the county palatine of Chester and the bishopric of Durham upon petitions preferred for that purpose in the reign of King Henry the eighth and Charles the first, the preamble of which statutes counts upon the petitions from those places as setting forth that being in their general civil jurisdiction exempted from the common law courts, etc., yet being subject to the general authority of Parliament, were taxed in common with the rest of the kingdom, which taxes by reason of their having no members in Parliament to represent their affairs, often proved hard and injurious, etc., and upon that ground they had the privilege of sending members granted them—and if this, say they, could be a reason in the case of Chester and Durham, how much more so in the case of America.

Thus I have given you, I think, the substance of the arguments on both sides of that great and important question of the right and also of the expediency of taxing America by authority of Parliament. I cannot, however, content myself without giving you a sketch of what the aforementioned Mr. Barré said in answer to some remarks made by Mr. Charles Townshend in a speech of his upon this subject. I ought here to tell you that the debate upon the American stamp bill came on before the House for the first time last Wednesday, when the same was opened by Mr. Grenville, the Chancellor of the Exchequer, in a pretty lengthy speech, and in a very able, and I think, in a very candid manner he opened the nature of the tax, urged the necessity of it, endeavoured to obviate all objections to it—and took occasion to desire the House to give the bill a most serious and cool consideration and not suffer themselves to be influenced by any resentments which might have been kindled from anything they might have heard out of doors— alluding, I suppose, to the New York and Boston Assemblies' speeches and votes—that this was a matter of revenue which was of all things the most interesting to the subject, etc. The argument was taken up by several who opposed the bill (viz.) by Alderman Beckford, who, and who only, seemed to deny the authority of Parliament, by Col. Barré, Mr. Jackson, Sir William Meredith, and some others. Mr. Barré, who by the way, I think, and I find I am not alone in my opinion, is one of the finest speakers that the House can boast of, having been some time in America as an officer in the army, and having while there, as I had known before, con- tracted many friendships with American gentlemen, and I believe entertained much more favourable opinions of them than some of his profession have done, delivered a very handsome and moving speech upon the bill and against the same, concluding by saying that he was very sure that most who should hold up their hands to the bill must be under a necessity of acting very much in the dark, but added, perhaps as well in the dark as any way.

After him Mr. Charles Townshend spoke in favour of the bill— took notice of several things Mr. Barré had said, and concluded with the following or like words: and now will these Americans, children planted by our care, nourished up by our indulgence until they are grown to a degree of strength and opulence, and protected by our arms, will they grudge to contribute their mite to relieve us from the heavy weight of that burden which we lie under? When he had done, Mr. Barré rose, and having explained something which he had before said and which Mr. Townshend had been remarking upon, he then took up the before mentioned concluding words of Mr. Townshend, and in a most spirited and I thought an almost inimitable manner, said:

They planted by your care? No! Your oppressions planted 'em in America. They fled from your tyranny to a then uncultivated and unhospitable country where they exposed themselves to almost all the hardships to which human nature is liable, and among others to the cruelties of a savage foe, the most subtle, and I take upon me to say, the most formidable of any people upon the face of God's earth. And yet, actuated by principles of true English liberty, they met all these hardships with pleasure, compared with those they suffered in their own country, from the hands of those who should have been their friends.

They nourished by your indulgence? They grew by your neglect of 'em. As soon as you began to care about 'em, that care was exercised in sending persons to rule over 'em, in one department and another, who were perhaps the deputies of deputies to some member of this house, sent to spy out their liberty, to misrepresent their actions and to prey upon 'em; men whose behaviour on many occasions has caused the blood of those sons of liberty to recoil within them; men promoted to the highest seats of justice; some who to my knowledge were glad by going to a foreign country to escape being brought to the bar of a court of justice in their own.

They protected by your arms? They have nobly taken up arms in your defence, have exerted a valour amidst their constant and laborious industry for the defence of a country, whose frontier while drenched in blood, its interior parts have yielded all its little savings to your emolument. And believe me, remember I this day told you so, that same spirit of freedom which actuated that people at first, will accompany them still. But prudence forbids me to explain myself further. God knows I do not at this time speak from motives of party heat; what I deliver are the genuine sentiments of my heart; however superior to me in general knowledge and experience the reputable body of this House may be, yet I claim to know more of America than most of you, having seen and been conversant in that country. The people I believe are as truly loyal as any subjects the king has, but a people jealous of their liberties and who will vindicate them if ever they should be violated; but the subject is too delicate and I will say no more.

These sentiments were thrown out so entirely without premeditation, so forceably and so firmly, and the breaking off so beautifully abrupt, that the whole House sat a while as amazed, intently looking and without answering a word.

I own I felt emotions that I never felt before and went the next morning and thanked Col. Barré in behalf of my country for his noble and spirited speech.

However, sir, after all that was said, upon a division of the House upon the question there was about 250 to about 50 in favour of the bill.

The truth is, I believe some who inclined rather against the bill voted for it, partly because they are loath to break the measures of the ministry, and partly because they don't undertake to inform themselves in the fullest manner upon the subject. The bill comes on to a second reading tomorrow when ours and the Massachusetts petitions will be presented and perhaps [there] may be some further debate upon the subject, but to no purpose, I am very sure, as to the stopping or preventing the Act taking place.

The agents of the colonies have had several meetings, at one of which they were pleased to desire Mr. Franklin and myself as having lately come from America and knowing more intimately the sentiments of the people, to wait on Mr. Grenville, together with Mr. Jackson and Mr. Garth, who, being agents are also members of Parliament, to remonstrate against the stamp bill, and to propose in case any tax must be laid upon America, that the several colonies might be permitted to lay the tax themselves. This we did Saturday before last. Mr. Grenville gave us a full hearing—told us he took no pleasure in giving the Americans so much uneasiness as he found he did—that it was the duty of his office to manage the revenue—that he really was made to believe that considering the whole of the circumstances of the mother country and the colonies, the lat[t]er could and ought to pay something, and that he knew of no better way than that now pursuing to lay such tax, but that if we could tell of a better, he would adopt it. We then urged the method first mentioned as being a method the people had been used to—that it would at least seem to be their own act and prevent that uneasiness and jealousy which otherwise we found would take place—that they could raise the money best by their own officers, etc.

Mr. Jackson told him plainly that he foresaw [by] the measure now pursuing, by enabling the Crown to keep up an armed force of its own in America and to pay the governors in the king's governments, and all with the Americans' own money, the assemblies in the colonies would be subverted—that the governors would have no occasion as for any ends of their own or of the Crown, to call 'em, and that they never would be called together in the king's governments. Mr. Grenville warmly rejected the thought, said no such thing was intended nor would, he believed, take place. Indeed, I understand since, there is a clause added to the bill applying the monies that shall be raised to the protecting and defending America *only*. Mr. Grenville asked us if we could agree upon the several proportions each colony should raise. We told him no. He said he did not think anybody here was furnished with materials for that purpose; not only so, but there would be no certainty that every colony would raise the sum enjoined and to be obliged to be at the expense of making stamps to compel some one or two provinces to do their duty, and that perhaps for one year only, would be very inconvenient; not only so, but the colonies by their constant increase will be constantly varying in their proportions of numbers and ability and which a stamp bill will always keep pace with, etc.

Upon the whole he said he had pledged his word for offering the stamp bill to the House, that the House would hear all our objections and would do as they thought best; he said he wished we would preserve a coolness and moderation in America; that he had no need to tell us that resentments indecently and unbecomingly expressed on one side the water would naturally produce resentments on tother side, and that we could not hope to get any good by a controversy with the mother country; that their ears will always be open to any remonstrances from the Americans with respect to this bill, both before it takes effect and after, if it shall take effect, which shall be expressed in a becoming manner, that is, as becomes subjects of the same common prince.

I acquainted you in my last that Mr. Whately, one of the secretaries of the Treasury, and who had under his care and direction the business of preparing the stamp bill, had often conferred with me on the subject. He wanted, I know, information of the several methods of transfer, law process, etc., made use of in the colony, and I believe has been also very willing to hear all objections that could be made to the bill or any part of it. This task I was glad to undertake, as I very well knew the information I must give would operate strongly in our favour; as the number of our law-suits, deeds, tavern licences, and in short, almost all the objects of the intended taxation and duties are so very numerous in the colony that the knowledge of them would tend to the imposing a duty so much the lower as the objects were more in number. This effect, I flatter myself, it has had in some measure. Mr. Whately, to be sure, tells me I may fairly claim the honour of having occasioned the duty's being much lower than was intended, and three particular things that were intended to be taxed I gave him no peace till he dropped; these were licences for marriage—a duty that would be odious in a new country where every encouragement ought to be given to matrimony, and where there was little portion; commissions of the justices of peace, which office was, generally speaking, not profitable and yet necessary for the good order and government of the people; and notes of hand which with us were given and taken so very often for very small sums.

After all, I believe the people in America will think the sums that will be raised will be quite enough, and I wish they mayn't find it more distressing than the people in power here are aware of.

The merchants in London are alarmed at these things; they have had a meeting with the agents and are about to petition Parliament upon the Acts that respect the trade of North America.

What the event of these things will be I don't know, but am pretty certain that wisdom will be proper and even very necessary, as well as prudence and good discretion to direct the councils of America.

16. The Virginia Resolves Introduced in the House of Burgesses by Patrick Henry
May 30, 1765

Resolved, That the first adventurers and settlers of this His Majesty's Colony and Dominion of Virginia brought with them, and transmitted to their posterity, and all other His Majesty's

SOURCE: J. P. Kennedy, ed., Journals of the House of Burgesses of Virginia, 1761–1765, 359–360.

subjects since inhabiting in this His Majesty's said Colony, all the liberties, privileges, franchises, and immunities, that have at any time been held, enjoyed, and possessed, by the people of Great Britain.

Resolved, That by two royal charters, granted by King James the First, the colonists aforesaid are declared entitled to all liberties, privileges, and immunities of denizens and natural subjects, to all intents and purposes, as if they had been abiding and born within the realm of England.

Resolved, That the taxation of the people by themselves, or by persons chosen by themselves to represent them, who can only know what taxes the people are able to bear, or the easiest method of raising them, and must themselves be affected by every tax laid on the people, is the only security against a burthensome taxation, and the distinguishing characteristick of British freedom, without which the ancient constitution cannot exist.

Resolved, That His Majesty's liege people of this his most ancient and loyal Colony have without interruption enjoyed the inestimable right of being governed by such laws, respecting their internal polity and taxation, as are derived from their own consent, with the approbation of their sovereign, or his substitute; and that the same hath never been forfeited or yielded up, but hath been constantly recognized by the kings and people of Great Britain.

Resolved therefore, That the General Assembly of this Colony have the only and sole exclusive right and power to lay taxes and impositions upon the inhabitants of this Colony, and that every attempt to vest such power in any person or persons whatsoever other than the General Assembly aforesaid has a manifest tendency to destroy British as well as American freedom.

Resolved, That His Majesty's liege people, the inhabitants of this Colony, are not bound to yield obedience to any law or ordinance whatever, designed to impose any taxation whatsoever upon them, other than the laws or ordinances of the General Assembly aforesaid.

Resolved, That any person who shall, by speaking or writing, assert or maintain that any person or persons other than the General Assembly of this Colony, have any right or power to impose or lay any taxation on the people here, shall be deemed an enemy to His Majesty's Colony.

17. The Boston Stamp Act Riot of August 15, 1765: Governor Francis Bernard to Lord Halifax

Castle William, August 15, 1765

My Lords,

I am extremely concerned, that I am obliged to give your Lordships the Relation that is to follow; as it will reflect disgrace upon this Province, and bring the Town of Boston under great difficulties. Two or three months ago, I thought that this People would have submitted to the Stamp Act without actual Opposition. Murmurs indeed were continually heard, but they seemed to be such as would in time die away; But the publishing the Virginia Resolves proved an Alarm bell to the disaffected. From that time an infamous weekly Paper, which is printed here, has swarmed with libells of the most atrocious kind. These have been urged with so much Vehemence and so industriously repeated, that I have considered them as preludes to Action. But I did not think, that it would have commenced so early, or be carried to such Lengths, as it has been.

Yesterday Morning at break of day was discovered hanging upon a Tree in a Street of the Town an Effigy, with inscriptions, shewing that it was intended to represent Mr Oliver, the Secretary, who had lately accepted the Office of Stamp Distributor. Some of the Neighbours offered to take it down, but they were given to know, that would not be permitted. Many Gentlemen, especially some of the Council, treated it as a boyish sport, that did not deserve the Notice of the Governor and Council. But I did not think so. However I contented myself with the Lt. Governor, as Chief Justice, directing the Sheriff to order his Officers to take down the Effigy; and I appointed a Council to meet in the Afternoon to consider what should be done, if the Sheriff's Officers were obstructed in removing the Effigy.

Source: The House of Lords Manuscripts for January 14, 1766— photocopy in the Library of Congress.

Before the Council met, the Sheriff reported, that his Officers had endeavoured to take down the Effigy: but could not do it without imminent danger of their lives. The Council met, I represented this Transaction to them as the beginning in my Opinion, of much greater Commotions. I desired their Advice, what I should do upon this Occasion. A Majority of the Council spoke in form against doing anything but upon very different Principles: some said, that it was trifling Business, which, if let alone, would subside of itself, but, if taken notice of would become a serious Affair. Others said, that it was a serious Affair already; that it was a pre-concerted Business, in which the greatest Part of the Town was engaged; that we had no force to oppose to it, and making an Opposition to it, without a power to support the Opposition, would only inflame the People; and be a means of extending the mischief to persons not at present the Objects of it. Tho' the Council were allmost unanimous in advising, that nothing should be done, they were averse to having such advice entered upon the Council Book. But I insisted upon their giving me an Answer to my Question, and that it should be entered in the Book; when, after a long altercation, it was avoided by their advising me to order the Sheriff to assemble the Peace Officers and preserve the peace which I immediately ordered, being a matter of form rather than of real Significance.

It now grew dark when the Mob, which had been gathering all the Afternoon, came down to the Town House, bringing the Effigy with them, and knowing we were sitting in the Council Chamber, they gave three Huzzas by way of defiance, and passed on From thence they went to a new Building, lately erected by Mr Oliver to let out for Shops, and not quite finished: this they called the Stamp Office, and pulled it down to the Ground in five minutes. From thence they went to Mr Oliver's House; before which they beheaded the Effigy; and broke all the Windows next the Street; then they carried the Effigy to Fort hill near Mr Oliver's House where they burnt the Effigy in a Bonfire made of the Timber they had pulled down from the Building. Mr Oliver had removed his family from his House, and remained himself with a few friends, when the Mob returned to attack the House. Mr Oliver was prevailed upon to retire, and his friends kept Possession of the House. The Mob finding the Doors barricaded, broke down the whole fence of the Garden towards fort hill, and coming on beat in all the doors and Windows of the Garden front, and entered the House, the Gentlemen there retiring. As soon as they had got possession, they searched about for Mr Oliver, declaring they would kill him; finding that he had left the House, a party set out to search two neighbouring Houses, in one of which Mr Oliver was, but happily they were diverted from this pursuit by a Gentleman telling them, that Mr Oliver was gone with the Governor to the Castle. Otherwise he would certainly have been murdered. After 11 o'clock the Mob seeming to grow quiet, the (Lt. Governor) Chief Justice and the Sheriff ventured to go to Mr Oliver's House to endeavour to perswade them to disperse. As soon as they began to speak, a Ringleader cried out, The Governor and the Sheriff! to your Arms, my boys! Presently after a volley of Stones followed, and the two Gentlemen narrowly escaped thro' favour of the Night, not without some bruises. I should have mentioned before, that I sent a written order to the Colonel of the Regiment of Militia, to beat an Alarm; he answered, that it would signify nothing, for as soon as the drum was heard, the drummer would be knocked down, and the drum broke; he added, that probably all the drummers of the Regiment were in the Mob. Nothing more being to be done, The Mob were left to disperse at their own Time, which they did about 12 o'clock.

18. Resolves of the Stamp Act Congress
October 19, 1765

The members of this Congress, sincerely devoted with the warmest sentiments of affection and duty to His Majesty's person and Government, inviolably attached to the present happy establishment of the Protestant succession, and with minds deeply impressed by a sense of the present and impending misfortunes of the British colonies on this continent; having considered as maturely as time will permit the circumstances of the said colonies, esteem it our indispensable duty to make the following declara-

SOURCE: H. Niles, ed., *Principles and Acts of the Revolution in America* (1822, reprinted New York, 1876), 163.

tions of our humble opinion respecting the most essential rights and liberties of the colonists, and of the grievances under which they labour, by reason of several late Acts of Parliament.

I. That His Majesty's subjects in these colonies owe the same allegiance to the Crown of Great Britain that is owing from his subjects born within the realm, and all due subordination to that august body the Parliament of Great Britain.

II. That His Majesty's liege subjects in these colonies are intitled to all the inherent rights and liberties of his natural born subjects within the kingdom of Great Britain.

III. That it is inseparably essential to the freedom of a people, and the undoubted right of Englishmen, that no taxes be imposed on them but with their own consent, given personally or by their representatives.

IV. That the people of these colonies are not, and from their local circumstances cannot be, represented in the House of Commons in Great Britain.

V. That the only representatives of the people of these colonies are persons chosen therein by themselves, and that no taxes ever have been, or can be constitutionally imposed on them, but by their respective legislatures.

VI. That all supplies to the Crown being free gifts of the people, it is unreasonable and inconsistent with the principles and spirit of the British Constitution, for the people of Great Britain to grant to His Majesty the property of the colonists.

VII. That trial by jury is the inherent and invaluable right of every British subject in these colonies.

VIII. That the late Act of Parliament, entitled *An Act for granting and applying certain stamp duties, and other duties, in the British colonies and plantations in America, etc.*, by imposing taxes on the inhabitants of these colonies; and the said Act, and several other Acts, by extending the jurisdiction of the courts of Admiralty beyond its ancient limits, have a manifest tendency to subvert the rights and liberties of the colonists.

IX. That the duties imposed by several late Acts of Parliament, from the peculiar circumstances of these colonies, will be extremely burthensome and grievous; and from the scarcity of specie, the payment of them absolutely impracticable.

X. That as the profits of the trade of these colonies ultimately center in Great Britain, to pay for the manufactures which they are obliged to take from thence, they eventually contribute very largely to all supplies granted there to the Crown.

XI. That the restrictions imposed by several late Acts of Parliament on the trade of these colonies will render them unable to purchase the manufactures of Great Britain.

XII. That the increase, prosperity, and happiness of these colonies depend on the full and free enjoyments of their rights and liberties, and an intercourse with Great Britain mutually affectionate and advantageous.

XIII. That it is the right of the British subjects in these colonies to petition the King or either House of Parliament.

Lastly, That it is the indispensable duty of these colonies to the best of sovereigns, to the mother country, and to themselves, to endeavour by a loyal and dutiful address to His Majesty, and humble applications to both Houses of Parliament, to procure the repeal of the Act for granting and applying certain stamp duties, of all clauses of any other Acts of Parliament, whereby the jurisdiction of the Admiralty is extended as aforesaid, and of the other late Acts for the restriction of American commerce.

V

The Repeal of the Stamp Act

While opposition to the Stamp Act was building rapidly in America, a movement for its repeal was gaining ground in London. Merchants involved in trade with America petitioned Parliament to strike down the act. Leading the forces in Parliament against the Stamp Act was the redoubtable William Pitt. In his speech of January 14, 1766, Pitt challenged the constitutionality of the entire Grenville program. An examination before the House of Commons made clear the depth of opposition in America to the new tax measure.

Parliament coupled its repeal of the Stamp Act with the passage of the Declaratory Act asserting Parliament's full authority to legislate for America "in all cases whatsoever." Thus Parliament kept the constitutional issue alive; while, in the view of the then Chief Justice and Lieutenant Governor of Massachusetts, Thomas Hutchinson, as set forth in a letter to the province's former governor, Thomas Pownall, radical leaders in America continued to exploit the issues to enlarge their own power base.

19. William Pitt's Speech on the Repeal of the Stamp Act January 14, 1766

IT IS a long time Mr. Speaker, since I have attended in Parliament. When the resolution was taken in the house to tax America, I was ill in bed. If I could have endured to have been carried in my bed, so great was the agitation of my mind for the consequence, I would have solicited some kind hand to have laid me down on this floor,

SOURCE: Correspondence of William Pitt, Earl of Chatham (4 vols., London, 1838–1840), II, 369–372.

to have borne my testimony against it. It is now an act that has passed: I would speak with decency of every act of this house, but I must beg the indulgence of the house to speak of it with freedom.

I hope a day may soon be appointed to consider the state of the nation with respect to America. I hope gentlemen will come to this debate with all the temper and impartiality that his Majesty recommends, and the importance of the subject requires—a subject of greater importance than ever engaged the attention of this house, that subject only excepted, when, near a century ago, it was the question, whether you yourselves were to be bound or free.

In the mean time, as I cannot depend upon health for any future day, such is the nature of my infirmities, I will beg to say a few words at present, leaving the justice, the equity, the policy, the expediency of the act, to another time. I will only speak to one point, a point which seems not to have been generally understood—I mean to the right. Some gentlemen [alluding to Mr. Nugent] seem to have considered it as a point of honour. If gentlemen consider it in that light, they leave all measures of right and wrong, to follow a delusion that may lead to destruction. It is my opinion that this kingdom has no right to lay a tax upon the colonies, to be sovereign and supreme in every circumstance of government and legislation whatsoever. They are the subjects of this kingdom, equally entitled with yourselves to all the natural rights of mankind and the peculiar privileges of Englishmen.

Equally bound by its laws, and equally participating of the constitution of this free country, the Americans are the sons, not the bastards of England. Taxation is no part of the governing or legislative power. The taxes are a voluntary gift and grant of the Commons alone. In legislation the three estates of the realm are alike concerned; but the concurrency of the Peers and the Crown to a tax, is only necessary to close with the form of a law.

The gift and grant is of the Commons alone. In ancient days, the Crown, the Barons, and the Clergy, possessed the lands. In those days, the Barons and the clergy gave and granted to the Crown. They gave and granted what was their own. At present, since the discovery of America, and other circumstances permitting, the Commons are become the proprietors of the land. The Crown has divested itself of its great estates. The Church (God bless it) has but a pittance. The property of the Lords, compared with that of the Commons, is as a drop of water in the ocean; and this House represents these Commons, the proprietors of the lands; and those proprietors virtually represent the rest of the inhabitants.

When, therefore, in this house we give and grant, we give and grant what is our own. But in an American tax, what do we do? We, your majesty's commons of Great Britain, give and grant to your Majesty, what? our own property?—No, we give and grant to your majesty the property of your Majesty's commons of America. It is an absurdity in terms.

The distinction between legislation and taxation is essentially necessary to liberty. The Crown, the Peers, are equally legislative powers with the Commons. If taxation be part of simple legislation, the Crown, the Peers, have rights in taxation as well as yourselves; rights they will claim, which they will exercise, whenever the principle can be supported by power.

There is an idea in some, that the colonies are virtually represented in this House. I would fain know by whom an American is represented here? Is he represented by any knight of the shire, in any county in this kingdom? Would to God that respectable representation was augmented to a greater number. Or will you tell him that he is represented by any representative of a borough,—a borough which, perhaps, no man ever saw? That is what is called the "rotten part of the constitution." It cannot continue a century. If it does not drop it must be amputated. The idea of a virtual representation of America in this House, is the most contemptible idea that ever entered into the head of man.—It does not deserve a serious consideration.

The Commons of America, represented in their several assemblies, have ever been in possession of the exercise of this, their constitutional right, of giving and granting their own money. They would have been slaves if they had not enjoyed it. At the same time, this kingdom, as the supreme governing and legislative power, has always bound the colonies by her laws, by her regulations, and restrictions in trade, in navigation, in manufactures, in every thing, except that of taking their money out of their pockets without their consent.

20. The Examination of Benjamin Franklin
Before the House of Commons
February 13, 1766

Q. What is your name, and place of abode?

A. Franklin, of Philadelphia.

Q. Do the Americans pay any considerable taxes among themselves?

A. Certainly many, and very heavy taxes.

Q. What are the present taxes in Pennsylvania, laid by the laws of the colony?

A. There are taxes on all estates real and personal, a poll tax, a tax on all offices, professions, trades and businesses, according to their profits; an excise on all wine, rum, and other spirits; and a duty of £10 per head on all Negroes imported, with some other duties.

Q. For what purposes are those taxes laid?

A. For the support of the civil and military establishments of the country, and to discharge the heavy debt contracted in the last war.

Q. How long are those taxes to continue?

A. Those for discharging the debt are to continue till 1772, and longer, if the debt should not be then all discharged. The others must always continue. . . .

Q. Are not the colonies, from their circumstances, very able to pay stamp duty?

A. In my opinion, there is not gold or silver enough in the colonies to pay the stamp duty for one year. . . .

Q. What may be the amount of one year's imports into Pennsylvania from Britain?

A. I have been informed that our merchants compute the imports from Britain to be above £500,000.

SOURCE: A Collection of Scarce and Interesting Tracts Written by Persons of Eminence upon the Most Important Political and Commercial Subjects (4 vols., London, 1787).

Q. What may be the amount of the produce of your province exported to Britain?

A. It must be small, as we produce little that is wanted in Britain. I suppose it cannot exceed £40,000.

Q. How then do you pay the balance?

A. The balance is paid by our produce carried to the West Indies and sold in our own islands, or to the French, Spaniards, Danes and Dutch; by the same carried to other colonies in North America, as to New England, Nova Scotia, Newfoundland, Carolina and Georgia; by the same carried to different parts of Europe, as Spain, Portugal and Italy. In all which places we receive either money, bills of exchange, or commodities that suit for remittance to Britain; which, together with all the profits on the industry of our merchants and mariners arising in those circuitous voyages, and the freights made by their ships, centre finally in Britain to discharge the balance and pay for British manufactures continually used in the province or sold to foreigners by our traders. . . .

Q. Do you think it right that America should be protected by this country and pay no part of the expense?

A. That is not the case. The Colonies raised, cloathed and payed during the last war, near 25,000 men and spent many millions.

Q. Were you not reimbursed by Parliament?

A. We were only reimbursed what, in your opinion, we had advanced beyond our proportion, or beyond what might reasonably be expected from us; and it was a very small part of what we spent. Pennsylvania, in particular, disbursed about £500,000, and the reimbursements, in the whole, did not exceed £60,000.

Q. You have said that you pay heavy taxes in Pennsylvania. What do they amount to in the pound?

A. The tax on all estates, real and personal is eighteen pence in the pound, fully rated; and the tax on the profits of trade and professions, with other taxes, do, I suppose, make full half a crown in the pound. . . .

Q. Do not you think the people of America would submit to pay the stamp duty if it was moderated?

A. No, never, unless compelled by force of arms. . . .

Q. What was the temper of America towards Great Britain before the year 1763?

A. The best in the world. They submitted willingly to the government of the Crown, and paid, in all their courts, obedience to acts of Parliament. Numerous as the people are in the several provinces, they cost you nothing in forts, citadels, garrisons, or armies, to keep them in subjection. They were governed by this country at the expense only of a little pen, ink and paper. They were led by a thread. They had not only a respect, but an affection for Great Britain; for its laws, its customs and manners, and even a fondness for its fashions, that greatly increased the commerce. Natives of Britain were always treated with particular regard; to be an Old-England man was, of itself, a character of some respect, and gave a kind of rank among us.

Q. And what is their temper now?

A. O, very much altered.

Q. Did you ever hear the authority of Parliament to make laws for America questioned till lately?

A. The authority of Parliament was allowed to be valid in all laws, except such as should lay internal taxes. It was never disputed in laying duties to regulate commerce.

Q. In what proportion hath population increased in America?

A. I think the inhabitants of all the provinces together, taken at a medium, double in about twenty-five years. But their demand for British manufactures increases much faster, as the consumption is not merely in proportion to their numbers, but grows with the growing abilities of the same numbers to pay for them. In 1723, the whole importation from Britain to Pennsylvania was about £15,000 sterling; it is now near half a million.

Q. In what light did the people of America use to consider the Parliament of Great Britain?

A. They considered the Parliament as the great bulwark and security of their liberties and privileges, and always spoke of it with the utmost respect and veneration. Arbitrary ministers, they thought, might possibly, at times, attempt to oppress them; but they relied on it, that the Parliament, on application, would always give redress. They remembered, with gratitude, a strong instance of this, when a bill was brought into Parliament with a clause to make royal instructions laws in the colonies, which the House of Commons would not pass, and it was thrown out.

Q. And have they not still the same respect for Parliament?

A. No, it is greatly lessened.

Q. To what cause is that owing?

A. To a concurrence of causes, the restraints lately laid on their trade, by which the bringing of foreign gold and silver into the Colonies was prevented; the prohibition of making paper money among themselves; and then demanding a new and heavy tax by stamps; taking away, at the same time, trials by juries, and refusing to receive and hear their humble petitions.

Q. Don't you think they would submit to the Stamp Act, if it was modified, the obnoxious parts taken out, and the duty reduced to some particulars of small moment?

A. No; they will never submit to it.

Q. What is your opinion of a future tax imposed on the same principle with that of the Stamp Act? How would the Americans receive it?

A. Just as they do this. They would not pay it.

Q. Have not you heard the resolutions of this House, and of the House of Lords, asserting the right of Parliament relating to America, including a power to tax the people there?

A. Yes, I have heard of such resolutions.

Q. What will be the opinion of the Americans on those resolutions?

A. They will think them unconstitutional and unjust. . . .

Q. If the Stamp Act should be repealed, would not the Americans think they could oblige the Parliament to repeal every external tax law now in force?

A. It is hard to answer questions of what people at such a distance will think.

Q. But what do you imagine they will think were the motives of repealing the act?

A. I suppose they will think that it was repealed from a conviction of its inexpediency, and they will rely upon it, that while the same inexpediency subsists, you will never attempt to make such another. . . .

Q. Before there was any thought of the Stamp Act, did they wish for a representation in Parliament?

A. No.

Q. Don't you know that there is, in the Pennsylvania charter, an express reservation of Parliament to lay taxes there?

A. I know there is a clause in the charter by which the King grants that he will levy no taxes on the inhabitants, unless it be with the consent of the assembly or by act of Parliament.

Q. How, then, could the assembly of Pennsylvania assert that laying a tax on them by the Stamp Act was an infringement of their rights?

A. They understood it thus; by the same charter, and otherwise, they are entitled to all the privileges and liberties of Englishmen; they find in the great charters, and the petition and declaration of rights, that one of the privileges of English subjects is, that they are not to be taxed but by their common consent. They have therefore relied upon it, from the first settlement of the province, that the Parliament never would, nor could, by color of that clause in the charter, assume a right of taxing them, till it had qualified itself to exercise such right by admitting representatives from the people to be taxed, who ought to make a part of that common consent.

Q. Are there any words in the charter that justify that construction?

A. "The common rights of Englishmen," as declared by Magna Charta, and the petition of right, all justify it.

Q. Does the distinction between internal and external taxes exist in the words of the charter?

A. No, I believe not.

Q. Then, may they not, by the same interpretation, object to the Parliament's right of external taxation?

A. They never have hitherto. Many arguments have been lately used here to show them that there is no difference, and that, if you have no right to tax them internally, you have none to tax them externally, or make any other law to bind them. At present they do not reason so; but in time they may possibly be convinced by these arguments. . . .

Q. Is not the post-office rate an internal tax laid by act of Parliament?

A. I have answered that.

Q. Are all parts of the Colonies equally able to pay taxes?

A. No, certainly; the frontier parts, which have been ravaged by the enemy, are greatly disabled by that means; and therefore, in such cases, are usually favored in our tax laws.

Q. Can we, at this distance, be competent judges of what favors are necessary?

A. The Parliament have supposed it, by claiming a right to make tax laws for America; I think it impossible. . . .

Q. If the Stamp Act should be repealed, would it induce the assemblies of America to acknowledge the rights of Parliament to tax them, and would they erase their resolutions?

A. No, never.

Q. Are there no means of obliging them to erase those resolutions?

A. None that I know of; they will never do it, unless compelled by force of arms.

Q. Is there a power on earth that can force them to erase them?

A. No power, how great soever, can force men to change their opinions. . . .

Q. What used to be the pride of Americans?

A. To indulge in the fashions and manufactures of Great Britain.

Q. What is now their pride?

A. To wear their old clothes over again, till they can make new ones.

21. The Declaratory Act
March 18, 1766

An Act for the better securing the dependency of his Majesty's Dominions in America Upon the Crown and Parliament of Great Britain

WHEREAS *several of the houses of representatives in his Majesty's colonies and plantations in America, have of late, against law, claimed to themselves, or to the general assemblies of the same, the sole and exclusive right of imposing duties and taxes upon his Majesty's subjects in the said colonies and plantations; and have, in pursuance of such claim, passed certain votes, resolutions, and orders, derogatory to the legislative authority of parliament, and inconsistent with the dependency of the said colonies and plantations upon the crown of Great Britain: . . . be it declared . . . , That the said colonies and plantations in America have been, are, and of right ought to be, subordinate unto, and dependent upon the imperial crown and parliament of Great*

SOURCE: D. Pickering, ed., *Statutes at Large*, XXVII, 19–20.

Britain; and that the King's majesty, by and with the advice and consent of the lords spiritual and temporal, and commons of *Great Britain,* in parliament assembled, had, hath, and of right ought to have, full power and authority to make laws and statutes of sufficient force and validity to bind the colonies and people of *America,* subjects of the crown of *Great Britain,* in all cases whatsoever.

II. And be it further declared . . . , That all resolutions, votes, orders, and proceedings, in any of the said colonies or plantations, whereby the power and authority of the parliament of *Great Britain,* to make laws and statutes as aforesaid, is denied, or drawn into question, are, and are hereby declared to be, utterly null and void to all intents and purposes whatsoever.

22. Thomas Hutchinson on the Collapse of Authority in Boston: Letter to Thomas Pownall March 8, 1766

SIR

I am very much obliged to you for your favour of December the 3d, under Mr. Hancock's cover. If I had received any letter from you before, since my misfortunes, I should have acknowledged it. Some of my letters from England I have reason to think stop by the way. I wish I could have had your sentiments in what manner those who wish well to America should conduct themselves, those I mean who are in America, for I am sure they never stood so much in need of advice. I have often had occasion to reflect upon your sentiments of the People of America, more justly formed, from the experience of a few years, than my own, from living among them all my days. A thought of independence I could not think it possible should enter into the heart of any man, in his senses, for ages to come. You have more than once hinted to me that I was mistaken and I am now convinced that I was so, and that the united endeavours of the friends to Britain and her colonies, in Europe and America, are necessary to restore the colonists to a true sense

SOURCE: Massachusetts Archives, lib. XXVI, 207–214.

of their duty and interest. It would be presumption in me to suggest measures to His Majesty's ministers. If I am capable of doing any service it must be by acquainting you with rise and progress of this taint of principles and the degree to which it prevails.

It is not more than two years since it was the general principle of the colonists, that in all matters of privilege or rights the determination of the Parliament of Great Britain must be decisive. They could not, it is true, alter the nature of things and the natural rights of an english man, to which no precise idea seems to have been affixed, would remain in him, but the exercise of that right, during the continuance of such determination or act, must be suspended. To oppose by an armed force the execution of any act of parliament, grand juries, without offence, have been often instructed was high treason, as well in America as in Europe, and that his Majesty as King of Great Britain had no subjects in any part of the world upon whom an act of the Parliament of Great Britain was not binding.

You will give me leave to mention to you how these principles have gradually changed, for others which approach very near to independence. You are sensible the Parliament had scarce in any instance imposed any tax or duty upon the colonies for the purpose of a revenue. The 18d. sugar duty was considered for the regulation of trade, the Molosses act of the 6th. of George the 2d was professedly designed meerly as a prohibition from the foreign islands, the Greenwich hospital duty was upon seamen who, generally, are rather inhabitants of the world than any colony, and the Post office was supposed to be established for publick convenience; and until the late act which lowered the duties upon molosses and sugar, with a professed design to raise a revenue from them, few people in the colonies had made it a question how far the Parliament, of right, might impose taxes upon them. When this first became a topick for conversation, few or none were willing to admit the right, but the power and, from thence the obligation to submit none would deny. The Massachusets assembly was the first representative body, which took this matter into consideration. Besides the act for raising a revenue from molosses, &c. there had been a resolve of the House of commons, that the parliament had a right to raise money from the colonies by internal taxes. A committee of the council and house were appointed to prepare an address to His

Majesty, or the Parliament, for relief. The committee soon determined the latter to be the most proper. I was chairman of the committee, but declined drawing any address. Several were prepared which expressed in strong terms an exclusive right in the assembly to impose taxes. I urged the ill policy, when they had the resolution of the house of commons before them, of sending an address, in express words, asserting the contrary and, after a fortnight spent, at the desire of the committee, I drew an address, which considered the sole Power of taxation as an indulgence which we prayed the continuance of, and this was unanimously agreed to. The proceeding of the general court was also approved and applauded out of doors, until the copy of an address from the assembly of New York was brought to Boston by Mr. Bayard, one of the city members. This was so high, that the heroes for liberty among us were ashamed of their own conduct and would have recalled what had been done here, if it had not been too late. Still this was not the general sense of the people. It was supposed the New York address and any others in the same strain would bring down the resentment of Parliament, but when news came, that the stamp act had passed and that no distinction was made in the addresses, it was then said, that if all the colonies had shewn the like firmness and asserted their rights the act would never have passed, and the promoter of the measure here was charged with treachery and from his dependence on the crown betraying his country.

It had not, however, been suggested that the act would not be executed and several persons, who are now for dying rather than submit to it, were then making interest with the distributor for places for themselves or friends. But soon after, the resolves of the Virginia assembly were sent hither. A new spirit appeared at once. An act of Parliament against our natural rights was ipso facto void and the people were bound to unite against the execution of it. You know the temper of the tradesmen of the town of Boston. They were inflamed, began the first violence against the distributor and then went on to more enormous acts, until they were struck with horror at looking back and thought they had done enough to deter all persons from giving the lest countenance to the act. This flame, by all the art of superior incendiaries, has been spread through this and every other colony upon the continent, and every where, it is the universal voice of all people, that if the stamp act must take place we are absolute slaves. There is no reasoning with them, you are immediately pronounced an enemy to your country.

It looks doubtful from your letter whether the act will be repealed. The general opinion is, among the most moderate, that nothing but superior force will carry it into execution. If you urge the invalidity of all instruments and law proceedings, it is immediately asked who will dare dispute them. Confusion, and convulsion, will be the inevitable consequence, how great or how durable it is not possible to judge.

If the act should be repealed, we shall still be in a deplorable condition. In the capital towns of several of the colonies and of this in particular, the authority is in the populace, no law can be carried into execution against their mind. I am not sure that the acts of trade will not be considered as grievous as the stamp act. I doubt whether, at present, any custom house officer would venture to make a seizure. In the country towns, in this province, I should hope the people in general would return to reason and be convinced of the necessity of supporting the authority of government. I do not mention this as a sufficient argument against external provision for the future support of government, but it may possibly be a reason for deferring for a short time, at lest in degree, any measures for that purpose, until the minds of the people are somewhat calmed, and the effect of the repeal, if that should be the case, shall appear.

I cannot avoid acquainting you with a further fact the consequence of the disaffected state of mind among the people and which I believe you have not a full conception of. When I first saw the proposals for lessening the consumption of english manufactures I took them to be mere puffs. The scheme for laying aside mourning succeeded to my surprize and scarce any body would now dare to wear black for the nearest relation. In this town, there is yet no very sensible alteration in other articles, but in the country, in general, there is a visible difference and the humour for being cloathed in homespun spreads every day not so much from oeconomy as to convince the people of England how beneficial the colonies have been to them, supposing the worth of any thing to be best known by the want of it.

A general representation of facts is all that is necessary to write to you, who know so perfectly the constitution of every colony, the disposition and temper of all the inhabitants; it is all that in prudence I ought to write to any body, considering the present prevailing jealousy in the minds of people improved, by a much more abandoned man than Clodius to render obnoxious every person who opposes his wicked schemes of popularity. I may safely say, that by some means or other the authority in the colonies first or last must be strengthened, that those are the most eligible which shall evidently appear, to be intended to preserve to them all the rights and liberties, which can consist with their connexion with their mother country. In this way, the present alienation may be removed and, instead of seeking to lessen the profit the mother country may make from trade and commerce with them, they will seek means to increase it, but while this alienation remains, although effectual means should be used to maintain a subordination, it will be impossible to continue equal advantages from trade as if it was removed.

It will be some amusement to you to have a more circumstantial account of the present model of government among us. I will begin with the lowest branch partly legislative partly executive. This consists of the rabble of the town of Boston headed by one Mackintosh who I imagine you never heard of. He is a bold fellow and as likely for a Massianello[1] as you can well conceive. When there is occasion to hang or burn effigies or pull down houses these are employed, but since government has been brought to a system they are some what controuled by a superior set consisting of the master masons carpenters &c of the town. When the Secretary was summoned to attend at the tree of liberty he sent to T. Daws to desire him to interpose and at lest procure leave for him to resign at the town house but after two or three consultations nothing more could be obtained than a promise of having no affront offered and a proposal to invite the principal persons of the town to accompany him.

When any thing of more importance is to be determined as opening the custom house or any matters of trade these are under the direction of a committee of merchants. Mr. Rowe at their head then Molyneux Solomon Davis &c but all affairs of a general nature opening all the courts of law &c. this is proper for a general meeting of the inhabitants of Boston where Otis with his mobbish

---

1. A corruption of [Tom]mas Anielo, a Neapolitan fisherman who headed an insurrection in 1647 against the Duke of Arcos.

eloquence prevails in every motion, and the town first determine what is necessary to be done and then apply either to the Governor and council or resolve that it is necessary the general court should meet and it must be a very extraordinary resolve indeed that is not carried into execution. The town applied to the governor in council to desire him to order the executive courts to do business with out stamps. This the council refused to advise to but advised him to recommend to the Justices of the inferior court for Suffolk to meet and determine whether at the court which was to be held in two or three days after they should proceed, but the town who kept their meeting alive by adjournment immediately upon receiving the answer resolved it was unsatisfactory. After this upon the motion of Otis they sent a committee to desire the governor not to prorogue the general court any further. When the court met the House resolved not above half a dozen dissenting that the courts ought to go on with business and sent to the council to concur. I opposed it as taking from the executive courts their right of judgment and moved the resolve should ly that if enquired after the house might be told it was extrajudicial. A day or two after I was charged in the news paper my name at large with declaring in council the vote was impertinent below the notice of the board and by usurping the president's place obtaining an undue influence &c. and the printers were directed to tell the author's name if required. Otis did not deny his being the author. A publication in the same paper had done a great deal towards raising the former storm against me and I expected a second shipwreck, and therefore moved to the council to send for the printers and if they should mention Otis as the author that the House should be applied to for justice upon one of their members, but the majority of the council were afraid and only ordered a vote to be published declaring the falshood of the account in the former paper. Although this had a tendency to appease the rage of the rabble against me yet it was so dishonorable to the council to contradict such an aspersion without any further notice that with the governor's approbation I excused my self from any further attendance that session. The board after this, instead of passing upon the resolve recommended to the Justices of the superior court to determine whether they would proceed or not at their next term. This they refused to do but gave it as their opinion that if the affairs of government continued in the present state they should find themselves under a necessity of proceeding. This was not satisfactory to the house who insisted that the board should pass on their resolve but they kept altercating upon it until the court was over by a long adjournment. A majority of the superior court I imagine will find the necessity they supposed they should. I hope to excuse my self from joining with them.

The majority of the house are not disaffected or unfriendly to government, but are afraid to act their judgment this boutefeu[2] threatning to print their names who vote against his measures. In council the valiant Brigadier Royall who has thrown up his commission is at the head of all popular measures and become a great orator. Erving Brattle Gray Otis and Bradbury and Sparhawk whose characters you well know are in the same box. Tyler is sometimes of one side and sometimes of the other.

It must be a pleasure to you sometimes to look back upon your old government, otherwise I should fear I had quite tired you with this long epistle.

I had wrote thus far the 8th. The constant intelligence every day or two of one occurrent and another which demonstrates that there is no authority subsisting in any of the colonies makes me doubt whether of our selves we shall ever return to a state of government and order. In the Jersies, New York and Connecticut there is a settled plan of union of the populace of those governments who correspond by Committees and are settling a committee to represent the whole. About a fortnight ago the distracted demagogue of Boston attacked my history of the colony and censured me in his news paper for charging the government with a mistake in imagining that an act of the colony was necessary to give force to an act of Parliament for regulating trade. A few days after upon a seizure of molosses and sugar at Newbury half a dozen boats well manned went after the officer took the goods from him and the boat he was in and left him all night upon the beach. A proclamation with promise of reward upon discovery is nothing more than the shew of authority, no man will venture a discovery and I imagine a few more such instances will make it settled law that no act but those of our legislatures can bind us.

2. French for "firebrand."

VI

The Conflict Expands

Only a year after the repeal of the Stamp Act, Parliament once again raised the constitutional issue by enacting the Townshend program. The Townshend Acts imposed import duties and were an attempt to by-pass the objections raised by some colonials, notably Daniel Dulany, Jr., and Benjamin Franklin, to levying "internal" taxes for the purpose of revenue. (Other colonials had sweepingly denied Parliament's right to levy any kind of tax.) The acts were promptly denounced in a learned, yet vigorous, pamphlet written by John Dickinson, a lawyer and rising political figure in the colonies of Delaware and Pennsylvania. In his best-selling Farmer's Letters Dickinson denied Parliament's right to tax the colonies for purposes of revenue. Included herein is Letter II of December 7, 1767. A month later, the Massachusetts House of Representatives, prodded by Samuel Adams, issued a Circular Letter which was forwarded to the other colonial legislatures asserting that Parliamentary taxation for the sole purpose of raising a revenue infringed upon "natural and constitutional rights." For their refusal to rescind the Circular Letter the Massachusetts Assembly was dissolved by its royal governor.

Thus it is seen how the Townshend program set off a chain reaction of intensified constitutional debate and British reprisals, the latter proving counterproductive. The stationing of the Customs Board in Boston sparked trouble from the start. The Board's strict enforcement of customs laws precipitated a series of clashes with British officials, the most notable occurring following the seizure of John Hancock's sloop Liberty for landing Madeira wine without payment of duty. Popular leaders prodded the merchants to reactivate nonimportation. After a faltering attempt initiated by New York in May, 1768, Boston adopted a sweeping nonimportation agreement, which other seaport towns also put into effect, including, after much pressure from the radical mechanics, the merchants of Charleston.

Deeply rooted in colonial America was a resentment of standing armies and a dislike of Old World militarism. That resentment was fanned by the Quartering Act (1765), requiring the civil authorities in the colonies to furnish barracks and supplies for British troops. The New York Assembly, suspended for its refusal to comply therewith, finally voted a nominal sum as a free gift, which the British ministry accepted, lifting the suspension. Tensions between populace and soldiers spread from New York to Boston, where British troops were stationed beginning in 1768. The Bostonians' constant harassment of the soldiers, inspired by grievances real and fancied, eventually touched off the "Boston Massacre."

The dispute between the colonies and the mother country was intensified by the transatlantic scandal over the Hutchinson letters. Benjamin Franklin had transmitted to Massachusetts Assembly Speaker Thomas Cushing letters by Thomas Hutchinson and Andrew Oliver, Governor and Lieutenant Governor of Massachusetts, respectively, to Thomas Whately, a member of the Grenville and North ministries. The letters, which recommended that the liberties of the province be restricted, were given to Franklin to show him that false advice from America went far toward explaining the obnoxious acts of the British government. Franklin sent the letters to Cushing, with an injunction that they were not to be copied or published but merely shown in the original to individuals in the province. But in June 1773 Samuel Adams read the letters before a secret session of the House of Representatives and later had the letters copied and printed. Although these letters were made public ostensibly against his wishes, Franklin was excoriated before the British Privy Council by Solicitor-General Alexander Wedderburn. The humiliation rankled for a long time. In the ministerial version of the confrontation, as reported by Israel Mauduit, Wedderburn couched his attack in temperate language, but other auditors disputed this. Wedderburn's excoriation of Franklin as a thief (Latin: fur) is preserved in the account of Benjamin Vaughan, an early editor of Franklin's writings. Both versions are included here.

23. Reaction to the Townshend Acts:
John Dickinson's *Farmer's Letters*, Letter II
December 7, 1767

THERE IS another late act of Parliament [the Townshend Act] which appears to me to be unconsitutional and as destructive to the liberty of these colonies as that mentioned in my last letter, that is, the act for granting the duties on paper, glass, etc.

The Parliament unquestionably possesses a legal authority to

SOURCE: P. L. Ford, ed., "The Writings of John Dickinson," Historical Society of Pennsylvania, Memoirs, XIV (2 vols., Philadelphia, 1895), I, 312–314, 316–321, passim.

regulate the trade of Great Britain and all her colonies. Such an authority is essential to the relation between a mother country and her colonies; and necessary for the common good of all. He who considers these provinces as states distinct from the British Empire has very slender notions of justice or of their interests. We are but parts of a whole, and therefore there must exist a power somewhere to preside and preserve the connection in due order. This power is lodged in the Parliament; and we are as much dependent on Great Britain as a perfectly free people can be on another.

I have looked over every statute relating to these colonies from their first settlement to this time, and I find every one of them founded on this principle, till the Stamp Act administration. All before are calculated to regulate trade and preserve or promote a mutually beneficial intercourse between the several constituent parts of the empire. And though many of them imposed duties on trade, yet those duties were always imposed with design to restrain the commerce of one part that was injurious to another, and thus to promote the general welfare. The raising a revenue thereby was never intended. . . . Never did the British Parliament, till the period above mentioned, think of imposing duties in America FOR THE PURPOSE OF RAISING A REVENUE. . . .

Here we may observe an authority expressly claimed and exerted to impose duties on these colonies; not for the regulation of trade; not for the preservation or promotion of a mutually beneficial intercourse between the several constituent parts of the empire, heretofore the sole objects of Parliamentary institutions; but for the single purpose of levying money upon us.

This I call an innovation, and a most dangerous innovation. It may perhaps be objected that Great Britain has a right to lay what duties she pleases upon her exports, and it makes no difference to us whether they are paid here or there. To this I answer: These colonies require many things for their use which the laws of Great Britain prohibit them from getting anywhere but from her. Such are paper and glass.

That we may be legally bound to pay any general duties on these commodities relative to the regulation of trade is granted; but we being obliged by the laws to take from Great Britain, any special duties imposed on their exportation to us only with intention to raise a revenue from us only are as much taxes upon us as those imposed by the Stamp Act.

What is the difference in substance and right whether the same sum is raised upon us by the rates mentioned in the Stamp Act, on the use of paper, or by these duties on the importation of it. It is only the edition of a former book, shifting a sentence from the end to the beginning. . . .

Some persons perhaps may say that this act lays us under no necessity to pay the duties imposed because we may ourselves manufacture the articles on which they are laid. . . . But can any man acquainted with America believe this possible? I am told there are but two or three glass-houses on this continent and but very few paper mills. And suppose more should be erected; a long course of years must elapse before they can be brought to perfection. This continent is a country of planters, farmers, and fishermen, not of manufacturers. The difficulty of establishing particular manufactures in such a country is almost insuperable. . . .

Inexpressible therefore must be our distresses in evading the late acts by the disuse of British paper and glass. Nor will this be the extent of our misfortune if we admit the legality of that act.

Great Britain has prohibited the manufacturing of iron and steel in these colonies without any objection being made to her right of doing it. The like right she must have to prohibit any other manufacture among us. Thus, she is possessed of an undisputed precedent on that point. This authority, she will say, is founded on the original intention of settling these colonies, that is, that she should manufacture for them, and that they should supply her with materials. The equity of this policy, she will also say, has been universally acknowledged by the colonies, who never have made the least objection to statutes for that purpose; and will further appear by the mutual benefits flowing from this usage, ever since the settlement of these colonies.

Our great advocate, Mr. Pitt, in his speeches on the debate concerning the repeal of the Stamp Act, acknowledged that Great Britain could restrain our manufacturers. His words were these: ". . . We may bind their trade, CONFINE THEIR MANUFACTURES, and exercise every power whatever except that of taking their money out of their pockets WITHOUT THEIR CONSENT."

Here, then, my dear countrymen, ROUSE yourselves and behold the ruin hanging over your heads. If you ONCE admit that Great Britain may lay duties upon her exportations to us, for the purpose of levying money on us only, she then will have nothing to do but to lay those duties on the articles which she prohibits us to manufacture—and the tragedy of American liberty is finished. . . . If Great Britain can order us to come to her for necessaries we want and can order us to pay what taxes she pleases before we take them away, or when we land them here, we are as abject slaves as France and Poland can show in wooden shoes and with uncombed hair.

24. The Seizure of John Hancock's Sloop *Liberty*: Thomas Hutchinson to Richard Jackson June 16, 1768

I REC'D today your very kind Letter by the [torn] Pacquet designed a month sooner but by a blunder in the Post Office was sent I suppose to Boston in Lincolnshire and returned. You will be amazed at the proceedings of our people since my last. The 9 [sic] in the evening the Cust. h. Officers seizd a Sloop belong. to M^r. H. one of the Boston Rep. for making a false entry. It is said a Cargo of Mad. Wine was landed in the night and the next morn. the master entred 4 or 5 pps and swore it was the whole of her Cargo. This was the town talk for several weeks but it was supposed nobody would dare make a seizure. The Offics differd in Opinion the Collect [or] thinking she might lay at the wharffe after she had the broad arrow but the Comptroller thot it best to move her under the Guns of the *Romney* which lay a quarter of a mile from the Shoar and made a signal for the man of war boats to come ashoar. The people upon the wharffe said there was no occasion she would ly safe and no Officer had a right to move her but the master of the Man of War cut her Moorings and carried her off. A Mob presently gathered and insulted the Custom H Offic^s and carried them in triumph as trespassers up the Wharffe tore their cloaths and bruised and otherways hurt them until one after another they escaped. The mob increased to 2 or 3000 chiefly sturdy boys and negroes and broke the windows of the Comptrollers house and then the Inspector's Williams and then went in search of the M of

SOURCE: Massachusetts Archives, XXVI, 310–312.

War's boats wch. not finding they took a boat belong^g to M^r. H. the Collector dragged her into the Common and burnt her and about one o'Clock dispersed. This was friday. Saturday and Sunday evenings are sacred. Monday it was supposed would produce something more important but in the aftern. printed tickets were put up in diff't quarters notifying the Sons of Lib. to meet the next day at 10 o'Clock at Liberty Hall or Lib. Tree which is all one to consult what was proper to be done in these times of Oppression and Distraction to preserve peace and order and maintain their Rights etc. This diverted the Evenings work but at the appointed time some thousands of the Rabble met but it being a rainy day they adjourned to Fan. Hall where a proposal was made to send the Constables to notify a legal Town meet. for the aftern. at [the] South Ch[urch] the Hall not being large eno accord. the same Convention met in the aft. under a new name and chose Otis their Moderator who after haranguing them some time from the Pulpit suffered them to harangue one another until they had agreed upon an Address to the G[overnor]. the most extrad. thing that has yet appeared and appointed 21 of their number to wait on him with it and then adjourned to the next day for an Answer. The G. let them know he could not comply with what they princip[ally] desired which was to order the *Romney* out of the Harb. but should be glad to do every thing for the good of the Town, and Prov. consist. with his Duty to the Crown etc. Upon receiving this Answer they adjourned until tomorrow evn'g to consider what further measures are proper. The Commis. Hulton Burch Paxton & Robi[nson] remained pretty easy Saturday and Sunday but Mond. morning early they sent a card to the G. to let him know they were going abroad the *Romney* and desired his orders for their Recept at the Castle which he readily gave. The Collect. and Comptroller and most of the other Officers of the Cust[oms] are also withdrawn and it is by no means advisable at present for any of them to return.

I have been with my family several weeks in the Country. The G. is at his house in the Country but goes to Council every day or two. Tuesday morning he sent one of his sons to me to desire me to come to him being in expect. of very import. news from Town. I went immed. when he acquainted me that he had been endeavouring all Saturday and Monday to prevail upon the C[ollector] to come into some spirited measures but all to no purpose, that when he sent his son away he was apprehensive he should receive such advices of the proceed. of the Sons of Lib. at Boston as that it would be necessary for him to withdraw but happily before my arrival he had more favorable accounts. It is now the talk among the Populace that neither the Commiss'rs nor the Comptroller shall be suffered to return to Town and just before noon today I saw a printed notification upon the Change requiring a full meet. tomorrow as the fate of the Prov. and of America depended upon the measures to be then taken.

It is very natural to ask where the Justices and Sheriffs are upon these occasions. The persons who are to assist the Sheriff in the execution of his Office are Sons of Liberty and determined to oppose him in every thing which shall be contrary to their Schemes. Some of the Justices are great favourers of them and those who are not are afraid of being sacrificed by them and will issue out no warrant to apprehend them. Let an Officer behave ever so ill even if he was to abet the Disorders he ought to suppress I do not think it would be practicable to remove him seeing it cannot be done without the advice of C. and they would be afraid to give the advice. . . .

25. Nonimportation Agreements: Boston, July 28, 1768, and Charleston, July 22, 1769

Boston Agreement, July 28, 1768

THE MERCHANTS and traders in the town of Boston, having taken into consideration the deplorable situation of the trade and the many difficulties it at present labours under on account of the scarcity of money, which is daily decreasing for want of other remittances to discharge our debts in Great Britain, and the large sums collected by the officers of the customs for duties on goods imported; the heavy taxes levied to discharge the debts contracted by the government in the late Warr; the embarrassments and re-

SOURCE: Price Papers, Massachusetts Historical Society.

strictions laid on the trade by the several late Acts of Parliament, together with the bad success of our cod fishery this season, and the discouraging prospect of the whale fishery, by which our principal sources of remittances are like to be greatly diminished, and we thereby rendered unable to pay the debts we owe the merchants in Great Britain, and to continue the importation of goods from thence:

We, the subscribers, in order to relieve the trade under those discouragements, and to promote industry, frugality, and œconomy, and to discourage luxury and every kind of extravagance, do promise and engage to and with each other as follows:

1st, That we will not send for or import from Great Britain this fall, either on our own account, or on commission, any other goods than what are already ordered for the fall supply.

2d, That we will not send for or import any kind of goods or merchandise from Great Britain, either on our own account, or on commissions, or any otherwise, from the 1st January 1769, to the 1st January 1770, except salt, coals, fish-hooks and lines, hemp, duck, bar lead and shot, wool-cards, and card-wire.

That we will not purchase of any factors, or others, any kind of goods imported from Great Britain from January 1769, to January 1770.

That we will not import on our own account, or on commission, or purchase from any who shall import from any other colony in America, from January 1769, to January 1770, any tea, glass, paper, or other goods commonly imported from Great Britain.

That we will not, from and after the 1st January 1769, import into the province any tea, paper, glass, or painters' colours, until the Act imposing duties on these articles shall have been repealed.

In Witness whereof we have hereunto sett our hands this 28th day of July 1768.

Charleston Agreement, July 22, 1769

It is with great Pleasure we now inform the Public, that, at a GENERAL MEETING of the Inhabitants of Charles-Town, and of the Places adjacent, the following ASSOCIATION was unanimously agreed

SOURCE: The South-Carolina Gazette, July 27, 1769.

to; which we have no Doubt, will be satisfactory to, and concurred with, by every Free-man in the Province.

We, His Majesty's dutiful and loving Subjects, the Inhabitants of SOUTH-CAROLINA, being sensibly affected with the great Prejudice done to GREAT-BRITAIN, and the abject and wretched Condition to which the BRITISH COLONIES are reduced by several Acts of Parliament lately passed; by *some of which* the Monies that the Colonists usually and chearfully spent in the Purchase of all Sorts of Goods imported from GREAT-BRITAIN, are now, to their great Grievance, wrung from them, without their Consent, or even their being represented, and applied by the Ministry, in Prejudice of, and without Regard to, the real Interest of GREAT-BRITAIN, or the Manufactures thereof, almost totally, to the Support of new-created Commissioners of Customs, Placemen, parasitical and novel ministerial Officers; and *by others of which* Acts, we are not only deprived of those invaluable Rights, Trial by our Peers and the Common Law, but are also made subject to the arbitrary and oppressive Proceedings of the Civil Law, justly abhorred and rejected by our Ancestors, the Free-Men of England, and finding, that the most dutiful and loyal Petitions from the Colonies ALONE, for Redress of those Grievances, have been rejected with Contempt, so that no Relief can be expected from that Method of Proceeding; and, being fully convinced of the absolute Necessity, of stimulating our Fellow Subjects and Sufferers in GREAT-BRITAIN to aid us, in this our Distress, and of joining the Rest of the Colonies, in some other loyal and vigorous Methods, that may most probably procure such Relief, which we believe may be most effectually promoted by strict OECONOMY, and by encouraging the MANUFACTURES of AMERICA in general, and of this Province in particular: WE THEREFORE, whose Names are underwritten, do solemnly promise, and agree to and with each other, That, until the Colonies be restored to their former Freedom, by the Repeal of the said Acts, we will most strictly abide by the following

RESOLUTIONS

I. That we will encourage and promote the Use of NORTH AMERICAN MANUFACTURES in general, and those of this Province in particular. And any of us, who are Venders thereof, do engage to sell and dispose of them, at the same Rates as heretofore.

II. That we will upon no Pretence whatsoever, either upon our own Account or on Commission, import into this Province, any of the Manufactures of GREAT-BRITAIN, or any other EUROPEAN or EAST-INDIA Goods, either from GREAT-BRITAIN, HOLLAND, or ANY OTHER PLACE, other than such as may have been shipped in Consequence of former Orders, excepting only NEGRO CLOTH, commonly called white and coloured PLAINS, not exceeding *One Shilling* and *Six Pence* Sterling per Yard, striped DUFFIL BLANKETS, OSNABURGS, coarse white LINENS, not exceeding *One Shilling* and *Six Pence* Sterling per Yard, CANVAS, BOLTING CLOTHS, DRUGS and FAMILY MEDICINES, PLANTATION and WORKMENS TOOLS, NAILS, FIRE ARMS, BAR STEEL, GUN POWDER, SHOT, LEAD, FLINTS, WIRE CARDS and CARD WIRE, MILL and GRIND STONES, FISH HOOKS, printed BOOKS and PAMPHLETS, SALT, COALS, and SALT-PETRE. And exclusive of these Articles, we do solemnly promise and declare, that we will immediately countermand all Orders to our Correspondents in GREAT-BRITAIN, for shipping any such Goods, Wares and Merchandize: And we will sell and dispose of the Goods we have on Hand, or that may arrive in Consequence of former Orders, at the same Rates as heretofore.

III. That we will use the utmost OECONOMY, in our Persons, Houses and Furniture; particularly, that we will give no MOURN-ING, or GLOVES or SCARVES at Funerals.

IV. That, from and after the 1st Day of *January* 1770, we will not IMPORT, BUY, or SELL, any NEGROES that shall be brought into this Province from AFRICA; nor, after the 1st Day of *October* next, any NEGROES that shall be imported from the WEST-INDIES, or ANY OTHER PLACE, excepting from AFRICA as aforesaid. And that, if any Goods or Negroes shall be sent to us, contrary to our Agreement in this Subscription, such GOODS shall be re-shipped or stored, and such Negroes re-shipped from this Province, and not by any Means offered for Sale therein.

V. That we will not purchase from, or sell for, any Masters of Vessels, transient Persons, or Non-Subscribers, any Kind of EURO-PEAN or EAST-INDIAN GOODS whatever, excepting COALS and SALT, after the 1st Day of *November* next.

VI. That as WINES are subject to a heavy Duty, we agree, not to import any on our Account or on Commission, or purchase from any Master of Vessel, transient Person, or Non-Subscriber, after the 1st Day of *January* next.

VIII. LASTLY, That we will not purchase any NEGROES imported, or any GOODS or MERCHANDIZE whatever, from any Resident in this Province, that refuses or neglects to sign this Agreement, within one Month from the Date hereof, excepting it shall appear he has been unavoidably prevented from doing the same. And every Subscriber who shall not, strictly or literally, adhere to this Agreement, according to the true Intent and Meaning hereof, ought to be treated with the utmost Contempt.

GIVEN under our Hand this twenty-second Day of July, 1769. SUBSCRIPTION PAPERS to be signed, are left with CHRISTOPHER GADSEN, Esq.; Messrs. ISAAC MOTTE, GEORGE ANCRUM, JOHN EDWARDS, JOHN NEUFVILLE, JOHN CORAM, JOHN WAGNER, ROBERT WELLS, CHARLES CROUCH, and at TIMOTHY's Printing-Office, in Broad-Street.

26. The Boston Massacre
March 5, 1770

THE TOWN of Boston affords a recent and melancholy demonstration of the destructive consequences of quartering troops among citizens in a time of peace, under a pretence of supporting the laws and aiding civil authority; every considerate and unprejudiced person among us was deeply impressed with the apprehension of these consequences when it was known that a number of regiments were ordered to this town under such a pretext, but in reality to enforce oppressive measures; to awe and control the legislative as well as executive power of the province, and to quell a spirit of liberty, which however it may have been basely opposed and even ridiculed by some, would do honour to any age or country. A few persons amongst us had determined to use all their influence to procure so destructive a measure with a view to their securely enjoying the profits of an American revenue, and unhappily both for Britain and this country they found means to effect it.

It is to Governor Bernard, the commissioners, their confidants and coadjutors, that we are indebted as the procuring cause of a

SOURCE: *The Boston Gazette and Country Journal*, March 12, 1770.

military power in this capital. The Boston Journal of Occurrences, as printed in Mr. Holt's *New York Gazette*, from time to time, afforded many striking instances of the distresses brought upon the inhabitants by this measure; and since those Journals have been discontinued, our troubles from that quarter have been growing upon us. We have known a party of soldiers in the face of day fire off a loaden musket upon the inhabitants, others have been pricked with bayonets, and even our magistrates assaulted and put in danger of their lives, when offenders brought before them have been rescued; and why those and other bold and base criminals have as yet escaped the punishment due to their crimes may be soon matter of enquiry by the representative body of this people. It is natural to suppose that when the inhabitants of this town saw those laws which had been enacted for their security, and which they were ambitious of holding up to the soldiery, eluded, they should more commonly resent for themselves; and accordingly it has so happened. Many have been the squabbles between them and the soldiery; but it seems their being often worsted by our youth in those rencounters, has only served to irritate the former. What passed at Mr. Gray's rope-walk has already been given the public and may be said to have led the way to the late catastrophe. That the rope-walk lads, when attacked by superior numbers, should defend themselves with so much spirit and success in the club-way, was too mortifying, and perhaps it may hereafter appear that even some of their officers were unhappily affected with this circumstance. Divers stories were propagated among the soldiery that served to agitate their spirits; particularly on the Sabbath that one Chambers, a sergeant, represented as a sober man, had been missing the preceding day and must therefore have been murdered by the townsmen. An officer of distinction so far credited this report that he entered Mr. Gray's rope-walk that Sabbath; and when required of by that gentleman as soon as he could meet him, the occasion of his so doing, the officer replied that it was to look if the sergeant said to be murdered had not been hid there. This sober sergeant was found on the Monday unhurt in a house of pleasure. The evidences already collected show that many threatenings had been thrown out by the soldiery, but we do not pretend to say that there was any preconcerted plan. When the evidences are published, the world will judge. We may, however, venture to declare that it appears too probable from their conduct that some of the soldiery aimed to draw and provoke the townsmen into squabbles, and that they then intended to make use of other weapons than canes, clubs, or bludgeons.

Our readers will doubtless expect a circumstantial account of the tragical affair on Monday night last; but we hope they will excuse our being so particular as we should have been, had we not seen that the town was intending an enquiry and full representation thereof.

On the evening of Monday, being the fifth current, several soldiers of the 29th Regiment were seen parading the streets with their drawn cutlasses and bayonets, abusing and wounding numbers of the inhabitants.

A few minutes after nine o'clock four youths, named Edward Archbald, William Merchant, Francis Archbald, and John Leech, jun., came down Cornhill together, and separating at Doctor Loring's corner, the two former were passing the narrow alley leading to Murray's barrack in which was a soldier brandishing a broad sword of an uncommon size against the walls, out of which he struck fire plentifully. A person of mean countenance armed with a large cudgel bore him company. Edward Archbald admonished Mr. Merchant to take care of the sword, on which the soldier turned round and struck Archbald on the arm, then pushed at Merchant and pierced through his clothes inside the arm close to the armpit and grazed the skin. Merchant then struck the soldier with a short stick he had; and the other person ran to the barrack and brought with him two soldiers, one armed with a pair of tongs, the other with a shovel. He with the tongs pursued Archbald back through the alley, collared and laid him over the head with the tongs. The noise brought people together; and John Hicks, a young lad, coming up, knocked the soldier down but let him get up again; and more lads gathering, drove them back to the barrack where the boys stood some time as it were to keep them in. In less than a minute ten or twelve of them came out with drawn cutlasses, clubs, and bayonets and set upon the unarmed boys and young folk who stood them a little while but, finding the inequality of their equipment, dispersed. On hearing the noise, one Samuel Atwood came up to see what was the matter; and entering the alley from dock square, heard the latter part of the combat; and when the boys had dispersed he met the ten or twelve soldiers aforesaid rushing down the alley towards the square and asked them if they intended to murder people? They answered Yes, by G-d, root and branch! With that one of them struck Mr. Atwood with a club which was repeated by another; and being unarmed, he turned to go off and received a wound on the left shoulder which reached the bone and gave him much pain. Retreating a few steps, Mr. Atwood met two officers and said, gentlemen, what is the matter? They answered, you'll see by and by. Immediately after, those heroes appeared in the square, asking where were the boogers? where were the cowards? But notwithstanding their fierceness to naked men, one of them advanced towards a youth who had a split of a raw stave in his hand and said, damn them, here is one of them. But the young man seeing a person near him with a drawn sword and good cane ready to support him, held up his stave in defiance; and they quietly passed by him up the little alley by Mr. Silsby's to King Street where they attacked single and unarmed persons till they raised much clamour, and then turned down Cornhill Street, insulting all they met in like manner and pursuing some to their very doors. Thirty or forty persons, mostly lads, being by this means gathered in King Street, Capt. Preston with a party of men with charged bayonets, came from the main guard to the commissioner's house, the soldiers pushing their bayonets, crying, make way! They took place by the custom house and, continuing to push to drive the people off, pricked some in several places, on which they were clamorous and, it is said, threw snow balls. On this, the Captain commanded them to fire; and more snow balls coming, he again said, damn you, fire, be the consequence what it will! One soldier then fired, and a townsman with a cudgel struck him over the hands with such force that he dropped his firelock; and, rushing forward, aimed a blow at the Captain's head which grazed his hat and fell pretty heavy upon his arm. However, the soldiers continued the fire successively till seven or eight or, as some say, eleven guns were discharged.

By this fatal manœuvre three men were laid dead on the spot and two more struggling for life; but what showed a degree of cruelty unknown to British troops, at least since the house of Hanover has directed their operations, was an attempt to fire upon or push with their bayonets the persons who undertook to remove the slain and wounded!

Mr. Benjamin Leigh, now undertaker in the Delph manufactory, came up; and after some conversation with Capt. Preston relative to his conduct in this affair, advised him to draw off his men, with which he complied.

The dead are Mr. Samuel Gray, killed on the spot, the ball entering his head and beating off a large portion of his skull.

A mulatto man named Crispus Attucks, who was born in Framingham, but lately belonged to New-Providence and was here in order to go for North Carolina, also killed instantly, two balls entering his breast, one of them in special goring the right lobe of the lungs and a great part of the liver most horribly.

Mr. James Caldwell, mate of Capt. Morton's vessel, in like manner killed by two balls entering his back.

Mr. Samuel Maverick, a promising youth of seventeen years of age, son of the widow Maverick, and an apprentice to Mr. Greenwood, ivory-turner, mortally wounded; a ball went through his belly and was cut out at his back. He died the next morning.

A lad named Christopher Monk, about seventeen years of age, an apprentice to Mr. Walker, shipwright, wounded; a ball entered his back about four inches above the left kidney near the spine and was cut out of the breast on the same side. Apprehended he will die.

A lad named John Clark, about seventeen years of age, whose parents live at Medford, and an apprentice to Capt. Samuel Howard of this town, wounded; a ball entered just above his groin and came out at his hip on the opposite side. Apprehended he will die.

Mr. Edward Payne of this town, merchant, standing at his entry door received a ball in his arm which shattered some of the bones.

Mr. John Green, tailor, coming up Leverett's Lane, received a ball just under his hip and lodged in the under part of his thigh, which was extracted.

Mr. Robert Patterson, a seafaring man, who was the person that had his trousers shot through in Richardson's affair, wounded; a ball went through his right arm, and he suffered a great loss of blood.

Mr. Patrick Carr, about thirty years of age, who worked with Mr. Field, leather breeches-maker in Queen Street, wounded; a ball entered near his hip and went out at his side.

A lad named David Parker, an apprentice to Mr. Eddy, the wheelwright, wounded; a ball entered in his thigh.

The people were immediately alarmed with the report of this horrid massacre, the bells were set a-ringing, and great numbers soon assembled at the place where this tragical scene had been acted. Their feelings may be better conceived than expressed; and while some were taking care of the dead and wounded, the rest were in consultation what to do in those dreadful circumstances. But so little intimidated were they, notwithstanding their being within a few yards of the main guard and seeing the 29th Regiment under arms and drawn up in King Street, that they kept their station and appeared, as an officer of rank expressed it, ready to run upon the very muzzles of their muskets. The lieutenant-governor soon came into the town house and there met some of his Majesty's Council and a number of civil magistrates. A considerable body of the people immediately entered the council chamber and expressed themselves to his honour with a freedom and warmth becoming the occasion. He used his utmost endeavours to pacify them, requesting that they would let the matter subside for the night and promising to do all in his power that justice should be done and the law have its course. Men of influence and weight with the people were not wanting on their part to procure their compliance with his Honour's request by representing the horrible consequences of a promiscuous and rash engagement in the night, and assuring them that such measures should be entered upon in the morning as would be agreeable to their dignity and a more likely way of obtaining the best satisfaction for the blood of their fellow townsmen. The inhabitants attended to these suggestions; and the regiment under arms being ordered to their barracks, which was insisted upon by the people, they then separated and returned to their dwellings by one o'clock. At three o'clock Capt. Preston was committed, as were the soldiers who fired, a few hours after him.

Tuesday morning presented a most shocking scene, the blood of our fellow citizens running like water through King Street and the Merchants' Exchange, the principal spot of the military parade for about eighteen months past. Our blood might also be tracked up to the head of Long Lane, and through divers other streets and passages.

At eleven o'clock the inhabitants met at Faneuil Hall; and after some animated speeches becoming the occasion, they chose a committee of fifteen respectable gentlemen to wait upon the lieutenant-governor in Council to request of him to issue his orders for the immediate removal of the troops.

27. The Hutchinson Letters Scandal: Solicitor-General Alexander Wedderburn's Attack on Benjamin Franklin Before the Privy Council and Benjamin Vaughan's Variant Version January 29, 1774

THUS FAR, then, the Governor's character stands fair and unimpeached. Whatever, therefore, be the foundation of this Address for his removal, it must be something done by him, or known of him, since his return from this service just before the arrival of these letters. Your Lordships will observe that his enemies don't attempt to point out a single action, during the four years in which he has been Governor, as a subject of complaint. The whole of this Address rests upon the foundation of these letters, written before the time when either of these gentlemen were possessed of the offices, from which the Assembly now ask their removal. They owe therefore all the ill-will which has been raised against them, and the loss of that confidence which the Assembly themselves acknowledge they had heretofore enjoyed, to Dr. Franklin's good office in sending back these letters to Boston. Dr. Franklin therefore stands in the light of the first mover and prime conductor of this whole contrivance against his Majesty's two Governors; and having by the help of his special confidents and party leaders, first made the Assembly *his* Agents in carrying on his own secret de-

SOURCE: Israel Mauduit, ed., *Letters of Governor Hutchinson and Lt. Governor Oliver . . . with the Speech of Mr. Wedderburn* (London, 1774), reprinted in Israel Mauduit, ed., *Franklin Before the Privy Council* (Philadelphia, 1860), 80–82, 93–94, 102–103.

signs, he now appears before your Lordships to give the finishing stroke to the work of his own hands.

How these letters came into the possession of any one but the right owners, is still a mystery for Dr. Franklin to explain. They who know the affectionate regard which the Whatelys had for each other, and the tender concern they felt for the honor of their brother's memory, as well as their own, can witness the distresses which this occasioned. My Lords, the late Mr. Whately was most scrupulously cautious about his letters. We lived for many years in the strictest intimacy; and in all those years I never saw a single letter written to him. These letters, I believe, were in his custody at his death. And I as firmly believe, that without fraud, they could not have been got out of the custody of the person whose hands they fell into. His brothers little wanted this additional aggravation to the loss of him. Called upon by their correspondents at Boston; anxious for vindicating their brother's honor and their own, they enquired; gave to the parties aggrieved all the information in their power; but never accused.

Your Lordships know the train of mischiefs which followed. But wherein had my late worthy friend or his family offended Dr. Franklin, that he should first do so great an injury to the memory of the dead brother, by secreting and sending away his letters; and then, conscious of what he had done, should keep himself concealed, till he had nearly, very nearly, occasioned the murder of the other.

After the mischiefs of this concealment had been left for five months to have their full operation, at length comes out a letter, which it is impossible to read without horror; expressive of the coolest and most deliberate malevolence. My Lords, what poetic fiction only had penned for the *breast* of a cruel African, Dr. Franklin has realized, and transcribed from his *own*. His too is the language of a Zanga:
"Know then 'twas I.
"I forged the letter—I disposed the picture—
"I hated, I despised, and I destroy." . . .

My Lords, Dr. Franklin's mind may have been so possessed with the idea of a Great American Republic, that he may easily slide into the language of the minister of a foreign independent state. A foreign Ambassador when residing here, just before the breaking out of a war, or upon particular occasions, may bribe a villain to steal or betray any state papers; he is under the command of another state, and is not amenable to the laws of the country where he resides; and the secure exemption from punishment may induce a laxer morality.

But Dr. Franklin, whatever he may teach the people at Boston, while he is here at least is a subject; and if a subject injure a subject, he is answerable to the law. And the Court of chancery will not much attend to his new self-created importance. . . .

Having turned out all other Governors, they[1] may at length hope to get one of their own. The letters from Boston, for two years past, have intimated that Dr. Franklin was aiming at Mr. Hutchinson's government. It was not easy before this to give credit to such surmises: but nothing surely but a too eager attention to an ambition of this sort, could have betrayed a wise man into such a conduct as we have now seen. Whether these surmises are true or not, your Lordships are much the best judges. If they should be true, I hope that Mr. Hutchinson will not meet with the less countenance from your Lordships, for his rival's being his accuser. Nor will your Lordships, I trust, from what you have heard, advise the having Mr. Hutchinson displaced, in order to make room for Dr. Franklin as a successor.

Benjamin Vaughan's Variant Version of the Wedderburn Denunciation

"The letters could not have come to Dr. Franklin," said Mr. Wedderburn, "by fair means. The writers did not give them to him; nor yet did the deceased correspondent, who from our intimacy would otherwise have told me of it: Nothing then will acquit Dr. Franklin of the charge of obtaining them by fraudulent or corrupt means, for the most malignant of purposes; unless he stole them, from the person who stole them. This argument is irrefragable.

1. The popular party in Massachusetts.

SOURCE: Benjamin Vaughan, ed., *Political, Miscellaneous, and Philosophical Pieces . . . Written by Benjamin Franklin* (London, 1779), p. 341.

"I hope, my lords, you will mark [and brand] the man, for the honour of this country, of Europe, and of mankind. Private correspondence has hitherto been held sacred, in times of the greatest party rage, not only in politics but religion. He has forfeited all the respect of societies and of men. Into what companies will he hereafter go with an unembarrassed face, or the honest intrepidity of virtue. Men will watch him with a jealous eye; they will hide their papers from him, and lock up their escritoires. He will henceforth esteem it a libel to be called *a man of letters; homo trium literarum!*"[2]

---

2. A man of three letters i.e., FUR (or *thief*).

VII

The Burgeoning of
Revolutionary Organizations

The opposition to British policy was spearheaded by extralegal organizations known as the Sons of Liberty, which came into prominence at the time of the Stamp Act. The Massachusetts Circular Letter of March 1768, which was sent to the other colonies urging repeal of the Townshend Acts, constituted another step toward intercolonial cooperation. The establishment of Committees of Correspondence in 1772–1773, to keep alive the revolutionary spirit which had been waning the previous two years, set up more systematic machinery of intercolonial cooperation and paved the way for the calling of the First Continental Congress.

28. Sons of Liberty: New London Agreement
December 25, 1765

CERTAIN RECIPROCAL and mutual agreements, concessions and associations made, concluded and agreed upon by and between the sons of liberty of the colony of *New York* of the one part, and the sons of liberty of the colony of *Connecticut* on the other part, this twenty-fifth day of December, in the sixth year of the reign of our sovereign Lord *George* the Third, by the grace of God, of *Great Britain, France*[1] and *Ireland* king, defender of the faith, and in the year of our Lord one thousand seven hundred and sixty-five.

The aforesaid parties taking into their most serious consideration

SOURCE: William Gordon, *The History of the Rise, Progress, and Establishment of the Independence of the United States of America* (London, 1788), I, 195–198.

1. The Kings of England still asserted their medieval claims over France.

the melancholy and unsettled state of *Great Britain* and her *North American colonies*, proceeding as they are fully persuaded, from a design in her most insidious and inveterate enemies, to alienate the affections of his majesty's most loyal and faithful subjects of *North America* from his person and government—Therefore to prevent as much as in us lies the dissolution of so inestimable an union, they do, in the presence of *Almighty God*, declare that they bear the most unshaken faith and true allegiance to his majesty King George the Third—that they are most affectionately and zealously attached to his royal person and family, and are fully determined to the utmost of their power, to maintain and support his crown and dignity, and the succession as by law established; and with the greatest cheerfulness they submit to his government, according to the known and just principles of the BRITISH CONSTITUTION, which they conceive to be founded on the eternal and immutable principles of justice and equity, and that every attempt to violate or wrest it, or any part of it from them, under whatever pretence, colour or authority, is an heinous sin against God, and the most daring contempt of the people, from whom (under God) all just government springs. From a sacred regard to all which, and a just sense of the impending evils that might befall them, in consequence of such a dreadful dissolution. They do hereby voluntarily, and of their own free will, as well for the support of his majesty's just prerogative and the British constitution as their own mutual security and preservation, agree and concede to associate, advise, protect, and defend each other in the peaceable, full and just enjoyment of their inherent and accustomed rights as British subjects of their respective *colonies*, not in the least desiring any alteration or innovation in the grand bulwark of their liberties and the wisdom of ages, but only to preserve it inviolate from the corrupt hands of its implacable enemies—And whereas a certain pamphlet has appeared in America in the form of an act of parliament, called and known by the name of the *Stamp-Act*, but has never been legally published or introduced, neither can it, as it would immediately deprive them of the most invaluable part of the British constitution, viz. the trial by juries, and the most just mode of taxation in the world, that is, of taxing themselves, rights that every British subject becomes heir to as soon as born. For the preservation of which, and every part of the British constitution, they do reciprocally resolve and determine to march with the utmost dispatch, at their own proper costs and expence, on the first proper notice, (which must be signified to them by at least six of the sons of liberty) with their whole force if required, and it can be spared, to the relief of those that shall, are, or may be in danger from the *stamp-act*, or its promoters and abettors, or any thing relative to it, on account of any thing that may have been done in opposition to its obtaining—And they do mutually and most fervently recommend it to each other to be vigilant in watching all those who, from the nature of their offices, vocations or dispositions, may be the most likely to introduce the use of stamped papers, to the total subversion of the British constitution and American liberty; and the same, when discovered, immediately to advise each other of, let them be of what rank or condition soever; and they do agree, that they will mutually, and to the utmost of their power, by all just ways and means, endeavour to bring all such betrayers of their country to the most condign punishment—And further, they do mutually resolve to defend the liberty of the press in their respective colonies from all unlawful violations and impediments whatever, on account of the said act, as the only means (under divine Providence) of preserving their lives, liberties and fortunes, and the same in regard to the judges, clerks, attornies, &c. that shall proceed without any regard to the *stamp-act*, from all pains, fines, mulcts, penalties, or any molestation whatever—And finally, that they will, to the utmost of their power, endeavour to bring about, accomplish, and perfect the like *association* with all the *colonies* on the continent for the like salutary purposes and no other.

29. Massachusetts' Circular Letter to the Other Colonial Legislatures February 11, 1768

THE House of Representatives of this province have taken into their serious consideration the great difficulties that must accrue to themselves and their constituents by the operation of several Acts

SOURCE: Alden Bradford, ed., *Speeches of the Governors of Massachusetts from 1765 to 1775* (Boston, 1818), 134–136.

of Parliament, imposing duties and taxes on the American colonies.

As it is a subject in which every colony is deeply interested, they have no reason to doubt but your house is deeply impressed with its importance, and that such constitutional measures will be come into as are proper. It seems to be necessary that all possible care should be taken that the representatives of the several assemblies, upon so delicate a point, should harmonize with each other. The House, therefore, hope that this letter will be candidly considered in no other light than as expressing a disposition freely to communicate their mind to a sister colony, upon a common concern, in the same manner as they would be glad to receive the sentiments of your or any other house of assembly on the continent.

The House have humbly represented to the ministry their own sentiments, that his Majesty's high court of Parliament is the supreme legislative power over the whole empire; that in all free states the constitution is fixed, and as the supreme legislative derives its power and authority from the constitution, it cannot overleap the bounds of it without destroying its own foundation; that the constitution ascertains and limits both sovereignty and allegiance, and, therefore, his Majesty's American subjects, who acknowledge themselves bound by the ties of allegiance, have an equitable claim to the full enjoyment of the fundamental rules of the British constitution; that it is an essential, unalterable right in nature, engrafted into the British constitution, as a fundamental law, and ever held sacred and irrevocable by the subjects within the realm, that what a man has honestly acquired is absolutely his own, which he may freely give, but cannot be taken from him without his consent; that the American subjects may, therefore, exclusive of any consideration of charter rights, with a decent firmness, adapted to the character of free men and subjects, assert this natural and constitutional right.

It is, moreover, their humble opinion, which they express with the greatest deference to the wisdom of the Parliament, that the Acts made there, imposing duties on the people of this province, with the sole and express purpose of raising a revenue, are infringements of their natural and constitutional rights; because, as they are not represented in the British Parliament, his Majesty's commons in Britain, by those Acts, grant their property without their consent.

This House further are of opinion that their constituents, considering their local circumstances, cannot, by any possibility, be represented in the Parliament; and that it will forever be impracticable, that they should be equally represented there, and consequently, not at all; being separated by an ocean of a thousand leagues. That his Majesty's royal predecessors, for this reason, were graciously pleased to form a subordinate legislature here, that their subjects might enjoy the unalienable right of a representation; also, that considering the utter impracticability of their ever being fully and equally represented in Parliament, and the great expense that must unavoidably attend even a partial representation there, this House think that a taxation of their constituents, even without their consent, grievous as it is, would be preferable to any representation that could be admitted for them there.

Upon these principles, and also considering that were the right in Parliament ever so clear, yet, for obvious reasons, it would be beyond the rules of equity that their constituents should be taxed on the manufactures of Great Britain here, in addition to the duties they pay for them in England, and other advantages arising to Great Britain, from the Acts of trade, this House have preferred a humble, dutiful, and loyal petition, to our most gracious sovereign, and made such representations to his Majesty's ministers, as they apprehended would tend to obtain redress.

They have also submitted to consideration, whether any people can be said to enjoy any degree of freedom if the Crown, in addition to its undoubted authority of constituting a governor, should appoint him such a stipend as it may judge proper, without the consent of the people, and at their expense; and whether, while the judges of the land, and other civil officers, hold not their commissions during good behaviour, their having salaries appointed for them by the Crown, independent of the people, hath not a tendency to subvert the principles of equity, and endanger the happiness and security of the subject.

In addition to these measures, the House have written a letter to their agent which he is directed to lay before the ministry; wherein they take notice of the hardships of the Act for preventing mutiny and desertion, which requires the governor and council to provide enumerated articles for the king's marching troops, and the people to pay the expenses; and also, the commission of the gentlemen appointed commissioners of the customs, to reside in America, which authorizes them to make as many appointments as they think fit, and to pay the appointees what sum they please, for whose malconduct they are not accountable; from whence it may happen that officers of the Crown may be multiplied to such a degree as to become dangerous to the liberty of the people, by virtue of a commission, which does not appear to this House to derive any such advantages to trade as many have supposed.

These are the sentiments and proceedings of this House; and as they have too much reason to believe that the enemies of the colonies have represented them to his Majesty's ministers, and to the Parliament, as factious, disloyal, and having a disposition to make themselves independent of the mother country, they have taken occasion, in the most humble terms, to assure his Majesty, and his ministers, that, with regard to the people of this province, and, as they doubt not, of all the colonies, the charge is unjust. The House is fully satisfied that your assembly is too generous and liberal in sentiment to believe that this letter proceeds from an ambition of taking the lead, or dictating to the other assemblies. They freely submit their opinions to the judgment of others; and shall take it kind in your house to point out to them anything further that may be thought necessary.

This House cannot conclude, without expressing their firm confidence in the king, our common head and father, that the united and dutiful supplications of his distressed American subjects will meet with his royal and favourable acceptance.

30. Committees of Correspondence: Virginia, March 12, 1773, and Massachusetts, March 28, 1773

Virginia Resolves, March 12, 1773

Whereas, the minds of his Majesty's faithful subjects in this colony have been much disturbed by various rumours and reports of proceedings tending to deprive them of their ancient, legal, and constitutional rights.

And whereas, the affairs of this colony are frequently connected with those of Great Britain, as well as of the neighbouring colonies,

SOURCE: *Journals of the House of Burgesses of Virginia, 1773– 1776* (Richmond, 1905–1910), 28.

which renders a communication of sentiments necessary; in order, therefore, to remove the uneasinesses and to quiet the minds of the people, as well as for the other good purposes above mentioned:

Be it resolved, that a standing committee of correspondence and inquiry be appointed to consist of eleven persons, to wit: the Honourable Peyton Randolph, Esquire; Robert Carter Nicholas, Richard Bland, Richard Henry Lee, Benjamin Harrison, Edmund Pendleton, Patrick Henry, Dudley Digges, Dabney Carr, Archibald Cary, and Thomas Jefferson, Esquires, any six of whom to be a committee, whose business it shall be to obtain the most early and authentic intelligence of all such Acts and resolutions of the British Parliament, or proceedings of administration, as may relate to or affect the British colonies in America, and to keep up and maintain a correspondence and communication with our sister colonies, respecting these important considerations; and the result of such their proceedings, from time to time, to lay before this House.

Resolved, that it be an instruction to the said committee that they do, without delay, inform themselves particularly of the principles and authority on which was constituted a court of inquiry, said to have been lately held in Rhode Island, with powers to transmit persons accused of offences committed in America to places beyond the seas to be tried.

The said resolutions being severally read a second time, were, upon the question severally put thereupon, agreed to by the House, *nemine contradicente.*

Resolved, that the speaker of this House do transmit to the speakers of the different assemblies of the British colonies on the continent, copies of the said resolutions, and desire that they will lay them before their respective assemblies, and request them to appoint some person or persons of their respective bodies, to communicate from time to time with the said committee.

Resolutions of the Massachusetts House of Representatives Agreeing to the Virginia Proposal, March 28, 1773

Whereas, the speaker hath communicated to this House a letter from the truly respectable House of Burgesses, in his Majesty's ancient colony of Virginia, enclosing a copy of the resolves entered into by them on the 12th of March last, and requesting that a

SOURCE: H. Niles, *Principles and Acts of the Revolution in America,* 94–95.

committee of this House may be appointed to communicate, from time to time, with a corresponding committee, then appointed by the said House of Burgesses in Virginia:

And, whereas this House is fully sensible of the necessity and importance of a union of the several colonies in America, at a time when it clearly appears that the rights and liberties of all are systematically invaded; in order that the joint wisdom of the whole may be employed in consulting their common safety:

Resolved, that this House have a very grateful sense of the obligations they are under to the House of Burgesses, in Virginia, for the vigilance, firmness and wisdom, which they have discovered, at all times, in support of the rights and liberties of the American colonies; and do heartily concur with their said judicious and spirited resolves.

Resolved, that a standing committee of correspondence and enquiry be appointed, to consist of fifteen members, any eight of whom to be a quorum; whose business it shall be to obtain the most early and authentic intelligence of all such Acts and resolutions of the British Parliament, or proceedings of administration as may relate to, or affect the British colonies in America, and to keep up and maintain a correspondence and communication with our sister colonies, respecting these important considerations: and the result of such their proceedings, from time to time, to lay before the House.

Resolved, that it be an instruction to the said committee, that they do, without delay, inform themselves particularly of the principles and authority, on which was constituted a court of enquiry, held in Rhode Island, said to be vested with powers to transport persons, accused of offences committed in America, to places beyond the seas, to be tried.

Resolved, that the said committee be further instructed to prepare and report to this House, a draft of a very respectful answer to the letter, received from the speaker of the honourable House of Burgesses in Virginia, and another, to a letter received from the speaker of the honourable House of Representatives, of the colony of Rhode Island; also, a circular letter to the several other houses of assembly on this continent, enclosing the aforesaid resolves, and requesting them to lay the same before their respective assemblies, in confidence, that they will readily and cheerfully comply with the wise and salutary resolves of the House of Burgesses, in Virginia.

[The committee of correspondence, chosen in pursuance of the resolves aforesaid, were Mr. Cushing (the speaker), Mr. Adams, Hon. John Hancock, Mr. William Phillips, Captain William Heath, Hon. Joseph Hawley, James Warren, Esq., R. Derby, Jun., Esq., Mr. Elbridge Gerry, J. Bowers, Esq., Jedediah Foster, Esq., Daniel Leonard, Esq., Captain T. Gardner, Capt. Jonathan Greenleaf, and J. Prescott, Esq.]

VIII

A Finger on the Trigger: The Tea Party and Its Aftermath

The Boston Tea Party and British retaliation marked a turning point in the relationship between the Crown and the colonies. Parliament countered with a series of punitive laws known as the "Intolerable Acts." As Arthur Lee, the agent for Massachusetts, wrote from London, the punishment of Boston was thought to be the first step toward inducing all America to acknowledge Parliament's right to tax the colonies. In this crisis the First Continental Congress was summoned to convene in September 1774. The Congress at once considered a proper course of action. The hopes of the conservatives rode on the Galloway Plan, which proposed an intercolonial legislature under Parliamentary jurisdiction. Despite the fact that Galloway's proposal was defeated by only six to five, the radicals quickly took control. They pushed through the Declaration of Colonial Rights and Grievances, which demanded an end to the restrictive legislation that Parliament had enacted since 1763. Then, after some dispute, the delegates approved the Continental Association, which required of each province a broad nonimportation and nonconsumption pledge and established extralegal machinery for its enforcement.

31. Boston Tea Party
December 16, 1773

JUST BEFORE the dissolution of the meeting, a number of brave and resolute men, dressed in the Indian manner, approached near the door of the Assembly, gave the war whoop, which rang through the house and was answered by some in the galleries, but silence being commanded, and a peaceable deportment was again enjoined till

SOURCE: *Massachusetts Gazette,* December 23, 1773.

the dissolution. The Indians, as they were then called, repaired to the wharf where the ships lay that had the tea on board, and were followed by hundreds of people to see the event of the transactions of those who made so grotesque an appearance. They, the Indians, immediately repaired on board Capt. Hall's ship, where they hoisted out the chests of tea, and when upon deck stove the chests and emptied the tea overboard; having cleared this ship, they proceeded to Capt. Bruce's and then to Capt. Coffin's brig. They applied themselves so dextrously to the destruction of this commodity that in the space of three hours they broke up 342 chests, which was the whole number in those vessels, and discharged their contents into the dock. When the tide rose it floated the broken chests and the tea insomuch that the surface of the water was filled therewith a considerable way from the south part of the town to Dorchester Neck, and lodged on the shores. There was the greatest care taken to prevent the tea from being purloined by the populace. One or two, being detected in endeavouring to pocket a small quantity, were stripped of their acquisitions and very roughly handled. It is worthy of remark that although a considerable quantity of goods were still remaining on board the vessels, no injury was sustained. Such attention to private property was observed that a small padlock belonging to the captain of one of the ships being broke, another was procured and sent to him. The town was very quiet during the whole evening and night following. Those persons who were from the country returned with a merry heart; and the next day joy appeared in almost every countenance, some on occasion of the destruction of the tea, others on account of the quietness with which it was effected. One of the Monday's papers says that the masters and owners are well pleased that their ships are thus cleared.

32. Intolerable Acts: Letter from Arthur Lee to His Brother, Francis L. Lee
April 2, 1774

MOST SINCERELY do I congratulate my dear brother, on the possession of that retirement, in which only can true tranquillity and happiness be enjoyed. Would to Heaven I could participate in the blissful retreat!

> Where peace, with ever blooming olive, crowns
> The gate; where honour's liberal hands effuse
> Unenvied treasures, and the snowy wings
> Of innocence and love protect the scene.

May providence watch over you, and protect you from that alarm, which, according to the poet,

> Through thickest shades, pursues the fond of peace.

How ought I to lament that my fortune and my temper are perpetually combating my inclination and my judgment. No man can see in a more amiable light, or feel a stronger desire of enjoying retirement, than I. Yet, unhappily, my fate has thrown me into public life, and the impatience of my nature makes me embark in it, with an impetuosity and imprudence, which increase the evils to which it is necessarily subject. The pursuit is as endless as it is turbulent and deceitful. One bubble is no sooner burst than another rises, with something new to engage and irritate its deluded pursuers. You will judge by this time, that I have nothing to say of my own situation and success, which can gratify the benevolent wishes you have the goodness to entertain for me. In my distresses you will also sympathize, for they are felt for our country. The parliament are now bringing the question to that decision, which makes me tremble for the virtue, the character, the liberties of my countrymen. They have passed an act to take away the port

SOURCE: R. H. Lee, *Life of Arthur Lee* (2 vols., Boston, 1829), I, 37–40.

of Boston, till every compensation is made for the tea, and perfect obedience is acknowledged. And then it is to be restored in such portions as the king pleases. What makes this more alarming is, that no accusation is brought against the town, no evidence produced to criminate it; and it is avowed, that this is the first step towards reducing all America to an acknowledgment of the right of parliament to impose taxes upon her, and to a submission to the exercise of that right.

The Americans who are here have thought it of so much consequence, that they have petitioned the three branches of the legislature against passing such a bill; but, as you may imagine, without success.

The next proceeding against Boston and the province is already announced in the house of commons. The selectmen and town-meetings are to be abolished. The governor is to be endued with the power of calling the citizens together, when and for what purpose he pleases. They are not to deliberate on any thing but what he dictates. The council and judges are to be suspended at the governor's pleasure. The constitution of juries is to be altered, so as to render them more manageable in finding bills and verdicts against the friends of liberty.

We are just informed that General Gage is going over immediately, with three regiments, as governor of Massachusetts, and commander-in-chief; that he is to collect an army about Boston, in order to impose these measures, and reduce the people to entire obedience.

The storm, you see, runs high; and it will require great prudence, wisdom, and resolution, to save our liberties from shipwreck. In my opinion, *there ought to be a general congress of the colonies;* and I think Annapolis would be the place, where it would be less liable to military interruption, than at New-York or Philadelphia. If you have virtue enough to resolve to stop, and to execute the resolution of stopping your exports and imports for one year, this country must do you justice. The shipping, manufactures, and revenue, depend so much on the tobacco and Carolina colonies, that they alone, by stopping their exports, would force redress. Such a measure should be attended with an address to the merchants, manufacturers, and traders of this country, stating the necessity which compels you to a measure injurious to them; professing every thing to flatter and conciliate them. Such a measure, operating at the general election, next April, would probably produce such a return of members, as would listen to truth and redress, not so much our grievances, as their own.

This is the only effectual measure I can conceive. If there is not virtue enough for it, I am afraid American liberty is no more; for you may depend upon it, that if they find the chains can be easily imposed, they will make them heavy, and rivet them fast.

It is impossible for me to describe how much I am grieved at these proceedings, and with what anxiety I look forward to the event. You know I have doubted the virtue of my countrymen. God grant, that I may be mistaken; that by a wise, temperate, and firm conduct, they may escape the blow intended, and preserve their freedom. The friends of liberty here, look to your conduct with great anxiety. They consider it as decisive, either to establish or overturn the present plan of despotism.

There is a spirit of violence, injustice, and persecution in administration, against every active friend of America, which makes that character perilous. I cannot see that any service can be done here until the event of these measures is seen, and the popular prejudices begin to abate. I am therefore determined to withdraw myself, by taking the advantage of a favourable opportunity of visiting Rome, for some months; from whence however, I shall return sooner, if any great event should hold out a probability of my being useful.

Mrs. Lee well knows the power of praise; and how ambitious I should be of meriting it from her. But, alas, I have not the powers of pleasing. Horrors only dwell on my imagination. Public corruption at present, and public calamity for the future, are the dismal objects which incessantly fill my mind. The busy haunts of men furnish more to lament than to rejoice in; to censure, than to praise. They are filled with scenes of false happiness and real misery, variety of vice and wretchedness. It is rural retirement only, rural innocence, rural tranquillity, which excite an uninterrupted flow of ideas, amiable and delightful. In these pleasing scenes, the perturbed spirits settle into a calm, productive of more real happiness, than all that the splendour of fortune, all that the pomp of power can bestow. It is there the golden age revives, and all things inspire the spirit of love and delight.

My best love awaits her. Remember me at Mt. Airy, Stradford, Chantilly, and wherever else you think the mention of my name will not be disagreeable.

Adieu, &c.

ARTHUR LEE

33. First Continental Congress: Joseph Galloway's Plan of Union September 28, 1774

RESOLVED. That the Congress will apply to his Majesty for a redress of grievances under which his faithful subjects in America labour; and assure him that the colonies hold in abhorrence the idea of being considered independent communities on the British government, and most ardently desire the establishment of a political union, not only among themselves, but with the mother state, upon those principles of safety and freedom which are essential in the constitution of all free governments, and particularly that of the British legislature; and as the colonies from their local circumstances cannot be represented in the Parliament of Great Britain, they will humbly propose to his Majesty and his two houses of Parliament, the following plan, under which the strength of the whole empire may be drawn together on any emergency, the interest of both countries advanced, and the rights and liberties of America secured.

A Plan of a Proposed Union Between Great Britain and the Colonies

That a British and American legislature, for regulating the administration of the general affairs of America, be proposed and established in America, including all the said colonies; within, and under which government, each colony shall retain its present con-

SOURCE: W. C. Ford, et al., eds., *Journals of the Continental Congress, 1774–1789* (34 vols., Washington, 1904–1937), I, 49 *et seq.*

stitution, and powers of regulating and governing its own internal police, in all cases whatsoever.

That the said government be administered by a president-general, to be appointed by the king, and a grand council, to be chosen by the representatives of the people of the several colonies, in their respective assemblies, once in every three years.

That the several assemblies shall choose members for the grand council in the following proportions, viz.

New Hampshire	Delaware Counties
Massachusetts Bay	Maryland
Rhode Island	Virginia
Connecticut	North Carolina
New York	South Carolina
New Jersey	Georgia
Pennsylvania	

Who shall meet at the city of   for the first time, being called by the president-general, as soon as conveniently may be after his appointment.

That there shall be a new election of members for the grand council every three years; and on the death, removal or resignation of any member, his place shall be supplied by a new choice, at the next sitting of assembly of the colony he represented.

That the grand council shall meet once in every year, if they shall think it necessary, and oftener, if occasions shall require, at such time and place as they shall adjourn to, at the last preceding meeting, or as they shall be called to meet at, by the president-general, on any emergency.

That the grand council shall have power to choose their speaker, and shall hold and exercise all the like rights, liberties and privileges as are held and exercised by and in the House of Commons of Great Britain.

That the president-general shall hold his office during the pleasure of the king, and his assent shall be requisite to all acts of the grand council, and it shall be his office and duty to cause them to be carried into execution.

That the president-general, by and with the advice and consent of the grand council, hold and exercise all the legislative rights, powers, and authorities necessary for regulating and administering all the general police and affairs of the colonies in which Great

Britain and the colonies, or any of them, the colonies in general, or more than one colony, are in any manner concerned, as well civil and criminal as commercial.

That the said president-general and the grand council be an inferior and distinct branch of the British legislature, united and incorporated with it, for the aforesaid general purposes; and that any of the said general regulations may originate and be formed and digested, either in the Parliament of Great Britain, or in the said grand council, and being prepared, transmitted to the other for their approbation or dissent; and that the assent of both shall be requisite to the validity of all such general acts or statutes.

That in time of war, all bills for granting aid to the Crown, prepared by the grand council, and approved by the president-general, shall be valid and passed into a law, without the assent of the British Parliament.

34. Declaration of Colonial Rights and Grievances October 1, 1774

WHEREAS, since the close of the last war the British Parliament, claiming a power of right to bind the people of America by statute in all cases whatsoever, hath in some Acts expressly imposed taxes on them, and in others, under various pretences, but in fact for the purpose of raising a revenue, hath imposed rates and duties payable in these colonies, established a board of commissioners with un-constitutional powers, and extended the jurisdiction of courts of admiralty, not only for collecting the said duties, but for the trial of causes merely arising within the body of a county.

And whereas, in consequence of other statutes, judges, who before held only estates at will in their offices, have been made dependent on the Crown alone for their salaries, and standing armies kept in times of peace:

And it has lately been resolved in Parliament, that by force of a

SOURCE: W. C. Ford, et al., eds., *Journals of the Continental Congress, 1774–1789*, I, 63–73.

statute, made in the thirty-fifth year of the reign of King Henry the eighth, colonists may be transported to England, and tried there upon accusations for treasons, and misprisions, or concealments of treasons committed in the colonies; and by a late statute, such trials have been directed in cases therein mentioned.

And whereas, in the last session of Parliament, three statutes were made; one, entitled "An Act to discontinue, in such manner and for such time as are therein mentioned, the landing and discharging, lading, or shipping of goods, wares and merchandise, at the town, and within the harbour of Boston, in the province of Massachusetts Bay in North America"; another entitled "An Act for the better regulating the government of the province of the Massachusetts Bay in New England"; and another entitled "An Act for the impartial administration of justice, in the cases of persons questioned for any act done by them in the execution of the law, or for the suppression of riots and tumults, in the province of the Massachusetts Bay in New England." And another statute was then made "for making more effectual provision for the government of the province of Quebec, etc." All which statutes are impolitic, unjust, and cruel, as well as unconstitutional, and most dangerous and destructive of American rights.

And whereas, assemblies have been frequently dissolved, contrary to the rights of the people, when they attempted to deliberate on grievances; and their dutiful, humble, loyal and reasonable petitions to the Crown for redress have been repeatedly treated with contempt by his Majesty's ministers of state:

The good people of the several colonies of New Hampshire, Massachusetts Bay, Rhode Island and Providence Plantations, Connecticut, New York, New Jersey, Pennsylvania, New Castle, Kent and Sussex on Delaware, Maryland, Virginia, North Carolina and South Carolina, justly alarmed at these arbitrary proceedings of Parliament and administration, have severally elected, constituted, and appointed deputies to meet and sit in general congress, in the city of Philadelphia, in order to obtain such establishment, as that their religion, laws, and liberties may not be subverted.

Whereupon the deputies so appointed being now assembled, in a full and free representation of these colonies, taking into their most serious consideration the best means of attaining the ends aforesaid, do, in the first place, as Englishmen, their ancestors in like cases have usually done, for asserting and vindicating their rights and liberties, declare,

That the inhabitants of the English colonies in North America, by the immutable laws of nature, the principles of the English constitution, and the several charters or compacts, have the following rights:

Resolved, N. C. D.[1] 1. That they are entitled to life, liberty and property, and they have never ceded to any sovereign power whatever, a right to dispose of either without their consent.

Resolved, N. C. D. 2. That our ancestors who first settled these colonies, were at the time of their emigration from the mother country, entitled to all the rights, liberties, and immunities of free and natural-born subjects, within the realm of England.

Resolved, N. C. D. 3. That by such emigration they by no means forfeited, surrendered, or lost any of those rights, but that they were, and their descendants now are, entitled to the exercise and enjoyment of all such of them, as their local and other circumstances enable them to exercise and enjoy.

Resolved, 4. That the foundation of English liberty, and of all free government, is a right in the people to participate in their legislative council: and as the English colonists are not represented, and from their local and other circumstances, cannot properly be represented in the British Parliament, they are entitled to a free and exclusive power of legislation in their several provincial legislatures, where their right of representation can alone be preserved, in all cases of taxation and internal polity, subject only to the negative of their sovereign, in such manner as has been heretofore used and accustomed. But, from the necessity of the case, and a regard to the mutual interest of both countries, we cheerfully consent to the operation of such Acts of the British Parliament, as are bona fide, restrained to the regulation of our external commerce, for the purpose of securing the commercial advantages of the whole empire to the mother country, and the commercial benefits of its respective members; excluding every idea of taxation, internal or external, for raising a revenue on the subjects in America, without their consent.

Resolved, N. C. D. 5. That the respective colonies are entitled to the common law of England, and more especially to the great and

1. Nemine Contradicente—without a dissenting vote.

inestimable privilege of being tried by their peers of the vicinage, according to the course of that law.

Resolved, 6. That they are entitled to the benefit of such of the English statutes as existed at the time of their colonization; and which they have, by experience, respectively found to be applicable to their several local and other circumstances.

Resolved, N. C. D. 7. That these, his Majesty's colonies, are likewise entitled to all the immunities and privileges granted & confirmed to them by royal charters, or secured by their several codes of provincial laws.

Resolved, N. C. D. 8. That they have a right peaceably to assemble, consider of their grievances, and petition the king; and that all prosecutions, prohibitory proclamations and commitments for the same, are illegal.

Resolved, N. C. D. 9. That the keeping a standing army in these colonies, in times of peace, without the consent of the legislature of that colony, in which such army is kept, is against law.

Resolved, N. C. D. 10. It is indispensably necessary to good government, and rendered essential by the English constitution, that the constituent branches of the legislature be independent of each other; that, therefore, the exercise of legislative power in several colonies, by a council appointed, during pleasure, by the Crown, is unconstitutional, dangerous, and destructive to the freedom of American legislation.

All and each of which the aforesaid deputies, in behalf of themselves and their constituents, do claim, demand, and insist on, as their indubitable rights and liberties; which cannot be legally taken from them, altered or abridged by any power whatever, without their own consent, by their representatives in their several provincial legislatures.

In the course of our inquiry, we find many infringements and violations of the foregoing rights, which, from an ardent desire, that harmony and mutual intercourse of affection and interest may be restored, we pass over for the present, and proceed to state such acts and measures as have been adopted since the last war, which demonstrate a system formed to enslave America.

Resolved, N. C. D. That the following Acts of Parliament are infringments and violations of the rights of the colonists; and that the repeal of them is essentially necessary in order to restore harmony between Great Britain and the American colonies, viz:

The several Acts of 4 Geo. III, c. 15 and c. 34; 5 Geo. III, c. 25; 6 Geo. III, c. 52; 7 Geo. III, c. 41 and c. 46; 8 Geo. III, c. 22, which impose duties for the purpose of raising a revenue in America, extend the powers of the admiralty courts beyond their ancient limits, deprive the American subject of trial by jury, authorize the judges' certificate to indemnify the prosecutor from damages that he might otherwise be liable to, requiring oppressive security from a claimant of ships and goods seized, before he shall be allowed to defend his property, and are subversive of American rights.

Also the 12 Geo. III, c. 24, entitled "An Act for the better securing his Majesty's dockyards, magazines, ships, ammunition, and stores", which declares a new offence in America, and deprives the American subject of a constitutional trial by a jury of the vicinage, by authorizing the trial of any person charged with the committing any offence described in the said Act, out of the realm, to be indicted and tried for the same in any shire or county within the realm.

Also the three Acts passed in the last session of Parliament, for stopping the port and blocking up the harbour of Boston, for altering the charter and government of the Massachusetts Bay, and that which is entitled "An Act for the better administration of justice", etc.

Also the Act passed in the same session for establishing the Roman Catholic religion in the province of Quebec, abolishing the equitable system of English laws, and erecting a tyranny there, to the great danger, from so total a dissimilarity of religion, law, and government of the neighbouring British colonies, by the assistance of whose blood and treasure the said country was conquered from France.

Also the Act passed in the same session for the better providing suitable quarters for officers and soldiers in his Majesty's service in North America.

Also that the keeping a standing army in several of these colonies, in time of peace, without the consent of the legislature of that colony in which such army is kept, is against law.

To these grievous acts and measures, Americans cannot submit, but in hopes that their fellow subjects in Great Britain will, on a revision of them, restore us to that state in which both countries found happiness and prosperity, we have for the present only resolved to pursue the following peaceable measures:

1. To enter into a non-importation, non-consumption, and non-exportation agreement or association.

2. To prepare an address to the people of Great Britain, and a memorial to the inhabitants of British America, and

3. To prepare a loyal address to his Majesty, agreeable to resolutions already entered into.

35. The Continental Association
October 18, 1774

WE, his Majesty's most loyal subjects, the delegates of the several colonies of New Hampshire, Massachusetts Bay, Rhode Island, Connecticut, New York, New Jersey, Pennsylvania, the three lower counties of Newcastle, Kent, and Sussex on Delaware, Maryland, Virginia, North Carolina, and South Carolina, deputed to represent them in a continental congress, held in the city of Philadelphia, on the 5th day of September, 1774, avowing our allegiance to his Majesty, our affection and regard for our fellow-subjects in Great Britain and elsewhere, affected with the deepest anxiety and most alarming apprehensions, at those grievances and distresses, with which his Majesty's American subjects are oppressed; and having taken under our most serious deliberation the state of the whole continent, find that the present unhappy situation of our affairs is occasioned by a ruinous system of colony administration, adopted by the British ministry about the year 1763, evidently calculated for enslaving these colonies, and with them, the British Empire. In prosecution of which system, various Acts of Parliament have been passed for raising a revenue in America, for depriving the American subjects, in many instances, of the constitutional trial by jury, exposing their lives to danger, by directing a new and illegal trial beyond the seas, for crimes alleged to have been committed in America; and in prosecution of the same system, several late, cruel and oppressive Acts have been passed, respecting the town of Boston and the Massachusetts Bay, and also an Act for extending the province of Quebec, so as to border on the

SOURCE: *Journals of the Continental Congress*, I, 75–80.

western frontiers of these colonies, establishing an arbitrary government therein, and discouraging the settlement of British subjects in that wide extended country; thus, by the influence of civil principles and ancient prejudices, to dispose the inhabitants to act with hostility against the free Protestant colonies, whenever a wicked ministry shall choose so to direct them.

To obtain redress of these grievances which threaten destruction to the lives, liberty, and property of his Majesty's subjects, in North America, we are of opinion that a non-importation, non-consumption, and non-exportation agreement, faithfully adhered to, will prove the most speedy, effectual, and peaceable measure: and therefore, we do, for ourselves, and the inhabitants of the several colonies whom we represent, firmly agree and associate, under the sacred ties of virtue, honour and love of our country, as follows:

1. That from and after the first day of December next, we will not import into British America, from Great Britain or Ireland, any goods, wares or merchandise whatsoever, or from any other place, any such goods, wares, or merchandise, as shall have been exported from Great Britain or Ireland; nor will we, after that day, import any East India tea from any part of the world; nor any molasses, syrups, paneles, coffee, or pimento, from the British plantations or from Dominica; nor wines from Madeira, or the Western Islands; nor foreign indigo.

2. We will neither import nor purchase any slave imported after the first day of December next; after which time we will wholly discontinue the slave trade and will neither be concerned in it ourselves, nor will we hire our vessels, nor sell our commodities or manufactures to those who are concerned in it.

3. As a non-consumption agreement, strictly adhered to, will be an effectual security for the observation of the non-importation, we, as above, solemnly agree and associate, that from this day we will not purchase or use any tea imported on account of the East India Company, or any on which a duty hath been or shall be paid; and from and after the first day of March next, we will not purchase or use any East India tea whatever; nor will we, nor shall any person for or under us, purchase or use any of those goods, wares or merchandise we have agreed not to import, which we shall know, or have cause to suspect, were imported after the first day of

December, except such as come under the rules and directions of the tenth article hereafter mentioned.

4. The earnest desire we have not to injure our fellow-subjects in Great Britain, Ireland, or the West Indies, induces us to suspend a non-exportation until the tenth day of September, 1775; at which time, if the said Acts and parts of Acts of the British Parliament hereinafter mentioned are not repealed, we will not, directly or indirectly, export any merchandise or commodity whatsoever to Great Britain, Ireland or the West Indies, except rice to Europe.

5. Such as are merchants, and use the British and Irish trade, will give orders, as soon as possible, to their factors, agents and correspondents, in Great Britain and Ireland, not to ship any goods to them, on any pretence whatsoever, as they cannot be received in America; and if any merchant residing in Great Britain or Ireland shall directly or indirectly ship any goods, wares, or merchandise for America, in order to break the said non-importation agreement, or in any manner contravene the same, on such unworthy conduct being well attested, it ought to be made public; and on the same being so done, we will not, from thenceforth, have any commercial connection with such merchant.

6. That such as are owners of vessels will give positive orders to their captains, or masters, not to receive on board their vessels any goods prohibited by the said nonimportation agreement, on pain of immediate dismission from their service.

7. We will use our utmost endeavours to improve the breed of sheep and increase their number to the greatest extent; and to that end we will kill them as seldom as may be, especially those of the most profitable kind; nor will we export any to the West Indies or elsewhere; and those of us who are or may become overstocked with, or can conveniently spare any sheep, will dispose of them to our neighbours, especially to the poorer sort, on moderate terms.

8. We will, in our several stations, encourage frugality, economy, and industry, and promote agriculture, arts, and the manufactures of this country, especially that of wool; and will discountenance and discourage every species of extravagance and dissipation, especially all horse-racing, and all kinds of gaming, cock-fighting, exhibitions of shows, plays, and other expensive diversions and entertainments; and on the death of any relation or friend, none of us, or any of our families, will go into any further mourning-dress than a black crepe or ribbon on the arm or hat, for gentlemen, and

a black ribbon and necklace for ladies, and we will discontinue the giving of gloves and scarves at funerals.

9. Such as are vendors of goods or merchandise will not take advantage of the scarcity of goods, that may be occasioned by this association but will sell the same at the rates we have been respectively accustomed to do for twelve months last past. And if any vendor of goods or merchandise shall sell any such goods on higher terms, or shall, in any manner, or by any device whatsoever violate or depart from this agreement, no person ought, nor will any of us deal with any such person, or his or her factor or agent, at any time thereafter, for any commodity whatever.

10. In case any merchant, trader, or other person, shall import any goods or merchandise after the first day of December, and before the first day of February next, the same ought forthwith, at the election of the owner, to be either reshipped or delivered up to the committee of the county or town wherein they shall be imported, to be stored at the risk of the importer until the non-importation agreement shall cease, or be sold under the direction of the committee aforesaid; and in the last mentioned case, the owner or owners of such goods shall be reimbursed out of the sales, the first cost and charges, the profit, if any, to be applied towards relieving and employing such poor inhabitants of the town of Boston as are immediate sufferers by the Boston Port Bill; and a particular account of all goods so returned, stored or sold to be inserted in the public papers; and if any goods or merchandises shall be imported after the said first day of February, the same ought forthwith to be sent back again, without breaking any of the packages thereof.

11. That a committee be chosen in every county, city, and town by those who are qualified to vote for representatives in the legislature, whose business it shall be attentively to observe the conduct of all persons touching this Association; and when it shall be made to appear to the satisfaction of a majority of any such committee that any person within the limits of their appointment has violated this Association, that such majority do forthwith cause the truth of the case to be published in the gazette; to the end that all such foes to the rights of British America may be publicly known, and universally condemned as the enemies of American liberty; and thenceforth we respectively will break off all dealings with him or her.

12. That the committee of correspondence, in the respective colonies, do frequently inspect the entries of their custom houses, and inform each other, from time to time, of the true state thereof, and of every other material circumstance that may occur relative to this Association.

13. That all manufactures of this country be sold at reasonable prices, so that no undue advantage be taken of a future scarcity of goods.

14. And we do further agree and resolve that we will have no trade, commerce, dealings, or intercourse whatsoever, with any colony or province in North America which shall not accede to, or which shall hereafter violate this Association, but will hold them as unworthy of the rights of freemen, and as inimical to the liberties of their country.

And we do solemnly bind ourselves and our constituents, under the ties aforesaid, to adhere to this Association, until such parts of the several Acts of Parliament passed since the close of the last war, as impose or continue duties on tea, wine, molasses, syrups, paneles, coffee, sugar, pimento, indigo, foreign paper, glass, and painters' colours imported into America, and extend the powers of the admiralty courts beyond their ancient limits, deprive the American subject of trial by jury, authorize the judge's certificate to indemnify the prosecutor from damages, that he might otherwise be liable to from a trial by his peers, require oppressive security from a claimant of ships or goods seized, before he shall be allowed to defend his property, are repealed. And until that part of the Act of the 12 Geo. III, c. 24, entitled "An Act for the better securing his Majesty's dock-yards, magazines, ships, ammunition, and stores," by which any persons charged with committing any of the offences therein described, in America, may be tried in any shire or county within the realm, is repealed—and until the four Acts, passed the last session of Parliament, viz. that for stopping the port and blocking up the harbour of Boston—that for altering the charter and government of the Massachusetts Bay—and that which is entitled "An act for the better administration of justice, etc."—and that "for extending the limits of Quebec, etc." are repealed. And we recommend it to the provincial conventions, and to the committees in the respective colonies, to establish such farther regulations as they may think proper, for carrying into execution this Association.

The foregoing Association being determined upon by the Congress, was ordered to be subscribed by the several members thereof; and thereupon, we have hereunto set our respective names accordingly.

IX

A Fear of Leveling

As the colonies veered closer to independence from Britain, many of
the more affluent colonists hesitated to take the decisive step. The
attempt to build a broad-based opposition to British policies had brought
into the political arena many artisans and small farmers, whose par-
ticipation aroused in the hearts of Establishment Patriots a genuine
fear of violent social upheaval. The harsh treatment of wealthy Tories
and royal officials at the hands of angry mobs in Massachusetts (as set
forth in a petition to the Provincial Congress) lent weight to the anxieties
both of the New York Patriot Gouverneur Morris and of Boston's
Doctor Joseph Warren, who later fell at Bunker Hill.

36. Rise of New York Mechanics:
Gouverneur Morris to Thomas Penn
May 20, 1774

DEAR SIR:

You have heard, and you will hear a great deal about politics,
and in the heap of chaff you may find some grains of good sense.
Believe me, sir, freedom and religion are only watchwords. We
have appointed a committee, or rather we have nominated one. Let
me give you the history of it. It is needless to premise that the
lower orders of mankind are more easily led by specious appearances than those of a more exalted station. This, and many similar
propositions, you know better than your humble servant.

The troubles in America during Grenville's administration put
our gentry upon this finesse. They stimulated some daring cox-

SOURCE: P. Force, ed., *American Archives*, 4th ser. (6 vols., Washington, 1837–1853), I, 342–343.

combs to rouse the mob into an attack upon the bounds of order and decency. These fellows became the Jack Cades of the day, the leaders in all the riots, the bell-wethers of the flock. The reason of the manœuvre in those who wished to keep fair with the government, and at the same time to receive the incense of popular applause, you will readily perceive. On the whole, the shepherds were not much to blame in a politic point of view. The bell-wethers jingled merrily and roared out liberty and property, and religion, and a multitude of cant terms which everyone thought he understood, and was egregiously mistaken. For you must know the shepherds kept the dictionary of the day, and like the mysteries of the ancient mythology, it was not for profane eyes or ears. This answered many purposes; the simple flock put themselves entirely under the protection of these most excellent shepherds. By and by, behold a great metamorphosis without the help of Ovid or his divinities, but entirely effectuated by two modern Genii, the god of Ambition and the goddess of Faction. The first of these prompted the shepherds to shear some of their flock, and then in conjunction with the other, converted the bell-wethers into shepherds. That we have been in hot water with the British Parliament ever since everybody knows. Consequently these new shepherds had their hands full of employment. The old ones kept themselves least in sight, and a want of confidence in each other was not the least evil which followed. The port of Boston has been shut up. These sheep, simple as they are, cannot be gulled as heretofore. In short, there is no ruling them, and now, to leave the metaphor, the heads of the mobility grow dangerous to the gentry, and how to keep them down is the question. While they correspond with the other colonies, call and dismiss popular assemblies, make resolves to bind the consciences of the rest of mankind, bully poor printers, and exert with full force all their other tribunitial powers, it is impossible to curb them.

But art sometimes goes farther than force, and therefore, to trick them handsomely a committee of patricians was to be nominated, and into their hands was to be committed the majesty of the people, and the highest trust was to be reposed in them by a mandate that they should take care, *quod respublica non capiat injuriam*.[1] The tribunes, through the want of good legerdemain in

---

1. That the republic should not suffer injury.

the senatorial order, perceived the finesse; and yesterday I was present at a grand division of the city, and there I beheld my fellow-citizens very accurately counting all their chickens, not only before any of them were hatched, but before above one half of the eggs were laid. In short, they fairly contended about the future forms of our government, whether it should be founded upon aristocratic or democratic principles.

I stood in the balcony, and on my right hand were ranged all the people of property, with some few poor dependents, and on the other all the tradesmen, etc., who thought it worth their while to leave daily labour for the good of the country. The spirit of the English constitution has yet a little influence left, and but a little. The remains of it, however, will give the wealthy people a superiority this time, but would they secure it they must banish all schoolmasters and confine all knowledge to themselves. This cannot be. The mob begin to think and to reason. Poor reptiles! It is with them a vernal morning; they are struggling to cast off their winter's slough, they bask in the sunshine, and ere noon they will bite, depend upon it. The gentry begin to fear this. Their committee will be appointed, they will deceive the people and again forfeit a share of their confidence. And if these instances of what with one side is policy, with the other perfidy, shall continue to increase and become more frequent, farewell aristocracy. I see, and I see it with fear and trembling, that if the disputes with Great Britain continue, we shall be under the worst of all possible dominions; we shall be under the domination of a riotous mob.

It is the interest of all men, therefore, to seek for reunion with the parent state. A safe compact seems, in my poor opinion, to be now tendered. Internal taxation is to be left with ourselves. The right of regulating trade to be vested in Great Britain, where alone is found the power of protecting it. I trust you will agree with me that this is the only possible mode of union. Men by nature are free as air. When they enter into society, there is, there must be, an implied compact, for there never yet was an express one, that a part of this freedom shall be given up for the security of the remainder. But what part? The answer is plain. The least possible, considering the circumstances of the society, which constitute what may be called its political necessity.

And what does this political necessity require in the present instance? Not that Britain should lay imposts upon us for the support of government, nor for its defence; not that she should regulate our internal police. These things affect us only. She can have no right to interfere. To these things we ourselves are competent. But can it be said that we are competent to the regulating of trade? The position is absurd, for this affects every part of the British Empire, every part of the habitable earth. If Great Britain, if Ireland, if America, if all of them are to make laws of trade, there must be a collision of these different authorities, and then who is to decide the *vis major*? To recur to this, if possible to be avoided, is the greatest of all great absurdities.

Political necessity, therefore, requires that this power should be placed in the hands of one part of the empire. Is it a question which part? Let me answer by taking another. Pray, which part of the empire protects trade? Which part of the empire receives almost immense sums to guard the rest? And what danger is in the trust? Some men object that England will draw all the profits of our trade into her coffers. All that she can, undoubtedly. But unless a reasonable compensation for his trouble be left to the merchant here, she destroys the trade, and then she will receive no profit from it.

37. Mobbism Versus the Establishment: Petition to the Massachusetts Legislature March 8, 1775

A WRITER in Boston addresses the Provincial Congress of Massachusetts as follows:—

Your assuming the government of Massachusetts Bay, makes it unnecessary for me to make any apology for addressing you in this public manner, further, than by acquainting you that it is to represent to you the distresses of some of those people, who, from a sense of their duty to the king, and a reverence for his laws, have behaved quietly and peaceably; and for which reason they have

SOURCE: Rivington's *Gazette*, March 9, 1775, reprinted in Frank Moore, *Diary of the American Revolution from Newspapers and Original Documents* (2 vols., New York, 1865), I, 37–42.

been deprived of their liberty, abused in their persons, and suffered such barbarous cruelties, insults, and indignities, besides the loss of their property, by the hands of lawless mobs and riots, as would have been disgraceful even for savages to have committed. The courts of justice being shut up in most parts of the province, and the justices of those courts compelled by armed force, headed by some who are members of your Congress, to refrain from doing their duties, at present it is rendered impracticable for those sufferers to obtain redress, unless it be by your interposition, or the aid of military force, which will be applied for in case this application fails.

A particular enumeration of all the instances referred to, is apprehended unnecessary, as many of your members are personally knowing to them, and for the information of any of you who may pretend ignorance of them, the following instances are here mentioned. In August last, a mob in Berkshire forced the justices of the court of Common Pleas from their seats, and shut up the courthouse. They also drove David Ingersoll from his house, and damaged the same, and he was obliged to leave his estate; after which his enclosures were laid waste. At Taunton, Daniel Leonard was driven from his house, and bullets fired into it by the mob, and he obliged to take refuge in Boston, for the supposed crime of obeying his Majesty's requisition as one of his council for this province. Colonel Gilbert, of Freetown, a firm friend to government, in August last being at Dartmouth, was attacked at midnight by a mob of about an hundred, but by his bravery, with the assistance of the family where he lodged, they were beaten off. The same night Brigadier Ruggles was also attacked by another party, who were routed after having painted and cut the hair off of one of his horses' mane and tail. Afterwards he had his arms taken from his dwellinghouse in Hardwick, all of which are not yet returned. He had at another time a very valuable English horse, which was kept as a stallion, poisoned, his family disturbed, and himself obliged to take refuge in Boston, after having been insulted in his own house, and twice on his way, by a mob.

The chief justice of the province in Middleborough, was threatened to be stopped on the highway in going to Boston court, but his firmness and known resolution, supporting government in this as well as many other instances, intimidated the mob from laying hands on him; he was also threatened with opposition in going into court, but the terror of the troops prevented. The whole bench were hissed by a mob as they came out of court. In September, Mr. Sewall, his Majesty's Attorney-General for Massachusetts Bay, was obliged to repair to Boston for refuge. His house at Cambridge was attacked by a mob, and his windows were broken, but the mob was beaten off by the gallant behavior and bravery of some young gentlemen of his family. About the same time the Lieutenant-Governor Oliver, president of his Majesty's council, was attacked at Cambridge, by a mob of about four thousand, and was compelled to resign his seat at the board, since which, upon further threats, he has been obliged to leave his estate, and take refuge with his family in Boston.

At Worcester, a mob of about five thousand collected, prevented the court of Common Pleas from sitting, (about one thousand of them had fire-arms,) and all drawn up in two files, compelled the judges, sheriffs, and gentlemen of the bar, to pass them with cap in hand, and read their disavowal of holding courts under the new acts of parliament, not less than thirty times in their procession. Daniel Oliver, Esq., of Hardwick, was disarmed by a mob, and has been obliged to take refuge in Boston, to the total loss of his business. Colonel Phips, the very reputable and highly esteemed sheriff of the county of Middlesex, by a large mob was obliged to promise not to serve any processes of courts, and to retire to Boston for protection from further insults. Colonel Saltonstall, the very humane sheriff of the county of Essex, has been obliged to take refuge in Boston, to screen himself from the violence of the mob. The court of Common Pleas was forbidden to sit at Taunton, by a large mob, with a justice acting as one of their committee. At Middleborough, Peter Oliver, Esq., was obliged to sign a paper, not to execute his office, under the new acts. At Springfield, the courts of Common Pleas and General Sessions of the peace, were prevented sitting by a large mob, who kept the justices from entering the court-house, and obliged them, the sheriff, and gentlemen of the bar, to desist, with their hats off, from holding any courts. Colonel Edson, one of his Majesty's council, has been driven from his house in Bridgewater, and kept from it ever since last August, for being a friend to government, and accepting his Majesty's appointment as counsellor.

The courts of General Session of the Peace and inferior courts of Common Pleas for the county of Plymouth, have been shut up. In

August, Colonel Putnam of Worcester, a firm friend to Government, had two fat cows stolen and taken from him, and a very valuable grist-mill burnt, and was obliged to leave a fair estate in Worcester, and retire to Boston, where he has been ever since, for his protesting against riots, &c. Colonel Murray, of Rutland, one of his Majesty's council, has been obliged to leave a large estate in the country, and repair to Boston to save himself from being handled by the mob, and compelled to resign his seat at council board. His house has been attacked, his family put in fear. Colonel Vassall, of Cambridge, from intolerable threats, and insolent treatment by mobs of his friends and himself, has left his elegant seat there, and retired to Boston, with his amiable family, for protection. John Borland, Esq., is in the same predicament with Colonel Vassall. Honorable John Chandler, Esq., judge of probate, &c., for the county of Worcester, has been obliged to retreat to Boston for protection, and leave his business, and a numerous family of hopeful youths behind him, with great reluctance, and who, before he came away, was ordered by the mob to hold his office till further orders.

The Plymouth protesters, addressers, and military officers, were compelled by a mob of two thousand, collected from Plymouth and Barnstable counties, to recant and resign their military commissions. Thomas Foster, Esq., an ancient gentleman, was obliged to run into the woods, and had like to have been lost, and the mob, although the justices, with Mr. Foster, were sitting in the town, ransacked his house, and damaged his furniture. He was obnoxious as a friend to government, and for that reason they endeavored to deprive him of his business, and to prevent even his taking the acknowledgment of a deed. Richard Clark, Esq., a consignee of the tea, was obliged to retire from Salem to Boston, as an asylum; and his son Isaac went to Plymouth to collect debts, but in the night was assaulted by a mob and obliged to get out of town at midnight. Jesse Dunbar, of Halifax, in Plymouth county, bought some fat cattle of Mr. Thomas the counsellor, and drove them to Plymouth for sale; one of the oxen being skinned and hung up, the committee came to him, and finding he bought it of Mr. Thomas, they put the ox into a cart, and fixing Dunbar in his belly, carted him four miles, and there made him pay a dollar, after taking three more cattle and a horse from him. The Plymouth mob delivered him to the Kingston mob, which carted him four miles further, and forced from him another dollar, then delivered him to the Duxborough mob, who abused him by throwing the tripe in his face, and endeavoring to cover him with it to the endangering his life. They then threw dirt at him, and after other abuses carried him to said Thomas's house, and made him pay another sum of money, and he not taking the beef, they flung it in the road and quitted him. Daniel Dunbar, of Halifax, an ensign of militia there, had his colors demanded by the mob, some of the selectmen being the chief actors. He refused; they broke into his house, took him out, forced him upon a rail, and after keeping him for two or three hours in such abuses, he was forced to give his colors up to save his life. A constable of Hardwick, for refusing to pay his collections, directly contrary to the oath of his office, was bound and confined six and thirty hours, and threatened with being sent to Simsbury mines. His wife being dangerously ill, he was released after signing a something which one of the mob had prepared for him. The mob committee of the county of York, ordered that no one should hire any of Sir William Pepperell's estates, buy no wood of him, or pay any debts due to him. In February, at Plymouth, a number of ladies attempted to divert themselves at their assembly room, but the mob collected, (the committee having met previous thereto,) and flung stones which broke the shutters and windows, and endangered their lives. They were forced to get out of the hall, and were pelted and abused to their own homes. After this the ladies diverted themselves by riding out, but were followed by a mob, pelted and abused, with the most indecent Billingsgate language. These things happened at the time when some of the people of Plymouth, in conjunction with the committee men from other towns in that county, aided and assisted by four dissenting clergymen, were presenting to General Gage, by their memorial, the peaceable state they were in before the arrival of a party of soldiers at Marshfield, in that county.

The Honorable Israel Williams, Esq., one who was appointed of his Majesty's new council, but had declined the office through infirmity of body, was taken from his house by the mob in the night, carried several miles, put into a room with a fire, the chimney at the top, the doors of the room closed, and kept there for many hours in the smoke, till his life was in danger; then he was carried home, after being forced to sign what they ordered, and a guard placed over him to prevent his leaving the house.

To recount the suffering of all from mobs, rioters, and trespassers, would take more time and paper than can be spared for that
purpose. It is hoped the foregoing will be sufficient to put you upon
the use of proper means and measures for giving relief to all that
have been injured by such unlawful and wicked practices.

38. Controlling the Militia:
Joseph Warren to Samuel Adams
Cambridge, May 26, 1775

DEAR SIR,—

I see more and more the necessity of establishing a civil government here, and such a government as shall be sufficient to control
the military forces, not only of this colony, but also such as shall be
sent to us from the other colonies. The continent must strengthen
and support with all its weight the civil authority here; otherwise
our soldiery will lose the ideas of right and wrong, and will plunder,
instead of protecting, the inhabitants. This is but too evident already; and I assure you *inter nos*, that, unless some authority
sufficient to restrain the irregularities of this army is established, we
shall very soon find ourselves involved in greater difficulties than
you can well imagine. The least hint from the most unprincipled
fellow, who has perhaps been reproved for some criminal behavior,
is quite sufficient to expose the fairest character to insult and abuse
among many; and it is with our countrymen as with all other men,
when they are in arms, they think the military should be upper-
most. I know very well, that, in the course of time, people will see
the error of such proceedings; but I am not sure it will be before
many disagreeable consequences may take place. The evil may now
be easily remedied. I know the temper of our people. They are
sensible, brave, and virtuous; and I wish they might ever continue
so. Mild and gentle regulations will be sufficient for them; but the
penalties annexed to the breach of those rules should be rigorously
inflicted. I would have such a government as should give every man

SOURCE: Richard Frothingham, *Life and Times of Joseph Warren*
(Boston, 1865), 495–496.

the greatest liberty to do what he pleases consistent with restrain-
ing him from doing any injury to another, or such a government as
would most contribute to the good of the whole, with the least
inconvenience to individuals. However, it is difficult to frame a
government *de novo* which will stand in need of no amendment.
Experience must point out defects. And, if the people should not
lose their morals, it will be easy for them to correct the errors in the
first formation of government. If they *should* lose *them*, what was
not good at first will be soon insupportable. My great wish therefore is, that we may restrain every thing which tends to weaken the
principles of right and wrong, more especially with regard to *property*. You may possibly think I am a little angry with my countrymen, or have not so good an opinion of them as I formerly had; but
that is not the case. I love,—I *admire* them. The errors they have
fallen into are natural and easily accounted for. A sudden alarm
brought them together, animated with the noblest spirit. They left
their houses, their families, with nothing but the clothes on their
backs, without a day's provision, and many without a farthing in
their pockets. Their country was in danger; their brethren were
slaughtered; their arms alone engrossed their attention. As they
passed through the country, the inhabitants gladly opened their
hospitable doors, and all things were in common. The enemies of
their country alone refused to aid and comfort the hungry soldier.
Prudence seemed to dictate that the force made use of to obtain
what ought voluntarily to have been given, should be winked at.
And it is not easy for men, especially when interest and the gratification of appetite are considered, to know how far they may continue
to tread in the path where there are no landmarks to direct them. I
hope care will be taken by the Continental Congress to apply an
immediate remedy, as the infection is caught by every new corps
that arrives.

X

The Coming of Independence

By early 1775 an open clash seemed imminent. Throughout the colonies militia companies drilled in earnest, while British troops were poised for action. Edmund Burke, still hoping to avert an armed conflict, delivered a masterful speech in Parliament pleading for conciliatory measures by the British government. But on April 19 fighting broke out at Lexington and soon spread to other points. The Second Continental Congress, which convened in May 1775, did not yet abandon hope for reconciliation. On July 5 it adopted the Olive Branch Petition drawn up by John Dickinson, which requested the King to forego further hostile actions until a settlement could be worked out. George III, however, flatly rejected the American offer.

The King's uncompromising attitude both before and during the war is clear from his extraordinarily frank correspondence with his chief minister, Lord North, on whom he kept the closest tabs, often writing him several times a day. With Burgoyne's capitulation at Saratoga in the fall of 1778, a storm broke over the heads of the North Ministry. North pressed the King to accept his resignation. Instead, George III preferred to remind North of the King's personal claim upon him (George III had paid £20,000 on North's personal debts). Indeed, the King was adamantly opposed to the prospect of having a government headed by William Pitt, now Lord Chatham, and kept North in office against his will. Chatham's fatal illness ended the immediate threat to the North Ministry.

In the interim between the sittings of the First and Second Continental Congresses the status of the colonies remained ambiguous. But Thomas Paine's blistering attack in January 1776 upon the institution of monarchy and on the abuses of that office under George III helped crystallize the sentiment for independence. On June 7, 1776, Richard Henry Lee, a delegate from Virginia, offered a resolution in Congress that the United States "are, and of right ought to be, free and independent States." The resolution was adopted on July 2, and two days later Congress approved the Great Declaration, which reflected the best Whig political thought in America.

39. Edmund Burke's Speech on
Conciliation with America
March 22, 1775

IN THIS character of the Americans, a love of freedom is the pre-
dominating feature which marks and distinguishes the whole: and
as an ardent is always a jealous affection, your colonies become
suspicious, restive, and untractable, whenever they see the least
attempt to wrest from them by force, or shuffle from them by
chicane, what they think the only advantage worth living for. This
fierce spirit of liberty is stronger in the English colonies probably
than in any other people of the earth; and this from a great variety
of powerful causes which, to understand the true temper of their
minds, and the direction which this spirit takes, it will not be amiss
to lay open somewhat more largely.

First, the people of the colonies are descendants of Englishmen.
England, Sir[1] is a nation, which still I hope respects, and formerly
adored, her freedom. The colonists emigrated from you, when this
part of your character was most predominant; and they took this
bias and direction the moment they parted from your hands. They
are therefore not only devoted to liberty, but to liberty according to
English ideas, and on English principles. Abstract liberty, like
other mere abstractions, is not to be found. Liberty inheres in some
sensible object; and every nation has formed to itself some favourite point which by way of eminence becomes the criterion of their
happiness. It happened, you know, Sir, that the great contests for
freedom in this country were from the earliest times chiefly upon
the question of taxing. Most of the contests in the ancient commonwealths turned primarily on the right of election of magistrates; or on the balance among the several orders of the state. The
question of money was not with them so immediate. But in England it was otherwise. On this point of taxes the ablest pens, and

SOURCE: *Works of Edmund Burke* (rev. ed., 12 vols., Boston, 1865–
1867), II, 120–182 *passim*.

1. The Speaker of the House.

most eloquent tongues, have been exercised; the greatest spirits have acted and suffered. In order to give the fullest satisfaction concerning the importance of this point, it was not only necessary for those who in argument defended the excellence of the English Constitution, to insist on this privilege of granting money as a dry point of fact, and to prove, that the right had been acknowledged in ancient parchments, and blind usages, to reside in a certain body called an House of Commons. They went much further; they attempted to prove, and they succeeded, that in theory it ought to be so, from the particular nature of the House of Commons, as an immediate representative of the people; whether the old records had delivered this oracle or not. They took infinite pains to inculcate, as a fundamental principle, that, in all monarchies, the people must in effect themselves mediately or immediately possess the power of granting their own money, or no shadow of liberty could subsist. The colonies draw from you, as with their life-blood, these ideas and principles. Their love of liberty, as with you, fixed and attached on this specifick point of taxing. Liberty might be safe, or might be endangered in twenty other particulars, without their being much pleased or alarmed. Here they felt its pulse; and as they found that beat, they thought themselves sick or sound. . . .

They were further confirmed in the pleasing errour, by the form of their provincial legislative assemblies. Their governments are popular in an high degree; some are merely popular; in all, the popular representative is the most weighty; and this share of the people in their ordinary government never fails to inspire them with lofty sentiments, and with a strong aversion from whatever tends to deprive them of their chief importance.

If any thing were wanting to this necessary operation of the form of government, religion would have given it a complete effect. Religion, always a principle of energy, in this new people, is no way worn out or impaired; and their mode of professing it is also one main cause of this free spirit. The people are Protestants and of that kind, which is the most adverse to all implicit submission of mind and opinion. This is a persuasion not only favourable to liberty, but built upon it. I do not think, Sir, that the reason of this averseness in the dissenting churches from all that looks like absolute government is so much to be sought in their religious tenets, as in their history. Every one knows that the Roman Catholick religion is at least coeval with most of the governments where it prevails; that it has generally gone hand in hand with them; and received great favour and every kind of support from authority. The church of England too was formed from her cradle under the nursing care of regular government. But the dissenting interests have sprung up in direct opposition to all the ordinary powers of the world; and could justify that opposition only on a strong claim to natural liberty. Their very existence depended on the powerful and unremitted assertion of that claim. All Protestantism, even the most cold and passive, is a sort of dissent. But the religion most prevalent in our northern colonies is a refinement on the principle of resistance; it is the dissidence of dissent; and the Protestantism of the protestant religion. This religion, under a variety of denominations, agreeing in nothing but in the communion of the spirit of liberty, is predominant in most of the northern provinces; where the Church of England, notwithstanding its legal rights, is in reality no more than a sort of private sect, not composing most probably the tenth of the people. The colonists left England when this spirit was high; and in the emigrants was the highest of all: and even that stream of foreigners, which has been constantly flowing into these colonies, has, for the greatest part, been composed of dissenters from the establishments of their several countries; and have brought with them a temper and character far from alien to that of a people with whom they mixed. . . .

Permit me, Sir, to add another circumstance in our colonies, which contributes no mean part towards the growth and effect of this untractable spirit. I mean their education. In no country perhaps in the world is the law so general a study. The profession itself is numerous and powerful; and in most provinces it takes the lead. The greater number of the deputies sent to the Congress were lawyers. But all who read, and most do read, endeavour to obtain some smattering in that science. I have been told by an eminent bookseller, that in no branch of his business, after tracts of popular devotion, were so many books as those in the law exported to the plantations. The colonists have now fallen into the way of printing them for their own use. I hear that they have sold nearly as many of Blackstone's Commentaries in America as in England. General Gage marks out this disposition very particularly in a letter on your table. He states, that all the people in his government are lawyers, or smatterers in law and that in Boston they have been enabled, by successful chicane, wholly to evade many parts of one of your capital penal constitutions. The smartness of debate will say, that this knowledge ought to teach them more clearly the rights of legislature, their obligations to obedience, and the penalties of rebellion. All this is mighty well. But my honourable and learned friend on the floor, who condescends to mark what I say for animadversion, will disdain that ground. He has heard, as well as I, that when great honours and great emoluments do not win over this knowledge to the service to the state, it is a formidable adversary to government. If the spirit be not tamed and broken by these happy methods, it is stubborn and litigious. *Abeunt studia in mores.*[2] This study renders men acute, inquisitive, dexterous, prompt in attack, ready in defence, full of resources. In other countries the people, more simple, and of a less mercurial cast, judge of an ill principle in government only by an actual grievance; here they anticipate the evil, and judge of the pressure of the grievance by the badness of the principle. They augur misgovernment at a distance; and snuff the approach of tyranny in every tainted breeze.

The last cause of this disobedient spirit in the colonies is hardly less powerful than the rest, as it is not merely moral, but laid deep in the natural constitution of things. Three thousand miles of ocean lie between you and them. No contrivance can prevent the effect of this distance, in weakening government. Seas roll, and months pass, between the order and the execution: and the want of a speedy explanation of a single point is enough to defeat a whole system. You have, indeed, winged ministers of vengeance, who carry their bolts in their pounces to the remotest verge of the sea. But there a power steps in, that limits the arrogance of raging passions and furious elements, and says, "So far shalt thou go, and no farther." Who are you, that should fret and rage, and bite the chains of nature?—Nothing worse happens to you, than does to all nations, who have extensive empire; and it happens in all the forms into which empire can be thrown. . . .

The temper and character, which prevail in our colonies, are I am afraid, unalterable by any human art. We cannot, I fear, falsify the pedigree of this fierce people, and persuade them that they are not sprung from a nation, in whose veins the blood of freedom circulates. The language in which they would hear you tell them this tale would detect the imposition; your speech would betray

2. Practice becomes custom.

you. An Englishman is the unfittest person on earth to argue another Englishman into slavery. . . .

If then, Sir, it seems almost desperate to think of any alternative course for changing the moral causes (and not quite easy to remove the natural) which produce prejudices irreconcilable to the late exercise of our authority; but that the spirit infallibly will continue; and, continuing, will produce such effects as now embarrass us; the second mode under consideration is to prosecute that spirit in its overt acts, as *criminal*.

At this proposition I must pause for a moment. The thing seems a great deal too big for my ideas of jurisprudence. It should seem, to my way of conceiving such matters, that there is a very wide difference in reason and policy, between the mode of proceeding on the irregular conduct of scattered individuals, or even of bands of men, who disturb order within the state, and the civil dissensions which may, from time to time, on great questions agitate the several communities which compose a great empire. It looks to me to be narrow and pedantick to apply the ordinary ideas of criminal justice to this great public contest. I do not know the method of drawing up such an indictment against an whole people. I cannot insult and ridicule the feelings of millions of my fellow creatures, as Sir Edward Coke insulted one excellent individual [Sir Walter Raleigh] at the bar. I am not ripe to pass sentence on the gravest public bodies, entrusted with magistracies of great authority and dignity, and charged with the safety of their fellow citizens, upon the very same title that I am. I really think, that for wise men this is not judicious; for sober men, not decent; for minds tinctured with humanity, not mild and merciful.

Perhaps, Sir, I am mistaken in my idea of an empire, as distinguished from a single state or kingdom. But my idea of it is this; that an empire is the aggregate of many states, under one common head; whether this head be a monarch or a presiding republic. It does, in such constitutions, frequently happen (and nothing but this dismal, cold, dead uniformity of servitude can prevent its happening) that the subordinate parts have many local privileges and immunities. Between these privileges and the supreme common authority, the line may be extremely nice. Of course disputes, often too, very bitter disputes, and much ill blood, will arise. But though every privilege is an exemption (in the case) from the ordinary exercise of the supreme authority, it is no denial of it. The claim of a privilege seems rather *ex vi termini*,[3] to imply a superiour power. For to talk of the privileges of a state or of a person, who has no superiour, is hardly any better than speaking nonsense. Now, in such unfortunate quarrels among the component parts of a great political union of communities, I can scarcely conceive any thing more completely imprudent than for the head of the empire to insist that, if any privilege is pleaded against his will, or his acts, that his whole authority is denied; instantly to proclaim rebellion, to beat to arms, and to put the offending provinces under the ban. Will not this, Sir, very soon teach the provinces to make no distinctions on their part? Will it not teach them that the government, against which a claim of liberty is tantamount to high treason, is a government to which submission is equivalent to slavery? It may not always be quite convenient to impress dependent communities with such an idea. . . .

If then the removal of the causes of this spirit of American liberty be, for the greater part, or rather entirely, impracticable; if the ideas of criminal process be inapplicable, or, if applicable, are in the highest degree inexpedient, what way yet remains? No way is open, but the third and last—to comply with the American spirit as necessary; or, if you please to submit to it, as a necessary evil.

If we adopt this mode; if we mean to conciliate and concede; let us see of what nature the concession ought to be; to ascertain the nature of our concession, we must look at their complaint. The colonies complain that they have not the characteristic mark and seal of British freedom. They complain that they are taxed in a Parliament in which they are not represented. If you mean to satisfy them at all, you must satisfy them with regard to this complaint. If you mean to please any people, you must give them the boon which they ask; not what you may think better for them, but of a kind totally different. Such an act may be a wise regulation, but it is no concession; whereas our present theme is the mode of giving satisfaction.

Sir, I think you must perceive that I am resolved this day to have nothing at all to do with the question of the right of taxation. Some gentlemen startle—but it is true: I put it totally out of the question. It is less than nothing in my consideration. I do not indeed wonder, nor will you, Sir, that gentlemen of profound learn-

3. From the term itself.

ing are fond of displaying it on this profound subject. But my consideration is narrow, confined, and wholly limited to the policy of the question. . . . The question with me is not whether you have a right to render your people miserable; but whether it is not your interest to make them happy. It is not, what a lawyer tells me, I may do; but what humanity, reason, and justice tell me I ought to do. Is a politic act the worse for being a generous one? . . .

Such is steadfastly my opinion of the absolute necessity of keeping up the concord of this empire by a unity of spirit, though in diversity of operations, that, if I were sure the colonists had, at their leaving this country, sealed a regular compact of servitude; that they had solemnly abjured all the rights of citizens; that they had made a vow to renounce all ideas of liberty for them and their prosperity, to all generations, yet I should hold myself obliged to conform to the temper I found universally prevalent in my own day, and to govern two million of men, impatient of servitude, on the principles of freedom. I am not determining a point of law; I am restoring tranquillity; and the general character and situation of a people must determine what sort of government is fitted for them. That point nothing else can or ought to determine.

My idea therefore, without considering whether we yield as matter of right, or grant as matter of favour, is *to admit the people of our colonies into an interest in the Constitution*; and, by recording that admission in the journals of Parliament, to give them as strong an assurance as the nature of the thing will admit, that we mean for ever to adhere to that solemn declaration of systematic indulgence. . . .

But, Sir, I am sure that I shall not be misled, when, in a case of constitutional difficulty, I consult the genius of the English Constitution. Consulting at that oracle (it was with all due humility and piety) I found four capital examples in a similar case before me: those of Ireland, Wales, Chester, and Durham. . . .

But your legislative authority is perfect with regard to America; was it less perfect in Wales, Chester, and Durham? But America is virtually represented. What! does the electric force of virtual representation more easily pass over the Atlantic than pervade Wales, which lies in your neighbourhood; or than Chester and Durham, surrounded by abundance of representation that is actual and palpable? But, Sir, your ancestors thought this sort of virtual representation, however ample, to be totally insufficient for the freedom of the inhabitants of territories that are so near, and comparatively so inconsiderable. How then can I think it sufficient for those which are infinitely greater, and infinitely more remote?

You will now, Sir, perhaps imagine that I am on the point of proposing to you a scheme for a representation of the colonies in Parliament. Perhaps I might be inclined to entertain such thought; but a great flood stops me in my course. *Opposuit natura*—I cannot remove the eternal barriers of the creation. . . . When we cannot give the benefit as we would wish, let us not refuse it altogether. If we cannot give the principal, let us find a substitute. But how? Where? What substitute?

Fortunately I am not obliged for the ways and means of the substitute to tax my own unproductive invention. I am not even obliged to go to the rich treasury of the fertile framers of imaginary commonwealths; not to the Republic of Plato, nor to the Utopia of More, not to the Oceana of Harrington. It is before me—It is at my feet, *and the rude swain treads daily on it with his clouted shoon.* I only wish you to recognize, for the theory, the ancient constitutional policy of this kingdom with regard to representation, as that policy has been declared in acts of Parliament; and, as to the practice, to return to that mode which an uniform experience has marked out to you, as best; and in which you walked with security, advantage, and honour, until the year 1763.

My resolutions therefore mean to establish the equity and justice of a taxation of America by *grant*, and not by *imposition*. To mark the *legal competency* of the colony assemblies for the support of their government in peace, and for public aids in time of war. To acknowledge that this legal competency has had *a dutiful and beneficial exercise; and that experience has shewn the benefit of their grants, and the futility of parliamentary taxation as a method of supply.* . . .

It is said, indeed, that this power of granting, vested in American assemblies, would dissolve the unity of the empire; which was preserved, entire, although Wales and Chester and Durham were added to it. Truly, Mr. Speaker, I do not know, what this unity means; nor has it ever been heard of that I know, in the constitutional policy of this country. The very idea of subordination of parts excludes this notion of simple and undivided unity. England is the head; but she is not the head and the members too. Ireland has ever had from the beginning a separate, but not an independent legislature; which, far from distracting, promoted the union of the whole. Everything was sweetly and harmoniously disposed through both islands for the conservation of English dominion, and the communication of English liberties. I do not see that the same principles might not be carried into twenty islands, and with the same good effect. This is my model with regard to America, as far as the internal circumstances of the two countries are the same. I know no other unity of this empire than I can draw from its example during these periods, when it seemed to my poor understanding more united than it is now, or than it is likely to be by the present methods. . . .

All this, I know well enough, will sound wild and chimerical to the profane herd of those vulgar and mechanical politicians who have no place among us; a sort of people who think that nothing exists but what is gross and material; and who therefore, far from being qualified to be directors of the great movement of empire, are not fit to turn a wheel in the machine. But to men truly initiated and rightly taught, these ruling and master principles, which, in the opinion of such men as I have mentioned, have no substantial existence, are in truth every thing, and all in all. Magnanimity in politics is not seldom the truest wisdom; and a great empire and little minds go ill together. If we are conscious of our situation, and glow with zeal to fill our places as becomes our station and ourselves, we ought to auspicate all our public proceedings on America, with the old warnings of the church, *Sursum corda!*[4] We ought to elevate our minds to the greatness of that trust to which the order of Providence has called us. By adverting to the dignity of this high calling, our ancestors have turned a savage wilderness into a glorious empire; and have made the most extensive, and the only honourable conquests; not by destroying, but by promoting, the wealth, the number, the happiness of the human race. Let us get an American revenue as we have got an American empire. English privileges have made it all that it is; English privileges alone will make it all it can be.

4. Lift up your hearts!

40. Battle of Lexington
April 19, 1775

ABOUT ten o'clock last night, the troops in Boston were discovered to be in motion in a very secret manner, and it was found they were embarking in boats which they had privately brought to the place in the evening at the lower end of the common. Expresses set off immediately to alarm the country, that they might be on their guard. When they were passing about a mile beyond Lexington, they were stopped by a party of officers who came out of Boston in the afternoon of that day, and were seen lurking in bye-places in the country until after dark. One of the expresses immediately fled, and was pursued a long distance by an officer, who, when he had overtaken him, presented a pistol and cried out, "You're a dead man if you don't stop!" but he kept on until he gained a house, when, stopping suddenly, he was thrown from his horse; and having the presence of mind to call out to the people of the house, "Turn out! turn out! I've got one of them!" the officer immediately retreated as fast as he had pursued. The other express [Paul Revere] after undergoing a strict examination, was allowed to depart.

The body of the troops, in the mean time, under the command of Lieutenant-Colonel Smith, had crossed the river and landed at Phipps' farm. They proceeded with great silence to Lexington, six miles below Concord. A company of militia, numbering about eighty men, had mustered near the meetinghouse. Just before sunrise the King's troops came in sight, when the militia began to disperse. The troops then set out upon the road, hallooing and huzzaing, and coming within a few rods of them, the commanding officer cried out in words to this effect, "Disperse, you damned rebels! damn you, disperse!" upon which the troops again huzzaed, and at the same time one or two officers discharged their pistols, which were instantaneously followed by the firing of four or five of the soldiers, and then there seemed to be a general discharge from

SOURCE: *Pennsylvania Journal*, May 24, 1775, reprinted in Frank Moore, *Diary of the American Revolution*, I, 63–67.

the whole. It is to be noticed, they fired upon the militia as they were dispersing agreeably to their command, and that they did not even return the fire. Eight of our men were killed, and nine wounded. The troops then laughed, and damned the Yankees, and said they could not bear the smell of gunpowder.

Soon after this action, the troops renewed their march to Concord, where they divided into parties, and went directly to the several places where the province stores were deposited. Each party was supposed to have a Tory pilot. One body went into the jail yard, and spiked and otherwise damaged the cannon belonging to the province, and broke and set fire to the carriages. They then entered a store and rolled out about a hundred barrels of flour, which they unheaded, and emptied about forty into the river. Some took possession of the town-house, which was soon after discovered to be on fire, but which was extinguished without much damage. Another party took possession of the North Bridge. About one hundred and fifty of the militia, who had mustered upon the alarm, coming towards the bridge, were fired upon by the troops, and two were killed upon the spot. Thus did the troops of Britain's King fire FIRST at two several times upon his loyal American subjects, and put a period to ten lives before one gun was fired upon them! Our people THEN returned the fire, and obliged the troops to retreat, who were soon joined by their other parties, but finding they were still pursued, the whole body moved back to Lexington, both troops and militia firing as they went.

During this time an express was sent to General Gage, who despatched a reinforcement under the command of Earl Percy, with two field-pieces. Upon the arrival of this reinforcement at Lexington, just as the retreating party had reached there, they made a stand, picking up their dead, took all the carriages they could find, and put their wounded thereon. Others of them—to their eternal disgrace be it spoken—were robbing and setting houses on fire, and discharging their cannon at the meeting-house.

While this was transacting a party of the militia at Menotomy, attacked a party of twelve of the enemy, who were carrying stores and provision, killed one of them and took possession of their arms and stores, without any loss.

The troops having halted about an hour at Lexington, found it necessary to make a second retreat, carrying with them many of their dead and wounded. This they continued from Lexington to Charlestown, with great precipitation, the militia closely following them, firing till they reached Charlestown Neck, where they arrived a little after sunset. Passing over the Neck the enemy proceeded up Bunker Hill and encamped for the night.

41. The Olive Branch Petition
July 5, 1775

WE, your Majesty's faithful subjects of the colonies of New Hampshire, Massachusetts Bay, Rhode Island and Providence Plantations, Connecticut, New York, New Jersey, Pennsylvania, the counties of New Castle, Kent, and Sussex on Delaware, Maryland, Virginia, North Carolina and South Carolina, in behalf of ourselves and the inhabitants of these colonies, who have deputed us to represent them in general congress, entreat your Majesty's gracious attention to this our humble petition.

The union between our mother country and these colonies, and the energy of mild and just government, produced benefits so remarkably important, and afforded such an assurance of their permanency and increase that the wonder and envy of other nations were excited, while they beheld Great Britain rising to a power the most extraordinary the world had ever known.

Her rivals, observing that there was no probability of this happy connection being broken by civil dissensions, and apprehending its future effects if left any longer undisturbed, resolved to prevent her receiving such continual and formidable accessions of wealth and strength by checking the growth of these settlements from which they were to be derived.

In the prosecution of this attempt, events so unfavourable to the design took place that every friend to the interests of Great Britain and these colonies entertained pleasing and reasonable expectations of seeing an additional force and extension immediately given

SOURCE: *Journals of the Continental Congress, 1774–1789*, II, 158–161.

to the operations of the union hitherto experienced, by an en-largement of the dominions of the Crown and the removal of ancient and warlike enemies to a greater distance.

At the conclusion, therefore, of the late war, the most glorious and advantageous that ever had been carried on by British arms, your loyal colonists having contributed to its success by such repeated and strenuous exertions as frequently procured them the distinguished approbation of your Majesty, of the late king, and of Parliament, doubted not but that they should be permitted, with the rest of the empire, to share in the blessings of peace, and the emoluments of victory and conquest. While these recent and honourable acknowledgments of their merits remained on record in the journals and acts of that august legislature, the Parliament, undefaced by the imputation or even the suspicion of any offence, they were alarmed by a new system of statutes and regulations adopted for the administration of the colonies, that filled their minds with the most painful fears and jealousies; and, to their inexpressible astonishment, perceived the dangers of a foreign quarrel quickly succeeded by domestic dangers, in their judgment, of a more dreadful kind.

Nor were their anxieties alleviated by any tendency in this system to promote the welfare of the mother country. For though its effects were more immediately felt by them, yet its influence appeared to be injurious to the commerce and prosperity of Great Britain.

We shall decline the ungrateful task of describing the irksome variety of artifices, practised by many of your Majesty's ministers, the delusive pretences, fruitless terrors, and unavailing severities that have, from time to time, been dealt out by them in their attempts to execute this impolitic plan, or of tracing through a series of years past, the progress of the unhappy differences be-tween Great Britain and these colonies, which have flowed from this fatal source.

Your Majesty's ministers, persevering in their measures, and proceeding to open hostilities for enforcing them, have compelled us to arm in our own defence, and have engaged us in a controversy so peculiarly abhorrent to the affections of your still faithful colonists that when we consider whom we must oppose in this contest, and if it continues, what may be the consequences, our own particular misfortunes are accounted by us only as parts of our distress.

Knowing to what violent resentments and incurable animosities, civil discords are apt to exasperate and inflame the contending parties, we think ourselves required by indispensable obligations to Almighty God, to your Majesty, to our fellow-subjects, and to ourselves, immediately to use all the means in our power not incompatible with our safety, for stopping the further effusion of blood, and for averting the impending calamities that threaten the British Empire.

Thus called upon to address your Majesty on affairs of such moment to America, and probably to all your dominions, we are earnestly desirous of performing this office with the utmost deference for your Majesty; and we therefore pray that your royal magnanimity and benevolence may make the most favourable construction of our expressions on so uncommon an occasion. Could we represent in their full force the sentiments that agitate the minds of us, your dutiful subjects, we are persuaded your Majesty would ascribe any seeming deviation from reverence in our language, and even in our conduct, not to any reprehensible intention, but to the impossibility of reconciling the usual appearances of respect with a just attention to our own preservation against those artful and cruel enemies who abuse your royal confidence and authority for the purpose of effecting our destruction.

Attached to your Majesty's person, family, and government, with all devotion that principle and affection can inspire, connected with Great Britain by the strongest ties that can unite societies, and deploring every event that tends in any degree to weaken them, we solemnly assure your Majesty that we not only most ardently desire the former harmony between her and these colonies may be restored, but that a concord may be established between them upon so firm a basis as to perpetuate its blessings, uninterrupted by any future dissensions, to succeeding generations in both countries, and to transmit your Majesty's name to posterity, adorned with that signal and lasting glory that has attended the memory of those illustrious personages whose virtues and abilities have extricated states from dangerous convulsions, and, by securing happiness to others, have erected the most noble and durable monuments to their own fame.

We beg leave further to assure your Majesty that notwithstanding the sufferings of your loyal colonists during the course of the present controversy, our breasts retain too tender a regard for the kingdom from which we derive our origin to request such a reconciliation as might in any manner be inconsistent with her dignity or her welfare. These, related as we are to her honour and duty as well as inclination, induce us to support and advance; and the apprehensions that now oppress our hearts with unspeakable grief being once removed, your Majesty will find your faithful subjects on this continent ready and willing at all times, as they ever have been, with their lives and fortunes to assert and maintain the rights and interests of your Majesty, and of our mother country.

We, therefore, beseech your Majesty that your royal authority and influence may be graciously interposed to procure us relief from our afflicting fears and jealousies, occasioned by the system before mentioned, and to settle peace through every part of your dominions, with all humility submitting to your Majesty's wise consideration whether it may not be expedient for facilitating those important purposes, that your Majesty be pleased to direct some mode by which the united applications of your faithful colonists to the throne, in pursuance of their common councils, may be improved into a happy and permanent reconciliation; and that, in the mean time, measures may be taken for preventing the further destruction of the lives of your Majesty's subjects; and that such statutes as more immediately distress any of your Majesty's colonies may be repealed.

For by such arrangements as your Majesty's wisdom can form for collecting the united sense of your American people, we are convinced your Majesty would receive such satisfactory proofs of the disposition of the colonists towards their sovereign and parent state that the wished for opportunity would soon be restored to them of evincing the sincerity of their professions by every testimony of devotion becoming the most dutiful subjects, and the most affectionate colonists.

That your Majesty may enjoy a long and prosperous reign, and that your descendants may govern your dominions with honour to themselves and happiness to their subjects, is our sincere and fervent prayer.

42. Resort to Force: Correspondence of King George III with Lord North November 18 and 19, 1774, March 15 – May 7, 1778

The King to Lord North, November 18, 1774, 12:48 P.M.

LORD NORTH,—

I am not sorry that the line of conduct seems now chalked out, which the enclosed dispatches thoroughly justify; the New England Governments are in a state of rebellion, blows must decide whether they are to be subject to this country or independent. . . .

November 19, 1774, 3:17 P.M.

LORD NORTH,—

I return the private letters received from Lieut.-General Gage; his idea of suspending the Acts appears to me the most absurd that can be suggested. The people are ripe for mischief, upon which the mother-country adopts suspending the measures she has thought necessary: this must suggest to the colonies a fear that alone prompts them to their present violence; we must either master them or totally leave them to themselves and treat them as aliens. I do not by this mean to insinuate that I am for advice [sic; advising]; new measures but I am for supporting those already undertaken.

SOURCE: The letters of 1774 are in W. B. Donne, ed., *The Correspondence of King George the Third with Lord North* (London, 1867), I, 214–216. Those from the year 1778 are found in Philip H. Stanhope, *History of England from the Peace of Utrecht to the Peace of Versailles, 1713–1783* (London, 1836–1854), VI, Appendix, p. xxxvi; Donne, *Corr. of King George the Third*, II, 149, 151, 153, 155; Sir John Fortescue, ed., *Correspondence of King George III, 1760–1783* (London, 1928), IV, No. 2329.

March 15(?), 1778

LORD NORTH—

On a subject that has for many months engrossed my thoughts, I cannot have the smallest difficulty instantly to answer the letter I have just received from you. My sole wish is to keep you at the head of the Treasury and as my Confidential Minister that end obtained, I am willing through your Channel to accept any description of person that will come devotedly to the support of your administration and as such do not object to Lord Shelburne and Mr. Barré who personally perhaps I dislike as much as Alderman Wilkes, and I cannot give you a strong proof of my desire to forward any thing you wish than taking this unpleasant step.

But I declare in the strongest and most solemn manner that though I do not object to your addressing yourself to Lord Chatham yet that you must acquaint him that I shall never address myself to him but through you and a clear explanation that he is to step forth to support an Administration whenever you are to be first Lord of the Treasury and Chancellor of the Exchequer; and that I cannot consent to have any conversation with him until the Ministry is formed that if he comes into this I will as he supports you receive him with open arms. I leave the whole arrangement to you provided Lord Suffolk Lord Weymouth and my two able lawyers are satisfied as to this situation; but chuse Ellis for Secretary of War in preference to Barré who in that event will get a more lucrative employment but will not be so near my person.

Having said this I will only add to put before your eyes my most inmost thoughts, that no advantage to this country nor personal danger can ever make me address myself for assistance either to Lord Chatham or any other branch of the Opposition honestly I would rather lose the Crown I now wear than bear the ignominy of possessing it under their shackles, I might write volumes if I would state my feeling of my mind; but I have honestly fairly, and affectionately told you the whole of my mind, and what I will never depart from.

Should Lord Chatham wish to see me before he gives an answer, I shall most certainly refuse it. I have had enough of personal negotiation and neither my dignity nor feelings will ever let me again submit to it.

Men of less principle and honesty than I pretend to may look on public measures and opinions as a game, I always act from conviction and certainly never can say but that I am shocked at the base Arts all these men have used therefore cannot go towards them; if they come to your assistance I will accept them.

You have now full powers to act, but I do not expect Lord Chatham and his crew will come to your assistance, but if they do not I trust the rest of the arrangements will greatly strengthen as it will give efficacy to Administration. Thurlowe as Chancellor, Yorke as Secretary of State will be efficient men. Numbers we have already, Lord Dartmouth as Steward and Lord Weymouth as Privy Seal will please them both, I am certain Lord Weymouth's conduct on the last vacancy of the Seals gives him a right to this change if agreeable to him.[1]

March 16, 1778, 8:28 A.M.

MY DEAR LORD—

As you are now thoroughly apprized of the whole of my thoughts and feelings, you cannot want any explanation of my opinion of the language held to Mr. Eden the last evening; it is so totally contrary to the only ground upon which I could have accepted the services of that perfidious man that I need not enter more fully upon, Lord Chatham as Dictator is planning a new Administration I appeal to my letter of yesterday if I did not clearly speak out upon [sic], if Lord Chatham agrees to support Your Administration or (if you like the expression better) the fundamentals of the present administration. Lord North the head of the Treasury, Lords Suffolk, Gower, and Weymouth in great offices to their own inclinations, Lord Sandwich in the Admiralty, Thurlow Chanr. and Wedderburne a Chief Justice; I will not object to see that great man when Lord Shelburne and Dunning with Barré are placed already in office but I solemnly declare nothing shall bring me to treat personally with Lord Chatham; what the D. of Northumberland told you yesterday is the old game over again; if I saw Lord Chatham he

1. The previously unidentified persons mentioned in this letter are Isaac Barré, an M.P. and follower of Shelburne; John Wilkes, the stormy petrel of British politics; the Earl of Suffolk, Secretary of State for the Northern Department; Lord Weymouth, Secretary of State for the Southern Department; and Welbore Ellis, who succeeded Lord Germain as Colonial Secretary in charge of the American War.

would insist on as total a change as Lord Shelburne has yesterday thrown out. Therefore my Dear Lord you will not understand that I entirely stick to what I wrote to you yesterday from which I will not change one jot.[2]

Lord North to the King, March 16, 1778

Lord North, Has the honour of receiving his Majesty's commands and begs leave to return his thanks for the repetition of his Majesty's great kindness towards him, which he is afraid may prove ruinous to the Public, and has, therefore, thought it his duty to lay his opinions frankly and fully before his Majesty. He would not have troubled him so often on a disagreeable subject, were he not perfectly convinced that the present system will not do; that it must break up in a very short time; that a change, which will become necessary, will be greater and accompanied with more disagreeable circumstances the longer it is delayed. The condition of the country is, indeed, most critical, and it is become next to impossible to carry on government, except upon a broad comprehensive plan which may in a great measure cripple opposition. There is no doubt but the opponents, perceiving that they stand on high ground, will urge their demands with great weight and perseverance, but, as Ld. Chatham's party is the smallest amongst the opposers of government, their demands will be the fewest and the most easily gratified. Lord North hopes that his Majesty will forgive the freedom with which he writes. The very dangerous situation of public affairs must be his excuse. Lord North mentioned yesterday to Lord Amherst[3] his intention of desiring his attendance in the Cabinet, and nominating him a Lieut. General on the Staff. He seemed much pleased with the distinction and express'd his readiness to give every assistance in his power.

The King to Lord North, March 16, 1778, 12:10 P.M.

LORD NORTH—

I am fully convinced that you are actuated alone from a wish not to conceal the most private corners of your breast in writing the letter you have just sent unto me; but my Dear Lord it is not

2. The Earls of Gower and Sandwich were Bedfordite members of the North Ministry; John Dunning, an M.P., was a follower of Shelburne.
3. Baron Jeffrey Amherst commanded the home forces.

private pique but an opinion formed on an experience of a Reign of now seventeen years, that makes me resolve to run any personal risque rather than submit to opposition; which every plan deviating from strengthening the present administration is more or less tending to, therefore I refer you to the genuine dictates of my heart which I put yesterday on paper and transmitted to you, and I am certain whilst I have no one object but to be of use to this country it is impossible I can be deserted and the road opened to a set of men who certainly would make me a slave for the remainder of my days and whatever they may pretend would go to the most unjustifiable lengths of cruelty and destruction of those who have stood forth in public office, of which you would be the first victim.

Lord North to the King, March 17, 1778

Lord North has the honour of returning the paper of Admiral Keppel to his Majesty. The majority of last night was owing to the situation and necessity of affairs, and not to any confidence the House seems to have in the administration. Lord North declared that he would not quit his post, unless his Majesty and the public were ready to fill it with an abler person, and this he thought it necessary to do in hopes that an arrangement might be made to his Majesty's satisfaction by his continuing in place and not throwing matters into confusion by a hasty retreat, but he does most earnestly intreat his Majesty to desist from making his continuance a necessary condition of any arrangement, as he fears, that no Ministry can be formed which will be able to carry this nation through its present difficulties unless the point of continuing Lord North at the head of the Treasury is given up. Whilst office was only vexatious and troublesome, Lord North, though always sensible of his being unequal to his Post, obey'd his Majesty's commands by remaining in the situation where his Majesty had thought proper to place him. Though he often solicited and pressed his dismission he thought that he ought not to do anything disagreeable to so good and gracious a Master, and therefore determined to wait till his Majesty should be pleased to release him. But the times have sadly changed their appearance and Lord North has too much reason to be afraid that a great part of our present distress is owing to the predilection which his Majesty has shewn to him, and to the perseverance with which he has continued him in office. The present situation of affairs requires *new* men and *able* men and Lord North would feel himself highly criminal if he should permit his interests and situation to stand in the way of any arrangement which may rescue his King and country from the present impending ruin. That he may be the victim selected by any new set of men is very possible but he has so much confidence in his own innocence and the protection of the Law that he does not fear the utmost of their resentment, and he will add, that capital punishment itself is, in Lord North's opinion, preferable to that constant anguish of mind which he feels from the consideration that his continuance in office is ruining his Majesty's affairs without resource. The nation may yet be saved, but much time is not left to do it in, and it can not be saved without a change of men, and particularly, of the first Lord of the Treasury. Lord North, therefore, most earnestly and humbly intreats his Majesty no longer to remain attach'd to that point, for, though Lord North will keep up a good countenance in public to prevent, if possible, the mischief that may arise from a contrary conduct, yet he can not continue much longer in office in any event, both because he is conscious that his continuance there is the ruin of the Public, and because his former incapacity is so much aggravated by his present distress of mind that he will soon be totally unfit for the performance of any ministerial duty. In this situation, he once more intreats that his situation may no longer be an absolute Bar to any negotiation from whence a prospect may arise of benefit to the country at this alarming crisis. The longer it is delay'd, the more unreasonable will be the terms press'd upon his Majesty, because every day will add strength to those whom his Majesty may think proper to invite to his service; If Lord Chatam had been admitted when he first gave signs of a separation from Ld. Rockingham,[4] he would have submitted to more reasonable terms than at present; he will now be more reasonable than he will be a fortnight hence, and sooner or later he or some other person in the opposition must be sent to, or this Nation is undone.

The King to Lord North, March 17, 1778, 10:35 A.M.

LORD NORTH—

I am grieved at your continually recurring to a subject on which we can never agree; your letter is certainly personally affectionate to

4. The Marquess of Rockingham, an "Old Whig" opposition leader.

me, and shews no signs of personal fear; but my Dear Lord no consideration in life shall make me stoop to Opposition; I am still ready to accept any part of them that will come to the assistance of my present efficient Ministers; but whilst any ten men in the kingdom will stand by me I will not give myself up into bondage; my Dear Lord I will rather risk my Crown than do what I think personally disgraceful, and whilst I have no wish but for the good and prosperity of my Country, it is impossible that the nation shall not stand by me; if they will not, they shall have another King, for I will never put my hand to what would make me miserable to the last hour of my life. . . .

March 17, 1778, 5:40 p.m.

LORD NORTH—

Though your Messenger did not wait for an answer, I could not help just sending this note to express my satisfaction at the first payment of the Loan having been made this day; this with the Majority that will appear in Parliament will I trust put my affairs on a respectable foot; indeed your standing forth at this particular juncture will do you credit for I trust you know me too well to doubt I can ever forget your conduct; indeed if real affection deserves any return you cannot fail exerting yourself on this Occasion for my service.

March 18, 1778, 8:35 a.m.

LORD NORTH—

A Majority in the House of Lords of 64, in the House of Commons of 150, and the first payment of the Loan made; had you the real Duty and Affection for my Person that I know is deep rooted in Your heart, common honesty and that Sense of honour which must reside in the breast of every Man born of a Noble family, would oblige You at this hour to stand firmly to the Aid of Him who thinks he deserves the assistance of every honest Man. Therefore let Thurloe[5] have notice that the Great Seal is ready to be placed in his hands and the Sollicitor that exertion will be used to accomplish whatever is his wish; that done, but not till then, I am open to the plan of Ministry proposed by You on Sunday; for I will never retract any propositions I have assented to, and the Appear-

5. Edward Thurlow, attorney general in the North government, soon to become chancellor.

ance of Parliament Yesterday may render those You had sounded more pliable than before they knew what effect the perfidious conduct of France[6] might have on the minds of Men; but my dear Lord I cannot help urging that I will never agree to the acceptance of the Services of any part of the Opposition but to add strength to Your Administration; it is a desire of going the utmost lengths my feelings will permit, that to give You ease I consent to what gives me infinite pain; but any further, even that consideration cannot make me go, and rather than be shackled by those desperate Men (if the Nation will not stand by Me, which I can never suppose) I will rather see any form of Government introduced into this Island and lose my Crown than wear it as a disgrace. . . .

Lord North to the King, May 7, 1778, 1:00 P.M.

SIR—

. . . The Ministry were violently attacked yesterday upon the departure of Mr. D'Estaign's Squadron,[7] and, indeed, the cry begins to rise so high against us that nothing can prevent the utmost confusion and distress, but a material change in the Ministry. I foretold this moment to your Majesty some time ago, and, indeed, the only blame that can fall upon your Majesty is that you have continued me so long in the Administration, notwithstanding your experience of my insufficiency, and my constant and earnest desire of retreat. But I am culpable, I am afraid, in a very great degree, in not having done what my own knowledge of my defects made it my duty to do. At present, my disgrace is, in a manner, certain, whether I continue in office or leave it. But it is of the utmost importance to prevent the ruin and disgrace of the Country, which must be the consequence of my remaining in the Cabinet, where I never could, nor can decide between different opinions; I have this instant, while I am writing, received the honour of your Majesty's commands; I certainly told your Majesty that I would not resign, but it was in confidence that your Majesty would speedily make an arrangement and dismiss me from your service. Indeed, indeed, Sir, it is too serious; my mind always weak, is now ten times weaker than it was, and I have difficulties ten times greater to encounter than ever I had. If your Majesty does not allow me to retire, you

6. France's treaty of alliance with America.
7. Comte d'Estaing, French vice admiral, whose fleet sailed for America.

and this country are ruin'd; as to myself, I said before, that my disgrace is already compleat, nothing can put me in a worse situation than I am; but your Majesty's affairs are by no means desperate, if they are put into good hands. Your Majesty and this nation may be extricated with honour out of our present difficulties. Let me die disgraced for that I can not now avoid, but let me not go to the grave with the guilt of having been the ruin of my King and Country.

I write this from a calm conviction of the truth of what I say, and of the necessity of attending to it. I never was less agitated in any important moment in my life, and I really deliver it as the best advice that I can offer to my Prince, to whom by allegiance, by duty, by gratitude and every tye I certainly owe the best counsel I can give.

43. Thomas Paine's *Common Sense*
January 10, 1776

SOCIETY IN every state is a blessing, but government even in its best state is but a necessary evil; in its worst state an intolerable one; for when we suffer, or are exposed to the same miseries *by a government*, which we might expect in a country *without government*, our calamity is heightened by reflecting that we furnish the means by which we suffer. Government, like dress, is the badge of lost innocence; the palaces of kings are built on the ruins of the bowers of paradise. For were the impulses of conscience clear, uniform, and irresistibly obeyed, man would need no other lawgiver; but that not being the case, he finds it necessary to surrender up a part of his property to furnish means for the protection of the rest; and this he is induced to do by the same prudence which in every other case, advises him out of two evils to choose the least. Wherefore security being the true design and end of government, it unanswer-

SOURCE: M. D. Conway, ed., *Writings of Thomas Paine* (4 vols., New York, 1894–1896), I, 69, 71–74, 79–82, 84–90, 92–96, 99–101, 120. This excerpt is from Paine's third edition, published February 14, 1776.

ably follows, that whatever *form* thereof appears most likely to insure it to us, with the least expence and greatest benefit, is preferable to all others. . . .

I draw my idea of the form of government from a principle of nature, which no art can overturn, viz. that the more simple any thing is, the less liable it is to be disordered, and the easier repaired when disordered; and with this maxim in view, I offer a few remarks on the so much boasted constitution of England. That it was noble for the dark and slavish times in which it was erected, is granted. When the world was over-run with tyranny, the least remove therefrom was a glorious rescue. But that it is imperfect, subject to convulsions, and incapable of producing what it seems to promise, is easily demonstrated. . . .

I know it is difficult to get over local or long standing prejudices, yet if we will suffer ourselves to examine the component parts of the English constitution, we shall find them to be the base remains of two ancient tyrannies, compounded with some new republican materials.

First. The remains of monarchical tyranny in the person of the king.

Secondly. The remains of aristocratical tyranny in the persons of the peers.

Thirdly. The new republican materials in the persons of the commons, on whose virtue depends the freedom of England.

The two first, by being hereditary, are independent of the people; wherefore in a *constitutional sense* they contribute nothing towards the freedom of the state.

To say that the constitution of England is a *union* of three powers reciprocally *checking* each other, is farcical, either the words have no meaning, or they are flat contradictions.

To say that the commons are a check upon the king, presupposes two things:

First. That the king is not to be trusted without being looked after, or in other words, that a thirst for absolute power is the natural disease of monarchy.

Secondly. That the commons, by being appointed for that purpose, are either wiser or more worthy of confidence than the crown.

But as the same constitution which gives the commons a power to check the king by withholding the supplies gives afterwards the king a power to check the commons by empowering him to reject their other bills; it again supposes that the king is wiser than those whom it has already supposed to be wiser than him. A mere-absurdity.

There is something exceedingly riduculous in the composition of monarchy; it first excludes a man from the means of information, yet empowers him to act in cases where the highest judgment is required. The state of a king shuts him from the world, yet the business of a king requires him to know it thoroughly; wherefore the different parts, by unnaturally opposing and destroying each other, prove the whole character to be absurd and useless.

Some writers have explained the English constitution thus: The king, say they, is one, the people another; the peers are an house in behalf of the king, the commons in behalf of the people. But this hath all the distinctions of an house divided against itself; and though the expressions be pleasantly arranged, yet when examined, they appear idle and ambiguous; and it will always happen, that the nicest construction that words are capable of when applied to the description of something which either cannot exist, or is too incomprehensible to be within the compass of description, will be words of sound only, and tho' they may amuse the ear, they cannot inform the mind, for this explanation includes a previous question, viz. *How came the king by a power which the people are afraid to trust, and always obliged to check?* Such a power could not be the gift of a wise people, neither can any power, which needs checking, be from God; yet the provision, which the constitution makes, supposes such a power to exist.

But the provision is unequal to the task; the means either cannot or will not accomplish the end, and the whole affair is a *felo de se;* for as the greater weight will always carry up the less, and as all the wheels of a machine are put in motion by one, it only remains to know which power in the constitution has the most weight, for that will govern; and tho' the others, or a part of them, may clog, or, as the phrase is, check the rapidity of its motion, yet so long as they cannot stop it, their endeavours will be ineffectual; the first moving power will at last have its way, and what it wants in speed, is supplied by time.

That the crown is this overbearing part in the English constitution, needs not be mentioned, and that it derives its whole consequence merely from being the giver of places and pensions, is self-evident; wherefore, though we have been wise enough to shut and lock a door against absolute monarchy, we at the same time have been foolish enough to put the crown in possession of the key. . . .

To the evil of monarchy we have added that of hereditary succession: and as the first is a degradation and lessening of ourselves, so the second, claimed as a matter of right, is an insult and an imposition on posterity. For all men being originally equals, no one by birth could have a right to set up his own family in perpetual preference to all others for ever, and though himself might deserve *some* decent degree of honours of his contemporaries, yet his descendants might be far too unworthy to inherit them. One of the strongest *natural* proofs of the folly of hereditary right in kings, is, that nature disapproves it, otherwise she would not so frequently turn it into ridicule by giving mankind an *Ass for a Lion*. . . .

England, since the conquest, hath known some few good monarchs, but groaned beneath a much larger number of bad ones; yet no man in his senses can say that their claim under William the Conquerer is a very honourable one. A French bastard landing with an armed banditti, and establishing himself king of England against the consent of the natives, is in plain terms a very paltry rascally original. It certainly hath no divinity in it. However, it is needless to spend much time in exposing the folly of hereditary right; if there are any so weak as to believe it, let them promiscuously worship the ass and the lion, and welcome. I shall neither copy their humility, nor disturb their devotion. . . .

But it is not so much the absurdity as the evil of hereditary succession which concerns mankind. Did it ensure a race of good and wise men, it would have the seal of divine authority, but as it opens a door to the *foolish*, the *wicked*, and the *improper*, it hath in it the nature of oppression. Men who look upon themselves born to reign, and others to obey, soon grow insolent; selected from the rest of mankind their minds are early poisoned by importance; and the world they act in differs so materially from the world at large, that they have but little opportunity of knowing its true interests, and when they succeed to the government, are frequently the most ignorant and unfit of any throughout the dominions. . . .

The most plausible plea which hath ever been offered in favour of hereditary succession, is, that it preserves a nation from civil wars; and were this true, it would be weighty; whereas, it is the most barefaced falsity ever imposed upon mankind. The whole history of England disowns the fact. Thirty kings and two minors have reigned in that distracted kingdom since the conquest, in which time there have been (including the revolution) no less than eight civil wars and nineteen rebellions. Wherefore instead of making for peace, it makes against it, and destroys the very foundation it seems to stand on. . . .

Volumes have been written on the subject of the struggle between England and America. Men of all ranks have embarked in the controversy, from different motives, and with various designs; but all have been ineffectual, and the period of debate is closed. Arms as the last resource decide the contest; the appeal was the choice of the King, and the Continent has accepted the challenge. . . .

The Sun never shined on a cause of greater worth. 'Tis not the affair of a City, a County, a Province, or a Kingdom; but of a Continent—of at least one eighth part of the habitable Globe. 'Tis not the concern of a day, a year, or an age; posterity are virtually involved in the contest, and will be more or less affected even to the end of time by the proceedings now. Now is the seed time of Continental union, faith, and honour. The least fracture now, will be like a name engraved with the point of a pin on the tender rind of a young oak; the wound will enlarge with the tree, and posterity read it in full grown characters.

By referring the matter from argument to arms, a new era for politics is struck—a new method of thinking hath arisen. All plans, proposals, etc. prior to the 19th of April, *i.e.* to the commencement of hostilities, are like the almanacks of the last year; which tho' proper then, are superceded and useless now. Whatever was advanced by the advocates on either side of the question then, terminated in one and the same point, viz. a union with Great Britain; the only difference between the parties was the method of effecting it; the one proposing force, the other friendship; but it hath so far happened that the first hath failed, and the second hath withdrawn her influence.

As much hath been said of the advantages of reconciliation, which like an agreeable dream, hath passed away and left us as we were, it is but right, that we should examine the contrary side of the argument, and enquire into some of the many material injuries which these Colonies sustain, and always will sustain, by being connected with and dependant on Great Britain. To examine that connection and dependance, on the principles of nature and common sense, to see what we have to trust to if separated, and what we are to expect if dependant.

I have heard it asserted by some, that as America hath flourished under her former connection with Great Britain, the same connection is necessary towards her future happiness, and will always have the same effect—Nothing can be more fallacious than this kind of argument:—we may as well assert that because a child has thrived upon milk, that it is never to have meat, or that the first twenty years of our lives is to become a precedent for the next twenty. But even this is admitting more than is true, for I answer, roundly, that America would have flourished as much, and probably much more had no European power taken any notice of her. The commerce by which she hath enriched herself are the necessaries of life, and will always have a market while eating is the custom of Europe.

But she has protected us say some. That she hath engrossed us is true, and defended the Continent at our expense as well as her own is admitted; and she would have defended Turkey from the same motive, viz. for the sake of trade and dominion.

Alas! we have been long led away by ancient prejudices and made large sacrifices to superstition. We have boasted the protection of Great Britain, without considering, that her motive was *interest* not *attachment*; and that she did not protect us from *our enemies* on *our account*, but from *her enemies* on *her own account*, from those who had no quarrel with us on any *other account*, and who will always be our enemies on the *same account*. Let Britain waive her pretensions to the continent, or the continent throw off the dependance, and we should be at peace with France and Spain were they at war with Britain. The miseries of Hanover's last war ought to warn us against connections.

It hath lately been asserted in parliament, that the colonies have no relation to each other but through the Parent Country, i.e. that Pennsylvania and the Jerseys, and so on for the rest, are sister Colonies by the way of England; this is certainly a very roundabout way of proving relationship, but it is the nearest and only true way of proving enemy-ship, if I may so call it. France and Spain never were, nor perhaps ever will be our enemies as *Americans*, but as our being the *subjects of Great Britain*.

But Britain is the parent country say some. Then the more shame upon her conduct. Even brutes do not devour their young, nor savages make war upon their families; wherefore, the assertion if true, turns to her reproach; but it happens not to be true, or only partly so, and the phrase, *parent* or *mother country*, hath been jesuitically adopted by the King and his parasites, with a low papistical design of gaining an unfair bias on the credulous weakness of our minds. Europe and not England is the parent country of America. This new World hath been the asylum for the persecuted lovers of civil and religious liberty from *every part* of Europe. Hither have they fled, not from the tender embraces of the mother, but from the cruelty of the monster; and it is so far true of England, that the same tyranny which drove the first emigrants from home, pursues their descendants still.

In this extensive quarter of the Globe, we forget the narrow limits of three hundred and sixty miles (the extent of England) and carry our friendship on a larger scale; we claim brotherhood with every European Christian, and triumph in the generosity of the sentiment.

It is pleasant to observe by what regular gradations we surmount the force of local prejudice as we enlarge our acquaintance with the World. A man born in any town in England divided into parishes, will naturally associate most with his fellow parishioners (because their intersts in many cases will be common) and distinguish him by the name of *neighbour*: if he meet him but a few miles from home, he drops the narrow idea of a street, and salutes him by the name of a *townsman*; if he travel out of the county and meet him in any other, he forgets the minor divisions of street and town, and calls him *countryman*, i.e. *countryman*: but if in their foreign excursions they should associate in France, or any other part of Europe, their local remembrance would be enlarged into that of *Englishmen*. And by a just parity of reasoning, all Europeans meeting in America, or any other quarter of the Globe, are *countrymen*; for England, Holland, Germany, or Sweden, when compared with the whole, stand in the same places on the larger scale, which the divisions of street, town, and county do on the smaller ones; distinctions too limited for Continental minds. Not one third of the inhabitants, even of this province [Pennsylvania], are of English descent. Wherefore, I reprobate the phrase of parent or mother country applied to England only, as being false, selfish, narrow and ungenerous.

But admitting that we were all of English descent, what does it amount to? Nothing. Britain, being now an open enemy, extinguishes every other name and title: and to say that reconciliation is our duty, is truly farcical. The first king of England, of the present line (William the Conqueror) was a Frenchman, and half the Peers of England are descendants from the same country; wherefore, by the same method of reasoning, England ought to be governed by France. . . .

I challenge the warmest advocate for reconciliation, to shew a single advantage that this Continent can reap by being connected with Great Britain. I repeat the challenge, not a single advantage is derived. Our corn will fetch its price in any market in Europe, and our imported goods must be paid for, buy them where we will.

But the injuries and disadvantages which we sustain by that connection are without number, and our duty to mankind at large, as well as to ourselves, instruct us to renounce the alliance: Because, any submission to, or dependance on Great Britain, tends directly to involve this Continent in European wars and quarrels.
. . . Europe is too thickly planted with Kingdoms, to be long at peace, and whenever a war breaks out between England and any foreign power, the trade of America goes to ruin, *because of her connection with Britain.* . . . Every thing that is right or reasonable pleads for separation. The blood of the slain, the weeping voice of nature cries, 'TIS TIME TO PART. Even the distance at which the Almighty hath placed England and America, is a strong and natural proof, that the authority of the one over the other, was never the design of Heaven. . . .

Though I would carefully avoid giving unnecessary offence, yet I am inclined to believe that all those who espouse the doctrine of reconciliation, may be included within the following descriptions. Interested men, who are not to be trusted, weak men who *cannot see,* prejudiced men who *will not see,* and a certain set of moderate men who think better of the European world than it deserves; and this last class, by an ill-judged deliberation, will be the cause of more calamities to this continent, than all the other three. . . .

I am not induced by motives of pride, party or resentment to espouse the doctrine of separation and independence; I am clearly, positively, and conscientiously persuaded that 'tis the true interest of this continent to be so; that every thing short of that is mere patchwork, that it can afford no lasting felicity,—that it is leaving the sword to our children, and shrinking back at a time, when a little more, a little further, would have rendered this continent the glory of the earth.

As Britain hath not manifested the least inclination towards a compromise, we may be assured that no terms can be obtained worthy the acceptance of the continent, or any ways equal to the expense of blood and treasure we have been already put to. . . .

But admitting that matters were now made up, what would be the event? I answer, the ruin of the Continent. And that for several reasons.

First.—The powers of governing still remaining in the hands of the king, he will have a negative over the whole legislation of this Continent: And as he hath shewn himself such an inveterate enemy to liberty, and discovered such a thirst for arbitrary power, is he, or is he not, a proper man to say to these Colonies, *You shall make no laws but what I please!* ? . . . To bring the matter to one point, is the power who is jealous of our prosperity, a proper power to govern us? Whoever says *No* to this question is an *Independent,* for independency means no more than whether we shall make our own laws, or, whether the King the greatest enemy this Continent hath, or can have, shall tell us, *there shall be no laws but such as I like.* . . . And in order to shew that reconciliation now is a dangerous doctrine, I affirm, *that it would be policy in the King at this time, to repeal the acts for the sake of reinstating himself in the government of the provinces;* In order that HE MAY ACCOMPLISH BY CRAFT AND SUBTLETY, IN THE LONG RUN, WHAT HE CANNOT DO BY FORCE AND VIOLENCE IN THE SHORT ONE. Reconciliation and ruin are nearly related.

Secondly.—That as even the best terms which we can expect to obtain, can amount to no more than a temporary expedient, or a kind of government by guardianship, which can last no longer than till the Colonies come of age, so the general face and state of things in the interim will be unsettled and unpromising: Emigrants of property will not choose to come to a country whose form of government hangs but by a thread, and who is every day tottering on the brink of commotion and disturbance; And numbers of the present inhabitants would lay hold of the interval to dispose of their effects, and quit the Continent.

But the most powerful of all arguments is, that nothing but independance, *i.e.* a continental form of government, can keep the peace of the Continent, and preserve it inviolate from civil wars. I dread the event of a reconciliation with Britain now, as it is more than probable, that it will be followed by a revolt some where or other, the consequences of which may be far more fatal than all the malice of Britain. . . .

Where there are no distinctions, there can be no superiority; perfect equality affords no temptation. The Republics of Europe are all, (and we may say always) in peace. Holland and Switzerland, are without wars, foreign or domestic: Monarchical governments, it is true, are never long at rest; the crown itself is a temptation to enterprising ruffians at home; and that degree of pride and insolence ever attendant on regal authority, swells into a rupture with foreign powers in instances, where a republican government by being formed on more natural principles, would negociate the mistake.

If there is any true cause for fear respecting independance, it is because no plan is yet laid down. Men do not see their way out—Wherefore, as an opening into that business I offer the following hints; at the same time modestly affirming, that I have no other opinion of them myself, than that they may be the means of giving rise to something better. Could the straggling thoughts of individuals be collected, they would frequently form materials for wise and able men to improve into useful matter.

Let the assemblies be annual with a president only. The representation more equal. Their business wholly domestic, and subject to the authority of a Continental Congress.

Let each Colony be divided into six, eight or ten convenient districts, each district to send a proper number of Delegates to Congress, so that each Colony send at least thirty. The whole number in Congress will be at least 390. Each congress to sit and to choose a president by the following method. When the Delegates are met, let a Colony be taken from the whole thirteen Colonies by lot, after which let the Congress choose (by ballot) a president from out of the Delegates of that province. In the next Congress let a Colony be taken by lot from twelve only, omitting that Colony from which the president was taken in the former Congress, and so proceeding on till the whole thirteen shall have had their proper rotation. And in order that nothing may pass into a law but what is satisfactorily just, not less than three fifths of the Congress to be called a majority—He that will promote discord under a government so equally formed as this, would have joined Lucifer in his revolt.

But as there is a peculiar delicacy from whom, or in what manner this business must first arise, and as it seems most agreeable and consistent, that it should come from some intermediate body between the governed and the governors, that is, between the Congress and the People Let a CONTINENTAL CONFERENCE be held in the following manner, and for the following purpose.

A Committee of twenty–six members of congress, viz. Two for each Colony. Two Members from each House of Assembly, or Provincial convention; and five Representatives of the people at large, to be chosen in the capital city or town of each Province, for, and in behalf of the whole Province, by as many qualified voters as shall think proper to attend from all parts of the Province for that purpose: or if more convenient, the Representatives may be chosen in two or three of the most populous parts thereof. In this CONFERENCE thus assembled, will be united the two grand principles of business, *knowledge* and *power*. The members of Congress, Assemblies, or Conventions, by having had experience in national concerns, will be able and useful counsellors, and the whole, being impowered by the people, will have a truly legal authority.

The conferring members being met, let their business be to frame a CONTINENTAL CHARTER, or Charter of the United Colonies; (answering, to what is called the Magna Charta of England) fixing the number and manner of choosing Members of Congress, Members of Assembly, with their date of sitting; and drawing the line of business and jurisdiction between them: Always remembering, that our strength and happiness is Continental, not Provincial. Securing freedom and property to all men, and above all things, the free exercise of religion, according to the dictates of conscience; with such other matter as is necessary for a charter to contain. Immediately after which, the said conference to dissolve, and the bodies which shall be chosen conformable to the said charter, to be the Legislators and Governors of this Continent, for the time being: Whose peace and happiness, may God preserve. AMEN.

Should any body of men be hereafter delegated for this or some similar purpose, I offer them the following extracts from that wise observer on Governments. Dragonetti. "The science" says he "of the Politician consists in fixing the true point of happiness and freedom. Those men would deserve the gratitude of ages, who should discover a mode of government that contained the greatest sum of individual happiness, with the least national expense."

But where, say some, is the King of America? I'll tell you,

Friend, he reigns above, and doth not make havoc of mankind like the Royal Brute of Great Britain. Yet that we may not appear to be defective even in earthly honours, let a day be solemnly set apart for proclaiming the Charter; let it be brought forth placed on the Divine Law, the word of God; let a crown be placed thereon, by which the world may know, that so far as we approve of monarchy, that in America THE LAW IS KING. For as in absolute governments the King is law, so in free countries the law *ought* to be King; and there ought to be no other. But lest any ill use should afterwards arise, let the Crown at the conclusion of the ceremony be demolished, and scattered among the People whose right it is. . . .

O ye that love mankind! Ye that dare oppose not only the tyranny, but the tyrant, stand forth! Every spot of the old world is over-run with oppression. Freedom hath been hunted round the globe. Asia and Africa have long expelled her.—Europe regards her like a stranger, and England hath given her warning to depart. O! receive the fugitive, and prepare in time an asylum for mankind. . . .

On these grounds I rest the matter. And as no offer hath yet been made to refute the doctrine contained in the former editions of this pamphlet, it is a negative proof that either the doctrine cannot be refuted, or that the party in favour of it are too numerous to be opposed. Wherefore, instead of gazing at each other, with suspicious or doubtful curiosity, let each of us hold out to his neighbour the hearty hand of friendship, and united in drawing a line, which, like an act of oblivion, shall bury in forgetfulness every former dissension. Let the names of whig and tory be extinct; and let none other be heard among us, than those of a *good citizen, an open and resolute friend,* and a *virtuous supporter* of the RIGHTS OF MANKIND, and of the FREE AND INDEPENDENT STATES OF AMERICA.

44. Declaration of Independence
July 4, 1776

WHEN IN the Course of human events, it becomes necessary for one people to dissolve the political bands which have connected them with another, and to assume among the powers of the earth, the separate and equal station to which the Laws of Nature and of Nature's God entitle them, a decent respect to the opinions of mankind requires that they should declare the causes which impel them to the separation.

We hold these truths to be self-evident, that all men are created equal, that they are endowed by their Creator with certain unalienable Rights, that among these are Life, Liberty and the pursuit of Happiness.——That to secure these rights, Governments are instituted among Men, deriving their just powers from the consent of the governed,——That whenever any Form of Government becomes destructive of these ends, it is the Right of the People to alter or abolish it, and to institute new Government, laying its foundation on such principles and organizing its powers in such form, as to them shall seem most likely to effect their Safety and Happiness. Prudence, indeed, will dictate that Governments long established should not be changed for light and transient causes; and accordingly all experience hath shewn, that mankind are more disposed to suffer, while evils are sufferable, than to right themselves by abolishing the forms to which they are accustomed. But when a long train of abuses and usurpations, pursuing invariably the same Object evinces a design to reduce them under absolute Despotism, it is their right, it is their duty, to throw off such Government, and to provide new Guards for their future security.—— Such has been the patient sufferance of these Colonies; and such is now the necessity which constrains them to alter their former Systems of Government. The history of the present King of Great Britain is a history of repeated injuries and usurpations, all having in direct object the establishment of an absolute Tyranny over these States. To prove this, let Facts be submitted to a candid world.

He has refused his Assent to laws, the most wholesome and necessary for the public good.

He has forbidden his Governors to pass Laws of immediate and pressing importance, unless suspended in their operation till his Assent should be obtained; and when so suspended, he has utterly neglected to attend to them.

He has refused to pass other Laws for the accommodation of large districts of people, unless those people would relinquish the right of Representation in the Legislature, a right inestimable to them and formidable to tyrants only.

He has called together legislative bodies at places unusual, un-comfortable, and distant from the depository of their public Rec-ords, for the sole purpose of fatiguing them into compliance with his measures.

He has dissolved Representative Houses repeatedly, for opposing with manly firmness his invasions on the rights of the people.

He has refused for a long time, after such dissolutions, to cause others to be elected; whereby the Legislative powers, incapable of Annihilation, have returned to the People at large for their exer-cise; the State remaining in the mean time exposed to all the dangers of invasion from without, and convulsions within.

He has endeavoured to prevent the population of these States; for that purpose obstructing the Laws for Naturalization of For-eigners; refusing to pass others to encourage their migration hither, and raising the conditions of new Appropriations of Lands.

He has obstructed the Administration of Justice, by refusing his Assent to Laws for establishing Judiciary powers.

He has made Judges dependent on his Will alone, for the tenure of their offices, and the amount and payment of their salaries.

He has erected a multitude of New Offices, and sent hither swarms of Officers to harrass our people, and eat out their sub-stance.

He has kept among us, in times of peace, Standing Armies with-out the Consent of our legislatures.

He has affected to render the Military independent of and superior to the Civil power.

He has combined with others to subject us to a jurisdiction for-eign to our constitution, and unacknowledged by our laws; giving his Assent to their Acts of pretended Legislation:——

For quartering large bodies of armed troops among us:——

For protecting them, by a mock Trial, from punishment for any Murders which they should commit on the Inhabitants of these States:——

For cutting off our Trade with all parts of the world:——

For imposing Taxes on us without our Consent:——

For depriving us in many cases of the benefits of Trial by Jury:

For transporting us beyond Seas to be tried for pretended offences:——

For abolishing the free System of English Laws in a neighbour-ing Province, establishing therein an Arbitrary government, and enlarging its Boundaries so as to render it at once an example and fit instrument for introducing the same absolute rule into these Colonies:——

For taking away our Charters, abolishing our most valuable Laws, and altering fundamentally the Forms of our Governments:

For suspending our own Legislatures, and declaring themselves invested with power to legislate for us in all cases whatsoever.

He has abdicated Government here, by declaring us out of his Protection and waging War against us.

He has plundered our seas, ravaged our Coasts, burnt our towns, and destroyed the Lives of our people.

He is at this time transporting large Armies of foreign Mercenaries to compleat the works of death, desolation and tyranny, already begun with circumstances of Cruelty and perfidy scarcely paralleled in the most barbarous ages, and totally unworthy the Head of a civilized nation.

He has constrained our fellow Citizens taken Captive on the high Seas to bear Arms against their Country, to become the executioners of their friends and Brethren, or to fall themselves by their Hands.

He has excited domestic insurrections amongst us, and has endeavoured to bring on the inhabitants of our frontiers, the merciless Indian Savages, whose known rule of warfare, is an undistinguished destruction of all ages, sexes and conditions.

In every stage of these Oppressions We have Petitioned for Redress in the most humble terms: Our repeated Petitions have been answered only by repeated injury. A Prince, whose character is thus marked by every act which may define a Tyrant, is unfit to be the ruler of a free people.

Nor have We been wanting in attention to our British brethren. We have warned them from time to time of attempts by their legislature to extend an unwarrantable jurisdiction over us. We have reminded them of the circumstances of our emigration and settlement here. We have appealed to their native justice and magnanimity, and we have conjured them by the ties of our common kindred to disavow these usurpations, which, would inevitably interrupt our connections and correspondence. They too have been deaf to the voice of justice and of consanguinity. We must, therefore, acquiesce in the necessity, which denounces our separation, and hold them, as we hold the rest of mankind, Enemies in War, in Peace Friends.

We, therefore, the Representatives of the *United States of Amer-*

ica, in General Congress, Assembled, appealing to the Supreme Judge of the world for the rectitude of our intentions, do, in the Name, and by the authority of the good People of these Colonies, solemnly publish and declare, That these United Colonies are, and of Right ought to be *Free and Independent States*; that they are Absolved from all Allegiance to the British Crown, and that all political connection between them and the State of Great Britain, is and ought to be totaly dissolved; and that as Free and Independent States, they have full Power to levy War, conclude Peace, contract Alliances, establish Commerce, and to do all other Acts and Things which Independent States may of right do.

And for the support of this Declaration, with a firm reliance on the protection of divine Providence, we mutually pledge to each other our Lives, our Fortunes, and our sacred Honor.

XI

The Rise of
American Nationalism

A significant element in the movement for independence was a burgeoning nationalism. Up to the middle of the eighteenth century most
colonists felt strongly attached to their respective provinces, although
the Seven Year's War served to intensify their loyalty to the Empire. Benjamin Franklin was the foremost colonial advocate for the
Empire; he had devised a plan of action in 1754 (the Albany Plan of
Union), and as late as 1767 hoped for the representation in Parliament
of all parts of the Empire on an equitable basis, while he also visualized
the future greatness of America. A signally perceptive expression of the
spirit of nationalism evoked by the Revolutionary struggle was penned by
Michel-Guillaume Jean de Crèvecoeur, a native of France who had taken
up farming in Orange County, New York. There he wrote his classic
Letters from an American Farmer (1782), wherein he depicted the
American as a new man, the product of a new world.

45. Benjamin Franklin's Vision
of America: Letter to Lord Kames[1]
April 11, 1767

IT BECOMES a matter of great importance that clear ideas should be
formed on solid principles, both in Britain and America, of the true
political relation between them, and the mutual duties belonging
to that relation. Till this is done, they will be often jarring. I know
none whose knowledge, sagacity and impartiality qualify him so

SOURCE: John Bigelow, ed., The Works of Benjamin Franklin
(12 vols., New York, 1904–1905), IV, 280–286.

1. A Scottish jurist who was a close friend of Franklin's and one of his intimate correspondents.

thoroughly for such a service, as yours do you. I wish therefore you would consider it. You may thereby be the happy instrument of great good to the nation, and of preventing much mischief and bloodshed. I am fully persuaded with you, that a *Consolidating Union*, by a fair and equal representation of all the parts of this empire in Parliament, is the only firm basis on which its political grandeur and prosperity can be founded. Ireland once wished it, but now rejects it. The time has been, when the colonies might have been pleased with it; they are now *indifferent* about it; and if it is much longer delayed, they too will *refuse* it. But the pride of this people cannot bear the thought of it, and therefore it will be delayed. Every man in England seems to consider himself as a piece of a sovereign over America; seems to jostle himself into the throne with the King, and talks of *our subjects in the Colonies*. The Parliament cannot well and wisely make laws suited to the Colonies, without being properly and truly informed of their circumstances, abilities, temper, &c. This it cannot be, without representatives from thence: and yet it is fond of this power, and averse to the only means of acquiring the necessary knowledge for exercising it; which is desiring to be *omnipotent*, without being *omniscient*.

I have mentioned that the contest is likely to be revived. It is on this occasion. In the same session with the stamp act, an act was passed to regulate the quartering of soldiers in America; when the bill was first brought in, it contained a clause, empowering the officers to quarter their soldiers in private houses: this we warmly opposed, and got it omitted. The bill passed, however, with a clause, that empty houses, barns, &c., should be hired for them, and that the respective provinces where they were should pay the expence and furnish firing, bedding, drink, and some other articles to the soldiers *gratis*. There is no way for any province to do this, but by the Assembly's making a law to raise the money. The Pennsylvanian Assembly has made such a law: the New York Assembly has refused to do it: and now all the talk here is of sending a force to compel them.

The reasons given by the Assembly to the Governor, for the refusal, are, that they understand the act to mean the furnishing such things to soldiers, only while on their march through the country, and not to great bodies of soldiers, to be fixt as at present, in the province; the burthen in the latter case being greater than the inhabitants can bear: That it would put it in the power of the Captain-General to oppress the province at pleasure, &c. But there is supposed to be another reason at bottom, which they intimate, though they do not plainly express it; to wit, that it is of the nature of an *internal tax* laid on them by Parliament, which has no right so to do. Their refusal is here called *Rebellion*, and punishment is thought of.

Now waving that point of right, and supposing the Legislatures in America subordinate to the Legislature of Great Britain, one might conceive, I think, a power in the superior Legislature to forbid the inferior Legislatures making particular laws; but to enjoin it to make a particular law contrary to its own judgment, seems improper; an Assembly or Parliament not being an *executive* officer of Government, whose duty it is, in law-making, to obey orders, but a *deliberative* body, who are to consider what comes before them, its propriety, practicability, or possibility, and to determine accordingly: The very nature of a Parliament seems to be destroyed, by supposing it may be bound, and compelled by a law of a superior Parliament, to make a law contrary to its own judgment.

Indeed, the act of Parliament in question has not, as in other acts, when a duty is enjoined, directed a penalty on neglect or refusal, and a mode of recovering that penalty. It seems, therefore, to the people in America as a mere requisition, which they are at liberty to comply with or not, as it may suit or not suit the different circumstances of different provinces. Pennsylvania has therefore voluntarily complied. New York, as I said before, has refused. The Ministry that made the act, and all their adherents, call for vengeance. The present Ministry are perplext, and the measures they will finally take on the occasion, are yet unknown. But sure I am, that, if *Force* is used, great mischief will ensue; the affections of the people of America to this country will be alienated; your commerce will be diminished; and a total separation of interests be the final consequence.

It is a common, but mistaken notion here, that the Colonies were planted at the expence of Parliament, and that therefore the Parliament has a right to tax them, &c. The truth is, they were planted at the expence of private adventurers, who went over there to settle, with leave of the King, given by charter. On receiving this leave, and those charters, the adventurers voluntarily engaged to remain the King's subjects, though in a foreign country; a country which had not been conquered by either King or Parliament, but was possessed by a free people.

When our planters arrived, they purchased the lands of the natives, without putting King or Parliament to any expence. Parliament had no hand in their settlement, was never so much as consulted about their constitution, and took no kind of notice of them, till many years after they were established. I except only the two modern Colonies, or rather attempts to make Colonies, (for they succeed but poorly, and as yet hardly deserve the name of Colonies), I mean Georgia and Nova Scotia, which have hitherto been little better than Parliamentary jobs. Thus all the colonies acknowledge the King as their sovereign; his Governors there represent his person: Laws are made by their Assemblies or little Parliaments, with the Governor's assent, subject still to the King's pleasure to confirm or annul them: Suits arising in the Colonies, and differences between Colony and Colony, are determined by the King in Council. In this view, they seem so many separate little states, subject to the same Prince. The *sovereignty of the* King is therefore easily understood. But nothing is more common here than to talk of the *sovereignty* of PARLIAMENT, and the *sovereignty* of THIS NATION over the Colonies; a kind of sovereignty, the idea of which is not so clear, nor does it clearly appear on what foundation it is established. On the other hand, it seems necessary for the common good of the empire, that a power be lodged somewhere, to regulate its general commerce: this can be placed nowhere so properly as in the Parliament of Great Britain; and therefore, though that power has in some instances been executed with great partiality to Britain, and prejudice to the Colonies, they have nevertheless always submitted to it. Custom-houses are established in all of them, by virtue of laws made here, and the duties constantly paid, except by a few smugglers, such as are here and in all countries; but internal taxes laid on them by Parliament, are still and ever will be objected to, for the reasons that you will see in the mentioned Examination.

Upon the whole, I have lived so great a part of my life in Britain, and have formed so many friendships in it, that I love it, and sincerely wish it prosperity; and therefore wish to see that Union, on which alone I think it can be secured and established. As to America, the advantages of such a union to her are not so apparent.

She may suffer at present under the arbitrary power of this country; she may suffer for a while in a separation from it; but these are temporary evils that she will outgrow. Scotland and Ireland are differently circumstanced. Confined by the sea, they can scarcely increase in numbers, wealth and strength, so as to overbalance England. But America, an immense territory, favoured by Nature with all advantages of climate, soil, great navigable rivers, and lakes, &c. must become a great country, populous and mighty; and will, in a less time than is generally conceived, be able to shake off any shackles that may be imposed on her, and perhaps place them on the imposers. In the mean time, every act of oppression will sour their tempers, lessen greatly, if not annihilate the profits of your commerce with them, and hasten their final revolt; for the seeds of liberty are universally found there, and nothing can eradicate them. And yet, there remains among that people, so much respect, veneration and affection for Britain, that, if cultivated prudently, with kind usage, and tenderness for their privileges, they might be easily governed still for ages, without force, or any considerable expence. But I do not see here a sufficient quantity of the wisdom, that is necessary to produce such a conduct, and I lament the want of it. . . .

46. American Character:
Michel-Guillaume Jean de Crèvecoeur,
Letters from an American Farmer
1782

What Is an American?

I wish I could be acquainted with the feelings and thoughts which must agitate the heart and present themselves to the mind of an enlightened Englishman, when he first lands on this continent. He must greatly rejoice that he lived at a time to see this

SOURCE: Michel-Guillaume Jean de Crèvecoeur, *Letters from an American Farmer* (London, 1782, reprinted from the original edition New York, 1904), 48–91, *passim*.

fair country discovered and settled. He must necessarily feel a share of national pride when he views the chain of settlements which embellishes these extended shores. When he says to himself, this is the work of my countrymen, who, when convulsed by factions, afflicted by a variety of miseries and wants, restless and impatient, took refuge here. They brought along with them their national genius, to which they principally owe what liberty they enjoy, and what substance they possess. Here he sees the industry of his native country, displayed in a new manner, and traces in their works the embryos of all the arts, sciences, and ingenuity which flourish in Europe. Here he beholds fair cities, substantial villages, extensive fields, an immense country filled with decent houses, good roads, orchards, meadows, and bridges, where an hundred years ago all was wild, woody, and uncultivated!

What a train of pleasing ideas this fair spectacle must suggest! It is a prospect which must inspire a good citizen with the most heartfelt pleasure. The difficulty consists in the manner of viewing so extensive a scene. He is arrived on a new continent; a modern society offers itself to his contemplation, different from what he had hitherto seen. It is not composed, as in Europe, of great lords who possess everything, and of a herd of people who have nothing. Here are no aristocratical families, no courts, no kings, no bishops, no ecclesiastical dominion, no invisible power giving to a few a very visible one; no great manufacturers employing thousands, no great refinements of luxury. The rich and the poor are not so far removed from each other as they are in Europe.

Some few towns excepted, we are all tillers of the earth, from Nova Scotia to West Florida. We are a people of cultivators, scattered over an immense territory, communicating with each other by means of good roads and navigable rivers, united by the silken bands of mild government, all respecting the laws without dreading their power, because they are equitable. We are all animated with the spirit of industry, which is unfettered and unrestrained, because each person works for himself. If he travels through our rural districts, he views not the hostile castle, and the haughty mansion, contrasted with the clay-built hut and miserable cabin, where cattle and men help to keep each other warm and dwell in meanness, smoke, and indigence. A pleasing uniformity of decent competence appears throughout our habitations. The meanest of our log-houses is a dry and comfortable habitation. Lawyer or merchant are the fairest titles our towns afford; that of a farmer is the only appellation of the rural inhabitants of our country. It must take some time ere he can reconcile himself to our dictionary, which is but short in words of dignity and names of honor. There, on a Sunday, he sees a congregation of respectable farmers and their wives, all clad in neat homespun, well mounted, or riding in their own humble waggons. There is not among them an esquire, saving the unlettered magistrate. There he sees a parson as simple as his flock, a farmer who does not riot on the labor of others. We have no princes for whom we toil, starve, and bleed. We are the most perfect society now existing in the world. Here man is free as he ought to be; nor is this pleasing quality so transitory as many others are. Many ages will not see the shores of our great lakes replenished with inland nations, nor the unknown bounds of North America entirely peopled. Who can tell how far it extends? Who can tell the millions of men whom it will feed and contain? for no European foot has as yet travelled half the extent of this mighty continent!

The next wish of this traveller will be to know whence came these people? They are a mixture of English, Scotch, Irish, French, Dutch, Germans, and Swedes. From this promiscuous breed, that race now called Americans have arisen. The eastern provinces must indeed be excepted, as being the unmixed descendants of Englishmen. I have heard many wish that they had been more intermixed also. For my part, I am no wisher; and think it much better as it has happened. They exhibit a most conspicuous figure in this great and variegated picture. They too enter for a great share in the pleasing perspective displayed in these thirteen provinces. I know it is fashionable to reflect on them; but I respect them for what they have done; for the accuracy and wisdom with which they have settled their territory; for the decency of their manners; for their early love of letters; their ancient college, the first in this hemisphere; for their industry, which to me, who am but a farmer, is the criterion of every thing. There never was a people, situated as they are, who, with so ungrateful a soil, have done more in so short a time. Do you think that the monarchical ingredients which are more prevalent in other governments have purged them from all foul stains? Their histories assert the contrary.

In this great American asylum the poor of Europe have by some means met together, and in consequence of various causes. To what purpose should they ask one another, what countrymen they are? Alas, two thirds of them had no country. Can a wretch who wanders about, who works and starves, whose life is a continual scene of sore affliction or pinching penury, can that man call England or any other kingdom his country? A country that had no bread for him, whose fields procured him no harvest, who met with nothing but the frowns of the rich, the severity of the laws, with jails and punishments; who owned not a single foot of the extensive surface of this planet? No! Urged by a variety of motives, here they came. Every thing has tended to regenerate them; new laws, a new mode of living, a new social system; here they are become men. In Europe they were as so many useless plants, wanting vegetative mould and refreshing showers. They withered, and were mowed down by want, hunger, and war. But now, by the power of transplantation, like all other plants, they have taken root and flourished! Formerly they were not numbered in any civil lists of their country, except in those of the poor. Here they rank as citizens. By what invisible power has this surprising metamorphosis been performed? By that of the laws and that of their industry. The laws, the indulgent laws, protect them as they arrive, stamping on them the symbol of adoption. They receive ample rewards for their labors. These accumulated rewards procure them lands. Those lands confer on them the title of freeman; and to that title every benefit is affixed which men can possibly require. This is the great operation daily performed by our laws.

From whence proceed these laws? From our government. Whence that government? It is derived from the original genius and strong desire of the people, ratified and confirmed by the crown. This is the great chain which links us all, this is the picture which every province exhibits, Nova Scotia excepted. There the crown has done all. Either there were no people who had genius, or it was not much attended to. The consequence is that the province is very thinly inhabited indeed. The power of the crown, in conjunction with the musketos, has prevented men from settling there. Yet some parts of it flourished once, and it contained a mild harmless set of people. But for the fault of a few leaders the whole were banished. The greatest political error the crown ever committed in America was to cut off men from a country which wanted nothing but men.

What attachment can a poor European emigrant have for a

country where he had nothing? The knowledge of the language, the love of a few kindred as poor as himself, were the only cords that tied him. His country is now that which gives him land, bread, patriotism, and consequence. *Ubi panis ibi patria*,[1] is the motto of all emigrants. What, then is the American, this new man? He is either an European, or the descendant of an European. Hence that strange mixture of blood, which you will find in no other country. I could point out to you a family, whose grandfather was an Englishman, whose wife was Dutch, whose son married a French woman, and whose present four sons have now four wives of different nations. He is an American, who, leaving behind all his ancient prejudices and manners, receives new ones from the new mode of life he has embraced, the new government he obeys, and the new rank he holds. He becomes an American by being received in the broad lap of our great *Alma Mater*.

Here individuals of all nations are melted into a new race of men, whose labors and posterity will one day cause great change in the world. Americans are the western pilgrims, who are carrying along with them that great mass of arts, sciences, vigor, and industry, which began long since in the east. They will finish the great circle. The Americans were once scattered all over Europe. Here they are incorporated into one of the finest systems of population which has ever appeared, and which will hereafter become distinct by the power of the different climates they inhabit. The American ought, therefore, to love this country much better than that wherein either he or his forefathers were born. Here the rewards of his industry follow with equal steps the progress of his labor. His labor is founded on the basis of nature, *self-interest*. Can it want a stronger allurement? Wives and children, who before in vain demanded of him a morsel of bread, now, fat and frolicsome, gladly help their father to clear those fields whence exuberant crops are to arise to feed and to clothe them all; without any part being claimed, either by a despotic prince, a rich abbot, or a mighty lord. Here religion demands but little of him; a small voluntary salary to the minister and gratitude to God. Can he refuse these? The American is a new man, who acts upon new principles. He must therefore entertain new ideas and form new opinions. From involuntary idleness, servile dependence, penury, and useless labor, he has

1. Where my bread is earned, there is my country.

passed to toils of a very different nature, rewarded by ample substance.—This is an American. . . .

He who would wish to see America in its proper light and have a true idea of its feeble beginnings and barbarous rudiments, must visit our extended line of frontiers where the last settlers dwell, and where he may see the first labors of settlement, the mode of clearing the earth, in all their different appearances; where men are wholly left dependent on their native tempers, and on the spur of uncertain industry, which often fails, when not sanctified by the efficacy of a few moral rules. There, remote from the power of example, and check of shame, many families exhibit the most hideous parts of our society. They are a kind of forlorn hope, preceding by ten or twelve years the most respectable army of veterans which come after them. In that space, prosperity will polish some, vice and the law will drive off the rest, who uniting again with others like themselves will recede still farther; making room for more industrious people, who will finish their improvements, convert the log-house into a convenient habitation, and rejoicing that the first heavy labors are finished, will change in a few years that hitherto barbarous country into a fine, fertile, well regulated district.

Such is our progress, such is the march of the Europeans toward the interior parts of this continent. In all societies there are off-casts; this impure part serves as our precursors or pioneers. My father himself was one of that class; but he came upon honest principles, and was therefore one of the few who held fast. By good conduct and temperance, he transmitted to me his fair inheritance, when not above one in fourteen of his contemporaries had the same good fortune.

Forty years ago this smiling country was thus inhabited. It is now purged, a general decency of manners prevails throughout; and such has been the fate of our best countries.

Exclusive of those general characteristics, each province has its own, founded on the government, climate, mode of husbandry, customs, and peculiarity of circumstances. Europeans submit insensibly to these great powers, and become in the course of a few generations, not only Americans in general, but either Pennsylvanians, Virginians, or provincials under some other name. Whoever traverses the continent must easily observe those strong differences, which will grow more evident in time. The inhabitants of Canada,

Massachusetts, the middle provinces, the southern ones will be as different as their climates. Their only points of unity will be those of religion and language. . . .

Europe contains hardly any other distinctions but lords and tenants; this fair country alone is settled by freeholders, the possessors of the soil they cultivate, members of the government they obey, and the framers of their own laws, by means of their representatives. This is a thought which you have taught me to cherish; our difference from Europe, far from diminishing, rather adds to our usefulness and consequence as men and subjects. Had our forefathers remained there, they would only have crowded it, and perhaps prolonged those convulsions which had shook it so long. Every industrious European who transports himself here, may be compared to a sprout growing at the foot of a great tree; it enjoys and draws but a little portion of sap; wrench it from the parent roots, transplant it, and it will become a tree bearing fruit also. Colonists are therefore entitled to the consideration due to the most useful subjects; a hundred families barely existing in some parts of Scotland will here in six years cause an annual exportation of 10,000 bushels of wheat; 100 bushels being but a common quantity for an industrious family to sell, if they cultivate good land. It is here, then, that the idle may be employed, the useless become useful, and the poor become rich. But by riches I do not mean gold and silver. We have but little of those metals. I mean a better sort of wealth, cleared lands, cattle, good houses, good clothes, and an increase of people to enjoy them.

There is no wonder that this country has so many charms, and presents to Europeans so many temptations to remain in it. A traveller in Europe becomes a stranger as soon as he quits his own kingdom; but it is otherwise here. We know, properly speaking, no strangers. This is every person's country. The variety of our soils, situations, climates, governments, and produce hath something which must please everybody. No sooner does an European arrive, no matter of what condition, than his eyes are opened upon the fair prospect. He hears his language spoke. He retraces many of his own country manners. He perpetually hears the names of families and towns with which he is acquainted. He sees happiness and prosperity in all places disseminated. He meets with hospitality, kindness, and plenty everywhere. He beholds hardly any poor. He seldom hears of punishments and executions, and he wonders at the elegance of our towns, those miracles of industry and freedom. He cannot admire enough our rural districts, our convenient roads, good taverns, and our many accommodations. He involuntarily loves a country where everything is so lovely. When in England he was a mere Englishman. Here he stands on a larger part of the globe, not less than its fourth part, and may see the productions of the North in iron and naval stores, the provisions of Ireland, the grain of Egypt, the indigo, the rice of China. He does not find, as in Europe, a crowded society, where every place is overstocked. He does not feel that perpetual collision of parties, that difficulty of beginning, that contention which oversets so many.

There is room for everybody in America. Has he any particular talent or industry? He exerts it in order to procure a livelihood, and it succeeds. Is he a merchant? The avenues of trade are infinite. Is he eminent in any respect? He will be employed and respected. Does he love a country life? Pleasant farms present themselves. He may purchase what he wants, and thereby become an American farmer. Is he a laborer, sober and industrious? He need not go many miles, nor receive many informations before he will be hired, well fed at the table of his employer, and paid four or five times more than he can get in Europe. Does he want uncultivated lands? Thousands of acres present themselves, which he may purchase cheap. Whatever be his talents or inclinations, if they are moderate, he may satisfy them. . . .

An European, when he first arrives, seems limited in his intentions, as well as in his views; but he very suddenly alters his scale. Two hundred miles formerly appeared a very great distance. It is now but a trifle. He no sooner breathes our air than he forms schemes and embarks in designs he never would have thought of in his own country. There the plenitude of society confines many useful ideas, and often extinguishes the most laudable schemes which here ripen into maturity. Thus Europeans become Americans. . . .

Let me select one as an epitome of the rest. He is hired, he goes to work, and works moderately. Instead of being employed by a haughty person, he finds himself with his equal, placed at the substantial table of the farmer, or else at an inferior one as good. His wages are high, his bed is not like that bed of sorrow on which he used to lie. If he behaves with propriety and is faithful, he is caressed and becomes, as it were, a member of the family. He

begins to feel the effects of a sort of resurrection. Hitherto he had
not lived, but simply vegetated. He now feels himself a man, because he is treated as such. The laws of his own country had overlooked him in his insignificancy. The laws of this cover him with
their mantle. Judge what an alteration there must arise in the mind
and thoughts of this man. He begins to forget his former servitude
and dependence. His heart involuntarily swells and glows. This first
swell inspires him with those new thoughts which constitute an
American. . . .

What an epocha in this man's life! He is become a freeholder,
from perhaps a German boor—he is now an American, a Pennsylvanian, an English subject. He is naturalized. His name is enrolled
with those of the other citizens of the province. Instead of being a
vagrant, he has a place of residence. He is called the inhabitant of
such a county, or of such a district, and for the first time in his life
counts for something, for hitherto he had been a cipher. I only repeat what I have heard many say, and no wonder their hearts should
glow, and be agitated with a multitude of feelings, not easy to describe. From nothing to start into being; from a servant to the rank
of a master; from being the slave of some despotic prince, to become a free man, invested with lands, to which every municipal
blessing is annexed! What a change indeed! It is in consequence of
that change, that he becomes an American.

This great metamorphosis has a double effect; it extinguishes all
his European prejudices. He forgets that mechanism of subordination, that servility of disposition which poverty had taught him;
and sometimes he is apt to forget it too much, often passing from
one extreme to the other. If he is a good man, he forms schemes of
future prosperity. He proposes to educate his children better than
he has been educated himself. He thinks of future modes of conduct, feels an ardor to labor he never felt before. Pride steps in, and
leads him to everything that the laws do not forbid. He respects
them. With a heartfelt gratitude he looks toward the east, toward
that insular government from whose wisdom all his new felicity is
derived, and under whose wings and protection he now lives. These
reflections constitute him the good man and the good subject.

Ye poor Europeans, ye, who sweat and work for the great—ye,
who are obliged to give so many sheaves to the church, so many to
your lords, so many to your government, and have hardly any left
for yourselves—ye, who are held in less estimation than favorite

hunters or useless lap-dogs—ye, who only breathe the air of nature, because it cannot be withheld from you; it is here that ye can conceive the possibility of those feelings I have been describing; it is here the laws of naturalization invite every one to partake of our great labors and felicity, to till unrented, untaxed lands! . . .

After a foreigner from any part of Europe is arrived, and become a citizen, let him devoutly listen to the voice of our great parent, which says to him, "Welcome to my shores, distressed European; bless the hour in which thou didst see my verdant fields, my fair navigable rivers, and my green mountains! If thou wilt work, I have bread for thee; if thou wilt be honest, sober, and industrious, I have greater rewards to confer on thee—ease and independence. I will give thee fields to feed and clothe thee; a comfortable fireside to sit by, and tell thy children by what means thou hast prospered; and a decent bed to repose on. I shall endow thee, beside, with the immunities of a freeman. If thou wilt carefully educate thy children, teach them gratitude to God, and reverence to that government, that philanthropic government, which has collected here so many men and made them happy, I will also provide for thy progeny; and to every good man this ought to be the most holy, the most powerful, the most earnest wish he can possibly form, as well as the most consolatory prospect when he dies. Go thou, and work and till, thou shalt prosper, provided thou be just, grateful and industrious."

XII

The Loyalists

The American Revolution displayed many of the aspects of a civil war, since a significant minority of the colonists remained faithful to England or chose to be neutral. The depth of their antipathy to the Revolutionary cause varied, as did their backgrounds. Some were indeed Establishment figures like young Peter Van Schaack, who by marriage belonged to one of the leading families in New York. Others, like Jonathan Boucher, were Anglican clergymen. Still others were back-country Tories, like the group from Anson County, North Carolina, whose address to their royal Governor is herein included. After the war began, numerous Loyalists went into exile either in Canada or in England. Yet some, like American-born Thomas Hutchinson, lamented their fate and yearned for their motherland.

47. Revolution Unjustified: Journal of Peter Van Schaack January 1776

THE ONLY foundation of all legitimate governments is certainly a compact between the rulers and the people, containing mutual conditions, and equally obligatory on both the contracting parties. No question can therefore exist, at this enlightened day, about the lawfulness of resistance, in cases of gross and palpable infractions on the part of the governing power. It is impossible, however, clearly to ascertain every case which shall effect a dissolution of this contract; for these, though always tacitly implied, are never expressly declared, in any form of government.

SOURCE: H. C. Van Schaack, *Life of Peter Van Schaack* (New York, 1842), 54–57.

As a man is bound by the sacred ties of conscience to yield obedience to every act of the legislature so long as the government exists, so, on the other hand, he owes it to the cause of liberty to resist the invasion of those rights which, being inherent and unalienable, could not be surrendered at the institution of the civil society of which he is a member. In times of civil commotions, therefore, an investigation of those rights which will necessarily infer an inquiry into the nature of government, becomes the indispensable duty of every man.

There are perhaps few questions relating to government of more difficulty than that at present subsisting between Great Britain and the Colonies. It originated about the *degree* of subordination we owe to the British Parliament, but by a rapid progress it seems now to be whether we are members of the empire or not. In this view, the principles of Mr. Locke and other advocates for the rights of mankind are little to the purpose. His treatise throughout presupposes rulers and subjects of the *same state*, and upon a supposition that we are members of the empire, his reasonings, if not inapplicable, will be found rather to militate against our claims; for he holds the necessity of a *supreme power*, and the necessary existence of *one legislature* only in every society, in the strongest terms.

Here arises the doubt: if we are parts of the same state, we cannot complain of a *usurpation*, unless in a qualified sense, but we must found our resistance upon an *undue and oppressive* exercise of a power we recognize. In short, our reasonings must resolve into one or the other of the following three grounds, and our right of resistance must be founded upon either the first or third of them; for either, first, we owe no obedience to any acts of Parliament; or, secondly, we are bound by all acts to which British subjects in Great Britain would, if passed with respect to them, owe obedience; or, thirdly, we are subordinate in a certain degree, or, in other words, certain acts may be valid in Britain which are not so here.

Upon the first point I am exceedingly clear in my mind, for I consider the Colonies as members of the British empire, and subordinate to the Parliament. But, with regard to the second and third, I am not so clear. The necessity of a supreme power in every state strikes me very forcibly; at the same time, I foresee the destructive consequences of a right in Parliament to bind us in all cases whatsoever. To obviate the ill effects of either extreme, some middle way should be found out, by which the benefits to the empire should be secured arising from the doctrine of a supreme power, while the abuses of that power to the prejudice of the colonists should be guarded against; and this, I hope, will be the happy effect of the present struggle.

The basis of such a compact must be the securing to the Americans the essential rights of Britons, but so modified as shall best consist with the general benefit of the whole. If upon such a compact we cannot possess the specific privileges of the inhabitants of Great Britain (as for instance a representation in Parliament we cannot), this must not be an obstacle; for there is certainly a point in which the general good of the whole, with the least possible disadvantage to every part, does centre, though it may be difficult to discern it, and every individual part must give way to the general good. . . .

It may be said that these principles terminate in passive obedience: far from it. I perceive that several of the acts exceed those bounds which, of right, ought to circumscribe the Parliament. But my difficulty arises from this, that, taking the whole of the acts complained of together, they do not, I think, manifest a system of slavery, but may fairly be imputed to human frailty and the difficulty of the subject. Most of them seem to have sprung out of particular occasions, and are unconnected with each other, and some of them are precisely of the nature of other acts made before the commencement of his present Majesty's reign, which is the era when the supposed design of subjugating the colonies began. If these acts have exceeded what is and ought to be declared to be the line of right, and thus we have been sufferers in some respects by the undefined state of the subject, it will also, I think, appear from such a union, when established, if past transactions are to be measured by the standard hereafter to be fixed, that we have hitherto been deficient in other respects, and derived benefit from the same unsettled state.

In short, I think those acts may have been passed without a preconcerted plan of enslaving us, and it appears to me that the more favorable construction ought ever to be put on the conduct of our rulers. I cannot therefore think the government dissolved; and as long as the society lasts, the power that every individual gave the society when he entered into it can never revert to the individuals again, but will always remain in the community.

If it be asked how we come to be subject to the authority of the British Parliament, I answer, by the same compact which entitles us to the benefits of the British constitution and its laws; and that we derive advantage even from some kind of subordination, whatever the degree of it should be, is evident because, without such a controlling common umpire, the colonies must become independent states, which would be introductive of anarchy and confusion among ourselves.

Some kind of dependence being then, in my idea, necessary for our own happiness, I would choose to see a claim made of a constitution which shall concede this point, as, before that is done by us and rejected by the mother country, I cannot see any principle of regard for my country which will authorize me in taking up arms, as absolute *dependence* and *independence* are two extremes which I would avoid; for, should we succeed in the latter, we shall still be in a sea of uncertainty and have to fight among ourselves for that constitution we aim at.

There are many very weighty reasons besides the above to restrain a man from taking up arms, but some of them are of too delicate a nature to be put upon paper; however, it may be proper to mention what does *not* restrain *me*. It is not from apprehension of the consequences should America be subdued, or the hopes of any favor from government, both which I disclaim; nor is it from any disparagement of the cause my countrymen are engaged in, or a desire of obstructing the present measures.

48. Fear of Anarchy: Jonathan Boucher's Sermon on Civil Liberty, Passive Obedience, and Nonresistance Preached at Queen Anne Parish, Prince George's County, Maryland
1775

HENCE IT follows, that we are free, or otherwise, as we are governed by law, or by the mere arbitrary will, or wills, of any individual, or any number of individuals. And liberty is not the setting at nought

SOURCE: Jonathan Boucher, *A View of the Causes and Consequences of the American Revolution* (London, 1797), 509–543. Original sermon printed, Philadelphia, 1775.

and despising established laws—much less the making our own wills the rule of our own actions, or the actions of others—and not bearing (whilst yet we dictate to others) the being dictated to, even by the laws of the land; but it is the being governed by law, and by law only. The Greeks described Eleutheria, or Liberty, as the daughter of Jupiter, the supreme fountain of power and law. And the Romans, in like manner, always drew her with the pretor's wand, (the emblem of legal power and authority,) as well as with the cap. Their idea, no doubt, was, that liberty was the fair fruit of just authority, and that it consisted in men's being subjected to law. The more carefully well devised restraints of law are enacted, and the more rigorously they are executed in any country, the greater degree of civil liberty does that country enjoy. To pursue liberty, then, in a manner not warranted by law, whatever the pretence may be, is clearly to be hostile to liberty: and those persons who thus *promise you liberty*, are themselves the *servants of corruption*.

Civil liberty [says an excellent writer] is a severe and a restrained thing; implies, in the notion of it, authority, settled subordinations, subjection, and obedience; and is altogether as much hurt by too little of this kind, as by too much of it. And the love of liberty, when it is indeed the love of liberty, which carries us to withstand tyranny, will as much carry us to reverence authority, and to support it; for this most obvious reason, that one is as necessary to the being of liberty as the other is destructive of it. And, therefore, the love of liberty which does not produce this effect, the love of liberty which is not a real principle of dutiful behaviour towards authority, is as hypocritical as the religion which is not productive of a good life. Licentiousness is, in truth, such an excess of liberty as is of the same nature with tyranny. For, what is the difference betwixt them, but that one is lawless power exercised under pretence of authority, or by persons vested with it; the other, lawless power exercised under pretence of liberty, or without pretence at all? A people, then, must always be less free in proportion as they are more licentious; licentiousness being not only different from liberty, but directly contrary to it—a direct breach upon it.

True liberty, then, is a liberty to do every thing that is right, and the being restrained from doing any thing that is wrong. So far from our having a right to do every thing that we please, under a notion of liberty, liberty itself is limited and confined—but limited and confined only by laws which are at the same time both it's foundation and it's support. . . .

Ashamed of this shallow device, that government originated in superior strength and violence, another party, hardly less numerous, and certainly not less confident than the former, fondly deduce it from some imaginary compact. They suppose that, in the decline perhaps of some fabulous age of gold, a multitude of human beings, who, like their brother beasts, had hitherto ranged the forests, *without guide, over-seer, or ruler*—at length convinced, by experience, of the impossibility of living either alone with any degree of comfort or security, or together in society, with peace, without government, had (in some lucid interval of reason and reflection) met together in a spacious plain, for the express purpose of framing a government. Their first step must have been the transferring to some individual, or individuals, some of those rights which are supposed to have been inherent in each of them: of these it is essential to government that they should be divested; yet can they not, rightfully, be deprived of them, otherwise than by their own consent. Now, admitting this whole supposed assembly to be perfectly equal as to rights, yet all agreed as to the propriety of ceding some of them, on what principles of equality is it possible to determine, either who shall relinquish such a portion of his rights, or who shall be invested with such new accessory rights? By asking another to exercise jurisdiction over me, I clearly confess that I do not think myself his equal; and by consenting to exercise such authority, he also virtually declares that he thinks himself superior. And, to establish this hypothesis of a compact, it is farther necessary that the whole assembly should concur in this opinion—a concurrence so extremely improbable, that it seems to be barely possible. The supposition that a large concourse of people, in a rude and imperfect state of society, or even a majority of them, should thus rationally and unanimously concur to subject themselves to various restrictions, many of them irksome and unpleasant, and all of them contrary to all their former habits, is to suppose them possessed of more wisdom and virtue than multitudes in any instance in real life have ever shewn. Another difficulty respecting this notion may yet be mentioned. Without a power of life and death, it will, I presume, be readily admitted that there could be no government. Now, admitting it to be possible that men, from motives of public and private utility, may be induced to submit to many heavy penalties, and even to corporal punishment, inflicted by the sentence of the law, there is an insuperable objection to any man's giving to another a power over his life: this objection is, that no man has such power over his own life; and cannot therefore transfer to another, or to others, be they few or many, on any conditions, a right which he does not himself possess. He only who gave life, can give the authority to take it away: and as such authority is essential to government, this argument seems very decidedly to prove, not only that government did not originate in any compact, but also that it was originally from God. . . .

Accordingly, when man was made, his Maker did not turn him adrift into a shoreless ocean, without star or compass to steer by. As soon as there were some to be governed, there were also some to govern: and the first man, by virtue of that paternal claim, on which all subsequent governments have been founded, was first invested with the power of government. For, we are not to judge of the Scriptures of God, as we do of some other writings; and so, where no express precept appears, hastily to conclude that none was given. On the contrary, in commenting on the Scriptures, we are frequently called upon to find out the precept from the practice. Taking this rule, then, for our direction in the present instance, we find, that, copying after the fair model of heaven itself, wherein there was government even among the angels, the families of the earth were subjected to rulers, at first set over them by God: *for, there is no power, but of God; the powers that be are ordained of God.* The first father was the first king: and if (according to the rule just laid down) the law may be inferred from the practice, it was thus that all government originated; and monarchy is it's most ancient form.

Little risque is run in affirming, that this idea of the patriarchal origin of government has not only the most and best authority of history, as far as history goes, to support it; but that it is also by far the most natural, most consistent, and most rational idea. Had it pleased God not to have interfered at all in the case, neither directly nor indirectly, and to have left mankind to be guided only by their own uninfluenced judgments, they would naturally have been led to the government of a community, or a nation, from the natural and obvious precedent of the government of a family. In confirmation of this opinion, it may be observed, that the patriarchal scheme is that which always has prevailed, and still does prevail, among the most enlightened people: and (what is no slight attestation of it's truth) it has also prevailed, and still does prevail, among the most unenlightened. According to Vitruvius, the rudiments of architecture are to be found in the cottage: and, according to Aristotle, the first principles of government are to be traced to private families. Kingdoms and empires are but so many larger families: and hence it is that our Church, in perfect conformity with the doctrine here inculcated, in her explication the fifth commandment, from the obedience due to parents, wisely derives the congenial duty of *honouring the king and all that are put in authority under him.* . . .

Even where the Scriptures are silent, they instruct: for, in general, whatever is not therein commanded is actually forbidden. Now, it is certain that mankind are nowhere in the Scriptures commanded to resist authority; and no less certain that, either by direct injunction, or clear implication, they are commanded to be *subject to the higher powers:* and this subjection is said to be enjoined, not for our sakes only, but also for the Lord's sake. The glory of God is much concerned, that there should be good government in the world: it is, therefore, the uniform doctrine of the Scriptures, that it is under the deputation and authority of God alone that *kings reign and princes decree justice.* Kings and princes (which are only other words for supreme magistrates) were doubtless created and appointed, not so much for their own sakes, as for the sake of the people committed to their charge: yet are they not, therefore, the creatures of the people. So far from deriving their authority from any supposed consent or suffrage of men, they receive their commission from Heaven; they receive it from God, the source and original of all power. However obsolete, therefore, either the sentiment or the language may now be deemed, it is with the most perfect propriety that the supreme magistrate, whether consisting of one or of many, and whether denominated an emperor, a king, an archon, a dictator, a consul, or a senate, is to be regarded and venerated as the vice-regent of God. . . .

49. Loyalism in the Back Country: Address of Inhabitants of Anson County, North Carolina, to Governor Josiah Martin [March 10] 1775

MOST EXCELLENT GOVERNOR:

Permit us, in behalf of ourselves, and many others of His Majesty's most dutiful and loyal subjects within the County of Anson, to take the earliest opportunity of addressing your Excellency, and expressing our abomination of the many outrageous attempts now forming on this side the Atlantick, against the peace and tranquility of His Majesty's Dominions in North America, and to witness to your Excellency, by this our Protest, a disapprobation and abhorrence of the many lawless combinations and unwarrantable practices actually carrying on by a gross tribe of infatuated anti-Monarchists in the several Colonies in these Dominions; the baneful consequence of whose audacious contrivance can, in fine, only tend to extirpate the fundamental principles of all Government, and illegally to shake off their obedience to, and dependance upon, the imperial Crown and Parliament of Great Britain; the infection of whose pernicious example being already extended to this particular County, of which we now bear the fullest testimony.

It is with the deepest concern (though with infinite indignation) that we see in all public places and papers disagreeable votes, speeches and resolutions, said to be entered into by our sister Colonies, in the highest contempt and derogation of the superintending power of the legislative authority of Great Britain. And we further, with sorrow, behold their wanton endeavors to vilify and arraign the honour and integrity of His Majesty's most honourable Ministry and Council, tending to sow the seeds of discord and sedition, in open violation of their duty and allegiance.

We are truly invigorated with the warmest zeal and attachment

SOURCE: W. L. Saunders, ed., *Colonial Records of North Carolina* (10 vols., Raleigh, 1886–1890), IX, 1161–1164.

in favour of the British Parliament, Constitution and Laws, which our forefathers gloriously struggled to establish, and which are now become the noblest birthright and inheritance of all Britannia's Sons.

We should be criminally wanting in respect and gratitude to the names of those ancestors, and ill deserve the protection of that Superiour Parliamentary power, could we tamely suffer its authority to be so basely controverted and derided, without offering our protest to your Excellency against such ignominious disobedience and reproach; for we consider that, under Divine Providence, it is solely upon the wisdom and virtue of that superior legislative might that the safety of our lives and fortunes, and the honour and welfare of this country, do most principally depend.

Give us leave, therefore, Sir, to express our utter detestation and abhorrence of the late unjustifiable violation of publick commercial credit in the Massachusetts Government.

We protest against it with the utmost disdain, as the wicked experiment of a most profligate and abandoned Republican faction, whereby the general repose and tranquility of His Majesty's good subjects on this Continent are very much endangered and impaired. We think it indispensibly necessary, and our duty at this alarming crisis, to offer this memorial and protest to your Excellency, against all such enthusiastick transgressions, (more especially the late ones committed by the common cause Deputies within this Province,) to the intent that it may be delivered down to posterity, that our hands were washed pure and clear of any cruel consequences, lest the woful calamities of a distracted country should give birth to sedition and insurrection, from the licentiousness of a concert prone to rebellion.

And we cannot omit expressing further to your Excellency, that we consider all such associations at this period of a very dangerous fatality against your Excellency's good Government of this Province, being calculated to distress the internal welfare of this Country, to mislead the unwary ignorant from the paths of their duty, and to entail destruction upon us, and wretchedness upon our posterity.

We do, most excellent Governor, with all obedience and humility, profess and acknowledge, in our consciences, that a law of the high Court of Parliament of Great Britain is an exercise of the highest authority that His Majesty's subjects can acknowledge upon earth, and that we do believe it hath legal power to bind every subject in that land, and the dominions thereunto belonging. And we do, moreover, with all duty and gratitude, acknowledge and reverence in the utmost latitude an Act of Parliament made in the sixth year of the reign of his present most sacred Majesty, entitled "An Act for the better securing the dependance of His Majesty's Dominions in America, on the Crown and Parliament of Great Britain."

And we do further beg leave to express our detestation of the many scandalous and ignorant deliberations on the power of that Parliament in the control of His Majesty's Provincial Charters. For could the doctrine of such unruly propositions possibly exist, or should their insolent attempt unhappily prevail, it must at once extinguish those Laws and that Constitution which are the glory of the British Empire and the envy of all Nations around it.

We are truly sensible that those invaluable blessings which we have hitherto enjoyed under His Majesty's auspicious Government, can only be secured to us by the stability of his Throne, supported and defended by the British Parliament, the only grand bulwark and guardian of our civil and religious liberties.

Duty and affection oblige us further to express our grateful acknowledgements for the inestimate blessings flowing from such a Constitution. And we do assure your Excellency that we are determined, by the assistance of Almighty God, in our respective stations, steadfastly to continue His Majesty's loyal Subjects, and to contribute all in our power for the preservation of the publick peace; so, that, by our unanimous example, we hope to discourage the desperate endeavours of a deluded multitude, and to see a misled people turn again from their atrocious offences to a proper exercise of their obedience and duty.

And we do furthermore assure your Excellency, that we shall endeavor to cultivate such sentiments in all those under our care, and to warm their breasts with a true zeal for His Majesty, and affection for his illustrious family. And may the Almighty God be pleased to direct his Councils, his Parliament, and all those in authority under him, that their endeavors may be for the advancement of piety, and the safety, honour and welfare of our Sovereign and his Kingdoms, that the malice of his enemies may be assuaged, and their evil designs confounded and defeated; so that all the world may be convinced that his sacred person, his Royal family, his Parliament, and our country, are the special objects of Devine dispensation and Providence.

[Signed by two hundred and twenty-seven of the inhabitants of the county of Anson.]

50. An Exile's Lament:
Thomas Hutchinson's Diary from England
April 1776 to October 1779

April 27, 1776

It is certain that a prodigeous armament is preparing, and will be very soon sailing in one large body after another, until the whole is gone for America. The destination of the several parts, I am not able to tell you. As the command will be in the two brothers,[1] one by sea the other by land, people are less inquisitive than otherwise they would be. I do not think a choice of men could have been made more generally satisfactory to the kingdom, and under Providence, I think we may found a reasonable hope for a more favourable summer than the last. We Americans are plenty here, and very cheap. Some of us at first coming, are apt to think ourselves of importance, but other people do not think so, and few, if any of us are much consulted, or enquired after.

September 16, 1776

I don't remember ever to have seen the town so thin of people since I have been in London. My own anxiety, from the state of my country, keeps me in town. The two last days the wind has been at east, so that we hardly expect an arrival until it has blown two or three days at west again, which quarter it is in to-day. My children from Brompton Row [Thomas's] dined with me to-day, and the High Street family [Dr. P. Oliver's] came to drink tea. This is some

SOURCE: P. O. Hutchinson, *The Diary and Letters of His Excellency Thomas Hutchinson, Esq.* (2 vols., London, 1886), 40, 95, 156, 193, 212, 257, 272, 290.

1. Admiral Viscount Richard Howe and Sir William Howe.

alleviation—to have my children and grand-children; but we are all in a state of exile from a country, which of all others is most dear to me, notwithstanding the unjust cruel treatment I have received from it.

August 16, 1777

Sensibly more feeble, and had a bad day. In this kind of life the days and nights pass incredibly swift, and I am six months older and nearer to my own death, than when my daughter's illness began; and it appears like the dream of a night.[2]

March 19, 1778

Called on Mr. Ellis. Laments the universal despondency: should not wonder if this afternoon the Americans were acknowledged Independent—a term they always avoided as a Religious distinction, but will always boast of as a Civil character. After all, I shall never see that there were just grounds for this revolt. I see that the ways of Providence are mysterious, but I abhor the least thought that all is not perfectly right, and ordered by infinite rectitude and wisdom.

August 1, 1778

The calm among all sorts of people is astonishing. It looks just the same as one might expect it would, if the English and French fleets were parading in the Channel upon friendly terms; and yet every minute some decisive stroke, some say, may be expected. The British forces in America are mouldering away—the Commissioners treated with neglect—and all considered as a matter of indifference. Why don't Government withdraw its forces, and leave the Americans to that Independence which the Ministry seem to expect they will attain to?

May 15, 1779

Doctor Gardiner and Col. Pickman called on me from Bristol, and dined—with two Auchmutys, Col. Chandler, and Treas. Gray. They are all anxious to return to America, except Gray. He and Ch. Just. Oliver, and Secretary Flucker, wish to have some provision in

2. His daughter Peggy, who died in the latter part of September.

England, and never much think of America. I can see reasons which are personal for each of them. I have more of the old Athenians in me; and though I know not how to reason upon it, I feel a fondness to lay my bones in my native soil, and to carry those of my dear daughter with me.

August 19, 1779

A letter from Dr. Murray. A young man there from Providence, Rh. Island, tells him the people abuse me as much as ever. This is my misfortune, as I wished for the esteem of none so much as of my own countrymen. I think it is not bias which satisfied me that what Tacitus observes was natural in his day is the cause—*Odisse quem laeseris.*[3]

October 19, 1779

Nothing can be more polite than my entertainment has been. The oeconomy is too steady, or has too much sameness, to please for a long time together. The Library is always open to everybody. The first appearance of my Lord and Lady[4] is in the breakfast room exactly at ten. Breakfast is over about eleven: everyone takes care of himself, and does just what he pleases until half after three, when all meet at dinner: between five and six the ladies withdraw: the gentlemen generally go into the Library—some chat, others take up books; at eight a call to one of the drawing-rooms to tea or coffee; which over, if there is company disposed to cards, any who don't like them converse, or take their books: exact at ten the sideboard is laid with a few light things upon it, that anybody disposed to supper may take it: and exact at eleven, as many servants as there are of gentlemen and ladies, come in with each of them two wax candles, and in procession we follow to the Gallery at the head of the great staircase, and file off to different rooms. This is high life: but I would not have parted with my humble cottage at Milton for the sake of it.

---

3. To hate the person whom you have injured.
4. Lord and Lady Hardwicke of Wimpole Hall, Cambridgeshire.

XIII

The Need for
Central Government

After independence was declared, it became evident that a coordinating authority was needed to conduct the war. The question was how much authority should be conferred upon a central government. Since the colonists had just rebelled from one empire, it was natural that they should have concern about entrusting too much authority to any remote government. According to Thomas Burke, a states' rights spokesman from North Carolina, "unlimited power [could] not be safely trusted to any man or set of men on Earth." The Articles of Confederation adopted by Congress proved a concession to the states' rights group, for effective power was withheld from the central government. Ratification of the Articles was deferred until March 1781, as the state of Maryland refused to ratify until all states claiming western lands had ceded them to the United States.

51. Fear of Strong Government: Thomas Burke to Governor Richard Caswell of North Carolina March 11, 1777

SIR

Our adjournment from Baltimore has put all our Proceedings to a stand and our unsettled Situation has prevented my writing to you as often as I at first Intended. I believe you have no cause to regret it, for I had nothing to communicate worth your attention.

The more experience I acquire, the stronger is my Conviction,

SOURCE: E. C. Burnett, *Letters of the Members of the Continental Congress* (8 vols., Washington, 1921–1936), II, 294–296.

that *unlimited Power can not be safely Trusted* to any man or set of men on Earth. No men have undertaken to exercise authority with Intentions more generous and disinterested than the Congress and none seem to have fewer or more feeble motives for increasing the Power of their body Politic. What could Induce Individuals blest with peaceable domestic affluence to forego all the enjoyment of a pleasing home, to neglect their private affairs, and at the expence of all their time and some part of their private fortunes, to attend public Business under many Insurmountable Difficulties and Inconveniences? What but a generous Zeal for the public? And what can Induce such men to Endeavour at increasing the Power with which they are Invested, when their Tenure of it must be exceedingly Dangerous and precarious and can bring them Individually neither pleasure or profit? this is a Question I believe cannot be answered but by a plain declaration that Power of all kinds has an Irresistible propensity to increase a desire for itself. it gives the Passion of ambition a Velocity which Increases in its progress, and this is a passion which grows in proportion as it is gratified. I hope sir you will pardon me these Reflections. I know they have not escaped you. but I find my attendance in Congress, short as it has been, obtrudes them on me every day. great part of our time is consumed in debates, whose object on one side is to increase the Power of Congress, and on the other to restrain it. The advocates do not always keep the same side of the Contest. the same persons who on one day endeavour to carry through some Resolutions, whose Tendency is to increase the Power of Congress, are often on an other day very strenuous advocates to restrain it. from this I infer that no one has entertained a concerted design to increase the Power; and the attempts to do it proceed from Ignorance of what such a Being ought to be, and from the Delusive Intoxication which Power Naturally imposes on the human Mind. . . .

These and many other considerations make me earnestly wish that the Power of Congress was accurately defined and that there were adequate Check provided to prevent any Excess. I am also exceedingly desirous to have particular Instructions relative to some Heads which I shall Inclose to you to be laid before the assembly. One thing now embarasses me very much. it is this. Whenever any Matter wherein the Jurisdiction or authority of Congress is contested is debated, it is usual to lay it over undetermined. by the rule of secrecy you know, Sir, I am not at liberty to communicate anything before it is determined and therefore cannot Consult the State upon it. in these cases all our time is lost, for nothing is entered on the Journals, and nothing therefore can give Testimony hereafter that such points were contested, and even reject[ed] by a majority as is indeed the usual case. Relative to the measures Intended to be pursued by Congress I have nothing new to add. they are Endeavouring at a foreign alliance, and have some hopes of success. they will Increase as much as possible their Naval Force, and are using every Endeavour to recruit a strong army to take the Field early in the Spring. their Endeavours in this respect will be ineffectual if not earnestly seconded by the States. I have no doubt Sir of your most particular attention to this Important object. I am often suggesting to Congress that the Civil Power of the States is the best Instrument for calling forth their Proportion of Exertions in this or any Cause, but they hear with reluctance any thing that looks like the Interposition of such a Power in Military affairs, tho' no one will venture directly to oppose or reject it. I need not repeat to you my own Thoughts on this subject. you have often heard me deliver them. I have not yet altered my Opinion. With respect to Intelligence I will enclose you the papers and anything not contained in them I will subjoin.

I enclose you an abstract of the Debates in Congress on every Question of any Consequence that has been determined in Congress since my last. By these you will see what has been decided, and why. You will from them also better Judge of the various Opinions, or rather the fluctuations of Opinion in Congress. this is an Evil from which nothing but experience, and a better Constitution of Congress can deliver us. my own Opinions, being those in which my Country is particularly Interested, I wish her to be fully informed of. I shall submit them to you Sir as her principal Guardian, with all the simplicity of unadorned Truth, and when they are reprehensible I wish them to be reproved, that the public servants in this Department[1] may better learn their Duty, and that I in particular may be Instructed not to give the sense of the State in a Manner which she may not approve. The last Matter in the abstract will shew you that even thus early, men so eminent as members of Congress, are willing to explain away any Power that

1. Congress.

stands in the way of their particular purposes. what may we not expect some time hence, when the Seat of Power shall become firm by Habit, and men will be accustomed to Obedience, and perhaps forgetful of the Original principles which gave rise thereto. I believe Sir the Root of the Evil is deep in human Nature. its growth may be kept down but it cannot be entirely extirpated. Power will sometime or other be abused unless men are well watched, and checked by something which they cannot remove when they please. . . .

Our expenses here Sir are incredible. every Horse is ten Shillings a Day, and every thing else is in proportion. It is now the 19th of March and since our arrival in this City we have done nothing. we had barely a Congress for a few days last week, but none this week yet. the few members in Town are closely engaged in Committees, and what I write is done in the time when other People are asleep. You will therefore not wonder, should you find it very Incorrect.

There are letters from Doctr. Franklin in France of the 10th of december. they represent a War in Europe as certainly iminent and we have received very particular marks of the Favor of the French Court, which I am not at liberty to disclose.

You will See a Resolution in the Papers recommending to the States to assess Blankets for the soldiery. This is absolutely Necessary, because such things can not otherwise be had in our State. . . .

Tis probable, Sir, the Assembly may make choice of some more able men to serve in this Department. I should be very far from deeming it an Injury to me, and I am certain it could be none to the State. I have resolved very early in this Dispute to decline no service that my country require me to perform altho almost all offices are equally out of my way, and none are desirable to me. But if the Assembly shall think proper to direct me to continue in this Department, I hope I may be allowed to return to my private affairs for a few weeks in the Summer. if I have this permission I promise Sir that I will not avail myself of it to the delay or prejudice of public Business. . . .

52. Articles of Confederation:
Voted by Congress
November 15, 1777

To ALL to whom these Presents shall come, we the undersigned Delegates of the States affixed to our Names send greeting. Whereas the Delegates of the United States of America in Congress assembled did on the fifteenth day of November in the Year of our Lord One Thousand Seven Hundred and Seventy seven, and in the Second Year of the Independence of America agree to certain articles of Confederation and perpetual Union between the States of Newhampshire, Massachusetts-bay, Rhodeisland and Providence Plantations, Connecticut, New York, New Jersey, Pennsylvania, Delaware, Maryland, Virginia, North-Carolina, South-Carolina and Georgia in the Words following, viz. "Articles of Confederation and perpetual Union between the states of Newhampshire, Massachusetts-bay, Rhodeisland and Providence Plantations, Connecticut, New-York, New-Jersey, Pennsylvania, Delaware, Maryland, Virginia, North-Carolina, South-Carolina and Georgia.

Art. I. The Stile of this confederacy shall be "The United States of America."

Art. II. Each state retains its sovereignty, freedom and independence, and every Power, Jurisdiction and right, which is not by this confederation expressly delegated to the United States, in Congress assembled.

Art. III. The said states hereby severally enter into a firm league of friendship with each other, for their common defence, the security of their Liberties, and their mutual and general welfare, binding themselves to assist each other, against all force offered to, or attacks made upon them, or any of them, on account of religion, sovereignty, trade, or any other pretence whatever.

Art. IV. The better to secure and perpetuate mutual friendship

SOURCE: J. D. Richardson, *Messages and Papers of the Presidents, 1789–1897* (10 vols., Washington, 1896–1899), I, 9 et seq.

and intercourse among the people of the different states in this union, the free inhabitants of each of these states, paupers, vagabonds and fugitives from Justice excepted, shall be entitled to all privileges and immunities of free citizens in the several states; and the people of each state shall have free ingress and regress to and from any other state, and shall enjoy therein all the privileges of trade and commerce, subject to the same duties, impositions and restrictions as the inhabitants thereof respectively, provided that such restriction shall not extend so far as to prevent the removal of property imported into any state, to any other state of which the Owner is an inhabitant; provided also that no imposition, duties or restriction shall be laid by any state, on the property of the united states, or either of them.

If any Person guilty of, or charged with treason, felony, or other high misdemeanor in any state, shall flee from Justice, and be found in any of the united states, he shall upon demand of the Governor or executive power, of the state from which he fled, be delivered up and removed to the state having jurisdiction of his offence.

Full faith and credit shall be given in each of these states to the records, acts and judicial proceedings of the courts and magistrates of every other state.

Art. V. For the more convenient management of the general interests of the united states, delegates shall be annually appointed in such manner as the legislature of each state shall direct, to meet in Congress on the first Monday in November, in every year, with a power reserved to each state, to recall its delegates, or any of them, at any time within the year, and to send others in their stead, for the remainder of the Year.

No state shall be represented in Congress by less than two, nor by more than seven Members; and no person shall be capable of being a delegate for more than three years in any term of six years; nor shall any person, being a delegate, be capable of holding any office under the united states, for which he, or another for his benefit receives any salary, fees or emolument of any kind.

Each state shall maintain its own delegates in a meeting of the states, and while they act as members of the committee of the states.

In determining questions in the united states, in Congress assembled, each state shall have one vote.

Freedom of speech and debate in Congress shall not be impeached or questioned in any Court, or place out of Congress, and the members of congress shall be protected in their persons from arrests and imprisonments, during the time of their going to and from, and attendance on congress, except for treason, felony, or breach of the peace.

Art. VI. No state without the Consent of the united states in congress assembled, shall send any embassy to, or receive any embassy from, or enter into any conference, agreement, or alliance or treaty with any King, prince or state; nor shall any person holding any office of profit or trust under the united states, or any of them, accept of any present, emolument, office or title of any kind whatever from any king, prince or foreign state; nor shall the united states in congress assembled, or any of them, grant any title of nobility.

No two or more states shall enter into any treaty, confederation or alliance whatever between them, without the consent of the united states in congress assembled, specifying accurately the purposes for which the same is to be entered into, and how long it shall continue.

No state shall lay any imposts or duties, which may interfere with any stipulations in treaties, entered into by the united states in congress assembled, with any king, prince or state, in pursuance of any treaties already proposed by congress, to the courts of France and Spain.

No vessels of war shall be kept up in time of peace by any state, except such number only, as shall be deemed necessary by the united states in congress assembled, for the defence of such state, or its trade; nor shall any body of forces be kept up by any state in time of peace, except such number only, as in the judgment of the united states, in congress assembled, shall be deemed requisite to garrison the forts necessary for the defence of such state; but every state shall always keep up a well regulated and disciplined militia, sufficiently armed and accoutred, and shall provide and constantly have ready for use, in public stores, a due number of field pieces and tents, and a proper quantity of arms, ammunition and camp equipage.

No state shall engage in any war without the consent of the united states in congress assembled, unless such state be actually invaded by enemies, or shall have received certain advice of a resolution being formed by some nation of Indians to invade such state, and the danger is so imminent as not to admit of a delay, till the united states in congress assembled can be consulted: nor shall any state grant commissions to any ships or vessels of war, nor letters of marque or reprisal, except it be after a declaration of war by the united states in congress assembled, and then only against the kingdom or state and the subjects thereof, against which war has been so declared, and under such regulations as shall be established by the united states in congress assembled, unless such state be infested by pirates, in which case vessels of war may be fitted out for that occasion, and kept so long as the danger shall continue, or until the united states in congress assembled shall determine otherwise.

Art. VII. When land-forces are raised by any state for the common defence, all officers of or under the rank of colonel, shall be appointed by the legislature of each state respectively by whom such forces shall be raised, or in such manner as such state shall direct, and all vacancies shall be filled up by the state which first made the appointment.

Art. VIII. All charges of war, and all other expences that shall be incurred for the common defence or general welfare, and allowed by the united states in congress assembled, shall be defrayed out of a common treasury, which shall be supplied by the several states, in proportion to the value of all land within each state, granted to or surveyed for any Person, as such land and the buildings and improvements thereon shall be estimated according to such mode as the united states in congress assembled, shall from time to time direct and appoint. The taxes for paying that proportion shall be laid and levied by the authority and direction of the legislatures of the several states within the time agreed upon by the united states in congress assembled.

Art. IX. The united states in congress assembled, shall have the sole and exclusive right and power of determining on peace and war, except in the cases mentioned in the sixth article—of sending and receiving ambassadors—entering into treaties and alliances, provided that no treaty of commerce shall be made whereby the legislative power of the respective states shall be restrained from imposing such imposts and duties on foreigners, as their own people are subjected to, or from prohibiting the exportation or importation of any species of goods or commodities whatsoever—of establishing rules for deciding in all cases, what captures on land or water shall be legal, and in what manner prizes taken by land or naval forces in the service of the united states shall be divided or appropriated—of granting letters of marque and reprisal in times of peace—appointing courts for the trial of piracies and felonies committed on the high seas and establishing courts for receiving and determining finally appeals in all cases of captures, provided that no member of congress shall be appointed a judge of any of the said courts.

The united states in congress assembled shall also be the last resort on appeal in all disputes and differences now subsisting or that hereafter may arise between two or more states concerning boundary, jurisdiction or any other cause whatever; which authority shall always be exercised in the manner following. Whenever the legislative or executive authority or lawful agent of any state in controversy with another shall present a petition to congress, stating the matter in question and praying for a hearing, notice thereof shall be given by order of congress to the legislative or executive authority of the other state in controversy, and a day assigned for the appearance of the parties by their lawful agents, who shall then be directed to appoint by joint consent, commissioners or judges to constitute a court for hearing and determining the matter in question: but if they cannot agree, congress shall name three persons out of each of the united states, and from the list of such persons each party shall alternately strike out one, the petitioners beginning, until the number shall be reduced to thirteen; and from that number not less than seven, nor more than nine names as congress shall direct, shall in the presence of congress be drawn out by lot, and the persons whose names shall be so drawn or any five of them, shall be commissioners or judges, to hear and finally determine the controversy, so always as a major part of the judges who shall hear the cause shall agree in the determination: and if either party shall neglect to attend at the day appointed, without shewing reasons, which congress shall judge sufficient, or being present shall refuse to strike, the congress shall proceed to nominate three persons out of each state, and the secretary of congress shall strike in behalf of such party absent or refusing; and the judgment and sentence of the court to be appointed, in the manner before prescribed, shall be final and conclusive; and if any of the parties shall refuse to submit to the authority of such court, or to appear to defend their claim or cause, the court shall nevertheless proceed to pronounce sentence, or judgment, which shall in like manner be final and decisive, the judgment or sentence and other proceedings being in either case transmitted to congress, and lodged among the acts of congress for the security of the parties concerned: provided that every commissioner, before he sits in judgment, shall take an oath to be administered by one of the judges of the supreme or superior court of the state, where the cause shall be tried, "well and truly to hear and determine the matter in question, according to the best of his judgment, without favour, affection or hope of reward"; provided also that no state shall be deprived of territory for the benefit of the united states.

All controversies concerning the private right of soil claimed under different grants of two or more states, whose jurisdictions as they may respect such lands, and the states which passed such grants are adjusted, the said grants or either of them being at the same time claimed to have originated antecedent to such settlement of jurisdiction, shall on the petition of either party to the congress of the united states, be finally determined as near as may be in the same manner as is before prescribed for deciding disputes respecting territorial jurisdiction between different states.

The united states in congress assembled shall also have the sole and exclusive right and power of regulating the alloy and value of coin struck by their own authority, or by that of the respective states—fixing the standard of weights and measures throughout the united states—regulating the trade and managing all affairs with the Indians, not members of any of the states, provided that the legislative right of any state within its own limits be not infringed or violated—establishing and regulating post-offices from one state to another, throughout all the united states, and exacting such postage on the papers passing thro' the same as may be requisite to defray the expences of the said office—appointing all officers of the land forces, in the service of the united states, excepting regimental officers—appointing all the officers of the naval forces, and commissioning all officers whatever in the service of the united states—making rules for the government and regulation of the said land and naval forces, and directing their operations.

The united states in congress assembled shall have authority to appoint a committee, to sit in the recess of congress, to be denominated "A Committee of the States," and to consist of one delegate from each state; and to appoint such other committees and civil officers as may be necessary for managing the general affairs of the united states under their direction—to appoint one of their number to preside, provided that no person be allowed to serve in the office of president more than one year in any term of three years; to ascertain the necessary sums of Money to be raised for the service of the united states, and to appropriate and apply the same for defraying the public expences—to borrow money, or emit bills on the credit of the united states, transmitting every half year to the respective states an account of the sums of money so borrowed or emitted,—to build and equip a navy—to agree upon the number of land forces and to make requisitions from each state for its quota, in proportion to the number of white inhabitants in such state; which requisition shall be binding, and thereupon the legislature of each state shall appoint the regimental officers, raise the men and cloath, arm and equip them in a soldier like manner, at the expence of the united states, and the officers and men so cloathed, armed and equipped shall march to the place appointed, and within the time agreed on by the united states in congress assembled: But if the united states in congress assembled shall, on consideration of circumstances judge proper that any state should not raise men, or should raise a smaller number than its quota, and that any other state should raise a greater number of men than the quota thereof, such extra number shall be raised, officered, cloathed, armed and equipped in the same manner as the quota of such state, unless the legislature of such state shall judge that such extra number cannot be safely spared out of the same, in which case they shall raise officer, cloath, arm and equip as many of such extra number as they judge can be safely spared. And the officers and men so cloathed, armed and equipped, shall march to the place appointed, and within the time agreed on by the united states in congress assembled.

The united states in congress assembled shall never engage in a war, nor grant letters of marque and reprisal in time of peace, nor enter into any treaties or alliances, nor coin money, nor regulate the value thereof, nor ascertain the sums and expences necessary for the defence and welfare of the united states, or any of them, nor emit bills, nor borrow money on the credit of the united states, nor appropriate money, nor agree upon the number of vessels of war, to be built or purchased, or the number of land or sea forces to be raised, nor appoint a commander in chief of the army or navy, unless nine states assent to the same: nor shall a question on any other point, except for adjourning from day to day be determined, unless by the votes of a majority of the united states in congress assembled.

The congress of the united states shall have power to adjourn to any time within the year, and to any place within the united states, so that no period of adjournment be for a longer duration than the space of six Months, and shall publish the Journal of their proceedings monthly, except such parts thereof relating to treaties, alliances or military operations as in their judgment require secrecy; and the yeas and nays of the delegates of each state on any question shall be entered on the Journal, when it is desired by any delegate; and the delegates of a state, or any of them, at his or their request shall be furnished with a transcript of the said Journal, except such parts as are above excepted, to lay before the legislatures of the several states.

Art. X. The committee of the states, or any nine of them, shall be authorised to execute, in the recess of congress, such of the powers of congress as the united states in congress assembled, by the consent of nine states, shall from time to time think expedient to vest them with; provided that no power be delegated to the said committee, for the exercise of which, by the articles of confederation, the voice of nine states in the congress of the united states assembled is requisite.

Art. XI. Canada acceding to this confederation, and joining in the measures of the united states, shall be admitted into, and entitled to all the advantages of this union: but no other colony shall be admitted into the same, unless such admission be agreed to by nine states.

Art. XII. All bills of credit emitted, monies borrowed and debts contracted by, or under the authority of congress, before the assembling of the united states, in pursuance of the present confederation, shall be deemed and considered as a charge against the united states, for payment and satisfaction whereof the said united states, and the publc faith are hereby solemnly pledged.

Art. XIII. Every state shall abide by the determinations of the united states in congress assembled, on all questions which by this confederation are submitted to them. And the Articles of this confederation shall be inviolably observed by every state, and the

union shall be perpetual; nor shall any alteration at any time hereafter be made in any of them; unless such alteration be agreed
to in a congress of the united states, and be afterwards confirmed
by the legislatures of every state.

AND WHEREAS it hath pleased the Great Governor of the World
to incline the hearts of the legislatures we respectively represent in
congress, to approve of, and to authorize us to ratify the said articles of confederation and perpetual union. KNOW YE that we the
under-signed delegates, by virtue of the power and authority to us
given for that purpose, do by these presents, in the name and in
behalf of our respective constituents, fully and entirely ratify and
confirm each and every of the said articles of confederation and
perpetual union, and all and singular the matters and things therein
contained: And we do further solemnly plight and engage the
faith of our respective constituents, that they shall abide by the
determinations of the united states in congress assembled, on all
questions, which by the said confederation are submitted to them.
And that the articles thereof shall be inviolably observed by the
states we respectively represent, and that the union shall be perpetual. In Witness whereof we have hereunto set our hands in
Congress. Done at Philadelphia in the state of Pennsylvania the
ninth Day of July in the Year of our Lord one Thousand seven
Hundred and Seventy-eight, and in the third year of the independence of America.

53. Maryland Blocks Ratification
of the Articles of Confederation:
Instructions to Delegates
December 15, 1778

GENTLEMEN,

Having conferred upon you a trust of the highest nature, it is
evident we place great confidence in your integrity, abilities and
zeal to promote the general welfare of the United States, and the

SOURCE: W. C. Ford, et al., eds., *Journals of the Continental
Congress, 1774–1789*, XIV, 619–622.

particular interest of this state, where the latter is not incompatible with the former; but to add greater weight to your proceedings in Congress, and to take away all suspicion that the opinions you there deliver, and the votes you give, may be the mere opinions of individuals, and not resulting from your knowledge of the sense and deliberate judgment of the state you represent, we[1] think it our duty to instruct you as followeth on the subject of the confederation, a subject in which, unfortunately, a supposed difference of interest has produced an almost equal division of sentiments among the several states composing the union: We say a supposed difference of interests; for, if local attachments and prejudices, and the avarice and ambition of individuals, would give way to the dictates of a sound policy, founded on the principles of justice, (and no other policy but what is founded on those immutable principles deserves to be called sound,) we flatter ourselves this apparent diversity of interests would soon vanish; and all the states would confederate on terms mutually advantageous to all; for they would then perceive that no other confederation than one so formed can be lasting. Although the pressure of immediate calamities, the dread of their continuance from the appearance of disunion, and some other peculiar circumstances, may have induced some states to accede to the present confederation, contrary to their own interests and judgments, it requires no great share of foresight to predict, that when those causes cease to operate, the states which have thus acceded to the confederation will consider it as no longer binding, and will eagerly embrace the first occasion of asserting their just rights and securing their independence. Is it possible that those states, who are ambitiously grasping at territories, to which in our judgment they have not the least shadow of exclusive right, will use with greater moderation the increase of wealth and power derived from those territories, when acquired, than what they have displayed in their endeavours to acquire them? we think not; we are convinced the same spirit which hath prompted them to insist on a claim so extravagant, so repugnant to every principle of justice, so incompatible with the general welfare of all the states, will urge them on to add oppression to injustice. If they should not be incited by a superiority of wealth and strength to oppress by open force their less wealthy and less powerful

1. The Maryland House of Delegates.

neighbours, yet the depopulation, and consequently the impover-ishment of those states will necessarily follow, which by an unfair construction of the confederation may be stripped of a common interest in, and the common benefits derivable from, the western country. Suppose, for instance, Virginia indisputably possessed of the extensive and fertile country to which she has set up a claim, what would be the probable consequences to Maryland of such an undisturbed and undisputed possession? they cannot escape the least discerning.

Virginia, by selling on the most moderate terms a small propor-tion of the lands in question, would draw into her treasury vast sums of money, and in proportion to the sums arising from such sales, would be enabled to lessen her taxes: lands comparatively cheap and taxes comparatively low, with the lands and taxes of an adjacent state, would quickly drain the state thus disadvanta-geously circumstanced of its most useful inhabitants, its wealth; and its consequence in the scale of the confederated states would sink of course. A claim so injurious to more than one half, if not to the whole of the United States, ought to be supported by the clearest evidence of the right. Yet what evidences of that right have been produced? what arguments alleged in support either of the evidence or the right; none that we have heard of deserving a seri-ous refutation.

It has been said that some of the delegates of a neighbouring state have declared their opinion of the impracticability of govern-ing the extensive dominion claimed by that state: hence also the necessity was admitted of dividing its territory and erecting a new state, under the auspices and direction of the elder, from whom no doubt it would receive its form of government, to whom it would be bound by some alliance or confederacy, and by whose councils it would be influenced: such a measure, if ever attempted, would certainly be opposed by the other states, as inconsistent with the letter and spirit of the proposed confederation. Should it take place, by establishing a sub-confederacy, *imperium in imperio*, the state possessed of this extensive dominion must then either submit to all the inconveniences of an overgrown and unwieldy govern-ment, or suffer the authority of Congress to interpose at a future time, and to lop off a part of its territory to be erected into a new and free state, and admitted into the confederation on such condi-tions as shall be settled by nine states. If it is necessary for the happiness and tranquillity of a state thus overgrown, that Congress should hereafter interfere and divide its territory; why is the claim to that territory now made and so pertinaciously insisted on? we can suggest to ourselves but two motives; either the declaration of relinquishing at some future period a portion of the country now contended for, was made to lull suspicion asleep, and to cover the designs of a secret ambition, or if the thought was seriously entertained, the lands are now claimed to reap an immediate profit from the sale. We are convinced policy and justice require that a country unsettled at the commencement of this war, claimed by the British crown, and ceded to it by the treaty of Paris, if wrested from the common enemy by the blood and treasure of the thirteen states, should be considered as a common property, subject to be parcelled out by Congress into free, convenient and independent governments, in such manner and at such times as the wisdom of that assembly shall hereafter direct. Thus convinced, we should betray the trust reposed in us by our constituents, were we to authorize you to ratify on their behalf the confederation, unless it be farther explained: we have coolly and dispassionately considered the subject; we have weighed probable inconveniences and hardships against the sacrifice of just essential rights; and do instruct you not to agree to the confederation, unless an article or articles be added thereto in conformity with our declaration: should we succeed in obtaining such article or articles, then you are hereby fully empowered to accede to the confederation.

That these our sentiments respecting the confederation may be more publicly known and more explicitly and concisely declared, we have drawn up the annexed declaration, which we instruct you to lay before Congress, to have it printed and to deliver to each of the delegates of the other states in congress assembled, copies thereof, signed by yourselves or by such of you as may be present at the time of the delivery; to the intent and purpose that the copies aforesaid may be communicated to our brethren of the United States, and the contents of the said declaration taken into their serious and candid consideration.

Also we desire and instruct you to move at a proper time, that these instructions be read to Congress by their secretary, and entered on the journals of Congress.

We have spoken with freedom, as becomes freemen, and we sincerely wish that these our representations may make such an

impression on that assembly as to induce them to make such addition to the articles of confederation as may bring about a permanent union.

A true copy from the proceedings of December 15, 1778.

Test,

J. DUCKETT, C.H.D.[2]

2. Clerk, House of Delegates.

XIV

The Military Front

At the start the war seemed to have pitted against one another extraordinarily mismatched adversaries. The British had the advantage of a well-trained and disciplined army, a strong navy to transport troops and protect supply lines, and abundant financial resources for hiring foreign troops. Nonetheless, in time the Patriot army of citizen-soldiers, fighting on their own ground, managed to tip the scales in their favor. Most important in the early stages of the war were the successes at Trenton and Princeton. Crossing the icy Delaware on December 26, 1776, General Washington and his men surprised and captured the Hessian garrison at Trenton. Eight days later at Princeton, Washington's main army drove the British back toward New Brunswick with heavy losses. The turning point of the war occurred in the fall of 1777 at Saratoga, where the British suffered a decisive defeat, which persuaded France to enter the contest. The second battle of Saratoga (October 7) is described here by Baroness Von Riedesel, wife of one of General Burgoyne's commanders. The end came four years later at Yorktown; and General Cornwallis' capitulation there is traced in his correspondence with Washington.

54. Battle of Trenton, December 26, 1776:
Newspaper Report in *Freeman's Journal* of Philadelphia
January 21, 1777

GENERAL WASHINGTON, finding it absolutely necessary to rouse the spirits of the army, which have been sorely depressed by the long

SOURCE: F. Moore, ed., *Diary of the American Revolution. From Newspapers and Original Documents* (2 vols., New York, 1860), I, 364–366.

eries of disasters which have attended us for almost the whole of
this month, resolved to attempt surprising a considerable body of
Hessians, quartered at Trenton, consisting of about nineteen hundred, and a detachment of British light horse. The plan was as
spiritedly executed as it was judiciously concerted, and terminated
in fully answering the warmest expectations of its projectors. Yesterday morning, orders were given for a large part of the army to
have three days' provisions ready cooked, and forty rounds a man,
and to be ready to march by three o'clock in the afternoon; accordingly the farthest brigades marched by two o'clock. About eleven
o'clock at night it began snowing, and continued so until daybreak,
when a most violent northeast storm came on, of snow, rain, and
hail together.

Early, the American army, which did not exceed twenty-four
hundred men, crossed the Delaware with several companies of artillery, and thirteen field-pieces, and formed in two divisions; one
commanded by General Greene, the other by General Sullivan,
and the whole by General Washington. The attack began about
seven o'clock by the van guard of Sullivan's division, who attacked
the Hessians' advanced guard, about a mile from the town. These
they soon drove, when the whole pushed with the utmost vigor for
the town, which they immediately entered. General Greene's division attacked the town on the other side at the same time. The
Hessians did as much as could be expected from people so surprised, but the impetuosity of our men was irresistible; fifteen
minutes decided the action, and the enemy threw down their arms
and surrendered prisoners of war. They consisted of three regiments of grenadiers and fusileers, and were equal to any troops the
Prince of Hesse could boast of. The troop of British dragoons,
without waiting to be charged, scampered off with the utmost expedition. Could the brigade under Colonel Ewing have landed below the town, as was intended, the light horse must inevitably have
been taken, as well as a considerable number of the Hessians who
got off; but the violence of the wind was such, and the quantity of
ice so great, that he found it impossible to cross. Our success,
though not complete, was great. The men behaved with the utmost bravery. Finding that their guns did not generally go off,
owing to their having been exposed to the snow and rain for six
hours, they charged bayonets, and, with three cheers, rushed like
bloodhounds upon the Hessians, who, astonished at their fury, fled

or threw down their arms; and it was owing to the ardor of the attack that so little blood was shed.

The army returned the same day, and, notwithstanding a continual pelting for twelve hours, of a most violent rain, hail, and snow-storm, we had only two men frozen to death. Luckily they found some hogsheads of rum at Trenton, large draughts of which alone preserved the lives of many. The soldiers behaved exceedingly well with respect to plundering, considering they were animated by revenge for past insults, exasperated by the injuries done their messmates taken at Fort Washington, and animated by every incentive that could work upon the license of a successful army. The general gave the Hessians all their baggage, and they have since gone to the western counties of Pennsylvania, with their packs unsearched. They were amazed at the generosity of the general, so opposite to their own conduct, and called him a very good rebel.

The enemy who lay at Bordentown soon had the alarm, which was communicated to all the parties along the river, who, after remaining under arms the whole day, in the evening marched off, leaving us to take possession of Bordentown, Mount Holly, and Burlington.

55. Battle of Princeton, January 7, 1777: Newspaper Report in *Pennsylvania Journal* of Philadelphia February 5, 1777

ON THE second instant, intelligence was received by express, that the enemy's army was advancing from Princeton towards Trenton, where the main body of the Americans were stationed. Two brigades under Brigadier-Generals Stephen and Fermoy, had been detached several days before, from the main body, to Maidenhead, and were ordered to skirmish with the enemy during their march, and to retreat to Trenton, as occasion should require. A body of men under command of Colonel Hand, were also ordered to meet

SOURCE: F. Moore, *Diary of the American Revolution*, I, 369–372.

the enemy, by which means their march was so much retarded as to give ample time for our forces to form, and prepare to give them a warm reception upon their arrival. Two field-pieces, planted upon a hill, at a small distance above the town, were managed with great advantage, and did considerable execution for some time; after which they were ordered to retire to the station occupied by our forces on the south side of the bridge, over the little river which divides the town into two parts, and opens at right angles into the Delaware. In their way through the town, the enemy suffered much by an incessant fire of musketry from behind the houses and barns. Their army had now arrived at the northern side of the bridge, whilst our army were drawn up, in order of battle, on the southern side. Our cannon played very briskly from this eminence, and were returned as briskly by the enemy. In a few minutes after the cannonade began, a very heavy discharge of musketry ensued, and continued for ten or fifteen minutes. During this action, a party of men were detached from our right wing, to secure a part of the river, which, it was imagined, from the motions of the enemy, they intended to ford. This detachment arrived at the pass very opportunely, and effected their purpose; after this the enemy made a feeble and unsupported attempt to pass the bridge, but this likewise proved abortive. It was now near six o'clock in the evening, and night coming on, closed the engagement. Our fires were built in due season, and were very numerous; and whilst the enemy were amused by these appearances, and preparing for a general attack the ensuing day, our army marched, at about one in the morning, from Trenton, on the south side of the creek, to Princeton. When they arrived near the hill, about one mile from the town, they found a body of the enemy formed upon it, and ready to receive them; upon which a spirited attack was made, both with field-pieces and musketry, and, after an obstinate resistance, and losing a considerable number of their men upon the field, those of them who could not make their escape, surrendered prisoners of war. We immediately marched on to the centre of the town, and there took another party of the enemy near the college. After tarrying a very short time in the town, General Washington marched his army from thence, towards Rocky Hill, and they are now near Morris-town, in high spirits, and in expectation of a junction with the rest of our forces, sufficiently seasonable to make a general attack upon the enemy, and prevent, at least, a considerable part of them from reaching their asylum in New York. It is difficult precisely to ascertain the loss we have sustained in the two engagements, but we think we have lost about forty men killed, and had near double the number wounded. In the list of the former are the brave Colonel Hazlet, Captain Shippen, and Captain Neal, who fell in the engagement upon the hill near Princeton; amongst the latter was Brigadier-General Mercer, who received seven wounds—five in his body, and two in his head, and was much bruised by the breech of a musket, of which bruises he soon after died. The loss sustained by the enemy was much greater than ours, as was easily discovered by viewing the dead upon the field, after the action. We have near a hundred of their wounded prisoners in the town, which, together with those who surrendered, and were taken in small parties endeavoring to make their escape, amount nearly to the number of four hundred, chiefly British troops. Six brass pieces of cannon have fallen into our hands, a quantity of ammunition, and several wagons of baggage. A Captain Leslie was found amongst the dead of the enemy, and was this day buried with the honors of war. A number of other officers were also found on the field, but they were not known, and were buried with the other dead. According to information from the inhabitants of Princeton, the number which marched out of it to attack our army, amounted to seven thousand men, under command of General Cornwallis. This body, as soon as they discovered that they were out-generaled by the march of General Washington, being much chagrined at their disappointment, (as it seems they intended to have cut our army to pieces, crossed the Delaware, and have marched immediately, without any further delay, to Philadelphia,) pushed with the greatest precipitation towards Princeton, where they arrived about an hour after General Washington had left it; and imagining he would endeavor to take Brunswick in the same manner, proceeded directly for that place. Our soldiers were much fatigued, the greatest part of them having been deprived of their rest the two preceding nights; otherwise we might, perhaps, have possessed ourselves of Brunswick. The enemy appear to be preparing to decamp and retire to New York, as they are much disgusted with their late treatment in New Jersey, and have a great inclination to rest themselves a little in some secure winter-quarters.

56. Battle of Saratoga:
Baroness Von Riedesel's Account
October 7–17, 1777

ON THE seventh of October, my husband, with the whole general staff, decamped. Our misfortunes may be said to date from this moment. . . . I observed considerable movement among the troops. My husband thereupon informed me that there was to be a reconnaissance, which, however, did not surprise me, as this often happened. On my way homeward I met many savages in their war dress, armed with guns. To my question where they were going, they cried out to me, "War! war!" which meant that they were going to fight. This completely overwhelmed me, and I had scarcely got back to my quarters when I heard skirmishing and firing, which by degrees became constantly heavier, until finally the noises became frightful. It was a terrible cannonade, and I was more dead than alive. . . .

On the ninth, we spent the whole day in a pouring rain, ready to march at a moment's warning. The savages had lost their courage, and they were seen in all directions going home. The slightest reverse of fortune discouraged them, especially if there was nothing to plunder. . . .

Toward evening, we at last came to Saratoga, which was only half an hour's march from the place where we had spent the whole day. I was wet through and through by the frequent rains and was obliged to remain in this condition the entire night, as I had no place whatever where I could change my linen. I, therefore, seated myself before a good fire and undressed my children; after which, we laid ourselves down together upon some straw. I asked General [William] Phillips, who came up to where we were, why we did not continue our retreat while there was yet time, as my husband had pledged himself to cover it and bring the army through.

SOURCE: Baroness Friederike Charlotte Luise von Riedesel, *Letters and Journals relating to the War of the American Revolution, and the Capture of the German Troops at Saratoga,* trans. William L. Stone (Albany, 1867), 116–137.

"Poor woman," answered he, "I am amazed at you! Completely wet through, have you still the courage to wish to go further in this weather! Would that you were only our commanding general! He halts because he is tired and intends to spend the night here and give us a supper."

In this latter achievement, especially, General Burgoyne was very fond of indulging. He spent half the nights in singing and drinking and amusing himself with the wife of a commissary who was his mistress and who, as well as he, loved champagne.

On the 10th, at seven o'clock in the morning, I drank some tea by way of refreshment; and we now hoped from one moment to another that at last we would again get under way. General Burgoyne, in order to cover our retreat, caused the beautiful houses and mills at Saratoga, belonging to General [Philip] Schuyler, to be burned. An English officer brought some excellent broth, which he shared with me, as I was not able to refuse his urgent entreaties.

Thereupon we set out upon our march, but only as far as another place not far from where we had started. The greatest misery and the utmost disorder prevailed in the army. The commissaries had forgotten to distribute provisions among the troops. There were cattle enough, but not one had been killed. More than thirty officers came to me, who could endure hunger no longer. I had coffee and tea made for them and divided among them all the provisions with which my carriage was constantly filled; for we had a cook who, although an arrant knave, was fruitful in all expedients and often in the night crossed small rivers in order to steal from the country people sheep, poultry, and pigs. He would then charge us a high price for them—a circumstance, however, that we only learned a long time afterward. . . .

The whole army clamored for a retreat, and my husband promised to make it possible, provided only that no time was lost. But General Burgoyne, to whom an order had been promised if he brought about a junction with the army of General Howe, could not determine upon this course, and lost everything by his loitering.

About two o'clock in the afternoon, the firing of cannon and small arms was again heard, and all was alarm and confusion. My husband sent me a message telling me to betake myself forthwith into a house which was not far from there. I seated myself in the calash with my children and had scarcely driven up to the house when I saw on the opposite side of the Hudson River five or six men with guns, which were aimed at us. Almost involuntarily I threw the children on the bottom of the calash and myself over them. At the same instant the churls fired and shattered the arm of a poor English soldier behind us, who was already wounded, and was also on the point of retreating into the house.

Immediately after our arrival a frightful cannonade began, principally directed against the house in which we had sought shelter, probably because the enemy believed, from seeing so many people flocking around it, that all the generals made it their headquarters. Alas! it harbored none but wounded soldiers, or women! We were finally obliged to take refuge in a cellar, in which I laid myself down in a corner not far from the door. My children lay down on the earth with their heads upon my lap, and in this manner we passed the entire night. A horrible stench, the cries of the children, and yet more than all this, my own anguish, prevented me from closing my eyes. On the following morning the cannonade again began, but from a different side. I advised all to go out of the cellar for a little while, during which time I would have it cleaned, as otherwise we would all be sick. They followed my suggestion, and I at once set many hands to work, which was in the highest degree necessary; for the women and children, being afraid to venture forth, had soiled the whole cellar.

After they had all gone out and left me alone, I for the first time surveyed our place of refuge. It consisted of three beautiful cellars, splendidly arched. I proposed that the most dangerously wounded of the officers should be brought into one of them; that the women should remain in another; and that all the rest should stay in the third, which was nearest the entrance. I had just given the cellars a good sweeping and had fumigated them by sprinkling vinegar on burning coals, and each one had found his place prepared for him—when a fresh and terrible cannonade threw us all once more into alarm. Many persons, who had no right to come in, threw themselves against the door. My children were already under the cellar steps, and we would all have been crushed if God had not given me strength to place myself before the door and with extended arms prevent all from coming in; otherwise, everyone of us would have been severely injured.

Eleven cannon balls went through the house, and we could plainly hear them rolling over our heads. One poor soldier, whose leg they were about to amputate, having been laid upon a table for this purpose, had the other leg taken off by another cannon ball, in the very middle of the operation. His comrades all ran off, and when they again came back they found him in one corner of the room, where he had rolled in his anguish, scarcely breathing. I was more dead than alive, though not so much on account of our own danger as for that which enveloped my husband, who, however, frequently sent to see how I was getting along and to tell me that he was still safe. . . .

In this horrible situation we remained six days. Finally, they spoke of capitulating, as by temporizing for so long a time our retreat had been cut off. A cessation of hostilities took place, and soon after this General Burgoyne requested the presence of all the generals and staff officers at a council of war, which was to be held early the next morning; in which he proposed to break the capitulation, already made with the enemy, in consequence of some false information just received. It was, however, finally decided that this was neither practicable nor advisable; and this was fortunate for us, as the Americans said to us afterward that had the capitulation been broken we all would have been massacred; which they could have done the more easily as we were not over four or five thousand men strong and had given them time to bring together more than twenty thousand. . . .

At last my husband sent to me a groom with a message that I should come to him with our children. I, therefore, again seated myself in my dear calash; and in the passage through the American camp I observed with great satisfaction that no one cast at us scornful glances. On the contrary, they all greeted me, even showing compassion on their countenances at seeing a mother with her little children in such a situation. I confess that I feared to come into the enemy's camp, as the thing was so entirely new to me.

When I approached the tents, a noble-looking man came toward me, took the children out of the wagon, embraced and kissed them, and then with tears in his eyes helped me also to alight. "You tremble," said he to me. "Fear nothing."

"No," replied I, "for you are so kind, and have been so tender toward my children, that it has inspired me with courage."

He then led me to the tent of General Gates, with whom I found Generals Burgoyne and Phillips, who were upon an extremely friendly footing with him.

Burgoyne said to me, "You may now dismiss all your apprehensions, for your sufferings are at an end."

I answered him that I should certainly be acting very wrongly to have any more anxiety when our chief had none, and especially when I saw him on such friendly footing with General Gates. All the generals remained to dine with General Gates.

The man who had received me so kindly came up and said to me, "It may be embarrassing to you to dine with all these gentlemen; come now with your children into my tent, where I will give you, it is true, a frugal meal, but one that will be accompanied by the best of wishes."

"You are certainly," answered I, "a husband and a father, since you show me so much kindness."

I then learned that he was the American General Schuyler. He entertained me with excellent smoked tongue, beefsteaks, potatoes, good butter, and bread. Never have I eaten a better meal. I was content. I saw that all around me were so likewise; but that which rejoiced me more than everything else was that my husband was out of danger. As soon as we had finished dinner, he invited me to take up my residence at his house, which was situated in Albany, and told me that General Burgoyne would also be there. I sent and asked my husband what I should do. He sent me word to accept the invitation; and as it was two days' journey from where we were, and already five o'clock in the afternoon; he advised me to set out in advance and to stay over night at a place distant about three hours' ride. General Schuyler was so obliging as to send with me a French officer, who was a very agreeable man and commanded those troops who composed the reconnoitering party of which I have before made mention. As soon as he had escorted me to the house where we were to remain, he went back. . . .

The day after this we arrived at Albany, where we had so often longed to be. But we came not, as we supposed we should, as victors. We were, nevertheless, received in the most friendly manner by the good General Schuyler and by his wife and daughters, who showed us the most marked courtesy, as, also, General Burgoyne, although he had—without any necessity it was said—caused their magnificently built houses to be burned. But they treated us as people who knew how to forget their own losses in the misfortunes of others.

Even General Burgoyne was deeply moved at their magnanimity

and said to General Schuyler, "Is it to me, who have done you so much injury, that you show so much kindness!"

"That is the fate of war," replied the brave man; "let us say no more about it."

We remained three days with them, and they acted as if they were very reluctant to let us go.

57. Capitulation at Yorktown, Virginia: Correspondence Between General George Washington and Earl Cornwallis October 17–18, 1781

Earl Cornwallis to General Washington,
York, 17 October, 1781

SIR,

I propose a cessation of hostilities for twenty-four hours, and that two officers may be appointed by each side, to meet at Mr. Moore's house, to settle terms for the surrender of the posts of York and Gloucester. I have the honor to be, &c.

CORNWALLIS

General Washington to Earl Cornwallis
Camp, before York, 17 October, 1781

MY LORD,

I have had the honor of receiving your Lordship's letter of this date.

An ardent desire to spare the further effusion of blood will readily incline me to listen to such terms for the surrender of your posts of York and Gloucester, as are admissible.

I wish, previously to the meeting of commissioners, that your Lordship's proposals in writing may be sent to the American lines,

SOURCE: Jared Sparks, ed., *Washington's Writings* (12 vols., New York, 1847), VIII, 530–532.

for which purpose a suspension of hostilities, during two hours from the delivery of this letter, will be granted.

I have the honor to be, &c.

GEORGE WASHINGTON

Earl Cornwallis to General Washington
York, half past four o'clock, P.M., *17 October, 1781*

SIR,

I have this moment been honored with your Excellency's letter dated this day.

The time limited for sending my answer will not admit of entering into the detail of articles; but the basis of my proposals will be, that the garrisons of York and Gloucester shall be prisoners of war, with the customary honors. And, for the conveniency of the individuals whom I have the honor to command, that the British shall be sent to Britain, and the Germans to Germany, under engagement not to serve against France, America, or their allies, until released or regularly exchanged. That all arms and public stores shall be delivered up to you; but that the usual indulgence of sidearms to officers, and of retaining private property, shall be granted to officers and soldiers, and that the interest of several individuals, in civil capacities and connected with us, shall be attended to.

If your Excellency thinks that a continuance of the suspension of hostilities will be necessary, to transmit your answer, I shall have no objection to the hour that you may propose.

I have the honor to be, &c.

CORNWALLIS

General Washington to Earl Cornwallis
Camp, before York, 18 October, 1781

MY LORD,

To avoid unnecessary discussion and delays, I shall at once, in answer to your Lordship's letters of yesterday, declare the general basis upon which a definitive treaty and capitulation must take place. The garrisons of York and Gloucester, including the seamen, as you propose, will be received prisoners of war. The condition annexed, of sending the British and German troops to the parts of Europe to which they respectively belong, is inadmissible. Instead of this, they will be marched to such parts of the country as can most conveniently provide for their subsistence; and the benevolent treatment of prisoners, which is invariably observed by the Americans, will be extended to them. The same honors will be granted to the surrendering army as were granted to the garrison of Charleston. The shipping and boats in the two harbours, with all their guns, stores, tackling, furniture, and apparel, shall be delivered in their present state to an officer of the navy, appointed to take possession of them.

The artillery, arms, accoutrements, military chest, and public stores of every denomination, shall be delivered unimpaired to the heads of the departments, to which they respectively belong.

The officers will be indulged in retaining their side-arms; and the officers and soldiers may preserve their baggage and effects; with this reserve, that property taken in the country will be reclaimed.

With regard to individuals in civil capacities, whose interest your Lordship wishes may be attended to, until they are more particularly described, nothing definitive can be settled.

I have to add, that I expect the sick and wounded will be supplied with their own hospital stores, and be attended by British surgeons, particularly charged with the care of them.

Your Lordship will be pleased to signify your determination, either to accept or reject the proposals now offered, in the course of two hours from the delivery of this letter, that commissioners may be appointed to digest the articles of capitulation, or a renewal of hostilities may take place.

I have the honor to be, &c.
GEORGE WASHINGTON

Earl Cornwallis to General Washington
York, 18 October, 1781

SIR,

I agree to open a treaty of capitulation upon the basis of the garrisons of York and Gloucester, including seamen, being prisoners of war, without annexing the condition of their being sent to Europe; but I expect to receive a compensation in the articles of capitulation for the surrender of Gloucester in its present state of defence.

I shall in particular desire, that the Bonetta sloop-of-war may be left entirely at my disposal, from the hour that the capitulation is signed, to receive an aid-de-camp to carry my despatches to Sir Henry Clinton. Such soldiers as I may think proper to send as passengers in her, to be manned with fifty men of her own crew, and to be permitted to sail without examination, when my despatches are ready; engaging on my part, that the ship shall be brought back and delivered to you, if she escapes the dangers of the sea, that the crew and soldiers shall be accounted for in future exchanges, that she shall carry off no officer without your consent, nor public property of any kind; and I shall likewise desire, that the traders and inhabitants may preserve their property, and that no person may be punished or molested for having joined the British troops.

If you choose to proceed to negotiation on these grounds, I shall appoint two field-officers of my army to meet two officers from you, at any time and place that you think proper, to digest the articles of capitulation. I have the honor to be, &c.

CORNWALLIS

XV

The Home Front

The American Revolution was waged on the home front as well as on the battlefield. Armies first had to be raised and then supplied with arms, powder, equipment, medicines, food, and clothing. The problems of supplying and maintaining an army in the field raised extraordinary difficulties for Congress, which, lacking effective taxing powers, was forced to resort to loans and paper money. To counteract inflation, an effort was made to hold wages and prices in line. The New Haven Convention, which comprised delegates from a number of states, was one of several attempts at stabilization.

The wartime emergency, with its consequent shortages, encouraged speculation and profiteering. In Pennsylvania a disgruntled mob attacked the residence of James Wilson, a noted lawyer and speculator who had defended merchants before price-control committees. The renowned artist, Charles Willson Peale, who as militia officer sought to restrain the rioters although sympathizing with their grievances, provides, in a report he prepared for Joseph Reed, President of the Pennsylvania Executive Council, a firsthand account of the incident. Profiteering by Maryland's Congressman Samuel Chase, who took advantage of inside information to make a secret purchase of grain for the French fleet, was denounced in public letters by young Alexander Hamilton.

Hamilton and a number of others believed that the solution to Congress' financial troubles was a central bank which would ensure a stable currency and provide the government with essential banking services. No later than the year 1780 he had formulated his fiscal and banking proposals and sent them on to a delegate in Congress; probably Robert Morris or General John Sullivan, active in Congress in financial measures, was the addressee. By the start of 1780, Congress had issued close to $200,000,000 in paper currency ("Continentals"); additional millions were outstanding in certificates for supplies requisitioned, issues of the loan office, and certificates given soldiers for their back pay. On March 18, 1780, Congress resolved to retire the bills in circulation by accepting them in payments due it at one-fortieth their face value. Almost coincidentally Robert Morris assumed the office of Superintendent of Finance and made substantial progress toward placing the country on a specie basis.

58. Holding the Wage-Price Line: New Haven Convention, Report of January 29, 1778

RESOLVED,

I. That the various kinds of Labour of Farmers, Mechanicks and others be set and affixed at rates not exceeding 75 per cent advance from what their respective labours were at in the same places in the several States aforesaid, through the various seasons of the year 1774.

II. That the price of Teaming and all kinds of Land transportation shall not exceed the rate of Five twelfths of a Continental dollar for the carriage of twenty hundred neat weight per mile, including all expenses attending the same.

III. That all kinds of American Manufactures or internal produce not particularly mentioned and regulated by this Convention be estimated at rates not exceeding 75 per cent from the prices they were usually sold at in the several parts of the respective States aforesaid in the year 1774, excepting Salt, Cordwood, Charcoal, Mutton, Lamb, Veal, small meats and Poultry of all kinds, Roots and Vegetables, the prices of which may be better regulated by the respective legislatures (if they shall judge it expedient) than by this Convention.

IV. That the price of Hemp, Flax, Sheep's-Wool, all kinds of Woollen and Linen Cloths, Hosiery of all kinds, Felt Hats, Wire and Wool-cards manufactured in America, shall not exceed the rate of cent per cent advance from the prices they were at in the several parts of the States aforesaid in the year 1774.

V. That the price of all kinds of European Goods, Wares and Merchandize, imported from foreign parts or brought into these States by Capture or otherwise shall not exceed the rate of one Continental dollar, for each shilling Sterling, prime cost of such Goods in Europe exclusive of all other Charges, when sold from

SOURCE: New Haven Colony Historical Society, Papers, III (1882), 52–54.

the Importer or Captor, excepting only the following articles, viz: All kinds of Woollen and Linen Goods and Checks suitable for the Army, Drugs and Medicines, Duck of all kinds, Cordage, Tin Plates, Copperas, Files, Allum, Brimstone, Felt Hats, Nails, Window Glass, Salt, Steel, Wire, Wool and Cotton-cards, Naval and Military Stores.

VI. That all Woollen Cloth, Blankets, Linens, Shoes, Stockings, Hats and other articles of cloathing suitable for the Army, heretofore imported, which are or shall be seized, and taken by order of authority, for the use of the army, shall be estimated at the above rate, with the addition of the stated allowance for land carriage, if any there be, to the place where taken.

VII. That the price of the following articles at the first Port of delivery, or place of manufacture, within these States, shall not exceed the rates to them affixed respectively, viz:

Good West India Rum, per Gallon by wholesale	£0	18s.
Good merchantable N. England ditto		12
Best Muscovado Sugar per hundred lbs.	10	0.1
All other Sugars in usual proportions, according to quality		
Best Molasses per Gallon by wholesale		9.1
Coffee not exceeding ¾ of a dollar per lb. by the hundred weight		
Good Merchantable Whiskey, per Gallon		7.1
Geneva, Brandy and all other distilled Spirits not herein enumerated, per Gallon not exceeding 12s.		12

VIII. That no Trader, Retailer or Vender of foreign Goods, Wares or Merchandize shall be allowed more than at the rate of 25 per cent. advance upon the price such Goods, wares or merchandize are or shall be first sold for by the Importer or Captor, agreeable to this regulation, with the addition only of cost and charges of transporting them by land at the rate of five-twelfths of a dollar per mile for transporting twenty hundred neat weight from the first port of delivery to the place where the same shall be sold and delivered by retail.

IX. That Innholders be not allowed more than 50 per cent advance on the wholesale price of all liquors or other foreign articles herein stated and by them sold in small quantities, allowing as aforesaid for charges of transporting. And all other articles of Entertainment, refreshment or Forage not to exceed 75 per cent advance on the prices the same were at in the same places in the year 1774.

X. That the articles enumerated in the following Table shall not be sold or disposed of at higher prices, in the respective States and places therein named, than at the rate set down and affixed to such articles respectively, with the addition only of the stated allowance for land carriage, if any there shall be. The same being estimated in lawful money at six shillings per Dollar.

The first column shows the price in New Hampshire.

The second in Massachusetts Bay and Rhode Island.

The third Connecticut, New York, New Jersey and Pennsylvania.

Merchantable Wheat, Peas, and White Beans, per Bushel	13s.	0d.	12s.	0d.	9s.	9d.
Merchantable Flour, per gross weight	36		33	4	27	
Rye or Rye Meal, per Bushel	7	6	7		6	6
Indian Corn, per Bushel	5	6	5	3	4	6
Oats, per Bushel	3	9	3	6	3	
Pork well fatted, from 100 lbs. to 150 lbs. per Hog, per lb.		8		7¼		5½
Ditto, weighing from 150 to 200 lbs.		8¼		7½		6
Ditto, weighing more than 200 lbs.		9		8		6½
Best American made Cheese, per lb.		10		10, 9		9

The following prices alike in all the States aforesaid:

Best Grass fed Beef, Hide and Tallow, per lb.	35s.	0d.
and in proportion for inferior quality		
Best stall fed ditto, with Hide and Tallow	48	
inferior in proportion, till July 1st.		
Good Butter per lb., by the Firkin or Cask,	1	3
per lb., in small quantity	1	4
Raw Hides, per lb.,		4½
and other skins in usual proportion		
Good, well tann'd Sole Leather, per lb.,	2	
Skins and all curried leather in due proportion		
Men's neat's leather Shoes, common sort	12	
Calf Skin ditto, best quality	15	
Women's and Children's in proportion		
Bloomery Iron at place of manufacture	£48 per ton	
Refined Iron do.	56	do.
Pig Iron, where made	18	do.
Best American manufactured Steel, fit for Edge Tools, per lb.	2s.	0d.
Common Steel, made in America	1	4

XI. *Resolved*, That it be recommended to the several Legislatures of these States that they cause the Laws they may enact to carry these resolves into execution to be in force from and after the 20th of March next with such penalties annexed as they shall judge effectual.

XII. Whereas it may be greatly subservient to the spirited and effectual execution of this plan of regulation of prices that each State represented in this Convention, should be assured that the others of them had stop'd the circulation of the Bills emitted on their respective Credits, and had resolved to carry all the other requisitions of Congress expressed in their resolves of Nov. 22 into execution. Therefore, *Resolved,* That the said States be desired as soon as may be, after the receipt of this Report, to write circular Letters to the other States, giving an account of their Resolutions and proceedings thereon.

Signed per order, Thos. Cushing, President
Attest, Henry Daggett, Secretary

59. Attack on "Fort Wilson," October 4, 1779: Statement of Charles Willson Peale

The rapidity of the depreciation of the Continental money was at this period such that those who retained it a few days could not purchase near the value which they had given for it.

This being a grievance greatly felt by those who had been most active in favour of the Revolution, and among them those who had on every occasion rendered their personal service in the militia, many of whom thought that this continual depreciation of their favourite paper was brought about by the machinations of their internal enemies. Very few indeed could trace the real or principal cause to its true source, viz. that of too great a quantity being issued and put into circulation. Taxation being too slow to obtain the necessary supply for the support of an army, Congress were continually obliged to be issuing more, although there was already so much in use as to have totally banished gold and silver in common dealings.

At the meeting of the militia of Philadelphia on the commons in 1779, a number of those active Whigs whose zeal would carry them any length in their favourite cause, and whose tempers had now become soured by the many insults they had met with from the

Source: W. B. Reed, *Life and Correspondence of Joseph Reed* (2 vols., Philadelphia, 1847), II, 423–426.

Tories, assembled at Burns' tavern, and after they had come to some resolutions, more passionate than judicious, that of sending away the wives and children of those men who had gone with the British, or were within the British lines, was adopted.

After these zealots had formed this design, they then began to devise the mode of carrying it into execution, and proposed to put themselves under some commander, and accordingly sent a messenger to request Captain Peale to attend them. But so soon as he was made acquainted with the business, he told them that he could not approve of the measure, as it would in the practice be found a difficult and dangerous undertaking; that the taking of women and children from their homes would cause much affliction and grief; that, when seen, the humanity of their fellow-citizens would be roused into an opposition to such a measure; that such attempts must of course fail. But all his arguments were in vain; they could not see these difficulties with a *determined* band. He then told them that the danger in case of a failure in such an attempt would be imminent to the commander of such a party. The reply was that General Washington could not take his command without running some risks, and that they in this undertaking would sacrifice their lives or effect it.

Captain Peale was at last obliged to refuse, and made the excuse that he was applied to by some of his friends to stand as a candidate at the then approaching election for members of the General Assembly; after which all further entreaty ceased, and he left them, and did not hear anything further of their proceedings until the Thursday following, when he received a notice that desired him, with Col. Bull, Major Boyd and Dr. Hutchinson, to meet the militia on the Monday following at Mrs. Burns' tavern on the common. Those persons so noticed having consulted together, all of them disapproved of the violent proceedings of the militia. Dr. Hutchinson said he would not attend the meeting; Peale and the other gentlemen conceived that they as good citizens were in duty bound to go and use their best endeavours to restrain, as far as they might be able, any violent and improper proceedings, and, in duty to themselves, at least to remonstrate in a public manner against having any part in the business.

After further consideration, Dr. Hutchinson agreed to meet them; Col. Bull, being dangerously ill, could not attend.

Accordingly, on that memorable Monday Dr. Hutchinson, Major Boyd and Captain Peale went to Mrs. Burns' tavern (where great numbers of the militia had already assembled), and they did use every argument in their power to prevent any further proceedings in that vain and dangerous undertaking. They represented the difficulty of selecting such characters as all could agree to be obnoxious amongst such a body of the people; that in such an attempt they must infallibly differ as to the object—of course no good purpose could be answered.

Among the militia were many Germans, whose attachment to the American cause was such that they disregarded every danger, and whose resentment at this time was most violently inveterate against all Tories. They only looked straight forward, regardless of consequences. In short, to reason with a multitude of devoted patriots assembled on such an occasion was in vain; and after Peale found all that could be said availed nought, he left them and went to his home, and afterwards to the President's, General Reed, whom he found was preparing to go out in order to prevent mischief, which he said was to be feared from the tidings then brought him. Captain Peale immediately returned to his home, where he had not long been before he heard the firing of small arms. He then began to think that he ought to prepare himself by getting his fire-arms in order, in case he should be under the necessity of making use of them; for no man could now know where the affair would end; and finding his wife and family very uneasy, he determined to stay within his own doors for the present time.

Shortly that tragical scene was ended, and very fortunately no more lives were lost.

The militia having taken two men who they conceived were inimical to the American cause, they were parading them up Walnut Street, and when they had got opposite James Wilson, Esq.'s house at the corner of Third Street, where a considerable number of gentlemen to the number of about thirty had collected and had armed themselves, amongst them Captain Campbell, commander of an invalid corps, this unfortunate person hoisted a window with a pistol in his hand, and some conversation having passed between him and the passing militia, a firing began, and poor Campbell was killed; a Negro boy at some distance from the house was also killed, and four or five persons badly wounded. The militia had now become highly exasperated, and had just broke into the house, and most probably would have killed every one assembled within those walls; but, very fortunately for them, General Reed with a number of the light horse appeared at this fortunate juncture and dispersed the militia. Numbers of them were taken and committed to the common jail, and a guard placed to prevent a rescue.

The next morning the officers of the militia and numbers of the people assembled at the Court House in Market Street, and the minds of the citizens generally seemed to be much distressed.

The militia of Germantown were beginning to assemble, and General Reed had sent Mr. Matlack, the Secretary of Council, to the officers of the militia, then assembled in Market Street, as above mentioned, to endeavour to keep them waiting until he could address the militia of Germantown, after which he would be with them.

Peale, hearing of this meeting at the Court House, went there, and found that the officers were exceedingly warm and full of resentment that any of the militia should be kept in durance in the jail; they appeared to be ripe for undertaking the release of the prisoners, and all Mr. Matlack's arguments, perhaps, would have been insufficient to keep them much longer from being active.

Several of the magistrates were present, and Peale whispered Mr. Matlack to know if he did not think it would be prudent to propose the taking bail for the persons and let them be released by the magistrates then present. This opinion was approved of as the most certain means to prevent disorder and perhaps a further shedding of blood. This measure being offered to the officers of the militia, they readily entered security for the personal appearance of the militia then confined at any future time for trial, and, in consequence, the prisoners were released by the magistrates' orders.

General Reed, having succeeded in preventing the Germantown militia from entering the city, came expecting to find things in the situation he had left them, and was not a little mortified to find that Mr. Matlack could not do as he had ordered. The people were assembled at the State House, and he publicly harangued them, after which, amongst a number of the officers and his particular acquaintance, he was blaming Mr. Matlack for not doing as he had requested him. Peale then told the General that Mr. Matlack ought not to suffer blame, for if the measure was wrong, that he was the unlucky person who had proposed that measure, which he then conceived was the best expedient, as it had the appearance of being a judicial act.

60. War on Profiteers:
Alexander Hamilton's Letters to New York *Journal*
October 16 and 26, 1778

Letter of October 16, 1778

Sir:—

While every method is taken to bring to justice those men whose principles and practices have been hostile to the present revolution, it is to be lamented that the conduct of another class, equally criminal, and, if possible, more mischievous, has hitherto passed with impunity, and almost without notice. I mean that tribe who, taking advantage of the times, have carried the spirit of monopoly and extortion to an excess which scarcely admits of a parallel. Emboldened by the success of progressive impositions, it has extended to all the necessaries of life. The exorbitant price of every article, and the depreciation upon our currency, are evils derived essentially from this source. When avarice takes the lead in a state, it is commonly the forerunner of its fall. How shocking is it to discover among ourselves, even at this early period, the strongest symptoms of this fatal disease.

There are men in all countries, the business of whose lives it is to raise themselves above indigence by every little art in their power. When these men are observed to be influenced by the spirit I have mentioned, it is nothing more than might be expected, and can only excite contempt. When others, who have characters to support, and credit enough in the world to satisfy a moderate appetite for wealth, in an honorable way, are found to be actuated by the same spirit, our contempt is mixed with indignation. But when a man, appointed to be the guardian of the State and the depositary of the happiness and morals of the people, forgetful of the solemn relation in which he stands, descends to the dishonest artifices of a mercantile projector, and sacrifices his conscience and his trust to

Source: "Publius," *N.Y. Journal, and the General Advertiser* (Poughkeepsie, John Holt), October 19 and 26, 1778.

pecuniary motives, there is no strain of abhorrence of which the human mind is capable, no punishment the vengeance of the people can inflict, which may not be applied to him with justice. If it should have happened that a member of C——ss had been this degenerate character, and has been known to turn the knowledge of secrets to which his office gave him access to the purposes of private profit, by employing emissaries to engross an article of immediate necessity to the public service, he ought to feel the utmost rigor of public resentment, and be detested as a traitor of the worst and most dangerous kind.

Letter of October 26, 1778

SIR:—

The honor of being a hero of a public panegyric is what you[1] could hardly have aspired to, either from your talents, or from your good qualities. The partiality of your friends has never given you credit for more than mediocrity in the former; and experience has proved that you are indebted for all your consequence to the reverse of the latter. Had you not struck out a new line of prostitution for yourself, you might still have remained unnoticed and contemptible—your name scarcely known beyond the little circle of your electors and clients, and recorded only in the journals of C——ss. But you have now forced yourself into view, in a light too singular and conspicuous to be overlooked, and have acquired an undisputed title to be immortalized in infamy. . . .

It is unfortunate for the reputation of Governor Johnstone,[2] and for the benevolent purposes of his royal master, that he was not acquainted with the frailties of your character before he made his experiment on men whose integrity was above temptation. If he had known you, and had thought your services worth purchasing, he might have played a sure game, and avoided the risk of exposing himself to contempt and ridicule. And you, sir, might have made your fortune at one decisive stroke.

It is a matter of curious inquiry, what could have raised you in the first instance, and supported you since in your present eleva-

1. Samuel Chase.
2. One of the commissioners sent over from England in 1778 to effect a reconciliation with America, Johnstone was accused of attempting to bribe American patriot leaders.

tion. I never knew a single man but was ready to do ample justice to your demerit. The most indulgent opinion of the qualifications of your head and heart could not offend the modest delicacy of your ear, or give the smallest cause of exultation to your vanity. It is your lot to have the peculiar privilege of being universally despised. Excluded from all resource to your abilities or virtues, there is only one way in which I can account for the rank you hold in the political scale. There are seasons in every country when noise and impudence pass current for worth; and in popular commotions especially, the clamors of interested and factious men are often mistaken for patriotism. You prudently took advantage of the commencement of the contest, to ingratiate yourself in the favor of the people, and gain an ascendant in their confidence by appearing a zealous assertor of their rights. No man will suspect you of the folly of public spirit—a heart notoriously selfish exempts you from any charge of this nature, and obliges us to resolve the part you took into opposite principles. A desire of popularity and a rivalship with the ministry will best explain them. Their attempt to confine the sale of a lucrative article of commerce to the East India Company, must have been more unpardonable in the sight of a *monopolist* than the most daring attack upon the public liberty. There is a vulgar maxim which has pointed emphasis in your case, and has made many notable patriots in this dispute.

It sometimes happens that a temporary caprice of the people leads them to make choice of men whom they neither love nor respect; and that they afterward, from an indolent and mechanical habit natural to the human mind, continue their confidence and support merely because they had once conferred them. I cannot persuade myself that your influence rests upon a better foundation, and I think the finishing touch you have given to the profligacy of your character must rouse the recollection of the people, and force them to strip you of a dignity which sets so awkwardly upon you, and consign you to that disgrace which is due to a scandalous perversion of your trust.

When you resolved to avail yourself of the extraordinary demand for the article of flour which the wants of the French fleet must produce, and which your official situation early impressed on your attention, to form connections, for monopolizing that article, and raising the price upon the public more than an hundred per cent; when by your intrigues and studied delays you protracted the

determination of the C-tt-e of C-ss on the proposals made by Mr.
W-sw-th, C-ss-y- G-n-l,[3] for procuring the necessary supplies for the
public use, to give your agents time to complete their purchases;—I
say when you were doing all this, and engaging in a traffic infamous
in itself, repugnant to your station, and ruinous to your country,
did you pause and allow yourself a moment's reflection on the
consequences? Were you infatuated enough to imagine you would
be able to conceal the part you were acting? Or had you conceived
a thorough contempt of reputation, and a total indifference to the
opinion of the world? Enveloped in the promised gratifications of
your avarice, you probably forgot to consult your understanding,
and lost sight of every consideration that ought to have regulated
the man, the citizen, the statesman.

I am aware that you could never have done what you have without first obtaining a noble victory over every sentiment of honor
and generosity. You have therefore nothing to fear from the re-
proaches of your own mind. Your insensibility secures you from
remorse. But there are arguments powerful enough to extort repen-
tance, even from a temper as callous as yours. You are a man of the
world, sir; your self-love forces you to respect its decisions, and your
utmost credit with it will not bear the test of your recent enormi-
ties, or screen you from the fate you deserve.

61. A National Bank: Alexander Hamilton
[Morristown, New Jersey, November 1779 to March 1780]

THE OBJECT of principal concern is the state of our currency. In my
opinion, all our speculations on this head have been founded in
error. Most people think that the depreciation might have been
avoided by provident arrangements in the beginning, without [any
aid] from abroad; and a great many of our [sanguine] politicians,
till very lately, imagined the money might still be restored by ex-

3. Jeremiah Wadsworth, Commissary General, whose proposals were being
considered by a Committee of Congress.

SOURCE: Hamilton Papers, Library of Congress, 1st series.

pedients with[in our]selves. Hence the delay in attempting to procure a foreign loan.

This idea proceeded from [an igno]rance of the real extent of our resources. The war, particularly in the first periods, [required] exertions beyond our strength, to which [neither] our population nor riches were equal. [We] have the fullest proof of this in the const[ant thin]ness of our armies, the impossibility, at [this time,] of recruiting them otherwise than by [compulsion,] the scarcity of hands in husbandry and [other oc]cupations, the decrease of our staple [commodi]ties, and the difficulty of every species [of supply.] I am aware that the badness of the [money] has its influence; but it [was ori]ginally an effect, not a cause, tho[ugh it] now partakes of the nature of both. A part of those [evils] would appear [were] our finances in a more flourishing cond[ition.] We experienced them before the [money] was materially depreciated; and they [contri]buted to its depreciation. The want [of men] soon obliged the public to pay extrav[agant] wages for them in every department. [Agri]culture languished from a defect [of] [hands.] The mechanic arts did the same. [The price] of every kind of labor increased, [and the] articles of foreign commerce, from the [interrup]tion it received, more than kept pace [with] other things.

The relative value of m[oney] being determined by the greater or less [portion] of labor and commodities which it [will pur]chase; whatever these gained in price, [that of] course lost in value.

The public expenditures, from the dearness of everything, necessarily became immense; great[er] in proportion than in other countries; and much beyond any revenues which the best concreted scheme of finance could have extracted from the natural funds of the State. No taxes, which the people were capable of bearing, on that quantity of money which is deemed a proper medium for this country (had it been gold instead of paper), would have been sufficient for the current exigencies of government.

The most opulent states of Europe, in a war of any duration, are commonly obliged to have recourse to foreign loans or subsidies. How, then, could we expect to do without them, and not augment the quantity of our artificial wealth beyond those bounds which were proper to preserve its credit? The idea was chimerical.

The quantity of money formerly in circulation among us is estimated at about thirty millions of dollars. This was barely sufficient for our interior commerce. Our exterior commerce was chiefly carried on by barter. We sent our commodities abroad, and brought back others in return. The balance of the principal branch was against us, and the little *specie* derived from others was transferred directly to the payment of that balance, without passing into home circulation. It would have been impracticable, by loans and taxes, to bring such a portion of the forementioned sum into the public coffers as would have answered the purposes of the war; nor could it have spared so considerable a part, without obstructing the operations of domestic commerce. Taxes are limited, not only by the quantity of wealth in a state, but by the temper, habits, and genius of the people; all which, in this country, conspired to render them moderate; and as to loans, men will not be prevailed upon to lend money to the public when there is a scarcity, and they can find a more profitable way of employing it otherwise, as was our case. . . .

From these reasonings it results, that it was not in the power of Congress, when their emissions had arrived at the thirty millions of dollars, to put a stop to them. They were obliged, in order to keep up the supplies, to go on creating artificial revenues by new emissions; and as these multiplied, their value declined. The progress of the depreciation might have been retarded, but it could not have been prevented. It was, in a great degree, necessary.

There was but one remedy; a foreign loan. All other expedients should rather have been considered as auxiliary. Could a loan have been obtained, and judiciously applied, assisted by a vigorous system of taxation, we might have avoided that excess of emissions which has ruined the paper. The credit of such a fund would have procured loans from the moneyed and trading men within ourselves; because it might have been so directed, as to have been beneficial to them in their commercial transactions abroad.

The necessity for a foreign loan is now greater than ever. Nothing else will retrieve our affairs. . . .

How this loan is to be employed is now the question; and its difficulty equal to its importance. Two plans have been proposed: one, to purchase up at once, in specie or sterling bills, all superfluous paper; and to endeavor, by taxes, loans, and economy, to hinder its returning into circulation. The remainder, it is supposed, would then recover its value. This, it is said, will reduce our public debt to the sterling cost of the paper. . . .

A great source of error in disquisitions of this nature, is the judging of events by abstract calculations; which, though geometrically true, are false as they relate to the concerns of beings governed more by passion and prejudice than by an enlightened sense of their interests. A degree of illusion mixes itself in all the affairs of society. The opinion of objects has more influence than their real nature. The quantity of money in circulation is certainly a chief cause of its decline; but we find it is depreciated more than five times as much as it ought to be by this rule. The excess is derived from opinion; a want of confidence. In like manner we deceive ourselves, when we suppose the value will increase in proportion as the quantity is lessened. Opinion will operate here also; and a thousand circumstances may promote or counteract the principle.

The other plan proposed is to convert the loan into merchandise, and import it on public account. This plan is incomparably better than the former. Instead of losing on the sale of its specie or bills, the public would gain a considerable profit on the commodities imported. The loan would go much further this way, towards supplying the expenses of the war; and a large stock of valuable commodities, useful to the army and to the country, would be introduced. This would affect the prices of things in general, and assist the currency. But the arts of monopolize[r]s would prevent its having so extensive and durable an influence as it ought to have.

A great impediment to the success of this, as well as the former scheme, will be the vast sums requisite for the current expenses. . . .

The farmers have the game in their own hands, and will make it very difficult to lower the price of their commodities. . . .

One measure, alone, can counterbalance these advantages of the farmers, and oblige them to contribute their proper quota to the support of government: a tax in kind.

This ought instantly to begin throughout the States. The present quantity of cash, though nominally enormous, would, in reality, be found incompetent to domestic circulation, were it not that a great part of our internal commerce is carried on by barter. For this reason, it is impossible, by pecuniary taxes, to raise a sum proportioned to the wants of the State. The money is no longer a general representative; and when it ceases to be so, the State ought to call for a portion of the thing represented; or, in other words, to tax in kind. This will greatly facilitate whatever plan of finance is adopted; because it will lessen the expenditures in cash, and make it the easier to retain what is drawn in. . . .

The only plan that can preserve the currency is one that will make it the *immediate* interest of the moneyed men to cooperate with government in its support. The country is in the same predicament in which France was previous to the famous Mississippi scheme, projected by Mr. Law.[1] Its paper money, like ours, had dwindled to nothing; and no efforts of the government could revive it, because the people had lost all confidence in its ability. Mr. Law, who had much more penetration than integrity, readily perceived that no plan could succeed which did not unite the interest and credit of rich individuals with those of the state; and upon this he framed the idea of his project, which, so far, agreed in principle with the Bank of England. The foundation was good, but the superstructure too vast. The proprietors aimed at unlimited wealth, and the government itself expected too much; which was the cause of the ultimate miscarriage of the scheme, and of all the mischiefs that befell the kingdom in consequence.

It will be our wisdom to select what is good in this plan, and in any others that have gone before us, avoiding their defects and excesses. Something on a similar principle in America will alone accomplish the restoration of paper credit, and establish a permanent fund for the future exigencies of government.

Article 1st. The plan I would propose is that of an American bank, instituted by authority of Congress for ten years, under the denomination of The Bank of the United States. . . .

I have confined the bank to the space of ten years, because this will be long enough to judge of its advantages and disadvantages; and the latter may be rectified by giving it a new form. I do not suppose it will ever be discontinued; because it seems to be founded on principles that must always operate well, and make it the interest, both of government and the company, to uphold it. But I suppose the plan capable of improvement, which experience will suggest.

I give one half of the whole property of the bank to the United

1. John Law, a Scottish financier, whose Mississippi Scheme (c. 1720) for the exploitation of French colonial trade and the settlement of Louisiana led to a speculative orgy and finally a pricking of the bubble.

States; because it is not only just but desirable to both parties. The United States contribute a great part of the stock; their authority is essential to the existence of the bank; their credit is pledged for its support. The plan would ultimately fail, if the terms were too favorable to the company, and too hard upon government. It might be encumbered with a debt which it could never pay, and be obliged to take refuge in a bankruptcy. The share which the State has in the profits will induce it to grant more ample privileges, without which the trade of the company might often be under restrictions injurious to its success. . . .

It may be objected that this plan will be prejudicial to trade, by making the government a party with a trading company; which may be a temptation to arrogate exclusive privileges, and thereby fetter that spirit of enterprise and competition on which the prosperity of commerce depends. But Congress may satisfy the jealousies on this head, by a solemn resolution not to grant exclusive privileges, which alone can make the objection valid. Large trading companies must be beneficial to the commerce of a nation, when they are not invested with these, because they furnish a capital with which the most extensive enterprises may be undertaken. There is no doubt the establishment proposed would be very serviceable at this juncture, merely in a commercial view; for private adventurers are not a match for the numerous obstacles resulting from the present posture of affairs. . . .

XVI

The Diplomatic Front

From July of 1775, when Jefferson and John Dickinson composed Congress' Declaration of the Causes and Necessity of Taking up Arms, the Patriots were convinced of the need to secure foreign aid. They were equally convinced of the perils of foreign alliances. France, anxious to redress the balance of power against England, generously provided indispensable aid—a long list of arms and supplies—to which the Spaniards also contributed initially. Even though America had not intended to move beyond a commercial alliance with France, the French court, fearing that the British after their defeat at Saratoga might come to terms with America, aligned themselves openly on the American side.

What the French feared did come to pass when, in the winter of 1778, the British dispatched a peace mission to America headed by the Earl of Carlisle. That mission was prepared to offer autonomy to America, a proposal that might well have prevented the conflict had it come in 1775, but was now too little and too late. Congress refused to receive the commissioners, who sought futilely to appeal to the American people directly.

Both in its specific provisions and in its significant omissions the terms of the military alliance concluded between France and the thirteen "United States of America" (each of the thirteen states was named in the treaty) proved central to Franco-American diplomatic relations. Thus, France guaranteed the "independence absolute and unlimited" of the United States, including its "possessions," but the treaty failed to define the territorial limits of the Thirteen States. The French were to oppose the American contention that these limits extended west to the Mississippi. During the dark days of the war France's foreign minister, the Comte de Vergennes, considered, as a possible way out of the dilemma posed by the pledge for American independence, a proposal advanced by Austro-Russian mediators that negotiations be undertaken with the Thirteen States separately, with a view to obtaining independence for some and dropping the claims for others, such as the Southern states that were presently occupied by the British army. Fortunately for the United States, the victory at Yorktown foreclosed the necessity of agreeing to a compromise peace so far as America was concerned. Furthermore, the treaty of alliance was not explicit on the subject of fishing rights off the Grand Bank, to which both France and the United States laid claim.

Peacemaking on the part of the allies was complicated by the separate alliance France made with Spain in 1779. At that time Spain joined the war as a cobelligerent of France but not as an ally of the insurgent Americans. The French commitment to Spain to continue the war until Gibraltar had been retaken from the English amounted to a unilateral change in the terms of the treaty between France and America. The failure of the allied siege of Gibraltar in the fall of 1782 blasted Spain's hopes of recovering the Rock.

Preliminary negotiations between the United States and Great Britain were conducted separately and in part secretly from France, although the French Court grudgingly approved the results of the negotiations. Since the preliminary treaty was considered a tentative draft, the Americans technically did not violate the provision of the treaty of alliance requiring the prior approval of either ally. Although the American commissioners—John Adams, Benjamin Franklin, and John Jay, and at the very last, Henry Laurens—yielded on minor matters, such as the issue of debts to British creditors and the forfeiture of Loyalist estates, they remained adamant on the crucial issue of complete and full independence, a continental domain for the thirteen seaboard states, and rights to share in the North American fisheries.

During the many months between the signing of the preliminary treaty on November 30, 1782, and the definitive treaty on September 3, 1783, the English failed to obtain a single modification of the terms of the preliminary treaty, while the Americans in turn were unable to wring trade concessions from the British, as a result of powerful lobbying by English shipping interests and of the widely shared view in England that America's economy was largely dependent on the English connection. The only change between the two drafts was the omission from the definitive treaty of the separate secret article which awarded to the British, should they secure Florida at the end of the war, a more advantageous northern boundary than the Americans were prepared to yield to the Spaniards. Since England was forced to re-cede Florida to Spain, while retaining possession of Gibraltar, that secret and embarrassing article no longer had relevance.

When Vergennes chided Franklin for concluding the preliminaries without the communication with the Court of France that Congress had prescribed in its instructions, the latter apologized for the indiscretion but stressed the need for further assistance. "The English, I just now learn, flatter themselves they have already divided us," Franklin placated the French minister, deftly adding, "I hope this little misunderstanding will therefore be kept secret, and that they will find themselves totally mistaken." When Robert R. Livingston, the American Secretary for Foreign Affairs, saw fit to rebuke Congress' peace commissioners for their secrecy while complimenting them on their gains, John Jay in a private letter warmly defended the course of his colleagues and himself.

Meanwhile the Earl of Shelburne had the doubly difficult task of selling the peace settlement to an obstinate king and a hostile Parliament. Standing on free-trade ground, his back to the wall, Shelburne, in a speech to the Lords, defended the sacrifices in America that his preliminary treaty imposed. Accepting the peace as a necessity, Parliament passed a vote of censure of the ministry, which spelled finis to Shelburne's public career.

62. Treaty of Alliance with France
February 6, 1778

Article I—If war should break out between France and Great Britain during the continuance of the present war between the United States and England, His Majesty [Louis XVI] and the said United States shall make it a common cause and aid each other mutually with their good offices, their counsels and their forces, according to the exigence of conjunctures, as becomes good and faithful allies.

ART. II.—The essential and direct end of the present defensive alliance is to maintain effectually the liberty, sovereignty and independence absolute and unlimited, of the said United States, as well in matters of government as of commerce.

ART. III.—The two contracting parties shall each on its own part, and in the manner it may judge most proper, make all the efforts in its power against their common enemy, in order to attain the end proposed.

ART. IV.—The contracting parties agree that in case either of them should form any particular enterprise in which the concurrence of the other may be desired, the party whose concurrence is desired, shall readily, and with good faith, join to act in concert for that purpose, as far as circumstances and its own particular situation will permit; and in that case, they shall regulate, by a particular convention, the quantity and kind of succour to be furnished,

SOURCE: W. M. Malloy, ed., *Treaties, Conventions, International Acts, Protocols, and Agreements between the United States of America and Other Powers* . . . (4 vols., Washington, D.C., 1910–1938), I, 479 et seq.

and the time and manner of its being brought into action, as well as the advantages which are to be its compensation.

Art. V.—If the United States should think fit to attempt the reduction of the British power, remaining in the northern parts of America, or the islands of Bermudas, those countries or islands, in case of success, shall be confederated with or dependent upon the said United States.

Art. VI.—The Most Christian King renounces forever the possession of the islands of Bermudas, as well as of any part of the continent of North America, which before the treaty of Paris in 1763, or in virtue of that treaty, were acknowledged to belong to the Crown of Great Britain, or to the United States, heretofore called British Colonies, or which are at this time or have lately been under the power of the King and Crown of Great Britain.

Art. VII.—If His Most Christian Majesty shall think proper to attack any of the islands situated in the Gulph of Mexico, or near that Gulph, which are at present under the power of Great Britain, all the said isles, in case of success, shall appertain to the Crown of France.

Art. VIII.—Neither of the two parties shall conclude either truce or peace with Great Britain without the formal consent of the other first obtained; and they mutually engage not to lay down their arms until the independence of the United States shall have been formally or tacitly assured by the treaty or treaties that shall terminate the war.

Art. IX.—The contracting parties declare, that being resolved to fulfil each on its own part the clauses and conditions of the present treaty of alliance, according to its own power and circumstances, there shall be no after-claim of compensation on one side or the other, whatever may be the event of the war.

Art. X.—The Most Christian King and the United States agree to invite or admit other powers who may have received injuries from England, to make common cause with them, and to accede to the present alliance, under such conditions as shall be freely agreed to and settled between all the parties.

Art. XI.—The two parties guarantee mutually from the present time and forever against all other powers, to wit: The United States to His Most Christian Majesty, the present possessions of the Crown of France in America, as well as those which it may acquire by the future treaty of peace: And His Most Christian

Majesty guarantees on his part to the United States their liberty, sovereignty and independence, absolute and unlimited, as well in matters of government as commerce, and also their possessions, and the additions or conquests that their confederation may obtain during the war, from any of the dominions now, or heretofore possessed by Great Britain in North America, conformable to the 5th and 6th articles above written, the whole as their possessions shall be fixed and assured to the said States, at the moment of the cessation of their present war with England.

ART. XII.—In order to fix more precisely the sense and application of the preceding article, the contracting parties declare, that in case of a rupture between France and England the reciprocal guarantee declared in the said article shall have its full force and effect the moment such war shall break out; and if such rupture shall not take place the mutual obligations of the said guarantee shall not commence until the moment of the cessation of the present war between the United States and England shall have ascertained their possessions.

ART. XIII.—The present treaty shall be ratified on both sides, and the ratifications shall be exchanged in the space of six months, or sooner if possible.

In faith whereof the respective Plenipotentiaries, to wit: On the part of the Most Christian King, Conrad Alexander Gerard, Royal Syndic of the city of Strasbourgh, and Secretary of His Majesty's Council of State; and on the part of the United States, Benjamin Franklin, Deputy to the General Congress from the State of Pennsylvania, and President of the Convention of the same State, Silas Deane, heretofore Deputy from the State of Connecticut, and Arthur Lee, Councellor at Law, have signed the above articles both in the French and English languages, declaring, nevertheless, that the present treaty was originally composed and concluded in the French language and they have hereunto affixed their seals.

Done at Paris, this sixth day of February, one thousand seven hundred and seventy-eight.

[SEAL.]   C. A. GERARD.
[SEAL.]   B. FRANKLIN.
[SEAL.]   SILAS DEANE.
[SEAL.]   ARTHUR LEE.

63. Carlisle Commission:
Letter to Henry Laurens, President,
and Other Members of Congress,
June 13, 1778; Congress' Rejection of the Carlisle
Proposals, June 17, 1778

GENTLEMEN,

With an earnest desire to stop the further effusion of blood and the calamities of war, we communicate to you, with the least possible delay after our arrival in this city, a copy of the communication with which his Majesty is pleased to honour us, as also the acts of parliament on which it is founded; and at the same time that we assure you of our most earnest desire to re-establish, on the basis of equal freedom and mutual safety, the tranquillity of this once happy empire, you will observe that we are vested with powers equal to the purpose, and such as are even unprecedented in the annals of our history. . . .

More effectually to demonstrate our good intentions, we think proper to declare, even in this our first communication, that we are disposed to concur in every satisfactory and just arrangement towards the following among other purposes:

To consent to a cessation of hostilities, both by sea and land. To restore free intercourse, to revive mutual affection, and restore the common benefits of naturalisation through the several parts of this empire. To extend every freedom to trade that our respective interests can require. To agree that no military force shall be kept up in the different states of North America, without the consent of the general congress, or particular assemblies. To concur in measures calculated to discharge the debts of America, and raise the value and credit of the paper circulation.

To perpetuate our union by a reciprocal deputation of an agent

SOURCE: *The Annual Register, or a View of the History, Politics, and Literature for the Year 1778* (London, 1779), 327–328.

or agents from the different states, who shall have the privilege of a seat and voice in the parliament of Great Britain; or, if sent from Britain, to have in that case a seat and voice in the assemblies of the different states to which they may be deputed respectively, in order to attend to the several interests of those by whom they are deputed.

In short, to establish the power of the respective legislatures in each particular state, to settle its revenue, its civil and military establishment, and to exercise a perfect freedom of legislation and internal government, so that the British states throughout North America, acting with us in peace and war, under our common sovereign, may have the irrevocable enjoyment of every privilege that is short of a total separation of interest, or consistent with that union of force on which the safety of our common religion and liberty depends.

In our anxiety for preserving those sacred and essential interests, we cannot help taking notice of the insidious interposition of a power which has from the first settlement of these colonies been actuated with enmity to us both. And notwithstanding the pretended date, or present form, of the French offers to America, yet it is notorious that these were made in consequence of the plans of accommodation previously concerted in Great Britain, and with a view to prevent our reconciliation, and to prolong this destructive war.

But we trust that the inhabitants of North-America, connected with us by the nearest ties of consanguinity, speaking the same language, interested in the preservation of similar institutions, remembering the former happy intercourse of good offices, and forgetting recent animosities, will shrink from the thought of becoming an accession of force to our late mutual enemy, and will prefer a firm, free and perpetual coalition with the parent state to an insincere and unnatural foreign alliance. . . .

If after the time that may be necessary to consider of this communication and transmit your answer, the horrors and devastations of war should continue, we call God and the world to witness that the evils which must follow are not to be imputed to Great Britain; and we cannot without the most real sorrow anticipate the prospect of calamities which we feel the most ardent desire to prevent. We are, with perfect respect, Gentlemen, your most obedient and most humble servants.

Congress' Rejection of the Carlisle Proposals

HENRY LAURENS TO THE EARL OF CARLISLE AND THE OTHER BRITISH COMMISSIONERS, JUNE 17, 1778

I have received the letter from your excellencies of the 9th instant, with the enclosures, and laid them before Congress. Nothing but an earnest desire to spare the further effusion of human blood could have induced them to read a paper containing expressions so disrespectful to his most Christian majesty, the good and great ally of these states, or to consider propositions so derogatory to the honor of an independent nation.

The acts of the British parliament, the commission from your sovereign, and your letter suppose the people of these states to be subjects of the crown of Great Britain, and are founded on the idea of dependence, which is utterly inadmissible.

I am further directed to inform your excellencies that Congress are inclined to peace, notwithstanding the unjust claims from which this war originated and the savage manner in which it hath been conducted. They will, therefore, be ready to enter upon the consideration of a treaty of peace and commerce not inconsistent with treaties already subsisting, when the king of Great Britain shall demonstrate a sincere disposition for that purpose. The only solid proof of this disposition will be an explicit acknowledgment of the independence of these states, or the withdrawing his fleets and armies.

SOURCE: W. C. Ford, et al., eds., *Journals of the Continental Congress, 1774–1789*, XI, 615.

64. John Jay's Defense of the American Peace Commissioners: Letter to Robert R. Livingston July 19, 1783

DEAR ROBERT:

Our Despatches by Barney must be ready the Day after Tomorrow. The many Letters I have written, and have still to write, by him, together with Conferences, Company, etc., keep me fully employed. You will therefore excuse my not descending so much to particulars, as both of us indeed might wish.

As little that passes in Congress is kept entirely secret, we think it prudent at least to postpone giving you a more minute Detail than you have already received, of the Reasons which induced us to sign the provisional articles without previously communicating them to the French Minister. For your private Satisfaction, however, I will make a few Remarks on that Subject.

Your Doubts respecting the Propriety of our Conduct in that Instance appear to have arisen from the following Considerations:

1. That we entertained and were influenced by Distrusts and Suspicions which do not seem to you to have been altogether well founded.
2. That we signed the articles without previously communicating them to this Court.

With Respect to the first. In our negociation with the British Commissioner, it was essential to insist on, and if possible, obtain, his Consent to four important concessions.

(1) That Britain should treat with us as being what we were, viz., an independent People. The French Minister thought this

SOURCE: John Jay Papers, Special Collections, Columbia University Libraries.

Demand premature, and that it ought to arise from, and not precede the Treaty.

(2) That Britain should agree to the *Extent* of Boundary we claimed. The French Minister thought our Demands on that head, extravagant in themselves, and as militating against certain views of Spain which he was disposed to favor.

(3) That Britain should admit our Right in common to the Fishery. The French Minister thought this Demand too extensive.

(4) That Britain should not insist on our reinstating the Tories. The French Minister argued that they ought to be reinstated.

Was it unnatural for us to conclude from these Facts that the French Minister was opposed to our succeeding on these four Points in the Extent we wished? It appeared evident that his Plan of a Treaty for America, was far from being such as America would have preferred; and as we disapproved of his model, we thought it imprudent to give him an opportunity of moulding our Treaty by it.

Whether the Minister was influenced by what he really thought best for us, or by what he really thought best for France, is a Question which however easy or difficult to decide, is not very important to the Point under Consideration. Whatever his motives may have been, certain it is that they were such as opposed our System; and as in private Life it is deemed imprudent to admit opponents to full Confidence, especially respecting the very Matters in Competition, so in public affairs the like Caution seems equally proper.

Secondly. But admitting the Force of this Reasoning, Why, when the articles were completed, did we not communicate them to the French Minister, *before* we proceeded to sign them? For the following Reasons:

The Expectations excited in England by Lord Shelbourn's Friends, that he would put a speedy Period to the war, made it necessary for him either to realize those Expectations, or prepare to quit his Place. The Parliament being to meet before his negociations with us were concluded, he found it expedient to adjourn it for a short Term, in Hopes of then meeting it with all the advantages that might be expected from a favorable Issue of the Negociation. Hence it was his Interest to draw it to a Close before that adjournment should expire; and to obtain that End both he and his Commissioner became less tenacious on certain Points than they would otherwise have been. Nay we have, and then had, good Reason to believe that the Latitude allowed by the British Cabinet for the Exercise of Discretion was exceeded on that occasion.

I must now remind you that the King of Great Britain had pledged himself, in Mr. Oswald's Commission, to confirm and ratify *not* what Mr. Oswald should *verbally* agree to, but what he should *formally sign his name and affix his Seal to.*

Had we communicated the articles when ready for signing, to the French Minister, he doubtless would have complimented us on the Terms of them; but, at the same Time he would have insisted on our postponing the Signature until the articles then preparing between France, Spain, and Britain should also be ready for signing—he having often intimated to us that we should all sign at the same Time and Place. This would have exposed us to a disagreeable Dilemma.

Had we agreed to postpone signing the articles, the British Cabinet might and probably would have taken advantage of it. They might (if better prospects had offered) have insisted that the articles were still *Res infectae;* that Mr. Oswald had exceeded the Limits of his Instructions, and for both these Reasons that they conceived themselves still at Liberty to dissent from his opinions, and to forbid his executing a Set of Articles which they could not approve of. It is true that this might not have happened, but it is equally true that it might, and therefore it was a Risque of too great Importance to be run. The whole Business would in that case have been set afloat again, and the Minister of France would have had an opportunity at least of approving the objections of the British Court, and of advising us to recede from Demands which in his opinion were immoderate, and too inconsistant with the Claims of Spain to meet with his Concurrence.

If on the other Hand, we had contrary to his advice and Request, refused to postpone the signing, it is natural to suppose that such Refusal would have given more offence to the French Minister, than our doing it without consulting him at all about the Matter.

Our withholding from him the Knowledge of these articles until after they were signed, was no violation of our Treaty with France, and therefore she has no Room for Complaint, on that Principle, against the United States.

Congress had indeed made and published a Resolution not to make peace but in Confidence and in Concurrence with France. So far as this Resolution declares against a *separate* peace, it has been incontestably observed; and admitting that the Words in Confidence and in Concurrence with France mean that we should mention to the French Minister and consult with him about every Step of our Proceedings, yet it is most certain that it was founded on a mutual Understanding that France would patronize our Demands, and assist us in obtaining the objects of them. France therefore by discouraging our Claims, ceased to be entitled to the Degree of Confidence respecting them, which was specified in the Resolution. It may be said that France must admit the Reasonableness of our Claims before we could properly expect that she should promote them. She knew what were our Claims before the Negociation commenced, tho she could only conjecture what Reception they would meet with from Britain. If she thought our Claims extravagant, she may be excusable for not countenancing them in their full Extent; but then we ought also to be excused for not giving her the full Confidence on those Subjects, which was promised on the implied Condition of her supporting them.

But Congress positively instructed us to do nothing without the advice and Consent of the French Minister, and we have departed from that Line of Conduct. This is also true; but then I apprehend that Congress marked out that Line of conduct for their own Sake, and not for the Sake of France. The Object of that Instruction was the supposed Interest of America, and not of France; and we were directed to ask the advice of the French Minister, because it was thought advantageous to our Country that we should receive and be governed by it. Congress *only* therefore have a Right to complain of our Departure from the Line of that Instruction.

If it be urged that Confidence ought to subsist between allies, I have only to remark that, as the French Minister did not consult us about his articles, nor make us any Communications about them, our giving him as little Trouble about our's did not violate any Principle of Reciprocity. . . .

65. Lord Shelburne's Defense
of the Preliminary Articles of Peace
Before the House of Lords
February 1783

THE Earl of *Shelburne* then rose. The lateness of the hour, my lords, said his lordship, will not suffer me to take the liberty of trespassing so far on your patience, as my feelings would prompt me to on the present occasion. I shall not address your passions—that candid province I will leave to those who have shewn such ability for its government to-night. As my conduct has been founded upon integrity—facts, and plain reasoning, will form its best support. I shall necessarily wave the consideration of the critical moment at which I stepped into the administration of the affairs of this country—a moment when, if there be any credit due to the solemn, public declarations of men, who seemed then, and seem now, to have the welfare of the state nearest to their hearts—every hope of renovated lustre was gone, and nothing but dreary despondency remained to the well-wishers of Great Britain. I am now speaking within memory, and consequently within proof. It is not for me to boast of my motives for standing forward at a period so alarming. My circumstances are not so secure as to render my conduct a matter of dubiety, and my own explanation of my feelings would, I flatter myself, fall far short of that credit which sympathy would give me in the minds of men, whose patriotism is not that of words: the ambition of advancing to the service of our country in an hour when even brave men shrink from the danger, is honourable, and I shall not be catechized for entertaining such an impulse. I make no merit of my hardihood, and when I speak of mine, I wish your lordships to understand me as speaking of the generous enterprize of my noble and honourable colleagues in administration. It was our duty as good citizens, when the state was

SOURCE: *The Parliamentary History of England* compiled by William Cobbett (36 vols., London, 1806–1820), XXIII, 407–420.

in danger, that all selfish apprehensions should be banished. I shall not, therefore, expatiate on my reasons for coming into office, but openly and candidly tell your lordships how I have conducted myself in it. A peace was the declared wish of the nation at that time. How was that to be procured best for the advantage of the country? Certainly by gaining the most accurate knowledge of the relative condition of the powers at war. Here a field of knowledge was required to be beaten, to which no one man, vast and profound as it is possible to picture human capacity, would by any means be supposed equal. Then if one man was inadequate to the whole task, the next question naturally is, what set of men are best qualified as auxiliaries in it? What is the skill required? A knowledge of trade and commerce, with all its relations, and an intimate acquaintance with military affairs, and all its concomitants. Were men of this description consulted previous to, and during the progress of the treaty now before your lordships? I answer, they were. And with this sanction, administration need assume no false brow of bravery, in combatting the glittering expressions of that hasty opposition that had been set up to the present terms.

Let us examine them, my lords, let us take the several assertions in their turn, and without wishing to intrude too much on your lordships time, I shall be pardoned for giving a distinct answer to each head of objection. Ministry, in the first place, is blamed for drawing the boundary they have done between the territories of the United States and those of our sovereign in Canada. I wish to examine every part of the treaties on the fair rule of the value of the district ceded—to examine it on the amount of the exports and imports, by which alone we could judge of its importance. The exports of this country to Canada, then, were only 140,000£., . . . has cost this country, on the average 800,000£. I have the vouchers in my pocket, should your lordships be inclined to examine the fact. But the trade is not given up, it is only divided, and divided for our benefit. I appeal to all men conversant with the nature of that trade, whether its best resources in Canada do not lie in the northward. What, then, is the result of this part of the treaty, so wisely, and with so much sincere love on the part of England clamoured against by noble lords? Why this. You have generously given America, with whom every call under Heaven urges you to stand on the footing of brethren, a share in a trade, the monopoly of which you sordidly preserved to yourselves, and the loss of the enormous sum of 750,000£. Monopolies, some way or other, are ever justly punished. They forbid rivalry, and rivalry is of the very essence of the well-being of trade. This seems to be the æra of protestantism in trade. All Europe appear enlightened, and eager to throw off the vile shackles of oppressive ignorant monopoly; that unmanly and illiberal principle, which is at once ungenerous and deceitful. A few interested Canadian merchants might complain; for merchants would always love monopoly, without taking a moment's time to think whether it was for their interest or not. I avow that monopoly is always unwise; but if there is any nation under heaven, who ought to be the first to reject monopoly, it is the English. Situated as we are between the old world and the new, and between the southern and northern Europe, all that we ought to covet upon earth is free trade, and fair equality. With more industry, with more enterprize, with more capital than any trading nation upon earth, it ought to be our constant cry, let every market be open, let us meet our rivals fairly, and we ask no more. It is a principle on which we have had the wisdom to act with respect to our brethren of Ireland: and, if conciliation be our view, why should we not reach it out also to America? Our generosity is not much, but, little as it is, let us give it with a grace. Indeed, to speak properly, it is not generosity to them, but œconomy to ourselves; and in the boundaries which are established we have saved ourselves the immense sum of 800,000£. a-year, and shewed to the Americans our sincere love and fair intentions, in dividing the little bit of trade which nature had laid at their doors; and telling them that we desired to live with them in communion of benefits, and in the sincerity of friendship. "But the Indians were abandoned to their enemies!" Noble lords have taken great pains to shew the immense value of these Indians; it was not unnatural for noble lords, who had made so lavish a use of these Indians, to complain of their loss; but those who abhorred their violence would think ministry had done wisely. The Americans knew best how to tame their savage natures. The descendants of the good William Penn would manage them better than all the Mr. Stuarts with all the Jewsharps, razors, trumpery, and jobs that we could contrive. "But our treaties with them bound us to everlasting protection!" This is one of those assertions which always sounds well, and is calculated to amuse the uninformed mind: but what is the meaning of *in perpetuo* in all treaties? That they shall endure as long as the parties are able to perform the conditions. This is the meaning of perpetual alliances; and in the present treaty with America, the Indian nations were not abandoned to their enemies; they were remitted to the care of neighbours, whose interest it was as much as ours to cultivate friendship with them, and who were certainly the best qualified for softening and humanizing their hearts. But I shall dismiss this subject, though it is blended with others, and proceed to the investigation of the rest of the objections to the treaties of pacification.

"Why have you given America the freedom of fishing in all your creeks and harbours, and especially on the banks of Newfoundland," say the noble objectors to this article? Why? because, in the first place, they could from their locality have exercised a fishery in that quarter for the first season (for there are two), in spite of all our efforts to repel them. In February the first season commences, and that is entirely at their devotion; for our people can never take their stations there so soon. With regard to the other season, let us again revert to what I have said respecting the fur trade; though we have not a monopoly, we have got such superior advantages in the article of drying, curing, and preparing our fish for market, from the exclusive command of the most contiguous shores, that a rivalry can only whet our industry to reap those benefits our preferable situation in this respect presents to us. "But why have you not stipulated a reciprocity of fishing in the American harbours and creeks?" I will tell your lordships:—because we have abundant employment in our own. Would not an American think it sordid in the extreme, nay, consider it bordering on madness, to covet the privilege of battening our cattle on some of their sterile wilds, when we had our own fertile savannahs to have recourse to? Such would be the opinion entertained of ministry, if it had childishly and avariciously made a stipulation of the nature the objectors think they ought to have. The broad and liberal policy on which the present treaty is formed, is in my opinion much more wise and beneficial than would have been the narrow and wretched plan of bargaining for every little particle of advantage which we might have procured, perhaps, by stickling in the negotiation. As to the masts, a noble lord said, we were to have in such abundance at Penobscot, I will oppose a fact to his bare assertion. I have in my pocket a certificate from one of the ablest surveyors in our service, captain Twiss, that there is not a tree there capable of being made into a mast.

But there remains somewhat in these provisional Articles still to be considered, which I have never reflected upon without feelings as pungent as any which the warmest admirers of the virtues of the loyalists can possibly have experienced. I mean the unhappy necessity of our affairs, which induced the extremity of submitting the fate of the property of these brave and worthy men to the discretion of their enemies. I have but one answer to give the House in this particular; it is the answer I gave my own bleeding heart. A part must be wounded, that the whole of the empire may not perish. If better terms could be had, think you, my lords, that I would not have embraced them? You all know my creed. You all know my steadiness. If it were possible to put aside the bitter cup the adversaries of this country presented to me, you know I would have done it; but you called for peace. To make it in the circumstances, which your lordships all know I stood in, was most arduous. In this point, nothing could be more grievous to me. Neither in public nor in private life is it my character to desert my friends. I had but the alternative, either to accept the terms, said Congress, of our recommendation to the states, in favour of the colonists, or continue the war. It is in our power to do no more than recommend. Is there any man who hears me, who will clap his hand on his heart, and step forward and say, I ought to have broken off the treaty? If there be, I am sure he neither knows the state of the country, nor yet has he paid any attention to the wishes of it. But still I do not despond with respect to the loyalists. I rely upon the wisdom, the honour, and the temper of the Congress. Their recommendation was all that in the nature of things we could procure. They were cautious in wording their treaty, lest they should possibly give offence to the new states, whose constitutions had not advanced to those habits of appearance and strength that banishes all suspicions; peremptory language is not the language of a new state. They must soften their applications. In all their measures for money, for men, they have used the word recommendation to the provincial assemblies; and it has always, or at least generally been paid respect to. And, believe me, they do the loyalists the offices not of friends, who surmise doubts on this occasion. But say the worst; and that after all, this estimable set of men are not received and cherished in the bosom of their own country: is England so lost to gratitude, and all the feelings of humanity, as not to afford them an asylum? Who can be so base as to think she will refuse it to them? Surely it cannot be that noble-minded man, who would plunge his country again knee-deep in blood, and saddle it with an expence of 20 millions for the purpose of restoring them. Without one drop of blood spilt, and without one-fifth of the expence of one year's campaign, happiness and easiness can be given the loyalists in as ample a manner as these blessings were ever in their enjoyment; therefore let the outcry cease on this head. But which of the two stiles of language is the more likely to assist the loyalists: the stile of the Address which declares the confidence of parliament in the good intentions of the Congress, or of the noble lords who declare that recommendation is nothing? It surely requires no great depth of penetration to distinguish between these things. . . .

I have now gone, as well as my memory serves me, through the detail of all the objections which have been made to the treaties; and, I trust, your lordships see from the facts to which I have all along referred you, the necessity and the policy of our conduct in this particular. Let me, before I conclude, call to your lordships minds the general state of this country, at the period in which the pacific negociations were set on foot. Were we not at the extremity of distress? Did not the boldest of us cry out for peace? Was not the object of the war accomplished? Was not the independence of America solemnly recognized by parliament? Could that independence be afterwards made a stipulation for the restoration of tranquillity? On an entire view of our affairs at that time, is there any honest, sensible man in the kingdom that will not say the powerful confederacy with whom we had then to contend had the most decided superiority over us? Had we scarce one taxable article that was not already taxed to the utmost extent? . . . It is easy for any bungler to pull down the fairest fabric, but is that a reason, my lords, he should censure the skill of the architect who reared it? But I fear I trespass, my lords, on your patience too long. The subject was near my heart, and you will pardon me, if I have been earnest in laying before your lordships our embarrassments, our difficulties, our views, and our reasons for what we have done. I submit them to you with confidence, and rely on the nobleness of your natures, that in judging of men who have hazarded so much for their country, you will not be guided by prejudice, nor influenced by party.

66. Treaty of Peace
September 3, 1783

ARTICLE. I.—His Britannic Majesty acknowledges the said United States, viz. New Hampshire, Massachusetts Bay, Rhode Island, and Providence Plantations, Connecticut, New York, New Jersey, Pennsylvania, Delaware, Maryland, Virginia, North Carolina, South Carolina, and Georgia, to be free, sovereign and independent States; that he treats with them as such, and for himself, his heirs and successors, relinquishes all claims to the Government, proprietary and territorial rights of the same, and every part thereof.

ART. II.—And that all disputes which might arise in future, on the subject of the boundaries of the said United States may be prevented, it is hereby agreed and declared, that the following are, and shall be their boundaries, viz.: From the northwest angle of Nova Scotia, viz.: that angle which is formed by a line drawn due north from the source of Saint Croix River to the Highlands; along the said Highlands which divide those rivers that empty themselves into the river St. Lawrence, from those which fall into the Atlantic Ocean, to the northwesternmost head of Connecticut River; thence down along the middle of that river, to the forty-fifth degree of north latitude; from thence, by a line due west on said latitude, until it strikes the river Iroquois or Cataraquy; thence along the middle of said river into Lake Ontario, through the middle of said lake until it strikes the communication by water between that lake and Lake Erie; thence along the middle of said communication into Lake Erie, through the middle of said lake until it arrives at the water communication between that lake and Lake Huron; thence along the middle of said water communication into the Lake Huron; thence through the middle of said lake to the water communication between that lake and Lake Superior; thence through Lake Superior northward of the Isles Royal and Phelipeaux, to the Long Lake; thence through the middle of said Long

SOURCE: W. M. Malloy, ed., *Treaties, Conventions, etc.*, I, 586 *et seq.*

Lake, and the water communication between it and the Lake of the Woods, to the said Lake of the Woods; thence through the said lake to the most northwestern point thereof, and from thence on a due west course to the river Mississippi; thence by a line to be drawn along the middle of the said river Mississippi until it shall intersect the northernmost part of the thirty-first degree of north latitude, South, by a line to be drawn due east from the determination of the line last mentioned, in the latitude of thirty-one degrees north of the Equator, to the middle of the river Appalachicola or Catahouche; thence along the middle thereof to its junction with the Flint River; thence straight to the head of St. Mary's River; and thence down along the middle of St. Mary's River to the Atlantic Ocean. East, by a line to be drawn along the middle of the river St. Croix, from its mouth in the Bay of Fundy to its source, and from its source directly north to the aforesaid Highlands, which divide the rivers that fall into the Atlantic Ocean from those which fall into the river St. Lawrence; comprehending all islands within twenty leagues of any part of the shores of the United States, and lying between lines to be drawn due east from the points where the aforesaid boundaries between Nova Scotia on the one part, and East Florida on the other, shall respectively touch the Bay of Fundy and the Atlantic Ocean; excepting such islands as now are, or heretofore have been, within the limits of the said province of Nova Scotia.

Art. III.—It is agreed that the people of the United States shall continue to enjoy unmolested the right to take fish of every kind on the Grand Bank, and on all the other banks of Newfoundland; also in the Gulph of Saint Lawrence, and at all other places in the sea where the inhabitants of both countries used at any time heretofore to fish. And also that the inhabitants of the United States shall have liberty to take fish of every kind on such part of the coast of Newfoundland as British fishermen shall use (but not to dry or cure the same on that island) and also on the coasts, bays and creeks of all other of His Britannic Majesty's dominions in America; and that the American fishermen shall have liberty to dry and cure fish in any of the unsettled bays, harbours and creeks of Nova Scotia, Magdalen Islands, and Labrador, so long as the same shall remain unsettled; but so soon as the same or either of them shall be settled, it shall not be lawful for the said fishermen to dry or cure fish at such settlements, without a previous agreement for that purpose with the inhabitants, proprietors or possessors of the ground.

Art. IV.—It is agreed that creditors on either side shall meet with no lawful impediment to the recovery of the full value in sterling money, of all *bona fide* debts heretofore contracted.

Art. V.—It is agreed that the Congress shall earnestly recommend it to the legislatures of the respective States, to provide for the restitution of all estates, rights and properties which have been confiscated, belonging to real British subjects, and also of the estates, rights and properties of persons resident in districts in the possession of His Majesty's arms, and who have not borne arms against the said United States. And that persons of any other description shall have free liberty to go to any part or parts of any of the thirteen United States, and therein to remain twelve months, unmolested in their endeavours to obtain the restitution of such of their estates, rights and properties as may have been confiscated; and that Congress shall also earnestly recommend to the several States a reconsideration and revision of all acts or laws regarding the premises, so as to render the said laws or acts perfectly consistent, not only with justice and equity, but with that spirit of conciliation which, on the return of the blessings of peace, should universally prevail. And that Congress shall also earnestly recommend to the several States, that the estates, rights and properties of such last mentioned persons, shall be restored to them, they refunding to any persons who may be now in possession, the *bona fide* price (where any has been given) which such persons may have paid on purchasing any of the said lands, rights or properties, since the confiscation. And it is agreed, that all persons who have any interest in confiscated lands, either by debts, marriage settlements or otherwise, shall meet with no lawful impediment in the prosecution of their just rights.

Art. VI.—That there shall be no future confiscations made, nor any prosecutions commenced against any person or persons for, or by reason of the part which he or they may have taken in the present war; and that no person shall, on that account, suffer any future loss or damage, either in his person, liberty or property; and that those who may be in confinement on such charges, at the time of the ratification of the treaty in America, shall be immediately set at liberty, and the prosecutions so commenced be discontinued.

Art. VII.—There shall be a firm and perpetual peace between

His Britannic Majesty and the said States, and between the subjects of the one and the citizens of the other, wherefore all hostilities, both by sea and land, shall from henceforth cease; All prisoners on both sides shall be set at liberty, and His Britannic Majesty shall, with all convenient speed, and without causing any destruction, or carrying away any negroes or other property of the American inhabitants, withdraw all his armies, garrisons and fleets from the said United States, and from every post, place and harbour within the same; leaving in all fortifications the American artillery that may be therein; And shall also order and cause all archives, records, deeds and papers, belonging to any of the said States, or their citizens, which, in the course of the war, may have fallen into the hands of his officers, to be forthwith restored and deliver'd to the proper States and persons to whom they belong.

Art. VIII.—The navigation of the river Mississippi, from its source to the ocean, shall forever remain free and open to the subjects of Great Britain, and the citizens of the United States.

Art. IX.—In case it should so happen that any place or territory belonging to Great Britain or to the United States, should have been conquer'd by the arms of either from the other, before the arrival of the said provisional articles in America, it is agreed, that the same shall be restored without difficulty, and without requiring any compensation. . . .

XVII

Building a Democratic Republic

With a few exceptions the Revolutionary elite maintained their hold on the leadership. The notable exception was Pennsylvania, where a radical faction seized control at the start of the war, only to be later ousted in what has been loosely termed a "counterrevolution." The Patriot leadership felt a certain propriety in resting their governments upon the consent of the governed and, in Massachusetts, in entrusting to a popularly elected constitutional convention the responsibility for drafting a constitution, which was then submitted to the voters for ratification. The Massachusetts voters rejected a 1778 draft but approved a new draft drawn up at a convention two years later.

The Founding Fathers believed that limits should be imposed on both government and popular power. The latter was effected through a division of powers—the system of checks and balances—and a bicameral legislature, as advocated by John Adams, whose pamphlet Thoughts on Government was written to refute Thomas Paine's advocacy of a unicameral legislature in his celebrated pamphlet Common Sense. Examples of limits imposed on government are the bills of rights of the state constitutions, of which two examples are included herein.

A quite different point of view was presented in a series of letters to the press by "Spartanus." This pseudonymous writer argued the case for a unicameral legislature along the lines previously suggested by Thomas Paine, as well as for frequent elections and seating popular control in the towns, and warned against the allegedly conspiratorial tactics of conservatives seeking to be returned to public favor.

67. Pittsfield, Massachusetts:
Petition, Remonstrance, and Address
December 26, 1775

THE Petition Remonstrance & Address of the Town of Pittsfield to the Honourable Board of Councellors & House of Representatives of the Province of the Massachusetts Bay in General Assembly now sitting in Watertown——

May it please your Honors,

The Inhabitants of the Town of Pittsfield unalterably attached to the Liberties of their Country & in the fullest Approbation of Congressional Measures, with all humility Deference & Candor beg leave to manifest the painful Anxieties & Distresses of our minds in this definitive Crisis not only in behalf of ourselves but this great & powerful Province, & declare our abhorrence of that Constitution now adopting in this province. Nothing but an invincible Love of Civil & religious Liberty for ourselves & future posterity has induced us to add to your accumulated Burdens at this Great Period.——

Our forefathers left the delightful Abodes of their native Country, passed a raging Sea that in these then solitary Climes they might enjoy Civil & religious Liberty, & never more feel the hand of Tyranny & Persecution; but that despotic persecuting power from which they fled reached them on these far distant shores the weight of which has been felt from their first Emigration to the present Day. After the Loss of the Charter of this province in the reign of Charles the second a popish Tyrant, a new one was obtained after the Revolution of King William of glorious Memory which was lame and essentially defective & yet was of great value for the support of tolerable order till we had grown up to our present strength to seek that by force of Arms which was then unjustly denied us.

The Nomination & appointment of our Governors by the King has been the Source of all the Evils & Calamities that have befallen

SOURCE: Massachusetts Archives, CLXXX, 150.

this province & the united Colonies. By this means a secret poison has been spread thro' out all our Towns & great Multitudes have been secured for the corrupt Designs of an abandoned Administration. Many of those Men who had drank of this baneful poison could not be confided in to aid & assist their Country in the present Contest, which [was] one Reason of the necessity of a Suppression of Government. At this Door all Manner of Disorders have been introduced into our Constitution till it has become an Engine of Oppression & deep Corruption & would finally, had it been continued, have brought upon us an eternal Destruction. The want of that one previlege of confessing Judgment in Cases of Debt has overwhelmed great Multitudes in Destruction & affoarded Encouragement to mercenary Lawyers to riot upon the spoils of the people.——

We have been ruled in this Country for many years past with a rod of Iron. The Tyranny, Despotism & oppression of our fellow Subjects in this Country have been beyond belief. Since the Suspension of Government we have lived in peace, Love, safety, Liberty & Happiness except the Disorders & Dissentions occasioned by the Tories. We find ourselves in Danger of [returning] to our former state & of undergoing a Yoke of Op[pression] which we are no longer able to bear.

We have calmly viewed the nature of our antient Mode of Government—its various sluices of Corruption & oppression—the dangerous Effects of nominating to office by those in power, & must pronounce it the most defective discordant & ruinous System of Government of any that has come under our Observation. We can discern no present necessity of adopting that mode of Government so generally reprobated by the good people of this province; or which will inevitably be so as soon as the great rational Majority of the people have had Time for proper Reflection. The adopting this Mode of Government to the length we have gone has in our view been hasty & precipitate. It was surprising to this Town & directly contrary to the Instructions given to their Representatives. By this Means a considerable Number of incurable Enemies to a better Constitution has been made & if once adopted by the people we shall perhaps never be able to rid ourselves of it again.

We have seen nothing done by the Continental Congress which leads us to conclude that they would limit us to this mode of Government. We do not know of their having given us any Advice that must necessarily be construed in Opposition to what they gave [the Gov]ernments of New Hampshire & South Carolina. ["] Who if they think it necessary are to chuse such form of Government as they in their Judgment shall think will best promote the happiness of the people & preserve peace & good order during the present dispute with Great Britain." Certainly the Continental Congress could have no Intention of forcing upon us a Constitution so detested by the people & so abhorrent to common Sense, & thus to reward us for our unparalleled Sufferings. We have been led to wish for new previleges which we still hope to obtain, or remain so far as we have done for some Time past in a State of Nature.——

We have with Decency & Moderation attended to the various Arguments of those Gentlemen lately created our Rulers, particularly we have heard it urged as the Advice of the [vene]rable Continental Congress, we have sufficiently attended to that & various other Arguments in favor of reassuming our antient Constitution, & are of opinion there is no such advice, the qualifying Expressions leaving ample room to new model our Constitution; but if there is, we are of opinion that unlimited passive obedience & Non-Resistance to any human power whatever is what we are now contending with Great Britain & to transfer that power to any other Body of Men is equally dangerous to our Security & happiness.——

We chuse to be known to future posterity as being of the Number of those who have timely protested against the Reassumption of this discordant Constitution, & shall be restless in our endeavours that we may obtain the previlege of electing our Civil & military officers. We assure your Honors that some of those who have been appointed to rule us are greatly obnoxious to people in General, especially those who have protested against the Just proceedings of a Congress lately held at Stockbridge. We beg leave further to assure your Honors that a Court has been held in this Town in a Clandestine Manner & great Dishonour hereby done to the Dignity of Magistracy.——

We therefore pray your Honors to issue out your orders to the good people of this province that their Votes may be collected in the Election of a Governor & Lieut Governor to act in Concert with the Honourable Board & house of Representatives. After which we pray that every Town may retain the previlege of nominating their Justice of the peace & every Country their Judges as well as the Soldiers of every Company of the Militia their officers. If the right of nominating to office is not invested in the people we are indifferent who assumes it whether any particular persons on this or the other side of the [w]ater. When such a Constitution is assumed you'll [fi]nd us the most meek & inoffensive Subjects of any in this province, though we would hope in such a case that the wisdom of our Rulers would not admit of collecting private Debts for the present as we imagine that Measure would be of great Detriment to our common cause as it would put much Money into the hands of our Enemies & create Divisions among ourselves. But if this Just & reasonable request is denied us, we pray that as we have lived in great love peace & good order in this County for more than 16 Months past in the most vigorous unintermitted Exertions in our Countrys cause, that you would dispense with a longer Suspension of this antient Mode of Government among us which we so much detest & abhor. The Government of our respective Committees is lenient & efficacious. But if it is necessary for the carrying into more effectual Execution the means of our Common safety that some Mode of government should be adopted we pray it may be one De novo agreeable to that formentioned Advice of the Continental Congress & no more of our antient form be retained than what is Just & reasonable. We hope in the Establishment of such a new Constitution regard will be had for such a broad Basis of Civil & religious Liberty as no Length of Time will corrupt & which will endure as long as the Sun & Moon shall endure. And as in Duty bound will ever pray.

[Per] Order of the Town Israel Dickinson Town Clerk. N.B. Upon the foregoing premise & on accoun[t] of obnoxious persons being appointed to rule us The Court of this County of Quarter Sessions is ordered to desist from any future Sessions.——

Our Resolves may be seen at Mr. Thomas's which were entered into at the same Time this petition was accepted by this Town——

68. Prescription for Democracy:
"Spartanus," "The Interest of America"
June 1776

IT IS proposed that we should be a proper Democracy, and form into a free popular Government. In my last I offered reasons why we should have but one branch of Legislature in a Province. I would propose whether each Province might not proceed something in the following manner: That the boundaries of the Province, County, Towns, Precincts, and Districts, for the present, continue as they have been; each County, City, Town, Precinct, or District, choose one, or such a number of persons as shall be thought proper, to represent them in Provincial Congress; the Provincial Congress yearly appoint a Committee of their number, (suppose three or five,) with a President, who should also be called the President of the Province; this President, with a majority of the Committee, to transact the publick business that shall be necessary in the recess of the Congress, and call together that body upon sudden emergencies, &c.; the Provincial Congress, once in a certain space of time, to choose all the publick officers whose business respects the whole Province, such as Judge of the Supreme Court, Treasurer, Secretary, Publick Notaries, Attorney-General, &c. There should be an annual Town-meeting, also a County-meeting, (but not on the same day,) through the Province, at which time each County should choose three or four Judges, a Sheriff, a County Attorney, &c., and each Town, Precinct and District choose not less than two, and not above seven, Justices of the Peace, and the other Town Officers as has been usual in these Provinces; yet it is probable the Judges and Justices, and some other officers, should not be rechosen oftener than once in three years. The laws of the Province (a very few excepted) to continue in force till they can be revised and formed into a new code. Where there is reference to *British* laws, an alteration may easily be made. Whether the Delegates for the Continental Congress should be

SOURCE: P. Force, ed., *American Archives*, 4th ser., VI, 994–996.

chosen by the Provincial Congress, or by each County choosing one for themselves, deserves well to be considered, and, if need be, the several Counties consulted upon that head.

The proper mode of Government is so easy and natural, that when a Congress is met, two or three Committees, taking several parts, might, in one day's time, form the whole plan so far as would be necessary for one session, some further requisition and alterations being left for future time.

As it is proposed we should form into a free popular Government, we should, as much as possible, guard against the disadvantages and difficulties that attend such a form of Government. We must, from the beginning, take all possible care, come into all proper methods, and use all proper means, to keep the Government pure. The grand difficulty of popular Government lies in election. If elections are free and regular, it will be impossible to shake a popular Government. Corruption and bribery, party spirit and animosities among a people, afford a threatening aspect. Rich and aspiring men there will always be, and these will endeavour to corrupt, bribe, and lead the populace. This will shake the foundation of a free State; and this is known by aspiring and ambitious men; hence they will always pursue this method. There are always a number of men in every State who seek to rise above their fellow-creatures, and would be so much above them as to have them and their estates at their disposal, and use them as their footstool to mount to what height they please. They would treat the rest of mankind as we do our cattle and horses, or as slaves are treated. We feed and take care of our horses, or they cannot do our business; we allow slaves food and raiment, or they cannot labour to advantage; so those rich and oppressive men would allow other people enough to till the country and manage manufactures to advantage, and if they are allowed the name of freedom, it is but a name; for all that can possibly be spared, beside maintaining their families, shall flow in some channel or other till it centres in the collective gulf of riches belonging to these aspiring men. Such men will always endeavour to corrupt, bribe, and influence the populace, too many of whom are often dependant upon them; and if people will not maintain their liberty and act for themselves at elections, without being bought and sold, or influenced by the rich and great, they will soon find themselves engulfed in the arbitrary Government. As the grand thing in popular Governments is to keep elections free and incorrupt, it is of importance that as many electors as possible should be in small bodies. It is not so easy to corrupt a great many small, distinct, distant bodies, as it is one large one. For this reason, besides some others, I think it would be better that each Town, District, or Precinct, should choose a Provincial Delegate or two, rather than the choice should be made by Counties; and to prevent the bad effects of corrupt elections, they should be often, they should ordinarily be annual; for if people find that they are bit, that they are imposed upon by intriguing, deceitful men, and oppressive measures are pursued, they will be wise enough at the next election to undo what they ignorantly and by imposition were led to do before. People will feel their oppression, and when they have severely felt, they will wake up from their lethargy, and not be so ready to take another sleepy dose. Frequent elections will happily tend to defeat the designs of aspiring men.

To keep elections free, we must have good laws; but this is not enough; it should, if possible, be a disgrace not to act according to law. A good custom will often do more than a good law. If it was thought mean and base for people to be bought and sold, or improperly biased at elections, they would avoid it. Persons of sense, reputation, and true love to their country, can do much to lead people into a manly, rational way of thinking and acting in this matter. It should be a maxim that no man be allowed to thrust himself into office; to seek it, to court it, is selfish and sordid. No one should be in place for his own sake, but for the good of the whole; and it savours too much of pride or covetousness for a man to put himself forward. Time have been in some part of *America* (I have known it) that a man could not more effectually disappoint himself than by letting it be known that he was desirous of an office or delegacy. No man should be allowed to come into place but such as the people choose, and desire that he would, for the sake of the publick good, take upon him such an arduous task. Government is a weight that will make a good man tremble. Every man that is fit for it will come to it with concern, and if it might be would much rather be excused.

I cannot conclude at present without expostulating with my countrymen on the head of elections. Many of you (many more than I should have expected) suffer yourselves to be imposed upon by evil-designing men. Why will you not act for yourselves at elections? Why will you be bought and sold, as I may say, or be influenced by some of the most dangerous of your fellow-creatures? Too much of it has been seen of late, and there is danger of much more in a short time. Will you be blinded? Will you be beguiled? Will you be overreached, circumvented, and kidnapped by designing men? There are numbers in our land disappointed, sadly disappointed. They were heretofore aspiring, they hoped they were rising, they had their schemes for preferment, they had great expectations; but they have met with a shock; things work contrary to them. What can they now do? They have no way left that they can brook or comply with, but by intriguing and planning specious appearances of friendship, and every art of deceit, to work themselves into place, where they can have influence to accomplish something agreeable to their party. They are with appearance of friendship, by one means or other, creeping into Offices, Committees, and Congresses. They leave no stone unturned, and the stone which they can turn to most advantage is corrupting and unduly influencing elections. They speak fair, they will join in the country's cause so far as will be best not to go too fast and run into danger; they appear to mean you great good will, but it is only appearance. Let them have their way, let them have it in their power, and they will soon again subject you to *British* tyranny, or to a tyranny and oppression among ourselves not much better. They will proceed from step to step until you are under their feet. Their apparent friendship now is in order to get a foot into the stirrup, and when they are once well in the saddle, you may be sure you shall be ridden till you are nothing but skin and bones. Do you ask how you shall know these men? Ask yourselves what these men were three years ago. What were then their views of Government? What were their pursuits? Who were their friends? What party were they of? Whose favour were they seeking? Did they then appear true friends to the country and the common people? Are they not men that are brought to the freedom which this country is coming to, with the greatest reluctance? And will you now believe they are so soon become friends? Can you now trust them to form your Government and make your laws? Can you be so credulous? Can you believe the professions of these men? Open your eyes, act for yourselves, trust men that are well known for a long time to have been friends to their country. Be upon your guard, and take the advice of those that are known to be true friends. Act for yourselves at every election.

SPARTANUS

69. John Adams'
Thoughts on Government
1776

My Dear Sir,[1]—

If I was equal to the task of forming a plan for the government of a colony, I should be flattered with your request, and very happy to comply with it; because, as the divine science of politics is the science of social happiness, and the blessings of society depend entirely on the constitutions of government, which are generally institutions that last for many generations, there can be no employment more agreeable to a benevolent mind than a research after the best.

Pope flattered tyrants too much when he said,

> For forms of government let fools contest,
> That which is best administered is best.

Nothing can be more fallacious than this. But poets read history to collect flowers, not fruits; they attend to fanciful images, not the effects of social institutions. Nothing is more certain, from the history of nations and nature of man, than that some forms of government are better fitted for being well administered than others.

We ought to consider what is the end of government, before we determine which is the best form. Upon this point all speculative politicians will agree, that the happiness of society is the end of government, as all divines and moral philosophers will agree that the happiness of the individual is the end of man. From this principle it will follow, that the form of government which communicates ease, comfort, security, or, in one word, happiness, to the greatest number of persons, and in the greatest degree, is the best.

1. The letter was first intended by Adams to be addressed to George Wythe, a delegate to Congress from Virginia.

Source: C. F. Adams, ed., *Works of John Adams*, IV, 193–200.

All sober inquirers after truth, ancient and modern, pagan and Christian, have declared that the happiness of man, as well as his dignity, consists in virtue. Confucius, Zoroaster, Socrates, Mahomet, not to mention authorities really sacred, have agreed in this.

If there is a form of government, then, whose principle and foundation is virtue, will not every sober man acknowledge it better calculated to promote the general happiness than any other form?

Fear is the foundation of most governments; but it is so sordid and brutal a passion, and renders men in whose breasts it predominates so stupid and miserable, that Americans will not be likely to approve of any political institution which is founded on it.

Honor is truly sacred, but holds a lower rank in the scale of moral excellence than virtue. Indeed, the former is but a part of the latter, and consequently has not equal pretensions to support a frame of government productive of human happiness.

The foundation of every government is some principle or passion in the minds of the people. The noblest principles and most generous affections in our nature, then, have the fairest chance to support the noblest and most generous models of government.

A man must be indifferent to the sneers of modern Englishmen, to mention in their company the names of Sidney, Harrington, Locke, Milton, Nedham, Neville, Burnet, and Hoadly. No small fortitude is necessary to confess that one has read them. The wretched condition of this country, however, for ten or fifteen years past, has frequently reminded me of their principles and reasonings. They will convince any candid mind, that there is no good government but what is republican. That the only valuable part of the British constitution is so; because the very definition of a republic is "an empire of laws, and not of men." That, as a republic is the best of governments, so that particular arrangement of the powers of society, or, in other words, that form of government which is best contrived to secure an impartial and exact execution of the laws, is the best of republics.

Of republics there is an inexhaustible variety, because the possible combinations of the powers of society are capable of innumerable variations.

As good government is an empire of laws, how shall your laws be made? In a large society, inhabiting an extensive country, it is impossible that the whole should assemble to make laws. The first necessary step, then, is to depute power from the many to a few of the most wise and good. But by what rules shall you choose your representatives? Agree upon the number and qualifications of persons who shall have the benefit of choosing, or annex this privilege to the inhabitants of a certain extent of ground.

The principal difficulty lies, and the greatest care should be employed, in constituting this representative assembly. It should be in miniature an exact portrait of the people at large. It should think, feel, reason, and act like them. That it may be the interest of this assembly to do strict justice at all times, it should be an equal representation, or, in other words, equal interests among the people should have equal interests in it. Great care should be taken to effect this, and to prevent unfair, partial, and corrupt elections. Such regulations, however, may be better made in times of greater tranquillity than the present; and they will spring up themselves naturally, when all the powers of government come to be in the hands of the people's friends. At present, it will be safest to proceed in all established modes, to which the people have been familiarized by habit.

A representation of the people in one assembly being obtained, a question arises, whether all the powers of government, legislative, executive, and judicial, shall be left in this body? I think a people cannot be long free, nor ever happy, whose government is in one assembly. My reasons for this opinion are as follow:—

1. A single assembly is liable to all the vices, follies, and frailties of an individual; subject to fits of humor, starts of passion, flights of enthusiasm, partialities, or prejudice, and consequently productive of hasty results and absurd judgments. And all these errors ought to be corrected and defects supplied by some controlling power.

2. A single assembly is apt to be avaricious, and in time will not scruple to exempt itself from burdens, which it will lay, without compunction, on its constituents.

3. A single assembly is apt to grow ambitious, and after a time will not hesitate to vote itself perpetual. This was one fault of the Long Parliament; but more remarkably of Holland, whose assembly first voted themselves from annual to septennial, then for life, and after a course of years, that all vacancies happening by death or otherwise, should be filled by themselves, without any application to constituents at all.

4. A representative assembly, although extremely well qualified, and absolutely necessary, as a branch of the legislative, is unfit to exercise the executive power, for want of two essential properties, secrecy and despatch.

5. A representative assembly is still less qualified for the judicial power, because it is too numerous, too slow, and too little skilled in the laws.

6. Because a single assembly, possessed of all the powers of government, would make arbitrary laws for their own interest, execute all laws arbitrarily for their own interest, and adjudge all controversies in their own favor.

But shall the whole power of legislation rest in one assembly? Most of the foregoing reasons apply equally to prove that the legislative power ought to be more complex; to which we may add, that if the legislative power is wholly in one assembly, and the executive in another, or in a single person, these two powers will oppose and encroach upon each other, until the contest shall end in war, and the whole power, legislative and executive, be usurped by the strongest.

The judicial power, in such case, could not mediate, or hold the balance between the two contending powers, because the legislative would undermine it. And this shows the necessity, too, of giving the executive power a negative upon the legislative, otherwise this will be continually encroaching upon that.

To avoid these dangers, let a distinct assembly be constituted, as a mediator between the two extreme branches of the legislature, that which represents the people, and that which is vested with the executive power.

Let the representative assembly then elect by ballot, from among themselves or their constituents, or both, a distinct assembly, which, for the sake of perspicuity, we will call a council. It may consist of any number you please, say twenty or thirty, and should have a free and independent exercise of its judgment, and consequently a negative voice in the legislature.

These two bodies, thus constituted, and made integral parts of the legislature, let them unite, and by joint ballot choose a governor, who, after being stripped of most of those badges of domination, called prerogatives, should have a free and independent exercise of his judgment, and be made also an integral part of the legislature. This, I know, is liable to objections; and, if you please, you may make him only president of the council, as in Connecti-cut. But as the governor is to be invested with the executive power, with consent of council, I think he ought to have a negative upon the legislative. If he is annually elective, as he ought to be, he will always have so much reverence and affection for the people, their representatives and counsellors, that, although you give him an independent exercise of his judgment, he will seldom use it in opposition to the two houses, except in cases the public utility of which would be conspicuous; and some such cases would happen.

In the present exigency of American affairs, when, by an act of Parliament, we are put out of the royal protection, and conse-quently discharged from our allegiance, and it has become neces-sary to assume government for our immediate security, the governor, lieutenant-governor, secretary, treasurer, commissary, at-torney-general, should be chosen by joint ballot of both houses. And these and all other elections, especially of representatives and counsellors, should be annual, there not being in the whole circle of the sciences a maxim more infallible than this, "where annual elections end, there slavery begins."

These great men, in this respect, should be, once a year,

> Like bubbles on the sea of matter borne,
> They rise, they break, and to that sea return.

This will teach them the great political virtues of humility, pa-tience, and moderation, without which every man in power be-comes a ravenous beast of prey.

This mode of constituting the great offices of state will answer very well for the present; but if by experiment it should be found inconvenient, the legislature may, at its leisure, devise other meth-ods of creating them, by elections of the people at large, as in Connecticut, or it may enlarge the term for which they shall be chosen to seven years, or three years, or for life, or make any other alterations which the society shall find productive of its ease, its safety, its freedom, or, in one word, its happiness.

A rotation of all offices, as well as of representatives and counsel-lors, has many advocates, and is contended for with many plausible arguments. It would be attended, no doubt, with many advantages; and if the society has a sufficient number of suitable characters to supply the great number of vacancies which would be made by such a rotation, I can see no objection to it. These persons may be allowed to serve for three years, and then be excluded three years, or for any longer or shorter term.

Any seven or nine of the legislative council may be made a quorum, for doing business as a privy council, to advise the governor in the exercise of the executive branch of power, and in all acts of state.

The governor should have the command of the militia and of all your armies. The power of pardons should be with the governor and council.

Judges, justices, and all other officers, civil and military, should be nominated and appointed by the governor, with the advice and consent of council, unless you choose to have a government more popular; if you do, all officers, civil and military, may be chosen by joint ballot of both houses; or, in order to preserve the independence and importance of each house, by ballot of one house, concurred in by the other. Sheriffs should be chosen by the freeholders of counties; so should registers of deeds and clerks of counties.

All officers should have commissions, under the hand of the governor and seal of the colony.

The dignity and stability of government in all its branches, the morals of the people, and every blessing of society depend so much upon an upright and skilful administration of justice, that the judicial power ought to be distinct from both the legislative and executive, and independent upon both, that so it may be a check upon both, as both should be checks upon that. The judges, therefore, should be always men of learning and experience in the laws, of exemplary morals, great patience, calmness, coolness, and attention. Their minds should not be distracted with jarring interests; they should not be dependent upon any man, or body of men. To these ends, they should hold estates for life in their offices; or, in other words, their commissions should be during good behavior, and their salaries ascertained and established by law. For misbehavior, the grand inquest of the colony, the house of representatives, should impeach them before the governor and council, where they should have time and opportunity to make their defence; but, if convicted, should be removed from their offices, and subjected to such other punishment as shall be thought proper.

A militia law, requiring all men, or with very few exceptions besides cases of conscience, to be provided with arms and ammunition, to be trained at certain seasons; and requiring counties, towns, or other small districts, to be provided with public stocks of ammunition and intrenching utensils, and with some settled plans for transporting provisions after the militia, when marched to defend their country against sudden invasions; and requiring certain districts to be provided with field-pieces, companies of matrosses, and perhaps some regiments of light-horse, is always a wise institution, and, in the present circumstances of our country, indispensable.

Laws for the liberal education of youth, especially of the lower class of people, are so extremely wise and useful, that, to a humane and generous mind, no expense for this purpose would be thought extravagant.

The very mention of sumptuary laws will excite a smile. Whether our countrymen have wisdom and virtue enough to submit to them, I know not; but the happiness of the people might be greatly promoted by them, and a revenue saved sufficient to carry on this war forever. Frugality is a great revenue, besides curing us of vanities, levities, and fopperies, which are real antidotes to all great, manly, and warlike virtues.

But must not all commissions run in the name of a king? No. Why may they not as well run thus, "The colony of——to A. B. greeting," and be tested by the governor?

Why may not writs, instead of running in the name of the king, run thus, "The colony of——to the sheriff," &c., and be tested by the chief justice?

Why may not indictments conclude, "against the peace of the colony of——and the dignity of the same?"

A constitution founded on these principles introduces knowledge among the people, and inspires them with a conscious dignity becoming freemen; a general emulation takes place, which causes good humor, sociability, good manners, and good morals to be general. That elevation of sentiment inspired by such a government, makes the common people brave and enterprising. That ambition which is inspired by it makes them sober, industrious, and frugal. You will find among them some elegance, perhaps, but more solidity; a little pleasure, but a great deal of business; some politeness, but more civility. If you compare such a country with the regions of domination, whether monarchical or aristocratical, you will fancy yourself in Arcadia or Elysium.

If the colonies should assume governments separately, they

should be left entirely to their own choice of the forms; and if a continental constitution should be formed, it should be a congress, containing a fair and adequate representation of the colonies, and its authority should sacredly be confined to these cases, namely, war, trade, disputes between colony and colony, the post-office, and the unappropriated lands of the crown, as they used to be called.

These colonies, under such forms of government, and in such a union, would be unconquerable by all the monarchies of Europe.

You and I, my dear friend, have been sent into life at a time when the greatest lawgivers of antiquity would have wished to live. How few of the human race have ever enjoyed an opportunity of making an election of government, more than of air, soil, or climate, for themselves or their children! When, before the present epocha, had three millions of people full power and a fair opportunity to form and establish the wisest and happiest government that human wisdom can contrive? I hope you will avail yourself and your country of that extensive learning and indefatigable industry which you possess, to assist her in the formation of the happiest governments and the best character of a great people. For myself, I must beg you to keep my name out of sight; for this feeble attempt, if it should be known to be mine, would oblige me to apply to myself those lines of the immortal John Milton, in one of his sonnets:—

> I did but prompt the age to quit their clogs
> By the known rules of ancient liberty,
> When straight a barbarous noise environs me
> Of owls and cuckoos, asses, apes, and dogs.

70. Two Bills of Rights:
Virginia, 1776, and Massachusetts, 1780

Virginia, June 12, 1776

A declaration of rights made by the representatives of the good people of Virginia, assembled in full and free convention; which rights do pertain to them and their posterity, as the basis and foundation of government.

SOURCE: F. N. Thorpe, ed., *Federal and State Constitutions* (7 vols., Washington, 1909), VII, 3812–3814.

1. That all men are by nature equally free and independent, and have certain inherent rights, of which, when they enter into a state of society, they cannot by any compact deprive or divest their posterity; namely, the enjoyment of life and liberty, with the means of acquiring and possessing property, and pursuing and obtaining happiness and safety.

2. That all power is vested in, and consequently derived from, the people; that magistrates are their trustees and servants, and at all times amenable to them.

3. That government is, or ought to be instituted for the common benefit, protection, and security of the people, nation, or community; of all the various modes and forms of government, that is best which is capable of producing the greatest degree of happiness and safety, and is most effectually secured against the danger of maladministration; and that when any government shall be found inadequate or contrary to these purposes, a majority of the community hath an indubitable, unalienable and indefeasible right to reform, alter or abolish it, in such manner as shall be judged most conducive to the public weal.

4. That no man, or set of men, are entitled to exclusive or separate emoluments or privileges from the community, but in consideration of publick services; which, not being descendible, neither ought the offices of magistrate, legislator or judge to be hereditary.

5. That the legislative and executive powers of the state should be separate and distinct from the judiciary; and that the members of the two first may be restrained from oppression, by feeling and participating the burthens of the people, they should, at fixed periods, be reduced to a private station, return into that body from which they were originally taken, and the vacancies be supplied by frequent, certain, and regular elections, in which all, or any part of the former members to be again eligible or ineligible, as the laws shall direct.

6. That elections of members to serve as representatives of the people in assembly, ought to be free; and that all men having sufficient evidence of permanent common interest with, and attachment to the community, have the right of suffrage, and cannot be taxed or deprived of their property for publick uses, without their own consent, or that of their representatives so elected, nor

bound by any law to which they have not, in like manner, assented for the public good.

7. That all power of suspending laws, or the execution of laws, by any authority without consent of the representatives of the people, is injurious to their rights, and ought not to be exercised.

8. That in all capital or criminal prosecutions a man hath a right to demand the cause and nature of his accusation, to be confronted with the accusers and witnesses, to call for evidence in his favour, and to a speedy trial by an impartial jury of his vicinage, without whose unanimous consent he cannot be found guilty; nor can he be compelled to give evidence against himself; that no man be deprived of his liberty, except by the law of the land or the judgment of his peers.

9. That excessive bail ought not to be required, nor excessive fines imposed, nor cruel and unusual punishments inflicted.

10. That general warrants, whereby an officer or messenger may be commanded to search suspected places without evidence of a fact committed, or to seize any person or persons not named, or whose offence is not particularly described and supported by evidence, are grievous and oppressive, and ought not to be granted.

11. That in controversies respecting property, and in suits between man and man, the ancient trial by jury is preferable to any other, and ought to be held sacred.

12. That the freedom of the press is one of the great bulwarks of liberty, and can never be restrained but by despotick governments.

13. That a well-regulated militia, composed of the body of the people trained to arms, is the proper, natural and safe defence of a free state; that standing armies in time of peace should be avoided as dangerous to liberty; and that in all cases the military should be under strict subordination to, and governed by, the civil power.

14. That the people have a right to uniform government; and, therefore, that no government separate from, or independent of the government of Virginia, ought to be erected or established within the limits thereof.

15. That no free government, or the blessings of liberty, can be preserved to any people, but by a firm adherence to justice, moderation, temperance, frugality and virtue, and by frequent recurrence to fundamental principles.

16. That religion, or the duty which we owe to our Creator, and the manner of discharging it, can be directed only by reason and

conviction, not by force or violence; and therefore all men are equally entitled to the free exercise of religion, according to the dictates of conscience; and that it is the mutual duty of all to practise Christian forbearance, love, and charity towards each other.

Massachusetts, 1780

ARTICLE I. All men are born free and equal, and have certain natural, essential, and unalienable rights; among which may be reckoned the right of enjoying and defending their lives and liberties; that of acquiring, possessing, and protecting property; in fine, that of seeking and obtaining their safety and happiness.

II. It is the right as well as the duty of all men in society, publicly, and at stated seasons, to worship the Supreme Being, the great Creator and Preserver of the universe. And no subject shall be hurt, molested, or restrained, in his person, liberty, or estate, for worshipping God in the manner and season most agreeable to the dictates of his own conscience; or for his religious profession of sentiments; provided he doth not disturb the public peace, or obstruct others in their religious worship. . . .

As the happiness of a people and the good order and preservation of civil government essentially depend upon piety, religion, and morality, and as these cannot be generally diffused through a community but by the institution of the public worship of God and of public instructions, in piety, religion, and morality. Therefore to promote their happiness and secure the good order and preservation of their government, the people of this commonwealth have a right to invest their legislature with power to authorize and require, and the legislature shall from time to time authorize and require, the several towns and other bodies—politic or religious societies, to make suitable provision, at their own expense, for the institution of the public worship of God and the support and maintenance of public Protestant teachers of piety, religion, and morality. . . .

And the people of this commonwealth . . . do invest their legislature with authority to enjoin upon all the subjects an attendance upon the instructions of the public teachers aforesaid. . . .

SOURCE: F. N. Thorpe, ed., *Federal and State Constitutions*, III, 1888–1893.

And every denomination of Christians, demeaning themselves peaceably and as good subjects of the commonwealth, shall be equally under the protection of the law; and no subordination of any one sect or denomination to another shall ever be established by law. . . .

IV. The people of this commonwealth have the sole and exclusive right of governing themselves, as a free, sovereign, and independent State, and do, and forever hereafter shall, exercise and enjoy every power, jurisdiction, and right, which is not, or may not hereafter be, by them expressly delegated to the United States of America, in Congress assembled.

V. All power residing originally in the people, and being derived from them, the several magistrates and officers of government, vested with authority, whether legislative, executive, or judicial, are their substitutes and agents, and are at all times accountable to them.

VI. No man, nor corporation, or association of men, have any other title to obtain advantages, or particular and exclusive privileges, distinct from those of the community, than what arises from the consideration of services rendered to the public; and this title being in nature neither hereditary, nor transmissible to children, or descendants, or relations by blood; the idea of a man born a magistrate, lawgiver, or judge, is absurd and unnatural.

VII. Government is instituted for the common good, for the protection, safety, prosperity, and happiness of the people and not for the profit, honor or private interest of any one man, family, or class of men; therefore the people alone have an incontestible unalienable, and indefeasible right to institute government; and to reform, alter, or totally change the same, when their protection, safety, prosperity, and happiness require it.

VIII. In order to prevent those who are vested with authority from becoming oppressors, the people have a right, at such periods and in such manner as they shall establish by their frame of government, to cause their public officers to return to private life; and to fill up vacant places by certain and regular elections and appointments.

IX. All elections ought to be free; and all the inhabitants of this commonwealth, having such qualifications as they shall establish by their frame of government, have an equal right to elect officers, and to be elected, for public employments.

X. Each individual of the society has a right to be protected by it in the enjoyment of his life, liberty, and property. . . . No part of the property of any individual can, with justice, be taken from him, or applied to public uses, without his own consent, or that of the representative body of the people. . . . And whenever the public exigencies require that the property of any individual should be appropriated to public uses, he shall receive a reasonable compensation therefor.

XI. Every subject of the commonwealth ought to find a certain remedy, by having recourse to the laws, for all injuries or wrongs which he may receive in his person, property, or character. He ought to obtain right and justice freely, and without being obliged to purchase it; completely, and without any denial; promptly, and without delay, conformably to the laws.

XII. No subject shall be held to answer for any crimes or offence, until the same is fully and plainly . . . described to him; or be compelled to accuse, or furnish evidence against himself. And every subject shall have a right to produce all proofs that may be favorable to him; to meet the witnesses against him face to face, and to be fully heard in his defence by himself, or his counsel, at his election. And no subject shall be arrested, or deprived of his life, liberty, or estate, but by the judgment of his peers, or the law of the land.

And the legislature shall not make any law that shall subject any person to a capital or infamous punishment, excepting for the government of the army and navy, without trial by jury. . . .

XIV. Every subject has a right to be secure from all unreasonable searches, and seizures, of his person, his houses, his papers, and all his possessions. . . . And no warrant ought to be issued but in cases, and with the formalities prescribed by the laws.

XV. In all controversies concerning property, and in all suits between two or more persons, . . . the parties have a right to a trial by jury; and this method of procedure shall be held sacred. . . .

XVI. The liberty of the press is essential to the security of freedom in a state; it ought not, therefore, to be restricted in this commonwealth.

XVII. The people have a right to keep and to bear arms for the common defence. And as, in time of peace, armies are dangerous to liberty, they ought not to be maintained without the consent of the legislature; and the military power shall always be held in an exact subordination to the civil authority, and be governed by it.

XVIII. A frequent recurrence to the fundamental principles of the constitution, and a constant adherence to those of piety, justice, moderation, temperance, industry and frugality, are absolutely necessary to preserve the advantages of liberty, and to maintain a free government. The people ought, consequently, to have a particular attention to all those principles, in the choice of their officers and representatives: and they have a right to require of their lawgivers and magistrates an exact and constant observance of them, in the formation and execution of the laws necessary for the good administration of the commonwealth.

XIX. The people have a right, in an orderly and peaceable manner to assemble to consult upon the common good; give instructions to their representatives, and to request of the legislative body, by the way of addresses, petitions, or remonstrances, redress of the wrongs done them, and of the grievances they suffer.

XX. The power of suspending the laws, or the execution of the laws, ought never to be exercised but by the legislature, or by authority derived from it, to be exercised in such particular cases only as the legislature shall expressly provide for.

XXI. The freedom of deliberation, speech, and debate, in either house of the legislature, is so essential to the rights of the people, that it cannot be the foundation of any accusation or prosecution, action or complaint, in any other court or place whatsoever.

XXII. The legislature ought frequently to assemble for the redress of grievances, for correcting, strengthening, and confirming the laws, and for making new laws, as the common good may require.

XXIII. No subsidy, charge, tax, impost, or duties ought to be established, fixed, laid, or levied, under any pretext whatsoever, without the consent of the people or their representatives in the legislature.

XXIV. Laws made to punish for actions done before the existence of such laws, and which have not been declared crimes by preceding laws, are unjust, oppressive, and inconsistent with the fundamental principles of a free government.

XXV. No subject ought, in any case, or in any time, to be declared guilty of treason or felony by the legislature.

XXVI. No magistrate or court of law shall demand excessive bail or sureties, impose excessive fines, or inflict cruel or unusual punishments.

XXVII. In time of peace, no soldier ought to be quartered in any house wihout the consent of the owner; and in time of war, such quarters ought not to be made but by the civil magistrate, in a manner ordained by the legislature.

XXVIII. No person can in any case be subject to law-martial, or to any penalties or pains, by virtue of that law, except those employed in the army or navy, and except the militia in actual service, but by authority of the legislature.

XXIX. It is essential to the preservation of the rights of every individual, his life, liberty, property, and character, that there be an impartial interpretation of the laws, and administration of justice. It is the right of every citizen to be tried by judges as free, impartial, and independent as the lot of humanity will admit. It is, therefore, not only the best policy, but for the security of the rights of the people, and of every citizen, that the judges of the supreme judicial court should hold their offices as long as they behave themselves well; and that they should have honorable salaries ascertained and established by standing laws.

XXX. In the government of this commonwealth, the legislative department shall never exercise the executive and judicial powers, or either of them: the executive shall never exercise the legislative and judicial powers, or either of them: the judicial shall never exercise the legislative and executive powers, or either of them: to the end it may be a government of laws and not of men.

71. Rejection of the Massachusetts Constitution of 1778: From the *Essex Result* 1778

RESULT OF the Convention of Delegates holden at Ipswich in the County of Essex, who were Deputed to take into Consideration the Constitution and Form of Government proposed by the Convention of the State of Massachusetts-Bay. Newbury-Port: Printed and Sold by John Mycall. 1778.

In Convention of Delegates from the several towns of Lynn,

SOURCE: Theophilus Parsons, Jr., *Memoir of Theophilus Parsons* (Boston, 1859), 359–402.

Salem, Danvers, Wenham, Manchester, Gloucester, Ipswich, Newbury-Port, Salisbury, Methuen, Boxford, & Topsfield, holden by adjournment at Ipswich, on the twenty-ninth day of April, one thousand seven hundred & seventy-eight.

Peter Coffin Esq; in the Chair.

The Constitution and form of Government framed by the Convention of this State, was read paragraph by paragraph, and after debate, the following votes were passed.

1. That the present situation of this State renders it best, that the framing of a Constitution therefor, should be postponed 'till the public affairs are in a more peaceable and settled condition.

2. That a bill of rights, clearly ascertaining and defining the rights of conscience, and that security of person and property, which every member in the State hath a right to expect from the supreme power thereof, ought to be settled and established, previous to the ratification of any constitution for the State.

3. That the executive power in any State, ought not to have any share or voice in the legislative power in framing the laws, and therefore, that the second article of the Constitution is liable to exception.

4. That any man who is chosen Governor, ought to be properly qualified in point of property—that the qualification therefor, mentioned in the third article of the Constitution, is not sufficient—nor is the same qualification directed to be ascertained on fixed principles, as it ought to be, on account of the fluctuation of the nominal value of money, and of property.

5. That in every free Republican Government, where the legislative power is vested in an house or houses of representatives, all the members of the State ought to be equally represented.

6. That the mode of representation proposed in the sixth article of the constitution, is not so equal a representation as can reasonably be devised.

7. That therefore the mode of representation in said sixth article is exceptionable.

8. That the representation proposed in said article is also exceptionable, as it will produce an unwieldy assembly.

9. That the mode of election of Senators pointed out in the Constitution is exceptionable.

10. That the rights of conscience, and the security of person and property each member of the State is entitled to, are not ascer-

tained and defined in the Constitution, with a precision sufficient to limit the legislative power—and therefore, that the thirteenth article of the constitution is exceptionable.

11. That the fifteenth article is exceptionable, because the numbers that constitute a quorum in the House of Representatives and Senate, are too small.

12. That the seventeenth article of the constitution is exceptionable, because the supreme executive officer is not vested with proper authority—and because an independence between the executive and legislative body is not preserved.

13. That the nineteenth article is exceptionable, because a due independence is not kept up between the supreme legislative, judicial, and executive powers, nor between any two of them.

14. That the twentieth article is exceptionable, because the supreme executive officer hath a voice, and must be present in that Court, which alone hath authority to try impeachments.

15. That the twenty second article is exceptionable, because the supreme executive power is not preserved distinct from, and independent of, the supreme legislative power.

16. That the twenty third article is exceptionable, because the power of granting pardons is not solely vested in the supreme executive power of the State.

17. That the twenty eighth article is exceptionable, because the delegates for the Continental Congress may be elected by the House of Representatives, when all the Senators may vote against the election of those who are delegated.

18. That the thirty fourth article is exceptionable, because the rights of conscience are not therein clearly defined and ascertained; and further, because the free exercise and enjoyment of religious worship is there said to be *allowed* to all the protestants in the State, when in fact, that free exercise and enjoyment is the natural and uncontroulable right of every member of the State.

A committee was then appointed to attempt the ascertaining of the true principles of government, applicable to the territory of the Massachusetts-Bay; to state the non-conformity of the constitution proposed by the Convention of this State to those principles, and to delineate the general outlines of a constitution conformable thereto; and to report the same to this Body.

This Convention was then adjourned to the twelfth day of May next, to be holden at Ipswich.

The Convention met pursuant to adjournment, and their committee presented the following report.

The committee appointed by this Convention at their last adjournment, have proceeded upon the service assigned them. With diffidence have they undertaken the several parts of their duty, and the manner in which they have executed them, they submit to the candor of this Body. When they considered of what vast consequence, the forming of a Constitution is to the members of this State, the length of time that is necessary to canvass and digest any proposed plan of government, before the establishment of it, and the consummate coolness, and solemn deliberation which should attend, not only those gentlemen who have reposed in them, the important trust of delineating the several lines in which the various powers of government are to move, but also all those, who are to form an opinion of the execution of that trust, your committee must be excused when they express a surprise and regret, that so short a time is allowed the freemen inhabiting the territory of the Massachusetts-Bay, to revise and comprehend the form of government proposed to them by the convention of this State, to compare it with those principles on which every free government ought to be founded, and to ascertain it's conformity or nonconformity thereto. All this is necessary to be done, before a true opinion of it's merit or demerit can be formed. This opinion is to be certified within a time which, in our apprehension, is much too short for this purpose, and to be certified by a people who, during that time, have had and will have their minds perplexed and oppressed with a variety of public cares. The committee also beg leave to observe, that the constitution proposed for public approbation, was formed by gentlemen, who, at the same time, had a large share in conducting an important war, and who were employed in carrying into execution almost all the various powers of government.

The committee however proceeded in attempting the task assigned them, and the success of that attempt is now reported.

The reason and understanding of mankind, as well as the experience of all ages, confirm the truth of this proposition, that the benefits resulting to individuals from a free government, conduce much more to their happiness, than the retaining of all their natural rights in a state of nature. These benefits are greater or less, as the form of government, and the mode of exercising the supreme power of the State, are more or less conformable to those principles of equal impartial liberty, which is the property of all men from their birth as the gift of their Creator, compared with the manners and genius of the people, their occupations, customs, modes of thinking, situation, extent of country, and numbers. If the constitution and form of government are wholly repugnant to those principles, wretched are the subjects of that State. They have surrendered a portion of their natural rights, the enjoyment of which was in some degree a blessing, and the consequence is, they find themselves stripped of the remainder. As an anodyne to compose the spirits of these slaves, and to lull them into a passively obedient state, they are told, that tyranny is preferable to no government at all; a proposition which is to be doubted, unless considered under some limitation. Surely a state of nature is more excellent than that, in which men are meanly submissive to the haughty will of an imperious tyrant, whose savage passions are not bounded by the laws of reason, religion, honor, or a regard to his subjects, and the point to which all his movements center, is the gratification of a brutal appetite. As in a state of nature much happiness cannot be enjoyed by individuals, so it has been conformable to the inclinations of almost all men, to enter into a political society so constituted, as to remove the inconveniences they were obliged to submit to in their former state, and, at the same time, to retain all those natural rights, the enjoyment of which would be consistent with the nature of a free government, and the necessary subordination to the supreme power of the state. . . .

The freemen inhabiting the territory of the Massachusetts-Bay are now forming a political society for themselves. Perhaps their situation is more favorable in some respects, for erecting a free government, than any other people were ever favored with. That attachment to old forms, which usually embarrasses, has no place amongst them. They have the history and experience of all States before them. Mankind have been toiling through ages for their information; and the philosophers and learned men of antiquity have trimmed their midnight lamps, to transmit to them instruction. We live also in an age, when the principles of political liberty, and the foundation of governments, have been freely canvassed, and fairly settled. Yet some difficulties we have to encounter. Not content with removing our attachment to the old government, perhaps we have contracted a prejudice against some part of it without foundation. The idea of liberty has been held up in so dazzling colours, that some of us may not be willing to submit that subordination necessary in the freest States. Perhaps we may say further, that we do not consider ourselves united as brothers, with an united interest, but have fancied a clashing of interests amongst the various classes of men, and have acquired a thirst of power, and a wish of domination, over some of the community. We are contending for freedom—Let us all be equally free—It is possible, and it is just. Our interests when candidly considered are one. Let us have a constitution founded, not upon party or prejudice—not one for to-day or to-morrow—but for posterity.

A republican form is the only one consonant to the feelings of the generous and brave Americans. Let us now attend to those principles, upon which all republican governments, who boast any degree of political liberty, are founded, and which must enter into the spirit of a FREE republican constitution. For all republics are not FREE.

All men are born equally free. The rights they possess at their births are equal, and of the same kind. Some of those rights are alienable, and may be parted with for an equivalent. Others are unalienable and inherent, and of that importance, that no equivalent can be received in exchange. Sometimes we shall mention the surrendering of a power to control our natural rights, which perhaps is speaking with more precision, than when we use the expression of parting with natural rights—but the same thing is intended. Those rights which are unalienable, and of that importance, are called the rights of conscience. We have duties, for the discharge of which we are accountable to our Creator and benefactor, which no human power can cancel. What those duties are, is determinable by right reason, which may be, and is called, a well informed conscience. What this conscience dictates as our duty, is so; and that power which assumes a controul over it, is an usurper; for no consent can be pleaded to justify the controul, as any consent in this case is void. The alienation of some rights, in themselves alienable, may be also void, if the bargain is of that nature, that no equivalent can be received. Thus, if a man surrender all his alienable rights, without reserving a controul over the supreme power, or a right to resume in certain cases, the surrender is void, for he becomes a slave; and a slave can receive no equivalent. Common equity would set aside this bargain.

When men form themselves into society, and erect a body

politic or State, they are to be considered as one moral whole, which is in possession of the supreme power of the State. This supreme power is composed of the powers of each individual collected together, and VOLUNTARILY parted with by him. No individual, in this case, parts with his unalienable rights, the supreme power therefore cannot controul them. Each individual also surrenders the power of controuling his natural alienable rights, ONLY WHEN THE GOOD OF THE WHOLE REQUIRES it. The supreme power therefore can do nothing but what is for the good of the whole; and when it goes beyond this line, it is a power usurped. If the individual receives an equivalent for the right of controul he has parted with, the surrender of that right is valid; if he receives no equivalent, the surrender is void, and the supreme power as it respects him is an usurper. If the supreme power is so directed and executed that he does not enjoy political liberty, it is an illegal power, and he is not bound to obey.

Over the class of unalienable rights the supreme power hath no controul, and they ought to be clearly defined and ascertained in a BILL OF RIGHTS, previous to the ratification of any constitution. The bill of rights should also contain the equivalent every man receives, as a consideration for the rights he has surrendered. This equivalent consists principally in the security of his person and property, and is also unassailable by the supreme power: for if the equivalent is taken back, those natural rights which were parted with to purchase it, return to the original proprietor, as nothing is more true, than that ALLEGIANCE AND PROTECTION ARE RECIPROCAL.

That state, (other things being equal) which has reposed the supreme power in the hands of one or a small number of persons, is the most powerful state. An union, expedition, secrecy and dispatch are to be found only here. Where power is to executed by a large number, there will not probably be either of the requisites just mentioned. Many men have various opinions: and each one will be tenacious of his own, as he thinks it preferable to any other; for when he thinks otherwise, it will cease to be his opinion. From this diversity of opinions results disunion; from disunion, a want of expedition and dispatch. And the larger the number to whom a secret is entrusted, the greater is the probability of it's disclosure. This inconvenience more fully strikes us when we consider that want of secrecy may prevent the successful execution of any measures, however excellently formed and digested.

But from a single person, or a very small number, we are not to expect that political honesty, and upright regard to the interest of the body of the people, and the civil rights of each individual, which are essential to a good and free constitution. For these qualities we are to go to the body of the people. The voice of the people is said to be the voice of God. No man will be so hardy and presumptuous, as to affirm the truth of that proposition in it's fullest extent. But if this is considered as the intent of it, that the people have always a disposition to promote their own happiness, and that when they have time to be informed, and the necessary means of information given them, they will be able to determine upon the necessary measures therefor, no man, of a tolerable acquaintance with mankind, will deny the truth of it.

Yet, when we are forming a Constitution, by deductions that follow from established principles, (which is the only good method of forming one for futurity,) we are to look further than to the bulk of the people, for the greatest wisdom, firmness, consistency, and perseverance. These qualities will most probably be found amongst men of education and fortune. From such men we are to expect genius cultivated by reading, and all the various advantages and assistances, which art, and a liberal education aided by wealth, can furnish. From these result learning, a thorough knowledge of the interests of their country, when considered abstractedly, when compared with the neighbouring States, and when with those more remote, and an acquaintance with it's produce and manufacture, and it's exports and imports. All these are necessary to be known, in order to determine what is the true interest of any state; and without that interest is ascertained, impossible will it be to discover, whether a variety of certain laws may be beneficial or hurtful. From gentlemen whose private affairs compel them to take care of their own household, and deprive them of leisure, these qualifications are not to be generally expected, whatever class of men they are enrolled in.

Let all these respective excellencies be united. Let the supreme power be so disposed and ballanced, that the laws may have in view the interest of the whole; let them be wisely and consistently framed for that end, and firmly adhered to; and let them be executed with vigour and dispatch.

Before we proceed further, it must be again considered, and kept always in view, that we are not attempting to form a temporary constitution, one adjusted only to our present circumstances. We wish for one founded upon such principles as will secure to us freedom and happiness, however our circumstances may vary. One that will smile amidst the declensions of European and Asiatic empires, and survive the rude storms of time. It is not therefore to be understood, that all the men of fortune of the present day, are men of wisdom and learning, or that they are not. Nor that the bulk of the people, the farmers, the merchants, the tradesmen, and labourers, are all honest and upright, with single views to the public good, or that they are not. In each of the classes there are undoubtedly exceptions, as the rules laid down are general. The proposition is only this. That among gentlemen of education, fortune and leisure, we shall find the largest number of men, possessed of wisdom, learning, and a firmness and consistency of character. That among the bulk of the people, we shall find the greatest share of political honesty, probity, and a regard to the interest of the whole, of which they compose the majority. That wisdom and firmness are not sufficient without good intentions, nor the latter without the former. The conclusion is, let the legislative body unite them all. The former are called the excellencies that result from an aristocracy; the latter, those that result from a democracy.

The supreme power is considered as including the legislative, judicial, and executive powers. The nature and employment of these several powers deserve a distinct attention.

The legislative power is employed in making laws, or prescribing such rules of action to every individual in the state, as the good of the whole requires, to be conformed to by him in his conduct to the governors and governed, with respect both to their persons and property, according to the several relations he stands in. What rules of action the good of the whole requires, can be ascertained only by the majority, for a reason formerly mentioned. Therefore the legislative power must be so formed and exerted, that in prescribing any rule of action, or, in other words, enacting any law, the majority must consent. This may be more evident, when the fundamental condition on which every man enters into society, is considered. No man consented that his natural alienable rights should be wantonly controuled: they were controulable, only when that controul should be subservient to the good of the whole; and that subserviency, from the very nature of government, can be determined but by one absolute judge. The minority cannot be that judge, because then there may be two judges opposed to each other, so that this subserviency remains undetermined. Now the enacting of a law, is only the exercise of this controul over the natural alienable rights of each member of the state; and therefore this law must have the consent of the majority, or be invalid, as being contrary to the fundamental condition of the original social contract. In a state of nature, every man had the sovereign controul over his own person. He might also have, in that state, a qualified property. Whatever lands or chattels he had acquired the peaceable possession of, were exclusively his, by right of occupancy or possession. For while they were unpossessed he had a right to them equally with any other man, and therefore could not be disturbed in his possession, without being injured; for no man could lawfully dispossess him, without having a better right, which no man had. Over this qualified property every man in a state of nature had also a sovereign controul. And in entering into political society, he surrendered this right of controul over his person and property, (with an exception to the rights of conscience) to the supreme legislative power, to be exercised by that power, *when the good of the whole demanded it.* This was all the right he could surrender, being all the alienable right of which he was possessed. The only objects of legislation therefore, are the person and property of the individuals which compose the state. If the law affects only the persons of the members, the consent of a majority of any members is sufficient. If the law affects the property only, the consent of those who hold a majority of the property is enough. If it affects, (as it will very frequently, if not always,) but the person and property, the consent of a majority of the members, and of those members also who hold a majority of the property, is necessary. If the consent of the latter is not obtained, their interest is taken from them against their consent, and their boasted security of property is vanished. Those who make the law, in this case give and grant what is not theirs. The law, in it's principles, becomes a second stamp act. Lord Chatham very finely ridiculed the British house of commons upon that principle. "You can give and grant," said he, "only your own. Here you give and grant, what? The property of the Americans." The people of the Massachusetts-Bay then thought his Lordship's ridicule well pointed. And would they be willing to merit the same? Certainly they will agree in the prin-

ciple, should they mistake the application. The laws of the province of Massachusetts-Bay adopted the same principle, and very
happily applied it. As the votes of proprietors of common and
undivided lands in their meetings, can affect only their property,
therefore it is enacted, that in ascertaining the majority, the votes
shall be collected according to the respective interests of the proprietors. If each member, without regard to his property, has equal
influence in legislation with any other, it follows, that some members enjoy greater benefits and powers in legislation than others,
when these benefits and powers are compared with the rights
parted with to purchase them. For the property-holder parts with
the controul over his person, as well as he who hath no property,
and the former also parts with the controul over his property, of
which the latter is destitute. Therefore to constitute a perfect law
in a free state, affecting the persons and property of the members,
it is necessary that the law be for the good of the whole, which is to
be determined by a majority of the members, and that majority
should include those, who possess a major part of the property in
the state.

The judicial power follows next after the legislative power; for it
cannot act, until after laws are prescribed. Every wise legislator
annexes a sanction to his laws, which is most commonly penal,
(that is) a punishment either corporal or pecuniary, to be inflicted
on the member who shall infringe them. It is the part of the
judicial power (which in this territory has always been, and always
ought to be, a court and jury) to ascertain the member who hath
broken the law. Every man is to be presumed innocent, until the
judicial power hath determined him guilty. When that decision is
known, the law annexes the punishment, and the offender is
turned over to the executive arm, by whom it is inflicted on him.
The judicial power hath also to determine what legal contracts
have been broken, and what member hath been injured by a
violation of the law, to consider the damages that have been sustained, and to ascertain the recompense. The executive power takes
care that this recompense is paid.

The executive power is sometimes divided into the external
executive, and internal executive. The former comprehends war,
peace, the sending and receiving ambassadors, and whatever concerns the transactions of the state with any other independent
state. The confederation of the United States of America hath

lopped off this branch of the executive, and placed it in Congress. We have therefore only to consider the internal executive power, which is employed in the peace, security and protection of the subject and his property, and in the defence of the state. The executive power is to marshal and command her militia and armies for her defence, to enforce the law, and to carry into execution all the orders of the legislative powers.

A little attention to the subject will convince us, that these three powers ought to be in different hands, and independent of one another, and so ballanced, and each having that check upon the other, that their independence shall be preserved—If the three powers are united, the government will be absolute, *whether these powers are in the hands of one or a large number*. The same party will be the legislator, accuser, judge and executioner; and what probability will an accused person have of an acquittal, however innocent he may be, when his judge will be also a party.

If the legislative and judicial powers are united, the maker of the law will also interpret it; and the law may then speak a language, dictated by the whims, the caprice, or the prejudice of the judge, with impunity to him—And what people are so unhappy as those, whose laws are uncertain. It will also be in the breast of the judge, when grasping after his prey, to make a retrospective law, which shall bring the unhappy offender within it; and this also he can do with impunity—The subject can have no peaceable remedy—The judge will try himself, and an acquittal is the certain consequence. He has it also in his power to enact any law, which may shelter him from deserved vengeance.

Should the executive and legislative powers be united, mischiefs the most terrible would follow. The executive would enact those laws it pleased to execute, and no others—The judicial power would be set aside as inconvenient and tardy—The security and protection of the subject would be a shadow—The executive power would make itself absolute, and the government end in a tyranny—Lewis the eleventh of France, by cunning and treachery compleated the union of the executive and legislative powers of that kingdom, and upon that union established a system of tyranny. France was formerly under a free government.

The assembly or representatives of the united states of Holland, exercise the executive and legislative powers, and the government there is absolute.

Should the executive and judicial powers be united, the subject would then have no permanent security of his person and property. The executive power would interpret the laws and bend them to his will; and, as he is the judge, he may leap over them by artful constructions, and gratify, with impunity, the most rapacious passions. Perhaps no cause in any state has contributed more to promote internal convulsions, and to stain the scaffold with it's best blood, than this unhappy union. And it is an union which the executive power in all states, hath attempted to form: if that could not be compassed, to make the judicial power dependent upon it. Indeed the dependence of any of these powers upon either of the others, which in all states has always been attempted by one or the other of them, has so often been productive of such calamities, and of the shedding of such oceans of blood, that the page of history seems to be one continued tale of human wretchedness.

The following principles now seem to be established.

1. That the supreme power is limited, and cannot controul the unalienable rights of mankind, nor resume the equivalent (that is, the security of person and property) which each individual receives, as a consideration for the alienable rights he parted with in entering into political society.

2. That these unalienable rights, and this equivalent, are to be clearly defined and ascertained in a BILL of RIGHTS, previous to the ratification of any constitution.

3. That the supreme power should be so formed and modelled, as to exert the greatest possible power, wisdom, and goodness.

4. That the legislative, judicial, and executive powers, are to be lodged in different hands, that each branch is to be independent, and further, to be so ballanced, and be able to exert such checks upon the others, as will preserve it from a dependence on, or an union with them.

5. That government can exert the greatest power when it's supreme authority is vested in the hands of one or a few.

6. That the laws will be made with the greatest wisdom, and best intentions, when men, of all the several classes in the state concur in the enacting of them.

7. That a government which is so constituted, that it cannot afford a degree of political liberty nearly equal to all it's members, is not founded upon principles of freedom and justice, and where any

member enjoys no degree of political liberty, the government, so far as it respects him, is a tyranny, for he is controuled by laws to which he has never consented.

8. That the legislative power of a state hath no authority to controul the natural rights of any of it's members, unless the good of the whole requires it.

9. That a majority of the state is the only judge when the general good does require it.

10. That where the legislative power of the state is so formed, that a law may be enacted by the minority, each member of the state does not enjoy political liberty. And

11. That in a free government, a law affecting the person and property of it's members, is not valid, unless it has the consent of a majority of the members, which majority should include those, who hold a major part of the property in the state.

It may be necessary to proceed further, and notice some particular principles, which should be attended to in forming the three several powers in a free republican government.

The first important branch that comes under our consideration, is the legislative body. Was the number of the people so small, that the whole could meet together without inconvenience, the opinion of the majority would be more easily known. But, besides the inconvenience of assembling such numbers, no great advantages could follow. Sixty thousand people could not discuss with candor, and determine with deliberation. Tumults, riots, and murder would be the result. But the impracticability of forming such an assembly, renders it needless to make any further observations. The opinions and consent of the majority must be collected from persons, delegated by every freeman of the state for that purpose. Every freeman, who hath sufficient discretion, should have a voice in the election of his legislators. To speak with precision, in every free state where the power of legislation is lodged in the hands of one or more bodies of representatives elected for that purpose, the person of every member of the state, and all the property in it, ought to be represented, because they are objects of legislation. All the members of the state are qualified to make the election, unless they have not sufficient discretion, or are so situated as to have no wills of their own; persons not twenty one years old are deemed of the former class, from their want of years and experience. The

municipal law of this country will not trust them with the disposition of their lands, and consigns them to the care of their parents
or guardians. Women what age soever they are of, are also considered as not having a sufficient acquired discretion; not from a
deficiency in their mental powers, but from the natural tenderness
and delicacy of their minds, their retired mode of life, and various
domestic duties. These concurring, prevent that promiscuous intercourse with the world, which is necessary to qualify them for
electors. Slaves are of the latter class and have no wills. But are
slaves members of a free government? We feel the absurdity, and
would to God, the situation of America and the tempers of it's
inhabitants were such, that the slave-holder could not be found in
the land.

The rights of representation should be so equally and impartially
distributed, that the representatives should have the same views,
and interests with the people at large. They should think, feel, and
act like them, and in fine, should be an exact miniature of their
constituents. They should be (if we may use the expression) the
whole body politic, with all it's property, rights, and priviledges,
reduced to a smaller scale, every part being diminished in just
proportion. To pursue the metaphor. If in adjusting the representation of freemen, any ten are reduced into one, all the other tens
should be alike reduced: or if any hundred should be reduced to
one, all the other hundreds should have just the same reduction.
The representation ought also to be so adjusted, that it should be
the interest of the representatives at all times, to do justice, therefore equal interest among the people, should have equal interest
among the body of representatives. The majority of the representatives should also represent a majority of the people, and the
legislative body should be so constructed, that every law affecting
property, should have the consent of those who hold a majority of
the property. The law would then be determined to be for the good
of the whole by the proper judge, the majority, and the necessary
consent thereto would be obtained: and all the members of the
State would enjoy political liberty, and an equal degree of it. If the
scale to which the body politic is to be reduced, is but a little
smaller than the original, or, in other words, if a small number of
freemen should be reduced to one, that is, send one representative,
the number of representatives would be too large for the public
good. The expences of government would be enormous. The body
would be too unwieldy to deliberate with candor and coolness. The

variety of opinions and oppositions would irritate the passions. Parties would be formed and factions engendered. The members would list under the banners of their respective leaders: address and intrigue would conduct the debates, and the result would tend only to promote the ambition or interest of a particular party. Such has always been in some degree, the course and event of debates instituted and managed by a large multitude.

For these reasons, some foreign politicians have laid it down as a rule, that no body of men larger than a hundred, would transact business well: and Lord Chesterfield called the British house of commons a mere mob, because of the number of men which composed it.

Elections ought also to be free. No bribery, corruption, or undue influence should have place. They stifle the free voice of the people, corrupt their morals, and introduce a degeneracy of manners, a supineness of temper, and an inattention to their liberties, which pave the road for the approach of tyranny, in all it's frightful forms.

The rights of representation should also be held sacred and inviolable, and for this purpose, representation should be fixed upon known and easy principles; and the constitution should make provision, that recourse should constantly be had to those principles within a very small period of years, to rectify the errors that will creep in through lapse of time, or alteration of situations. The want of fixed principles of government, and a stated regular recourse to them, have produced the dissolution of all states, whose consitutions have been transmitted to us by history.

But the legislative power must not be trusted with one assembly. A single assembly is frequently influenced by the vices, follies, passions, and prejudices of an individual. It is liable to be avaricious, and to exempt itself from the burdens it lays upon it's constituents. It is subject to ambition, and after a series of years, will be prompted to vote itself perpetual. The long parliament in England voted itself perpetual, and thereby, for a time, destroyed the political liberty of the subject. Holland was governed by one representative assembly annually elected. They afterwards voted themselves from annual to septennial; then for life; and finally exerted the power of filling up all vacancies, without application to their constituents. The government of Holland is now a tyranny *though a republic.*

The result of a single assembly will be hasty and indigested, and their judgments frequently absurd and inconsistent. There must be a second body to revise with coolness and wisdom, and to control with firmness, independent upon the first, either for their creation, or existence. Yet the first must retain a right to a similar revision and controul over the second.

Let us now ascertain some particular principles which should be attended to, in forming the executive power.

When we recollect the nature and employment of this power, we find that it ought to be conducted with vigour and dispatch. It should be able to execute the laws without opposition, and to controul all the turbulent spirits in the state, who should infringe them. If the laws are not obeyed, the legislative power is vain, and the judicial is mere pageantry. As these laws, with their several sanctions, are the only securities of person and property, the members of the state can confide in, if they lie dormant through failure of execution, violence and oppression will erect their heads, and stalk unmolested through the land. The judicial power ought to discriminate the offender, as soon after the commission of the offence, as an impartial trial will admit; and the executive arm to inflict the punishment immediately after the criminal is ascertained. This would have an happy tendency to prevent crimes, as the commission of them would awaken the attendant idea of punishment; and the hope of an escape, which is often an inducement, would be cut off. The executive power ought therefore in these cases, to be exerted with union, vigour, and dispatch. Another duty of that power is to arrest offenders, to bring them to trial. This cannot often be done, unless secrecy and expedition are used. The want of these two requisites, will be more especially inconvenient in repressing treasons, and those more enormous offences which strike at the happiness, if not existence of the whole. Offenders of these classes do not act alone. Some number is necessary to the compleating of the crime. Cabals are formed with art, and secrecy presides over their councils; while measures the most fatal are the result, to be executed by desperation. On these men the thunder of the state should be hurled with rapidity; for if they hear it roll at a distance, their danger is over. When they gain intelligence of the process, they abscond, and wait a more favourable opportunity. If that is attended with difficulty, they destroy all the evidence of their guilt, brave government, and deride the justice and power of the state.

It has been observed likewise, that the executive power is to act as Captain-General, to marshal the militia and armies of the state, and, for her defence, to lead them on to battle. These armies should always be composed of the militia or body of the people. Standing armies are a tremendous curse to a state. In all periods in which they have existed, they have been the scourge of mankind. In this department, union, vigour, secrecy, and dispatch are more peculiarly necessary. Was one to propose a body of militia, over which two Generals, with equal authority, should have the command, he would be laughed at. Should one pretend, that the General should have no controul over his subordinate officers, either to remove them or to supply their posts, he would be pitied for his ignorance of the subject he was discussing. It is obviously necessary, that the man who calls the militia to action, and assumes the military controul over them in the field, should previously know the number of his men, their equipments and residence, and the talents and tempers of the several ranks of officers, and their respective departments in the state, that he may wisely determine to whom the necessary orders are to be issued. Regular and particular returns of these requisites should be frequently made. Let it be enquired, are these returns to be made only to the legislative body, or a branch of it, which necessarily moves slow?— Is the General to go to them for information? intreat them to remove an improper officer, and give him another they shall chuse? and in fine is he to supplicate his orders from them, and constantly walk where their leading-strings shall direct his steps? If so, where are the power and force of the militia—where the union—where the dispatch and profound secrecy? Or shall these returns be made to him?—when he may see with his own eyes—be his own judge of the merit, or demerit of his officers—discern their various talents and qualifications, and employ them as the service and defence of his country demand. Besides, the legislative body or a branch of it is local—they cannot therefore personally inform themselves of these facts, but must judge upon trust. The General's opinion will be founded upon his own observations—the officers and privates of the militia will act under his eye: and, if he has it in his power immediately to promote or disgrace them, they will be induced to noble exertions. It may further be observed here, that if the subordinate civil or military executive officers are appointed by the legislative body or a branch of it, the former will become dependent upon the latter, and the necessary independence of either the legislative or executive powers upon the other is wanting. The legislative power will have that undue influence over the executive which will amount to a controul, for the latter will be their creatures, and will fear their creators.

One further observation may be pertinent. Such is the temper of mankind, that each man will be too liable to introduce his own friends and connexions into office, without regarding the public interest. If one man or a small number appoint, their connexions will probably be introduced. If a large number appoint, all their connexions will receive the same favour. The smaller the number appointing, the more contracted are their connexions, and for that reason, there will be a greater probability of better officers, as the connexions of one man or a very small number can fill but a very few of the offices. When a small number of men have the power of appointment, or the management in any particular department, their conduct is accurately noticed. On any miscarriage or imprudence the public resentment lies with weight. All the eyes of the people are converted to a point, and produce that attention to their censure, and that fear of misbehaviour, which are the greatest security the state can have, of the wisdom and prudence of its servants. This observation will strike us, when we recollect that many a man will zealously promote an affair in a public assembly, of which he is but one of a large number, yet, at the same time, he would blush to be thought the sole author of it. For all these reasons, the supreme executive power should be rested in the hands of one or of a small number, who should have the appointment of all subordinate executive officers. Should the supreme executive officer be elected by the legislative body, there would be a dependence of the executive power upon the legislative. Should he be elected by the judicial body, there also would be a dependence. The people at large must therefore designate the person, to whom they will delegate this power. And upon the people, there ought to be a dependence of all the powers in government, for all the officers in the state are but the servants of the people.

We have not noticed the navy-department. The conducting of that department is indisputably in the supreme executive power: and we suppose, that all the observations respecting the Captain-General, apply to the Admiral.

We are next to fix upon some general rules which should govern us in forming the judicial power. This power is to be independent upon the executive and legislative. The judicial power should be a court and jury, or as they are commonly called, the Judges and jury. The jury are the peers or equals of every man, and are to try all facts. The province of the Judges is to preside in and regulate all trials, and ascertain the law. We shall only consider the appointment of the Judges. The same power which appoints them, ought not to have the power of removing them, not even for misbehavior. That conduct only would then be deemed misbehavior which was opposed to the will of the power removing. A removal in this case for proper reasons, would not be often attainable: for to remove a man from an office, because he is not properly qualified to discharge the duties of it, is a severe censure upon that man or body of men who appointed him—and mankind do not love to censure themselves. Whoever appoints the judges, they ought not to be removable at pleasure, for they will then feel a dependence upon that man or body of men who hath the power of removal. Nor ought they to be dependent upon either the executive or legislative power for their salaries; for if they are, that power on whom they are thus dependent, can starve them into a compliance. One of these two powers should appoint, and the other remove. The legislative will not probably appoint so good men as the executive, for reasons formerly mentioned. The former are composed of a large body of men who have a numerous train of friends and connexions, and they do not hazard their reputations, which the executive will. It has often been mentioned that where a large body of men are responsible for any measures, a regard to their reputations, and to the public opinion, will not prompt them to use that care and precaution, which such regard will prompt one or a few to make use of. Let one more observation be now introduced to confirm it. Every man has some friends and dependents who will endeavor to snatch him from the public hatred. One man has but a few comparatively, they are not numerous enough to protect him, and he falls a victim to his own misconduct. When measures are conducted by a large number, their friends and connexions are numerous and noisy—they are dispersed through the State—their clamors stifle the execrations of the people, whose groans cannot even be heard. But to resume, neither will the executive body be the most proper judge when to remove. If this body is judge, it must also be the accuser, or the legislative body, or a branch of it, must be—If the executive body complains, it will be both accuser and judge—If the complaint is preferred by the legislative body, or a branch of it, when the judges are appointed by the legislative body, then a body of men who were concerned in the appointment, must in most cases complain of the impropriety of their own appointment. Let therefore the judges be appointed by the executive body—let their salaries be independent—and let them hold their places during good behaviour—Let their misbehaviour be determinable by the legislative body—Let one branch thereof impeach, and the other judge. Upon these principles the judicial body will be independent so long as they behave well and a proper court is appointed to ascertain their mal-conduct.

The Committee afterwards proceeded to consider the Constitution framed by the Convention of this State. They have examined that Constitution with all the care the shortness of the time would admit. And they are compelled, though reluctantly to say, that some of the principles upon which it is founded, appeared to them inconsonant, not only to the natural rights of mankind, but to the fundamental condition of the original social contract, and the principles of a free republican government. In that form of government the governor appears to be the supreme executive officer, and the legislative power is in an house of representatives and senate. It may be necessary to descend to a more particular consideration of the several articles of that constitution.

The second article thereof appears exceptionable upon the principles we have already attempted to establish, because the supreme executive officer hath a seat and voice in one branch of the legislative body, and is assisting in originating and framing the laws, the Governor being entitled to a seat and voice in the Senate, and to preside in it, and may thereby have that influence in the legislative body, which the supreme executive officer ought not to have.

The third article among other things, ascertains the qualifications of the Governor, Lieutenant Governor, Senators and Representatives respecting property—The estate sufficient to qualify a man for Governor is so small, it is hardly any qualification at all. Further, the method of ascertaining the value of the estates of the officers aforesaid is vague and uncertain as it depends upon the nature and quantity of the currency, and the encrease of property, and not upon any fixed principles. This article therefore appears to be exceptionable.

The sixth article regulates the election of representatives. So many objections present themselves to this article, we are at a loss which first to mention. The representation is grossly unequal, and it is flagrantly unjust. It violates the fundamental principle of the original social contract, and introduces an unwieldy and expensive house. Representation ought to be equal upon the principles formerly mentioned. By this article any corporation, however small, may send one representative, while no corporation can send more than one, unless it has three hundred freemen. Twenty corporations (of three hundred freemen in each) containing in the whole six thousand freemen, may send forty representatives, when one corporation, which shall contain six thousand two hundred and twenty, can send but nineteen. One third of the state may send a majority of the representatives, and all the laws may be enacted by a minority—Do all the members of the state then, enjoy political liberty? Will they not be controuled by laws enacted against their consent? When we go further and find, that sixty members make an house, and that the concurrence of thirty one (which is about one twelfth of what may be the present number of representatives) is sufficient to bind the persons and properties of the members of the State, we stand amazed, and are sorry that any well disposed Americans were so inattentive to the consequences of such an arrangement.

The number of representatives is too large to debate with coolness and deliberation, the public business will be protracted to an undue length and the pay of the house is enormous. As the number of freemen in the state encreases, these inconveniences will encrease; and in a century, the house of representatives will, from their numbers, be a mere mob. Observations upon this article crowd upon us, but we will dismiss it, with wishing that the mode of representation there proposed, may be candidly compared with the principles which have been already mentioned in the course of our observations upon the legislative power, and upon representation in a free republic.

The ninth article regulates the election of Senators, which we think exceptionable. As the Senators for each district will be elected by all the freemen in the state properly qualified, a trust is reposed in the people which they are unequal to. The freemen in the late province of Main, are to give in their votes for senators in the western district, and so, on the contrary. Is it supposeable that the freemen in the county of Lincoln can judge of the political merits of a senator in Berkshire? Must not the several corporations in the state, in a great measure depend upon their representatives for information? And will not the house of representatives in fact chuse the senators? That independence of the senate upon the house, which the constitution seems to have intended, is visionary, and the benefits which were expected to result from a senate, as one distinct branch of the legislative body, will not be discoverable.

The tenth article prescribes the method in which the Governor is to be elected. This method is open to, and will introduce bribery and corruption, and also originate parties and factions in the state. The Governor of Rhode-Island was formerly elected in this manner, and we all know how long a late Governor there, procured his re-election by methods the most unjustifiable. Bribery was attempted in an open and flagrant manner.

The thirteenth article ascertains the authority of the general court, and by that article we find their power is limited only by the several articles of the constitution. We do not find that the rights of conscience are ascertained and defined, unless they may be thought to be in the thirty-fourth article. That article we conceive to be expressed in very loose and uncertain terms. What is a *religious* profession and worship of God, has been disputed for sixteen hundred years, and the various sects of christians have not yet settled the dispute. What is a free exercise and enjoyment of religious worship has been, and still is, a subject of much altercation. And this free exercise and enjoyment is said to be *allowed* to the protestants of this state by the constitution, when we suppose it to be an unalienable right of all mankind, which no human power can wrest from them. We do not find any bill of rights either accompanying the constitution, or interwoven with it, and no attempt is made to define and secure that protection of the person and property of the members of the state, which the legislative and executive bodies cannot withhold, unless the general words *of confirming the right to trial by jury*, should be considered as such definition and security. We think a bill of rights ascertaining and clearly describing the rights of conscience, and that security of person and property, the supreme power of the state is bound to afford to all the members thereof, ought to be fully ratified, before, or at the same time with, the establishment of any constitution.

The fifteenth article fixes the number which shall constitute a quorum in the senate and house of representatives—We think these numbers much too small—This constitution will immediately introduce about three hundred and sixty members into the house. If sixty make a quorum, the house may totally change its members six different times; and it probably will very often in the course of a long session, be composed of such a variety of members, as will retard the public business, and introduce confusion in the debates, and inconsistency in the result. Besides the number of members, whose concurrence is necessary to enact a law, is so small, that the subjects of the state will have no security, that the laws which are to controul their natural rights, have the consent of a majority of the freemen. The same reasoning applies to the senate, though not so strikingly, as a quorum of that body must consist of nearly a third of the senators.

The eighteenth article describes the several powers of the Governor or the supreme executive officer. We find in comparing the several articles of the constitution, that the senate are the only court to try impeachments. We also conceive that every officer in the state ought to be amenable to such court. We think therefore that the members of that court ought never to be advisory to any officer in the state. If their advice is the result of inattention or corruption, they cannot be brought to punishment by impeachment, as they will be their own judges. Neither will the officer who pursues their advice be often, if ever, punishable, for a similar reason. To condemn this officer will be to reprobate their own advice—consequently a proper body is not formed to advise the Governor, when a sudden emergency may render advice expedient: for the senate advise, and are the court to try impeachments. We would now make one further observation, that we cannot discover in this article or in any part of the constitution that the executive power is entrusted with a check upon the legislative power, sufficient to prevent the encroachment of the latter upon the former— Without this check the legislative power will exercise the executive, and in a series of years the government will be as absolute as that of Holland.

The nineteenth article regulates the appointment of the several classes of officers. And we find that almost all the officers are appointed by the Governor and Senate. An objection formerly made occurs here. The Senate with the Governor are the court to remove these officers for misbehaviour. Those officers, in general, who are guilty of mal-conduct in the execution of their office, were improper men to be appointed. Sufficient care was not taken in ascertaining their political, military or moral qualifications. Will the senators therefore if they appoint, be a proper court to remove? Will not a regard to their own characters have an undue bias upon them? This objection will grow stronger, if we may suppose that the time will come when a man may procure his appointment to office by bribery. The members of that court therefore who alone can remove for misbehaviour, should not be concerned in the appointment. Besides, if one branch of the legislative body appoint the executive officers, and the same branch alone can remove them, the legislative power will acquire an undue influence over the executive.

The twenty-second article describes the authority the Governor shall have in all business to be transacted by him and the Senate. The Governor by this article must be present in conducting an impeachment. He has it therefore in his power to rescue a favourite from impeachment, so long as he is Governor, by absenting himself from the Senate, whenever the impeachment is to be brought forwards.

We cannot conceive upon what principles the twenty-third article ascertains the speaker of the house to be one of the three, the majority of whom have the power of granting pardons. The speaker is an officer of one branch of the legislative body, and hourly depends upon them for his existence in that character—he therefore would not probably be disposed to offend any leading party in the house, by consenting to, or denying a pardon. An undue influence might prevail and the power of pardoning be improperly exercised.—When the speaker is guilty of this improper exercise, he cannot be punished but by impeachment, and as he is commonly a favourite of a considerable party in the house, it will be difficult to procure the accusation; for his party will support him.

The judges by the twenty fourth article are to hold their places during good behaviour, but we do not find that their salaries are any where directed to be fixed. The house of representatives may therefore starve them into a state of dependence.

The twenty-eighth article determines the mode of electing and removing the delegates for Congress. It is by joint ballot of the house and Senate. These delegates should be some of the best men in the State. Their abilities and characters should be thoroughly investigated. This will be more effectually done, if they are elected by the legislative body, each branch having a right to originate or negative the choice, and removal. And we cannot conceive why they should not be elected in this manner, as well as all officers who are annually appointed with annual grants of their sallaries, as is directed in the nineteenth article. By the mode of election now excepted against, the house may choose their delegates, altho' every Senator should vote against their choice.

The thirty-fourth article respecting liberty of conscience, we think exceptionable, but the observations necessary to be made thereon, were introduced in animadverting upon the thirteenth article.

The Committee have purposely been as concise as possible in their observations upon the Constitution proposed by the Convention of this State—Where they thought it was non-conformable to the principles of a free republican government, they have ventured to point out the non-conformity—Where they thought it was repugnant to the original social contract, they have taken the liberty to suggest that repugnance—And where they were persuaded it was founded in political injustice, they have dared to assert it. . . .

[There follows a detailed scheme for the legislative, executive and judicial branches of government.]

The committee have only further to report, that the inhabitants of the several towns who deputed delegates for this convention, be seriously advised, and solemnly exhorted, as they value the political freedom and happiness of themselves and of their posterity, to convene all the freemen of their several towns in town meeting, for this purpose regularly notified, and that they do unanimously vote their disapprobation of the constitution and form of government, framed by the convention of this state; that a regular return of the same be made to the secretary's office, that it may there remain a grateful monument to our posterity of that consistent, impartial and persevering attachment to political, religious, and civil liberty, which actuated their fathers, and in defence of which, they bravely fought, chearfully bled, and gloriously died.

The above report being read was accepted.

Attest,

PETER COFFIN, Chairman

XVIII

Transforming Society

In the Revolutionary Era the spirit of reform touched not only the
structure of governmental institutions and the disestablishment of the
Church of England, but such diverse areas as real property law, penal
reform, and education. During this period a number of states outlawed
both entail and primogeniture. Leading the movement for such reforms
in Virginia was Thomas Jefferson, who, in his autobiography, described
the struggle to obtain the new legislation. Much more thoroughgoing
in his proposals for a reform of the legal system was the New England
critic, Benjamin Austin. Writing under the pseudonym of "Honestus,"
he would have drastically curbed English common law and restricted,
if not abolished, the professional lawyer. In the field of educational
reform Thomas Jefferson proved a leading exponent of public education.
In his Notes on Virginia (1782) he set forth proposals for both elemen-
tary and higher education.

72. Land Tenure: Thomas Jefferson's
Bill to Abolish Entails in Virginia
October 14, 1776

*A Bill to Enable Tenants in Tail to Convey Their Lands
in Fee-simple*

Whereas the perpetuation of property in certain families by
means of gifts made to them in fee-simple is contrary to good
policy, tends to deceive fair traders who give credit on the visible
possession of such estates, discourages the holder thereof from
taking care and improving the same, and sometimes does injury to
the morals of youth by rendering them independent of, and dis-

SOURCE: P. L. Ford, ed., *Works of Thomas Jefferson*, II, 268–270.

obedient to, their parents; and whereas the former method of docking such estates tail by special act of assembly formed for every particular case employed very much time of the legislature, was burthensome to the public, and also to the individual who made application for such acts:

Be it therefore enacted by [the General Assembly of the Commonwealth of Virginia] and it is hereby enacted by authority of the same that any person who now hath, or hereafter may have any estate in fee tail general or special in any lands or slaves in possession, or who now is or hereafter may be entitled to any such estate tail in reversion or remainder after the determination of any estate for life or lives or of any lesser estate, whether such estate hath been or shall be created by deed, will, act of assembly, or any other ways or means shall have full power to pass, convey, or assure in fee-simple or for any lesser estate the said lands or slaves, or use in lands or slaves or such reversion or remainder therein, or any part or parcel thereof, to any person or persons whatsoever by deed or deeds of feoffment, gift, grant, exchange, partition, lease, release, bargain, and sale, covenant to stand seized to uses, deed to lead uses, or by his last will and testament, or by any other mode or form of conveyance or assurance by which such lands or slaves, or use in lands or slaves, or such reversion or remainder therein might have been passed, conveyed or assured had the same been held in fee-simple by the person so passing, conveying or assuring the same: and such deed, will or other conveyance shall be good and effectual to bar the issue in tail and those in remainder and reverter as to such estate or estates so passed, conveyed, or assured by such deed, will, or other conveyance.

Provided nevertheless that such deed, will, or other conveyance shall be executed, acknowledged, or proved, and recorded in like manner as, and in all cases where, the same should have been done, had the person or persons so conveying or assuring held the said lands or slaves, or use of lands and slaves or such reversion or remainder in fee-simple.

On the 12th, I obtained leave to bring in a bill declaring tenants in tail to hold their lands in fee simple. In the earlier times of the colony, when lands were to be obtained for little or nothing, some provident individuals procured large grants; and, desirous of founding great families for themselves, settled them on their descendants in fee tail. The transmission of this property from generation to generation, in the same name, raised up a distinct set of families, who, being privileged by law in the perpetuation of their wealth, were thus formed into a Patrician order, distinguished by the splendor and luxury of their establishments. From this order, too, the king habitually selected his counsellors of State; the hope of which distinction devoted the whole corps to the interests and will of the crown. To annul this privilege, and instead of an aristocracy of wealth, of more harm and danger, than benefit, to society, to make an opening for the aristocracy of virtue and talent, which nature has wisely provided for the direction of the interests of society, and scattered with equal hand through all its conditions, was deemed essential to a well-ordered republic. To effect it, no violence was necessary, no deprivation of natural right, but rather an enlargement of it by a repeal of the law. For this would author-ize the present holder to divide the property among his children equally, as his affections were divided; and would place them, by natural generation, on the level of their fellow citizens. But this repeal was strongly opposed by Mr. Pendleton,[1] who was zealously attached to ancient establishments; and who, taken all in all, was the ablest man in debate I have ever met with. He had not indeed the poetical fancy of Mr. Henry, his sublime imagination, his lofty and overwhelming diction; but he was cool, smooth and persuasive; his language flowing, chaste and embellished; his conceptions quick, acute and full of resource; never vanquished: for if he lost the main battle, he returned upon you, and regained so much of it as to make it a drawn one by dexterous manœuvres, skirmishes in detail, and the recovery of small advantages which, little singly, were important all together. You never knew when you were clear of him, but were harassed by his perseverance, until the patience was worn down of all who had less of it than himself. Add to this, that he was one of the most virtuous and benevolent of men, the kindest friend, the most amiable and pleasant of companions, which ensured a favorable reception to whatever came from him. Finding that the general principle of entails could not be main-tained, he took his stand on an amendment which he proposed, instead of an absolute abolition, to permit the tenant in tail to convey in fee simple, if he chose it; and he was within a few votes of saving so much of the old law. But the bill passed finally for entire abolition.

1. Edmund Pendleton.

73. The Role of Lawyers: "Honestus's"
Observations on the Pernicious Practice of the Law
1786

SOME OBSERVATIONS on the pernicious practice of the LAW, addressed to the PEOPLE.

In my last, some observations were offered for the consideration of the Legislature, on the practice "of the law," as of late introduced amongst us by the "order" of lawyers. —It being a matter of serious concern, I hope it will not be thought unnecessary to draw the attention of my countrymen to this interesting subject. The observations in the former piece were not intended merely for *speculation*, and I hope they will not be considered of such *trifling moment* as to be treated with indifference; the people of this Commonwealth are too much *interested* in the decision, to rest satisfied with barely *hearing of the evils they suffer*, without some determinate resolutions to remedy them.

The questions are, *whether we will have this "order" so far established in this Commonwealth, as to rule over us; or, whether the people of this State do think themselves free from danger, while this "order" of men are permitted to continue in their present career?* These surely are questions worthy of our attention, and ought not to be passed over without *mature consideration*. There is scarcely a town throughout the Commonwealth, but has felt the effects of this "order," and many individuals, I doubt not, have reason to rue the day that any of this body became residents among them. Has good fellowship or brotherly harmony been promoted since their arrival? I presume not.

One reason of the pernicious practice of the law, and what gives great influence to this "order" is, *that we have introduced the whole body of English laws into our Courts;* why should these States be governed by British laws? Can we suppose them applicable to the circumstances of this country? Can the monarchical and aristocratical institutions of England, be consistent with the

SOURCE: Honestus [Benjamin Austin], *Observations on the Pernicious Practice of the Law* (Boston, 1786), pp. 7–26 passim.

republican principles of our constitution? Why should a young Republic be ruled by laws framed for the particular purpose of a monarchical government, or can laws which are applicable to King, Lords and Commons of England, be any way consonant to the Republican establishment of this Commonwealth? We may as well adopt the laws of the Medes and Persians. A great error, therefore, lies in our want of a proper system of laws, adapted to our particular state and circumstances: The numerous precedents brought from *Old English Authorities*, serve to embarrass all our judiciary causes, and answer no other purpose than to increase the influence of lawyers, as from such Authorities they can cull and select precedents to answer every purpose; the omnipotence of their laws can reconcile all contradictions: how absurd therefore, to introduce into our young Republic, the whole body of English laws? . . .

In Courts of Justice, all persons employed who have any *influence* in the cause, ought to be as *unbiassed* as possible; judges, jury, witnesses, &c. The *parties*, therefore, should not be permitted to offer any thing further than what can be produced simply from the evidence. A Court acting upon such principles, must be considered as the most equitable and judicious. In this impartial arrangement, therefore, with what propriety can we introduce a person to act in the character of a lawyer? Can this man be *unbiassed*, who has received a large reward, to involve the case (if necessary) in as much perplexity as possible? It may be said, that the lawyer stands in the place of his client, and may say *anything* in his defence; but is there not a material difference, between allowing a man to relate his own story, and employing a person who in *consideration of his fee,* may be influenced to *pervert the general principles of law?* No *"order" of men ought to be employed to speak to a cause, who are under a biass to misconstrue the laws;* and herein is the difference, between admitting a person to plead his own case, and employing a lawyer for this purpose; as the former must relate only plain matters of fact, but the latter (provided the cause is bad) may be led to warp the laws to answer his own particular purposes. Can the poor man (who cannot pay any of this "order") receive *equal advantage* with the rich, while such a body of men *exist,* who stand ready to speak on any *subject,* and like mercenary troops, can be hired to support any cause for the consideration of a large reward? Will not the rich opponent overpower the poor man, by the greatness of his gifts to his lawyers? This surely is permitting the evidence of an "order" purposely to deprive the "majority of persons" of the benefits of the laws, and putting it in the power of the "wealthy few" (*by the assistance of this* "order") to trample on the rights and property of the community. Wherein is the *necessity* of establishing an "order" of men, who, by their profession, have no *fixed* principle, but whose sentiments are oftentimes exposed for public sale to the *highest bidder.*

These considerations make me strenuous for the ABOLITION of the present mode of practice; and I might still urge the propriety of that plan proposed in the former papers, *that the evidence be delivered to the jury, and the points of law be explained by the Judges, without the intervention of lawyers.* In free governments all appeals to the laws should be on the plainest principles pos· sible: —By this method, the poor man stands on an *equality* with his wealthy neighbour; and every individual would receive equal benefit from the laws, without any tedious delays. If this simple mode was adopted, the dishonest would not dare to take the advantage of the honest, as they could not have any person *within the Court* to plead in their favour. The quibbles of law would not be so often urged. The paltry litigious causes amongst neighbours would not exist: Harmony and benevolence would more generally prevail, and agreeable to my motto,

> "Mutual passions, mutual charms might lend,
> And each to each be neighbour, father, friend."

Our Courts would become places of justice, as we should have no "order" to prevent the execution of it, and every individual would apply to the JUDGES with confidence becoming FREEMEN.

Some persons have a wonderful opinion of this "order," as *being necessary to explain the* MISTERIES *of the law.* —In the first place, the greatest part of those misteries are owing to the *existence* of this "order." The variety of *sophistry* introduced by these men, is the principal cause of the intricacy of our laws; any man of common abilities can easily distinguish between right and wrong (a tryal by Jury is on this principle) more especially when the parties are admitted to give a plain story, without any assistance from lawyers; I dare appeal to any man who has been on a Jury, whether the greatest puzzle did not arise from the *tedious loquacity* of the lawyers? *The most simple case can be made intricate by a person who is rewarded for this purpose.* Is it not as common to employ a lawyer for his art and cunning, as for his knowledge in the law? and do we not as often find him succeed by the former, as by the latter? For this purpose these lawyers are crying up the *intricacy of the law;* and by *hard words,* in all their judiciary proceedings, they deceive the people (like Romish priests in matters of religion) by vehemently asserting, that without the existence of this "order" the laws could not be executed. This however is a mere flight of *law craft;* from which good Lord deliver us.

The manner of employing these persons must show the impropriety and fatal tendency of such an "order" practising in a Court of Justice; sometimes half a dozen are employed or *retained on one side;* and a wealthy man may *silence a whole bar.* If then we allow this "order" to be "necessary," does not such practice deprive a poor man of every *necessary* means to obtain his plea?

It is said, *"that the Judges stand in need of the advice of the lawyers, as from the multiplicity of causes within their cognizance, they could not attend particularly to them, unless assisted by this 'order.'"* To which I answer, that if the decisions by references were binding, we should not have so great a number of cases before the Judges, as this mode would keep out of our Courts, the greatest part of our actions. The Judges, therefore, would be better able to attend the business than they are at present, as the vast *variety* of cases now before them, must be attended with delay and indecision. I dare appeal to those who are conversant in Courts, whether nineteen cases in twenty could not be decided as equitably by referees, as by a tedious court process? . . .

Provided there is *danger* of such a combination, is it not time that the PEOPLE should be guarded against it, by *abolishing* the "order"? If the inhabitants of this Commonwealth, should become subject to such impositions, as *previous agreements before their causes are brought to trial,* have we not the greatest reason to apprehend the most pernicious perversion of every judiciary process? —If this "order" should become *allied* by mutual correspondence through the State, might they not subvert every principle of law by their combination, and establish a perfect *aristocratical influence* thro' the Commonwealth? In short, what *security* have the people in the laws, while an "order" of men exist, *who have it in their power* to manage them, so as to answer their own particular purposes and emolument?

Further, if the individuals of this "order" are admitted into our Legislature to make laws, and at the same time can become so formidable by their professional attachments, is there not the greatest danger, that in a few years they will render themselves (as a combined body) absolute, both in the Legislative and Judicial branches? —What safety has the "majority of persons" as to their rights, liberties and property, when in the first instance the framing of our laws, are under the management of this "order"? This "order" therefore may, in time, exercise as unlimited authority as the Spanish inquisition.

74. Education: Thomas Jefferson's
Notes on Virginia, Answer to Query XIV
1782

ANOTHER OBJECT of the revisal is, to diffuse knowledge more generally through the mass of the people. This bill proposes to lay off every county into small districts of five or six miles square, called hundreds, and in each of them to establish a school for teaching, reading, writing, and arithmetic. The tutor to be supported by the hundred, and every person in it entitled to send their children three years gratis, and as much longer as they please, paying for it. These schools to be under a visitor who is annually to chuse the boy of best genius in the school, of those whose parents are too poor to give them further education, and to send him forward to one of the grammar schools, of which twenty are proposed to be erected in different parts of the country, for teaching Greek, Latin, Geography, and the higher branches of numerical arithmetic. Of the boys thus sent in one year, trial is to be made at the grammar schools one or two years, and the best genius of the whole selected, and continued six years, and the residue dismissed. By this means twenty of the best geniuses will be raked from the rubbish annually, and be instructed, at the public expence, so far as the grammar schools go. At the end of six years instruction, one half are to be discontinued (from among whom the grammar

SOURCE: P. L. Ford, ed., Works of Thomas Jefferson (12 vols., New York, 1904), III, 251–255.

schools will probably be supplied with future masters); and the other half, who are to be chosen for the superiority of their parts and disposition, are to be sent and continued three years in the study of such sciences as they shall chuse, at William and Mary college, the plan of which is proposed to be enlarged, as will be hereafter explained, and extended to all the useful sciences. The ultimate result of the whole scheme of education would be the teaching all the children of the State reading, writing, and common arithmetic; turning out ten annually, of superior genius, well taught in Greek, Latin, Geography, and the higher branches of arithmetic; turning out ten others annually, of still superior parts, who, to those branches of learning, shall have added such of the sciences as their genius shall have led them to; the furnishing to the wealthier part of the people convenient schools at which their children may be educated at their own expence. The general objects of this law are to provide an education adapted to the years, to the capacity, and the condition of everyone, and directed to their freedom and happiness. Specific details were not proper for the law. These must be the business of the visitors entrusted with its execution. The first stage of this education being the schools of the hundreds, wherein the great mass of the people will receive their instruction, the principal foundations of future order will be laid here. Instead, therefore, of putting the Bible and Testament into the hands of the children at an age when their judgments are not sufficiently matured for religious inquiries, their memories may here be stored with the most useful facts from Grecian, Roman, European and American history. The first elements of morality too may be instilled into their minds; such as, when further developed as their judgments advance in strength, may teach them how to work out their own greatest happiness, by shewing them that it does not depend on the condition of life in which chance has placed them, but is always the result of a good conscience, good health, occupation, and freedom in all just pursuits. Those whom either the wealth of their parents or the adoption of the State shall destine to higher degrees of learning, will go on to the grammar schools, which constitute the next stage, there to be instructed in the languages. The learning Greek and Latin, I am told, is going into disuse in Europe. I know not what their manners and occupations may call for; but it would be very ill-judged in us to follow their example in this instance. There is a certain period of life, say from eight to fifteen or sixteen years of age, when the mind like the body is not yet firm enough for laborious and close operations. If applied to such, it falls an early victim to premature exertion; exhibiting, indeed, at first, in these young and tender subjects, the flattering appearance of their being men while they are yet children, but ending in reducing them to be children when they should be men. The memory is then most susceptible and tenacious of impressions; and the learning of languages being chiefly a work of memory, it seems precisely fitted to the powers of this period, which is long enough too for acquiring the most useful languages, antient and modern. I do not pretend that language is science. It is only an instrument for the attainment of science. But that time is not lost which is employed in providing tools for future operation; more especially as in this case the books put into the hands of the youth for this purpose may be such as will at the same time impress their minds with useful facts and good principles. If this period be suffered to pass in idleness, the mind becomes lethargic and impotent, as would the body it inhabits if unexercised during the same time. The sympathy between body and mind during their rise, progress and decline, is too strict and obvious to endanger our being misled while we reason from the one to the other. As soon as they are of sufficient age, it is supposed they will be sent on from the grammar schools to the university, which constitutes our third and last stage, there to study those sciences which may be adapted to their views. By that part of our plan which prescribes the selection of the youths of genius from among the classes of the poor, we hope to avail the State of those talents which nature has sown as liberally among the poor as the rich, but which perish without use, if not sought for and cultivated. But of all the views of this law none is more important, none more legitimate, than that of rendering the people the safe, as they are the ultimate, guardians of their own liberty. For this purpose the reading in the first stage, where they will receive their whole education, is proposed, as has been said, to be chiefly historical. History, by apprising them of the past, will enable them to judge of the future; it will avail them of the experience of other times and other nations; it will qualify them as judges of the actions and designs of men; it will enable them to know ambition under every disguise it may assume; and knowing it, to defeat its views. In every government on earth is some trace of human weakness, some germ of corruption and degeneracy, which cunning will discover, and wickedness insensibly open, cultivate and improve. Every government degenerates when trusted to the rulers of the people alone. The people themselves therefore are its only safe depositories. And to render even them safe, their minds must be improved to a certain degree. This indeed is not all that is necessary, though it be essentially necessary. An amendment of our constitution must here come in aid of the public education. The influence over government must be shared among all the people. If every individual which composes their mass participates of the ultimate authority, the government will be safe; because the corrupting the whole mass will exceed any private resources of wealth; and public ones cannot be provided but by levies on the people. In this case every man would have to pay his own price. The government of Great Britain has been corrupted, because but one man in ten has a right to vote for members of parliament. The sellers of the government, therefore, get nine-tenths of their price clear. It has been thought that corruption is restrained by confining the right of suffrage to a few of the wealthier of the people; but it would be more effectually restrained by an extension of that right to such numbers as would bid defiance to the means of corruption.

Lastly, it is proposed, by a bill in this revisal, to begin a public library and gallery, by laying out a certain sum annually in books, paintings, and statues.

XIX

Slavery, the Negro, and the American Revolution

A struggle that at its start proclaimed the equality of all men and enumerated as unalienable rights, life, liberty, and the pursuit of happiness, could not fail to have an impact on the status of the black people in America. Lord Dunmore's proclamation offering liberty to indentured servants and slaves entering the King's service served not only to arouse Southern planters to a pitch of indignation but to underscore the ambivalent position of the Patriots on the subject of slavery. True, steps were taken in the Northern states to liberate slaves or to ameliorate their condition; and Southerners like Henry Laurens, who had moral qualms about slavery, might manumit their loyal slaves. In the hope of freedom some slaves fought on the Patriot side, while others made their way behind British lines and joined the Loyalist émigrés to Canada and Nova Scotia.

75. Lord Dunmore's Proclamation
November 7, 1775

As I have ever entertained hopes that an accommodation might have taken place between Great Britain and this Colony, without being compelled by my duty to this most disagreeable, but now absolutely necessary step, rendered so by a body of armed men, unlawfully assembled, firing on His Majesty's Tenders; and the formation of an Army, and that Army now on their march to attack His Majesty's Troops, and destroy the well-disposed subjects of this Colony: To defeat such treasonable purposes, and that all such traitors and their abettors may be brought to justice, and that

SOURCE: P. L. Force, ed., *American Archives*, 4th ser., III, 1385.

the peace and good order of this Colony may be again restored, which the ordinary course of the civil law is unable to effect, I have thought fit to issue this my Proclamation, hereby declaring, that until the aforesaid good purposes can be obtained, I do, in virtue of the power and authority to me given by His Majesty, determine to execute martial law, and cause the same to be executed throughout this Colony. And to the end that peace and good order may the sooner be restored, I do require every person capable of bearing arms to resort to His Majesty's standard, or be looked upon as traitors to His Majesty's crown and Government, and thereby become liable to the penalty the law inflicts upon such offences—such as forfeiture of life, confiscation of lands, etc., etc.: and I do hereby further declare all indented servants, Negroes or others (appertaining to Rebels) free, that are able and willing to bear arms, they joining His Majesty's Troops as soon as may be, for the more speedily reducing this Colony to a proper sense of their duty to His Majesty's crown and dignity. I do further order and require all His Majesty's liege subjects to retain their quit-rents, or any other taxes due, or that may become due, in their own custody, till such time as peace may be again restored to this, at present, most unhappy Country, or demanded of them for their former salutary purposes, by officers properly authorized to receive the same.

Given under my hand, on board the Ship *William*, off Norfolk, the 7th day of November, in the sixteenth year of His Majesty's reign.

DUNMORE

God Save the King!

76. A Carolina Planter's Denunciation of Slavery: Henry Laurens' Letter August 14, 1776

My Negroes there all to a Man are strongly attached to me, so are all of mine in this Country, hitherto not one of them has attempted to desert on the contrary those who are more exposed hold themselves always ready to fly from the Enemy in case of a sudden descent—many hundreds of that Colour have been stolen and decoyed by the Servants of King George the third—Captains of British Ships of War and Noble Lords have busied themselves in such inglorious pilferage to the disgrace of their Master and disgrace of their Cause.—these Negroes were first enslaved by the English—Acts of Parliament have established the Slave Trade in favour of the home residing English & almost totally prohibited the Americans from reaping any share of it—men of War Forts Castles Governors Companies & Committees are employed and authorized by the English Parliament to protect regulate and extend the Slave Trade—Negroes are brought by English Men and sold as Slaves to Americans—Bristol Liverpoole Manchester Birmingham etc., etc., live upon the Slave Trade—the British Parliament now employ their Men of War to steal those Negroes from the Americans to whom they had sold them, pretending to set the poor wretches free but basely trepan and sell them into tenfold worse Slavery in the West Indies, where probably they will become the property of English-Men again and of some who sit in Parliament; what meanness! what complicated wickedness appears in this scene! O England, how changed! how fallen!

You know my Dear Sir. I abhor Slavery, I was born in a Country where Slavery had been established by British Kings and Parliaments as well as by the Laws of that Country Ages before my existence, I found the Christian Religion and Slavery growing

SOURCE: A Letter from Henry Laurens to his Son John Laurens, August 14, 1776 (New York: Columbia University Libraries, private printing, 1964).

under the same authority and cultivation—I nevertheless disliked it—in former days there was no combatting the prejudices of Men supported by Interest, the day I hope is approaching when from principles of gratitude as well as justice every Man will strive to be foremost in shewing his readiness to comply with the Golden Rule; not less than £20000, Stg. would all my Negroes produce if sold at public Auction tomorrow I am not the Man who enslaved them. They are indebted to English Men for that favour, nevertheless I am devising means for manumitting many of them and for cutting off the entail of Slavery—great powers oppose me, the Laws and Customs of my Country, my own and the avarice of my Country Men—What will my Children say if I deprive them of so much Estate? these are difficulties but not insuperable.

I will do as much as I can in my time and leave the rest to a better hand.

I am not one of those who arrogate the peculiar care of Providence in each fortunate event, nor one of those who dare trust in Providence for defence and security of their own Liberty while they enslave and wish to continue in Slavery, thousands who are as well intitled to freedom as themselves.—I perceive the work before me is great. I shall appear to many as a promoter not only of strange but of dangerous doctrines, it will therefore be necessary to proceed with caution, you are apparently deeply Interested in this affair but as I have no doubts concerning your concurrence and approbation I most sincerely wish for your advice and assistance and hope to receive both in good time. . . .

77. Slave Enlistment Act of Rhode Island
February 14, 1778

WHEREAS, for the preservation of the rights and liberties of the United States, it is necessary that the whole powers of government should be exerted in recruiting the Continental battalions; and

SOURCE: J. R. Bartlett, ed., *Records of the Colony of Rhode Island and Providence Plantations, in New England* (10 vols., Providence, 1856–1865), VIII, 358–360.

whereas, His Excellency Gen. Washington hath enclosed to this state a proposal made to him by Brigadier General Varnum, to enlist into the two battalions, raising by this state, such slaves as should be willing to enter into the service; and whereas, history affords us frequent precedents of the wisest, the freest, and bravest nations having liberated their slaves, and enlisted them as soldiers to fight in defence of their country; and also whereas, the enemy, with a great force, have taken possession of the capital, and of a greater part of this state; and this state is obliged to raise a very considerable number of troops for its own immediate defence, whereby it is in a manner rendered impossible for this state to furnish recruits for the said two battalions, without adopting the said measure so recommended.

It is voted and resolved, that every able-bodied negro, mulatto, or Indian man slave, in this state, may enlist into either of the said two battalions, to serve during the continuance of the present war with Great Britain.

That every slave, so enlisting, shall be entitled to, and receive, all the bounties, wages, and encouragements, allowed by the Continental Congress, to any soldier enlisting into their service.

It is further voted and resolved, that every slave, so enlisting, shall, upon his passing muster before Col. Christopher Greene, be immediately discharged from the service of his master or mistress, and be absolutely FREE, as though he had never been encumbered with any kind of servitude or slavery.

And in case such slave shall, by sickness or otherwise, be rendered unable to maintain himself, he shall not be chargeable to his master or mistress; but shall be supported at the expense of the state.

And whereas, slaves have been, by the laws, deemed the property of their owners, and therefore compensation ought to be made to the owners for the loss of their service,—

It is further voted and resolved, that there be allowed, and paid by this state, to the owner, for every such slave so enlisting, a sum according to his worth; at a price not exceeding £120 for the most valuable slave; and in proportion for a slave of less value.

Provided, the owner of said slave shall deliver up to the officer, who shall enlist him, the clothes of the said slave; or otherwise he shall not be entitled to said sum.

And for settling and ascertaining the value of such slaves,—

It is further voted and resolved, that a committee of five be appointed, to wit:

One from each county; any three of whom, to be a quorum, to examine the slaves who shall be so enlisted, after they shall have passed muster, and to set a price upon each slave according to his value, as aforesaid.

It is further voted and resolved, that upon any able-bodied negro, mulatto, or Indian slave, enlisting as aforesaid, the officer who shall so enlist him, after he shall have passed muster, as aforesaid, shall deliver a certificate thereof, to the master or mistress of said negro, mulatto, or Indian slave; which shall discharge him from the service of his said master or mistress, as aforesaid.

It is further voted and resolved, that the committee who shall estimate the value of any slave, as aforesaid, shall give a certificate of the sum at which he may be valued, to the owner of said slave; and the general treasurer of this state is hereby empowered and directed to give unto the said owner of the said slave, his promissory note, as treasurer, as aforesaid, for the sum of money at which he shall be valued, as aforesaid, payable on demand, with interest at the rate of six per cent. per annum; and that said notes, which shall be so given, shall be paid with the money which is due to this state, and is expected from Congress; the money which has been borrowed out of the general treasury, by this Assembly, being first re-placed.

XX

Concluding Observations

Founding Fathers like George Washington, John Jay, and Alexander Hamilton recognized the need for building a national character and a national purpose. It remained for the South Carolina physician-historian David Ramsay to show how the spirit of American nationalism had expanded during the American Revolution until it permeated almost all branches of society. It is significant, too, that Ramsay recognized the reformist impulses that the Revolution had touched off, notably in the areas of culture and education, and that he discerned how the lead in the Revolutionary movement had been taken by self-made men. Over all, Ramsay would have agreed that the benefits from the Revolution outweighed its disadvantages, but he realized how wars contribute to a deterioration of both private and public morals, and how revolutions bring public authority into disrepute.

78. The American Revolution as Viewed by a Contemporary Historian: David Ramsay 1789

THE American Revolution, on the one hand, brought forth great vices; but on the other hand, it called forth many virtues, and gave occasion for the display of abilities which, but for that event, would have been lost to the world.

When the war began, the Americans were a mass of husbandmen, merchants, mechanics and fishermen; but the necessities of the country gave a spring to the active powers of the inhabitants, and set them on thinking, speaking and acting in a line far beyond that to which they had been accustomed.

SOURCE: David Ramsay, *History of the American Revolution* (2 vols., London, 1793), II, 315–325 *passim.*

The difference between nations is not so much owing to nature as to education and circumstances. While the Americans were guided by the leading strings of the mother country, they had no scope nor encouragement for exertion. All the departments of government were established and executed for them, but not by them. In the years 1775 and 1776 the country, being suddenly thrown into a situation that needed the abilities of all its sons, these generally took their places, each according to the bent of his inclination. As they severally pursued their objects with ardour, a vast expansion of the human mind speedily followed. This displayed itself in a variety of ways. It was found that their talents for great stations did not differ in kind, but only in degree, from those which were necessary for the proper discharge of the ordinary business of civil society.

In the bustle that was occasioned by the war, few instances could be produced of any persons who made a figure, or who rendered essential services, but from among those who had given specimens of similar talents in their respective professions. Those who from indolence or dissipation had been of little service to the community in time of peace, were found equally unserviceable in war. A few young men were exceptions to this general rule. Some of these, who had indulged in youthful follies, broke off from their vicious courses and on the pressing call of their country became useful servants of the public; but the great bulk of those who were the active instruments of carrying on the Revolution were self-made, industrious men. These who by their own exertions had established or laid a foundation for establishing personal independence, were most generally trusted and most successfully employed in establishing that of their country. In these times of action, classical education was found of less service than good natural parts, guided by common sense and sound judgment.

Several names could be mentioned of individuals who, without the knowledge of any other language than their mother tongue, wrote not only accurately, but elegantly, on public business. It seemed as if the war not only required, but created talents. Men whose minds were warmed with the love of liberty, and whose abilities were improved by daily exercise, and sharpened with a laudable ambition to serve their distressed country, spoke, wrote and acted with an energy far surpassing all expectations which could be reasonably founded on their previous acquirements.

The Americans knew but little of one another previous to the Revolution. Trade and business had brought the inhabitants of their seaports acquainted with each other, but the bulk of the people in the interior country were unaquainted with their fellow citizens. A Continental Army and a Congress composed of men from all the States by freely mixing together were assimilated into one mass. Individuals of both, mingling with the citizens, disseminated principles of union among men. Local prejudices abated. By frequent collision asperities were worn off, and a foundation was laid for the establishment of a nation out of discordant materials. Intermarriages between men and women of different States were much more common than before the war and became an additional cement to the union. Unreasonable jealousies had existed between the inhabitants of the eastern and the southern states; but on becoming better acquainted with each other, these in a great measure subsided. A wiser policy prevailed. Men of liberal minds led the way in discouraging local distinctions, and the great body of the people, as soon as reason got the better of prejudice, found that their best interests would be most effectually promoted by such practices and sentiments as were favorable to union.

Religious bigotry had broken in upon the peace of various sects before the American war. This was kept up by partial establishments, and by a dread that the Church of England through the power of the mother country would be made to triumph over all other denominations. These apprehensions were done away by the Revolution. The different sects, having nothing to fear from each other, dismissed all religious controversy. A proposal for introducing bishops into America before the war had kindled a flame among the dissenters; but the Revolution was no sooner accomplished than a scheme for that purpose was perfected, with the consent and approbation of all those sects who had previously opposed it. Pulpits which had formerly been shut to worthy men, because their heads had not been consecrated by the imposition of the hands of a bishop or of a presbytery, have since the establishment of independence been reciprocally opened to each other, whensoever the public convenience required it. The world will soon see the result of an experiment in politics, and be able to determine whether the happiness of society is increased by religious establishments, or diminished by the want of them.

Though schools and colleges were generally shut up during the war, yet many of the arts and sciences were promoted by it. The geography of the United States before the Revolution was but little known; but the marches of armies and the operations of war gave birth to many geographical enquiries and discoveries which otherwise would not have been made. A passionate fondness for studies of this kind and the growing importance of the country excited one of its sons, the Reverend Mr. Morse[1], to travel through every State of the Union and amass a fund of topographical knowledge far exceeding any thing heretofore communicated to the public.

The necessities of the States led to the study of tactics, fortifications, gunnery and a variety of other arts connected with war, and diffused a knowledge of them among a peaceable people who would otherwise have had no inducement to study them.

The abilities of ingenious men were directed to make farther improvements in the art of destroying an enemy. Among these, David Bushnell of Connecticut invented a machine for submarine navigation, which was found to answer the purpose of rowing horizontally at any given depth under water, and of rising or sinking at pleasure. To this was attached a magazine of powder, and the whole was contrived in such a manner as to make it practicable to blow up vessels by machinery under them. Mr. Bushnell also contrived sundry other curious machines for the annoyance of British shipping, but from accident they only succeeded in part. He destroyed one vessel in charge of Commodore Symonds, and a second one near the shore of Long-Island.

Surgery was one of the arts which was promoted by the war. From the want of hospitals and other aids, the medical men of America had few opportunities of perfecting themselves in this art, the thorough knowledge of which can only be acquired by practice and observation. The melancholy events of battles gave the American students an opportunity of seeing and learning more in one day than they could have acquired in years of peace. It was in the hospitals of the United States that Dr. Rush first discovered the method of curing the lock jaw by bark and wine, added to other invigorating remedies, which has since been adopted with success in Europe, as well as in the United States.

1. Jedidiah Morse, best remembered as the "father of American geography," whose *Geography Made Easy* (1784) was the first geography to be published in the United States.

The science of government has been more generally diffused among the Americans by means of the Revolution. The policy of Great Britain in throwing them out of her protection induced a necessity of establishing independent constitutions. This led to reading and reasoning on the subject. The many errors that were at first committed by unexperienced statesmen have been a practical comment on the folly of unbalanced constitutions and injudicious laws. The discussions concerning the new constitutions gave birth to much reasoning on the subject of government, and particularly to a series of letters signed Publius, but really the work of Alexander Hamilton, in which much political knowledge and wisdom were displayed, and which will long remain a monument of the strength and acuteness of the human understanding in investigating truth. . . .

As literature had in the first instance favoured the Revolution, so in its turn the Revolution promoted literature. The study of eloquence and of the belles lettres was more successfully prosecuted in America after the disputes between Great Britain and her colonies began to be serious than it had ever been before. The various orations, addresses, letters, dissertations and other literary performances which the war made necessary, called forth abilities where they were, and excited the rising generation to study arts which brought with them their own reward. Many incidents afforded materials for the favourites of the muses to display their talents. Even burlesquing royal proclamations by parodies and doggerel poetry had great effects on the minds of the people. A celebrated historian has remarked that the song of "Lillibullero" forwarded the revolution of 1688 in England. It may be truly affirmed that similar productions produced similar effects in America. Francis Hopkinson[2] rendered essential service to his country by turning the artillery of wit and ridicule on the enemy. Philip Freneau[3] laboured successfully in the same way. Royal proclamations and other productions which issued from royal printing presses were, by the help of warm imaginations, arrayed in such dresses as rendered them truly ridiculous. Trumbull[4] with a vein of

2. Statesman and jurist, but also renowned for his satiric poems.
3. Poet and satirist, later well known as a pro-Jeffersonian newspaper editor.
4. John Trumbull, literary leader of the "Hartford Wits," who also numbered David Humphreys, an aide-de-camp to Washington, Joel Barlow, and Timothy Dwight.

original Hudibrastic humour diverted his countrymen so much with the follies of their enemies that for a time they forgot the calamities of war. Humphries twined the literary with the military laurel by superadding the fame of an elegant poet to that of an accomplished officer. Barlow increased the fame of his country and of the distinguished actors in the Revolution by the bold design of an epic poem ably executed on the idea that Columbus foresaw in vision the great scenes that were to be transacted on the theater of that new world which he had discovered. Dwight struck out in the same line and at an early period of life finished an elegant work entitled *The Conquest of Canaan*, on a plan which has rarely been attempted. The principles of their mother tongue were first unfolded to the Americans since the Revolution by their countryman Webster.[5] Pursuing an unbeaten track, he has made discoveries in the genius and construction of the English language which had escaped the researches of preceding philologists.

These and a group of other literary characters have been brought into view by the Revolution. It is remarkable that of these Connecticut has produced an unusual proportion. In that truly republican state, every thing conspires to adorn human nature with its highest honours.

From the latter periods of the Revolution till the present time, schools, colleges, societies, and institutions for promoting literature, arts, manufactures, agriculture, and for extending human happiness, have been increased far beyond any thing that ever took place before the Declaration of Independence. Every state in the union has done more or less in this way, but Pennsylvania has done the most.

To overset an established government unhinges many of those principles which bind individuals to each other. A long time, and much prudence, will be necessary to reproduce a spirit of union and that reverence for government without which society is a rope of sand. The right of the people to resist their rulers, when invading their liberties, forms the corner stone of the American republics. This principle, though just in itself, is not favourable to the tranquility of present establishments. The maxims and measures which in the years 1774 and 1775 were successfully inculcated and adopted by American patriots for oversetting the established gov-

5. Noah Webster, educator and lexicographer, whose spelling book and dictionary were enormously influential in America.

ernment, will answer a similar purpose when recurrence is had to them by factious demagogues for disturbing the freest governments that were ever devised.

War never fails to injure the morals of the people engaged in it. The American war, in particular, had an unhappy influence of this kind. Being begun without funds or regular establishments, it could not be carried on without violating private rights; and in its progress it involved a necessity for breaking solemn promises and plighted public faith. The failure of national justice, which was in some degree unavoidable, increased the difficulties of performing private engagements, and weakened that sensibility to the obligations of public and private honor which is a security for the punctual performance of contracts.

In consequence of the war, the institutions of religion have been deranged, the public worship of the Deity suspended, and a great number of inhabitants deprived of the ordinary means of obtaining that religious knowledge which tames the fierceness and softens the rudeness of human passions and manners. Many of the temples dedicated to the service of the Most High were destroyed, and these, from a deficiency of ability and inclination, are not yet rebuilt. The clergy were left to suffer without proper support. The depreciation of the paper currency was particularly injurious to them. It reduced their salaries to a pittance, so insufficient for the maintenance that several of them were obliged to lay down their profession and engage in other pursuits. Public preaching, of which many of the inhabitants were thus deprived, seldom fails of rendering essential service to society by civilising the multitude and forming them to union. No class of citizens have contributed more to the Revolution than the clergy, and none have hitherto suffered more in consequence of it. From the diminution of their number and the penury to which they have been subjected, civil government has lost many of the advantages it formerly derived from the public instructions of that useful order of men.

On the whole, the literary, political and military talents of the citizens of the United States have been improved by the Revolution, but their moral character is inferior to what it formerly was. So great is the change for the worse that the friends of public order are loudly called upon to exert their utmost abilities in extirpating the vicious principles and habits which have taken deep root during the late convulsions.

DATE DUE

MAY 28 '72			
NOV 2 '82			
NOV 2 1982			
JAN 7 '85			
JAN 7 '86			
APR 3 0 '89			
MAR 31 '02			
GAYLORD			PRINTED IN U.S.A.